MASTERING
SPANISH

MASTERING SPANISH

THIRD EDITION

Laurel H. Turk

DePauw University

Aurelio M. Espinosa, Jr.

Stanford University

D. C. HEATH AND COMPANY

Lexington, Massachusetts   Toronto

Cover illustration "Familia Andina" by Héctor Poleo. Courtesy *Museum of Modern Art of Latin America,* OAS, Washington, D.C.

Photograph credits appear on page 385.

Published simultaneously in Canada.

Printed in the United States of America.

International Standard Book Number: 0–669–01713–2

Library of Congress Catalog Card Number: 78–20331

Mastering Spanish, Third Edition, is a second-year college program. It is designed to further the development of the language through review of the fundamentals of Spanish structure, to emphasize oral and reading comprehension, and to provide opportunity for self-expression in speaking and writing. Students who have completed one year of college Spanish or its equivalent in secondary school will find material which is essential for a good command of the language.

To fulfill these aims, the text consists of three *Repasos,* twelve regular lessons, twelve *Lecturas,* an art section, a section on Spanish letter writing, five appendices, and end vocabularies. The art section in color, the maps, and the illustrations provide the basis for a great variety of topics which supplement the material on the cultural background of the Spanish-American countries. Throughout the text, emphasis is placed on the acquisition of a practical vocabulary and on the active use of the language. The dialogues, which introduce the *Repasos* and regular lessons, deal with situations from daily life and are within the experience of present-day students.

Mastering Spanish is written so that it may be used as a logical extension of most basic, first-year programs. It provides ample material for a one-semester course which meets four times per week. In a course meeting three days per week, some of the exercises and/or *Lecturas* may be omitted without detriment to the over-all effectiveness of the text. If it is used in conjunction with other reading material in addition to the *Lecturas,* it may be necessary to carry over a few lessons into the second semester or even to spread them through the whole year.

The three *Repasos* are devoted largely to a review of all the simple and compound indicative tenses and of formal singular and plural and familiar singular command forms of the verb. This stress on verb forms is recognized as a necessity if the student is to gain complete mastery of the language. Each of the three reviews consists of a dialogue, followed by two groups of questions in Spanish, a section on pronunciation, a verb review including varied drill exercises, and, finally, a vocabulary list, which includes a few individual words and all the idiomatic phrases and expressions used in the dialogue and other parts of each lesson. In addition to the specific focus on developing a firm command of the verb forms, the *Preguntas sobre el diálogo* and the *Preguntas para conversar,* which are related to the contents of the dialogue, facilitate and reinforce comprehension and speaking. The entire verb review contained in these three lessons may be taken up before *Lección primera,* or certain sections may be assigned in conjunction with the regular lessons.

The twelve regular lessons contain: (1) a practical dialogue, with *Preguntas sobre el diálogo* and *Preguntas para conversar;* (2) a section on pronunciation and intonation (through *Lección diez*); (3) *Notas gramaticales,* with *Ejercicios* placed after the explanation of grammatical points; (4) a *Resumen,* which offers additional oral drills and short English sentences to be expressed in Spanish, and which summarizes the major points taken up in the lesson; and (5) a summary list of new words and expressions. A reading selection (*Lectura*) follows each lesson.

Throughout the text the headings as well as the directions are given in Spanish. In the *Pronunciación* and *Notas gramaticales* sections, however, the explanations are given in English to ensure comprehension. Additional grammatical terms and expressions for use in the classroom and laboratory are listed in Appendix B.

The pronunciation material constitutes a basic and effective survey of Spanish phonology, with special attention to intonation. This section is included through *Lección diez* to ensure that the student will continue to apply the principles involved in good Spanish pronunciation.

The *Notas gramaticales* give a systematic, logical, and pragmatic review of the fundamentals of Spanish structure. They are advanced in scope and include points frequently omitted in other texts. However, they retain their basic nature and emphasize general usage rather than exceptions. An important feature of the *Notas gramaticales* is that each major structure is immediately followed by appropriate and adequate drills. Wherever feasible, these exercises are devised so that they may be done orally by the student. The device of placing the exercises immediately after the grammatical summary enables the student to center his attention on the particular point under discussion and to review a maximum number of points in a relatively short time. This method of presentation also permits an easy division of each lesson into assignments. The sentences in the exercises are purposely kept short to encourage rapid drill work. The vocabulary of the drills is most often limited to words of high frequency, permitting the student to focus on the structure under consideration.

The *Lecturas* present reading and conversational material which is topically related to the dialogue of each lesson. The content of these narratives should be of interest to college students of today and at the same time should serve to widen their active vocabularies in Spanish. The meanings of certain new words, of idiomatic expressions not previously introduced, and of a limited number of difficult phrases or expressions are given in footnotes. The *Lecturas* are followed by exercises in which stress is again placed on developing expression and fostering the student's ability to use Spanish.

The sixteen-page section in full color on painting in Spanish America and the accompanying essay, *Lectura XI,* are a special feature of the book. Black and white illustrations supplement the information included in the *Lecturas.* All illustrations may serve as topical bases for oral and written expression.

For those who may wish to carry on social or commercial correspondence in Spanish, some commonly used phrases and formulas are given in the special section on letter writing, called *Cartas españolas.*

Appendix A contains a summary of Spanish pronunciation, with an explanation of terms used; Appendix B includes lists of expressions used in the classroom and the laboratory, grammatical terms, punctuation marks, and the abbreviations and signs used in the text; Appendix C gives the cardinal and ordinal numerals, the days of the week, the months of the year, the seasons, dates, and ways to express the time of day; Appendix D contains the regular verb paradigms and complete lists of verbs with various types of irregularity used in the text, as well as a few additional verbs which may be encountered in later study of Spanish; and Appendix E includes lists of verbs which are followed immediately by an infinitive without a preposition, verbs which require certain prepositions before an infinitive or other object, and verbs used in the text whose meanings change when used reflexively.

The Spanish-English vocabulary is intended to be complete, with the exception of a few proper and geographical names which are either identical in Spanish and English or whose meaning is clear, a few past participles used as adjectives when the infinitive is given, some of the titles of literary and artistic works mentioned in the *Lecturas,* the Spanish examples translated in the *Cartas españolas* section, and a few diminutives given in *Lección diez.* Idioms are listed under the most important word in the phrase, and, in most cases, cross listings are given. Irregular plural forms of nouns and adjectives are included only for those forms which are used in the plural in the text. The English-Spanish vocabulary contains only the English words used in the English-Spanish exercises.

In this edition of *Mastering Spanish,* the contents of the three *Repasos* have been reorganized to make for a more even length of the three units. The dialogues of the *Repasos* have been revised, rewritten, or replaced with new subject matter. The dialogues of the regular lessons have been revised to varying degrees; many have been rewritten and contain new subject matter; others, even though totally rewritten, are based on the same subject matter. In all cases they are followed by *Preguntas sobre el diálogo* and *Preguntas para conversar.* The pronunciation section, included in this edition through *Lección diez,* has been expanded and reorganized in order to permit a more systematic study of Spanish intonation. Some of the explanations and examples have been revised or changed. An effort has been made to clarify a few of the more difficult matters taken up in the *Notas gramaticales.* A great number of the examples used in the explanations, drawn largely from the new and revised dialogues, have been changed. The types of drill exercises, both oral and written, which appeared in the previous edition are largely unchanged, although individual exercises have been shortened, some lengthened, and others rewritten completely. The summary list of words and expressions included at the end of each lesson should serve as a valuable review for students and should avoid much vocabulary thumbing.

Major changes have been made in the *Lecturas.* Only one has been retained without change, three have been dropped and replaced with new topics of current interest, and the others modified. The content of each is closely related to that of the dialogue of the preceding lesson. Four types of exercises, in groups of three lessons each, accompany the *Lecturas:* guided composition in Spanish; questions in Spanish devised by students to be answered by their classmates; completion of dialogues, or of a letter, on designated topics; and the translation of English sentences into Spanish. The section on letter writing has been expanded in this edition, principally with the inclusion of new sample letters.

The *Workbook* has been completely revised. The exercises, except for a few on pronunciation, have been rewritten. They differ from the exercises in the text, including the ones for the *Lecturas*. A feature of the *Workbook* is the inclusion of five new comprehensive tests, each of which covers a unit of three lessons.

As an aid to the teacher and student, an innovative tape program accompanies the text, covering the dialogues, most of the oral exercises, including pronunciation, and the *Lecturas*. A comprehension exercise, based on each *Lectura*, has been included in the tape for each regular lesson and for the comprehensive tests; space is provided in the *Workbook* for the student's responses. The exercise consists of true-false statements, sentences to be completed in Spanish, questions to be answered in complete Spanish sentences, etc. The teacher who does not use the *Workbook* may want to duplicate, for students who listen to the tapes, the sections in the *Workbook* provided for these exercises.

In the preparation of this edition the authors wish to express their deep appreciation for the valuable suggestions and constructive criticism offered by colleagues who have used the earlier editions, and by the members of the staff of the Modern Language Department of D. C. Heath and Company.

L. H. T.

A. M. E., Jr.

CONTENTS

ADDITIONAL MATERIALS:

Workbook and Testing Program

Tapes
Number of reels: 8 7″ dual track
Speed: $3\frac{3}{4}$ ips
Running time: $9\frac{1}{2}$ hours (approximately)

MASTERING
SPANISH

Repaso de las formas del presente de indicativo de los verbos regulares ▪ Algunos verbos que tienen formas irregulares en el presente de indicativo ▪ Verbos que cambian la vocal radical en el presente de indicativo

REPASO PRIMERO

En la residencia de estudiantes

Comienza un nuevo año académico. Luis García se encuentra en su cuarto en una de las residencias universitarias, desempacando cajas y maletas. Carlos Suárez aparece en la puerta. Lo[1] acompaña su padre. Los dos llevan maletas.

Carlos. ¡Hola! ¿Es el cuarto número 24?

Luis. Sí. Pasen ustedes, por favor.

Carlos. Yo me llamo Carlos Suárez. Y tú eres Luis García, ¿verdad?

Luis. A la orden. Vamos a ser compañeros de cuarto.

Carlos. Quiero presentarte a mi padre.

Luis. (*Le da la mano.*) Mucho gusto, señor Suárez . . . ¿Necesitan ayuda? ¿Traen otras maletas?

Sr. Suárez. Quedan algunas cosas más en el coche. Pero no te molestes, Luis. Carlos y yo podemos traerlas en un momento.

Luis. Pues, ¡manos a la obra!

Carlos. (*Después de varios minutos.*) Bueno, ya está todo en el cuarto . . . Oye, Luis, ¿está abierto el comedor?

---

[1] See page 55 for the use of the direct object pronoun **lo** and **le** for *him, you* (formal m.).

Luis. Todavía no. Se sirve la primera comida esta noche. Pero hay varios restaurantes a unas cuadras de aquí.

Sr. Suárez. (*Mirando su reloj de pulsera.*) Son las doce menos cuarto ya. Luis, ¿por qué no nos acompañas a almorzar?

Carlos. Sí. Así nos puedes contar algo acerca de la universidad.

Luis. ¡Con mucho gusto! Hay varios lugares de interés por el camino.

Preguntas sobre el diálogo: 1. ¿Dónde se encuentra Luis García? 2. ¿Quién aparece en la puerta? 3. ¿Qué pregunta Carlos? 4. ¿Qué contesta Luis? 5. ¿Qué dice Luis cuando Carlos lo presenta a su padre? 6. ¿Qué tienen que traer al cuarto? 7. ¿Está abierto el comedor de la residencia? 8. ¿Qué hay a unas cuadras de la residencia?

Preguntas para conversar: 1. ¿Cuántas residencias de estudiantes hay en esta universidad? 2. ¿Vive usted en una residencia de estudiantes? 3. ¿Viven todos los estudiantes en residencias universitarias? 4. ¿Tiene usted un compañero (una compañera) de cuarto? 5. ¿Cómo se llama su compañero (compañera) de cuarto? 6. ¿Cuántas maletas tiene usted? 7. ¿A qué hora almuerza usted? 8. ¿A qué hora se sirve la comida en la residencia en que usted vive?

PRONUNCIACIÓN

American-Spanish pronunciation. The differences in pronunciation between American Spanish and Castilian or Peninsular Spanish are matters of some concern to teachers and students of Spanish. Since Spanish is spoken in so many different areas, it is only natural that there should be differences from country to country. In general, however, the pronunciation of educated persons differs only in two important respects:

1. In American Spanish (and also in southern Spain), **c** before **e** or **i**, and **z**, are not pronounced as interdental *th* (as in northern and central Spain) but as a dental **s**,[1] not unlike the English *s* in *sent*.

2. In some parts of Spain and quite generally in Spanish America, **ll** (pronounced somewhat like *lli* in *million* in other parts of Spain) is pronounced as the *y* sound in *yes*, with somewhat stronger friction than in English *y*.

In both cases the two variants are accepted as standard forms of pronunciation. Because of the geographic situation of our country in the Western Hemisphere, it seems natural to use the so-called American-Spanish pronunciation of these sounds in this book.

Certain other traits of American Spanish (and of some parts of Spain) are considered popular or regional and are generally avoided by educated persons. Some of these are: aspiration of **s** final in the word or syllable, that is, to pronounce **s** in such circumstances

---

[1] A few basic phonetic terms will be introduced in this text to allow for greater accuracy in the description of Spanish speech sounds. For a definition of the terms used, see Appendix A, pages 270–271.

as English *h*: **ehtoh campoh** for **estos campos**; confusion of l and r when final in the word or syllable: **comel** for **comer**; pronunciation of **y** (and **ll**) as English *z* in *azure*; retention of aspirate **h**, as in Old Spanish: **jumo** for **humo** (with silent **h**); pronunciation of Spanish **j** and **g** before **e** or **i** as English *h*. All these forms should be carefully avoided.

A. Review the sounds of **c** before **e** or **i**, of **z**, of **ll**, of **y**, of **g** before **e** or **i**, and of **j** (Appendix A, pages 273–274) and pronounce after your teacher:

1. aparece	conocer	García	necesitan	oración
2. almorzar	comienza	conduzco	razón	Suárez
3. ellos	hallar	llamar	llevan	llover
4. ayer	ayuda	oye	ya	yo
5. general	Jorge	cajas	humo	hora

B. Review the division of words into syllables and word stress in Appendix A, pages 271–272; then rewrite the words listed above in Exercise A, 1 and 2, dividing them into syllables, by means of a hyphen, and underlining the stressed syllables.

PARA REPASAR

To help you understand and use Spanish more readily, you will need to review some of the verbs and expressions used earlier in your study of the language.

1 Repaso de las formas del presente de indicativo de los verbos regulares

In Appendix D, page 288, review the forms of the present indicative tense of regular verbs. Some common verbs are:

comprar   *to buy*   mirar   *to look (at)*
esperar   *to wait (for), await; to hope, expect*   necesitar   *to need*
hablar   *to speak, talk*   tomar   *to take, drink, eat*
llevar   *to take, carry*   trabajar   *to work*

aprender (a + *inf.*)[1]   *to learn (to + inf.)*   comprender   *to understand*
comer   *to eat*   vender   *to sell*

abrir   *to open*   permitir   *to permit, allow, let*
escribir   *to write*   vivir   *to live*

---

[1] See Appendix B, page 283, for the abbreviations used in the text.

EJERCICIOS

A. Repitan la frase; luego, al oír un sujeto nuevo, substitúyanlo en la frase, cambiando la forma del verbo cuando sea necesario:

1. *Los estudiantes* toman café.
   (Yo, Jorge y yo, Tú, Usted, Ana y María)
2. *José* aprende a hablar español.
   (José y yo, Yo, Ustedes, Tú, Ramón y Luis)
3. ¿Escribes *tú* muchas cartas?
   (ustedes, yo, Carolina, los muchachos, tú y yo)

B. Para contestar afirmativamente[1] en español:

1. ¿Hablan ustedes español?
2. ¿Esperas tú el autobús?
3. ¿Necesitan ellos más tiempo?
4. ¿Compran ustedes muchas cosas?
5. ¿Aprenden ustedes a hablar bien?
6. ¿Come Luisa a las seis?
7. ¿Abren ustedes la puerta a veces?
8. ¿Escribo yo en la pizarra?

C. Para contestar negativamente[1] en español:

1. ¿Compras papel en la biblioteca?
2. ¿Espera Ricardo a Marta?
3. ¿Comes tarde todas las noches?
4. ¿Comen ustedes con Bárbara?
5. ¿Viven ustedes en el campo?
6. ¿Escribe Carlos una composición?

2   Algunos verbos que tienen formas irregulares en el presente de indicativo

Some common verbs with irregular forms in the present indicative are:

decir	*to say, tell*	**digo**	**dices**	**dice**	decimos	decís	**dicen**
estar	*to be*	**estoy**	**estás**	**está**	estamos	estáis	**están**
haber	*to have* (aux.)	**he**	**has**	**ha**	**hemos**	habéis	**han**
ir	*to go*	**voy**	**vas**	**va**	**vamos**	**vais**	**van**
oír	*to hear*	**oigo**	**oyes**	**oye**	oímos	oís	**oyen**
poder	*to be able, can*	**puedo**	**puedes**	**puede**	podemos	podéis	**pueden**
querer	*to wish, want*	**quiero**	**quieres**	**quiere**	queremos	queréis	**quieren**
ser	*to be*	**soy**	**eres**	**es**	**somos**	**sois**	**son**
tener	*to have* (possess)	**tengo**	**tienes**	**tiene**	tenemos	tenéis	**tienen**
venir	*to come*	**vengo**	**vienes**	**viene**	venimos	venís	**vienen**

---

[1] Adverbs of manner are often formed by adding **-mente** to the feminine singular of adjectives.

A number of irregular verbs have regular forms in the present indicative tense, except in the first person singular: **caer,** *to fall* **(caigo); dar,** *to give* **(doy); hacer,** *to do, make* **(hago); poner,** *to put, place* **(pongo); saber,** *to know* (a fact) **(sé); salir,** *to go out, leave* **(salgo); traer,** *to bring* **(traigo); valer,** *to be worth* **(valgo); ver,** *to see* **(veo).** Also irregular only in the first person singular are **conducir,** *to drive, conduct* **(conduzco); conocer,** *to know* (a person) **(conozco); escoger,** *to choose* **(escojo).**

See Appendix D, page 288, for accented forms in the present indicative tense of **enviar,** *to send,* and **continuar,** *to continue,* and for forms of verbs ending in **-uir: huir,** *to flee.*

EJERCICIOS

A. Repitan la frase; luego, repítanla otra vez, cambiando el sujeto y el verbo al plural.

MODELOS: Yo puedo salir.   Yo puedo salir.
                                           Nosotros podemos salir.

            ¿Tiene usted mucho tiempo?   ¿Tiene usted mucho tiempo?
                                           ¿Tienen ustedes mucho tiempo?

1. Yo doy paseos a menudo.
2. ¿Qué quiere usted hacer?
3. ¿Viene ella con mi tío?
4. Él tiene mucha suerte.
5. Yo les traigo regalos a veces.
6. ¿Dónde está ella ahora?
7. ¿Ve usted a Carolina?
8. Yo los pongo en el coche.
9. ¿Puede él esperar aquí?
10. ¿Le envía usted algo a Inés?
11. Mi hermana oye la música.
12. Yo escojo muchas cosas.

B. Lean en español, supliendo (*supplying*) la forma correcta del verbo entre paréntesis en el presente de indicativo:

1. (decir) —¿Qué le _____ tú a Margarita? —Yo no le _____ nada. 2. (estar) —¿Dónde _____ yo ahora? —Usted _____ cerca de la mesa. 3. (poder) —¿ _____ ustedes esperar unos minutos? —Sí, _____ esperar un rato. 4. (hacer) —¿Qué _____ usted esta tarde? —No _____ nada. 5. (ver) —¿ _____ ustedes estos mapas? —Sí, los _____ bien. 6. (saber) —¿ _____ usted si mi novia está en la clase? —No, no _____ si ella está en la clase. 7. (conocer) —¿ _____ tú a mi tía? —Sí, la _____ muy bien. 8. (salir) —¿ _____ yo de casa temprano? —Sí, usted _____ a las siete y media. 9. (ir) —¿ _____ usted a asistir a esta clase? —Sí, _____ a asistir a esta clase este semestre. 10. (venir) —¿Quién _____ a ayudar a Pablo? —Yo _____ a ayudarlo esta noche. 11. (ser) —¿ _____ tú estudiante? —Sí, _____ estudiante de esta universidad. 12. (continuar) —¿ _____ ustedes leyendo la novela? —Sí, _____ leyendo varias páginas cada día.

C. Para expresar en español:

1. I leave at a quarter after eight. 2. I don't know whether John is coming. 3. I see many cars in the street. 4. I go to the library. 5. I choose several books. 6. I put the

things on the table. 7. We hear the music. 8. We bring records to class. 9. We are lucky. 10. Do you (*fam. sing.*) want to attend this class? 11. Do you (*fam. sing.*) say that the secretary is in the office? 12. Do you (*pl.*) say that you can wait a few minutes?

3 Verbos que cambian la vocal radical (*Stem-changing verbs*) en el presente de indicativo

Some verbs of Class I are:

almorzar (ue) *to take (eat) lunch*	encontrar (ue) *to encounter, find*
cerrar (ie) *to close*	jugar (ue) *to play (a game)*
comenzar (ie) *to commence, begin, start*	pensar (ie) *to think;* + inf. *to intend*
contar (ue) *to count; to tell*	perder (ie) *to lose, miss*
despertar (ie) *to awaken; to wake up*	recordar (ue) *to recall, remember*
devolver (ue) *to return, give back*	sentarse (ie) *to sit down*
empezar (ie) *to begin, start*	volver (ue) *to return, come back*

cerrar	**cierro**	**cierras**	**cierra**	cerramos	cerráis	**cierran**
volver	**vuelvo**	**vuelves**	**vuelve**	volvemos	volvéis	**vuelven**
jugar	**juego**	**juegas**	**juega**	jugamos	jugáis	**juegan**

Some Class II verbs are:

divertirse (ie, i) *to have a good time, amuse oneself*	sentir (ie, i) *to feel, regret, be sorry*
preferir (ie, i) *to prefer*	dormir (ue, u) *to sleep*

sentir	**siento**	**sientes**	**siente**	sentimos	sentís	**sienten**
dormir	**duermo**	**duermes**	**duerme**	dormimos	dormís	**duermen**

Some Class III verbs are:

conseguir[1] (i, i) *to get, obtain*	seguir[1] (i, i) *to follow, continue*
pedir (i, i) *to ask (for), request*	servir (i, i) *to serve*
reír (i, i) *to laugh*	vestirse (i, i) *to dress oneself, get dressed*
repetir (i, i) *to repeat*	

pedir	**pido**	**pides**	**pide**	pedimos	pedís	**piden**
reír	**río**	**ríes**	**ríe**	reímos	reís	**ríen**

---

[1] See Appendix D, pages 297–298, for the first person singular present indicative of verbs with changes in spelling, including those ending in **-guir: conseguir (consigo), seguir (sigo).**

Estudiantes españoles se dirigen a sus clases en la universidad de Barcelona.

EJERCICIOS

A. Repitan la frase; luego, al oír un sujeto nuevo, substitúyanlo en la frase, cambiando la forma del verbo cuando sea necesario:

1. *Jaime* comienza a estudiar el diálogo.
   (*Yo, Vicente y yo, Tú, Enrique, Usted y él*)
2. *Nuestros amigos* prefieren esperar aquí.
   (*Tú, Yo, Dorotea y yo, Mis tíos, Usted*)
3. ¿Juegan *ustedes* al tenis?
   (*tú, Ramón y Luis, nosotros, yo, tu hermano*)
4. ¿Cuánto tiempo duerme *Juanita*?
   (*tú, ustedes, tu hermanito, él y yo, los niños*)
5. ¿Le pide *usted* a Clara un favor?
   (*Isabel, tú, yo, ustedes, nosotros*)

B. Para expresar en español:

1. I remember the word. 2. Paul begins to talk in Spanish. 3. Do you (*pl.*) intend to see the film? 4. Mary and I return home at a quarter after five. 5. The boys have a good time, don't they? 6. I ask for books in the library. 7. Do you (*fam. sing.*) sleep seven hours each night? 8. I always repeat the words. 9. Many students continue studying until midnight. 10. My mother serves coffee or chocolate.

Resumen de palabras y expresiones[1]

a clase   to class
a la orden   yes, at your service
a las (seis)   at (six) o'clock
a menudo   often, frequently
¿a qué hora?   at what time? when?
a veces   at times
académico, -a   academic
acerca de   *prep.* about, concerning
al + *inf.*   on, upon + *pres. part.*
aparecer   to appear, show up
asistir a   to attend
cerca de   *prep.* near
la caja   box, case
¿cómo se llama . . . ?   what's the name of . . . ?
compañero (compañera) de cuarto   roommate (*m.* and *f.*)
con mucho gusto   gladly, with great (much) pleasure
la cuadra   block (*city*)
¿cuánto tiempo?   how long (much time)?
dar la mano a (uno)   to shake hands with (one)
dar un paseo   to take a walk (stroll)
desempacar   to unpack
después de   *prep.* after
divertirse (ie, i) (mucho)   to have a (very) good time
en casa   at home
esta noche   tonight
jugar (ue) (a + *obj.*)   to play (*a game*)
los (las) dos   the two, both

¡manos a la obra!   (let's get) to work!
me llamo . . .   my name is . . .
✓mucho gusto   (I'm very) glad *or* pleased to meet *or* know you
¿(no es) verdad?   aren't you? isn't it (true)? *etc.*
ño te molestes   don't bother, never mind
otra vez   again, another time
oye   (*fam. sing.*) listen, hey, say
pase (n) usted (es)   come in
pensar (ie) + *inf.*   to intend, plan
✓por el camino   along the way
por favor   please (*at end of request*)
quedan algunas cosas más   a few more things remain (are left)
el reloj de pulsera   wrist watch
la residencia (de estudiantes)   (student) residence hall *or* dormitory
el resumen (*pl.* resúmenes)   summary
salir (de + *obj.*)   to leave, go out (of)
salir de casa   to leave home
son las (doce) menos cuarto   it is a quarter to (twelve)
tener (mucha) suerte   to be (very) fortunate *or* lucky
tener que + *inf.*   to have to, must
todas las noches   every night (evening)
todavía no   not yet
universitario, -a   university (*adj.*)
unos, -as   some, a few, about (*quantity*)
volver (ue) a casa   to return home

[1]All the expressions used in the dialogue and/or exercises of each lesson and all individual words not used in the active vocabularies of Turk, Espinosa, and Solé, *Foundation Course in Spanish*, Heath, 1978, are given in this section for reference.

Una estudiante toma notas de las explicaciones del profesor en la universidad de Barcelona, España.

Repaso de las formas del pretérito y del imperfecto de indicativo de los verbos regulares ▪ Algunos verbos que tienen formas irregulares en el pretérito de indicativo ▪ Otros tipos de verbos que tienen formas irregulares en el pretérito de indicativo ▪ Verbos que cambian la vocal radical, Grupos II y III, en el pretérito ▪ Verbos que tienen formas irregulares en el imperfecto de indicativo ▪ Repaso de las formas del participio presente

REPASO DOS

Luisa se matricula en la universidad

Luisa y Felipe viven en la misma residencia de estudiantes. Esta noche van a cenar juntos. Son las seis menos cuarto de la tarde. Luisa espera a Felipe en el vestíbulo de la residencia. Llega Felipe.

Felipe. ¡Hola, Luisa! ¿A qué hora saliste de la residencia esta mañana?

Luisa. Eran las nueve, más o menos. Me desayuné temprano y fui en seguida a matricularme.

Felipe. ¿Pudiste matricularte?

Luisa. Sí. Fue muy fácil. No hubo dificultades.[1]

Felipe. Pues, yo tengo que esperar hasta mañana. Varias de las clases que me interesaban estaban llenas.

Luisa. Mi consejero me dijo que iban a abrir algunas secciones nuevas.

Felipe. Casi siempre hay algunos cambios. Y, ¿qué hiciste después?

Luisa. Pasé por la librería y compré varios de los textos que voy a necesitar.

Felipe. ¿Sacaste la licencia para tu bicicleta?

---

[1] **No hubo dificultades,** *There were no difficulties.* The impersonal form **hubo** (pret. of **haber**) means *there was (were).*

Luisa. También. Te busqué para ir juntos a la oficina de policía, pero no te encontré.

Felipe. ¿Oíste lo que nos dijo el director anoche acerca de las bicicletas?

Luisa. Sí, que las bicicletas tenían muy corta vida en esta universidad.

Felipe. Pues, como mi bicicleta es nueva, pienso comprarme un candado fuerte.

Luisa. Afortunadamente la bicicleta que tengo es muy vieja. Nadie va a querer robármela.[1]

Felipe. Bueno, parece que podemos entrar en el comedor.

Luisa. Sí. Han abierto las puertas. Vamos a cenar.

Preguntas sobre el diálogo: 1. ¿Dónde espera Luisa a Felipe? 2. ¿A qué hora salió Luisa de la residencia? 3. ¿Qué hizo Luisa después de desayunarse? 4. ¿Por qué no pudo matricularse Felipe? 5. ¿Qué hizo Luisa después de matricularse? 6. ¿Dónde sacó Luisa la licencia para su bicicleta? 7. ¿Qué piensa comprarse Felipe? 8. ¿Qué dice Luisa de la bicicleta que ella tiene?

Preguntas para conversar: 1. ¿Tuvo usted dificultades al matricularse este año? 2. ¿Estaban llenas algunas de las clases que le interesaban a usted? 3. ¿Dónde compró usted los textos para sus clases? 4. ¿Cuántos textos necesita usted para la clase de español? 5. ¿Es útil tener una bicicleta? 6. ¿Desaparecen pronto las bicicletas en esta universidad? 7. ¿Es necesario sacar una licencia si uno tiene una bicicleta en esta universidad? 8. ¿Tenía usted una bicicleta cuando estaba en la escuela superior?

PRONUNCIACIÓN

A. Spanish **b** (and **v**), **d.** Each of these consonants (**b** and **v** are pronounced exactly alike) has two different sounds, a voiced stop sound and a voiced continuant sound.

When initial in a breath-group or when after **m** or **n** (also pronounced **m** in this case), whether within a word or between words, Spanish **b** (or **v**) is a voiced bilabial stop, like English *b* in *boy*, but somewhat weaker. In all other positions, it is a voiced bilabial continuant; the lips do not close completely as in stop **b**, but allow the breath to pass between them through a very narrow passage. When between vowels, the articulation is especially weak. Avoid the English *v* sound. Pronounce after your teacher:

1. bueno	también	vamos	varios	un vaso
2. abrir	estaban	llevan	nuevo	servir

At the beginning of a breath-group or when after **n** or **l**, Spanish **d** is a voiced dental stop, like English *d*, but with the tip of the tongue touching the inner surface of

---

[1] **robármela,** *to steal it from me.*

the upper teeth, rather than the ridge above the teeth as in English. In all other cases the tongue drops even lower and the **d** is pronounced as a voiced interdental continuant, like a weak English *th* in *this.* The sound is especially weak in the ending **-ado** and when final in a word before a pause. Pronounce after your teacher:

3. después	dijo	¿dónde?	mirando	el día
4. nadie	orden	tarde	verdad	le da

B. In Appendix A, pages 270–277, review the division of words into syllables, linking of words, and word stress; then write the last two exchanges of the dialogue on page 14, dividing them into breath-groups and syllables, indicating the linking of sounds between words by means of a linking sign, and underlining the syllables that are stressed.

PARA REPASAR

1 Repaso de las formas del pretérito y del imperfecto de indicativo de los verbos regulares

Review in Appendix D, pages 288–289, the forms of the preterit and imperfect indicative tenses of regular verbs.

EJERCICIO

Repitan la frase; luego, al oír un sujeto nuevo, substitúyanlo en la frase, cambiando la forma del verbo cuando sea necesario:

1. *Yo* no esperé a Tomás.
    (*Tú, Ud., Los estudiantes, Luisa y yo, Uds.*)
2. *Felipe* aprendió bien el diálogo.
    (*José y yo, Yo, Uds., Tú, Ana y Luis*)
3. *Ellos* miraban el mapa de México.
    (*Ella, Yo, Tú, El profesor, Isabel y yo*)
4. *Mis padres* vivían en la Argentina.
    (*El señor Díaz, Yo, Mi hermano y yo, Tú, Ud.*)

2   Algunos verbos que tienen formas irregulares en el pretérito de indicativo

Some common verbs are:

decir	**dije dijiste dijo dijimos dijisteis dijeron**
hacer	**hice hiciste hizo hicimos hicisteis hicieron**
querer	**quise quisiste quiso quisimos quisisteis quisieron**
venir	**vine viniste vino vinimos vinisteis vinieron**
andar	**anduve anduviste anduvo anduvimos anduvisteis anduvieron**
estar	**estuve estuviste estuvo estuvimos estuvisteis estuvieron**
poder	**pude pudiste pudo pudimos pudisteis pudieron**
poner	**puse pusiste puso pusimos pusisteis pusieron**
saber	**supe supiste supo supimos supisteis supieron**
tener	**tuve tuviste tuvo tuvimos tuvisteis tuvieron**
traer	**traje trajiste trajo trajimos trajisteis trajeron**
dar	**di diste dio dimos disteis dieron**
ir, ser	**fui fuiste fue fuimos fuisteis fueron**
ver	**vi** viste **vio** vimos visteis vieron

In the listed forms note that:

1. Four verbs have **i**-stems and six have **u**-stems. There are no written accents on any of the forms, and in the first eleven verbs the first person singular ends in **-e** and the third person singular ends in **-o**.
2. The third person singular of **hacer** is **hizo**; the third person plural ending of **decir** and of **traer** is **-eron**.
3. **Ir** and **ser** have the same forms.

A few verbs have special meanings in the preterit tense. The preterit of **saber** usually means *learned, found out*: **Anoche supe eso**, *Last night I learned that*; that of **tener** often means *got, received*: **Yo tuve una carta**, *I got (received) a letter*; that of **querer** often means *tried*: **Juan quiso hacer eso pero no pudo**, *John tried to do that but he couldn't*; that of **querer** used negatively often means *refused to, would not*: **Ellos no quisieron esperar**, *They refused to (would not) wait.*

EJERCICIOS

A. Para contestar afirmativamente:

1. ¿Tuviste que ir al centro?
2. ¿Tuvo que ir Carlos también?
3. ¿Hiciste una excursión ayer?
4. ¿Hizo Juan un viaje a México?

5. ¿Anduviste un rato?
6. ¿Dieron Uds. un paseo ayer?

7. ¿Fuiste de compras con Pablo?
8. ¿Fueron Uds. en taxi?

B. Para contestar negativamente:

1. ¿Estuviste en el centro anoche?
2. ¿Trajeron Uds. muchas fotos a clase?
3. ¿Pudiste trabajar ayer por la tarde?

4. ¿Vio Carlos un partido de fútbol?
5. ¿Vinieron Uds. a clase el sábado?
6. ¿Le dijiste la verdad a Carolina?

C. Repitan la frase; luego, repítanla otra vez, cambiando la forma del verbo al pretérito de indicativo:

1. Yo no hago nada por la mañana. 2. José y yo no vemos a nadie. 3. María no quiere ir al cine. 4. Los jóvenes no pueden esperar. 5. ¿Adónde vas en avión? 6. ¿Qué ves en la calle? 7. Oigo cantar a alguien. 8. ¿Quién te trae muchos regalos? 9. Mis padres no dicen eso. 10. Pongo los paquetes sobre la mesa. 11. Mi madre tiene que volver en autobús. 12. Él no sabe nada de particular.

D. Para expresar en español:

1. "I went at once to register," said Louise. 2. "It was easy. There were no difficulties." 3. Philip had to wait until the following day (in order) to register. 4. "What did you (*fam. sing.*) do afterwards?" 5. "I dropped by the bookstore and bought several texts." 6. Did you (*fam. sing.*) hear what the director said about (the) bicycles? 7. Did you (*pl.*) eat breakfast early? 8. Louise looked for Philip (in order) to go together to the police department.

3 Otros tipos de verbos que tienen formas irregulares en el pretérito de indicativo

1. Before the ending -é in the first person singular preterit, all verbs ending in -car change c to qu; those ending in -gar change g to gu, and those ending in -zar change z to c (see Appendix D, pages 298–300):

buscar	**busqué** buscaste buscó, etc.
llegar	**llegué** llegaste llegó, etc.
empezar (ie)	**empecé** empezaste empezó, etc.

2. Certain verbs ending in -er and -ir preceded by a vowel replace unaccented i by y in the third person singular and plural of the preterit. Accents must be written on the

other four forms. **Caer**, *to fall*, and **leer**, *to read*, have the same changes as **creer**, *to believe*, and **oír**, *to hear*:

| creer | creí | **creíste** | **creyó** | **creímos** | **creísteis** | **creyeron** |
| oír | oí | oíste | **oyó** | oímos | oísteis | **oyeron** |

3. Verbs ending in **-ducir** and **-uir** (except **-guir**) have irregular forms in the preterit and also in the present indicative. In Appendix D, review the forms of the models **conducir** and **huir**, page 299.

EJERCICIOS

A. Escriban cada frase, cambiando la forma del verbo al pretérito de indicativo; luego, lean la frase nueva en voz alta (*aloud*):

1. Yo no almuerzo hasta la una. 2. Llego tarde al partido. 3. Me acerco rápidamente al estadio. 4. Pago tres dólares por mi billete (boleto). 5. Le entrego el dinero al empleado. 6. Entro y busco un asiento. 7. Empiezo a sacar fotos de los jugadores. 8. Saco ocho o diez fotos. 9. Por la mañana juego al golf. 10. Por la tarde toco unos discos primero. 11. Luego, busco mi libro de español. 12. Por fin comienzo a estudiar. 13. Leo bien toda la lección. 14. Practico el diálogo varias veces. 15. A las cinco conduzco mi coche a casa de Ramón.

B. Repitan la frase; luego, repítanla otra vez, cambiando la forma del verbo[1] al pretérito de indicativo:

1. Ellos empiezan a matricularse. 2. Yo me despierto tarde. 3. ¿No cierras tu libro? 4. ¿No vuelven Uds. a las cinco? 5. Jorge le devuelve el dinero a su amigo. 6. Ella no recuerda el diálogo. 7. Carlos y yo lo recordamos muy bien. 8. Ellos pierden el autobús. 9. Carlos nunca piensa en Juanita. 10. ¿Se sienta Felipe en la sala de clase?

C. Para contestar afirmativamente:

1. ¿Buscaste varios textos?
2. ¿Tocaste la guitarra anoche?
3. ¿Jugaste al fútbol el sábado?
4. ¿Condujiste el coche al centro?
5. ¿Almorzaron Uds. a las doce?
6. ¿Oyeron Uds. la orquesta ayer?
7. ¿Creyeron Uds. lo que dijo Marta?
8. ¿Leyeron Uds. la novela?

[1] All verbs to be changed in this exercise are stem-changing verbs, Class I; remember that the stem vowel of these verbs does not change in the preterit. See Appendix D, pages 300–301, for verbs of this class used in the text.

4 Verbos que cambian la vocal radical, Grupos II y III, en el pretérito

Stem-changing verbs, Class II and Class III,[1] change **e** to **i** and **o** to **u** in the third person singular and plural of the preterit:

	3rd Singular	3rd Plural
sentir	**sintió**	**sintieron**
dormir	**durmió**	**durmieron**
pedir	**pidió**	**pidieron**

EJERCICIOS

A. Repitan la frase; luego, repítanla otra vez, cambiando la forma del verbo al pretérito:

1. Los muchachos se divierten. 2. María se divierte mucho también. 3. Ricardo prefiere ir a la residencia de estudiantes. 4. Ellos prefieren no acompañarlo. 5. Mi padre duerme la siesta. 6. Juan consigue un puesto. 7. ¿Le pide Ud. a él alguna cosa? 8. Los niños nunca me piden nada. 9. Mi hermano se viste rápidamente. 10. Mis hermanas se visten despacio. 11. ¿Sigue Ud. por este camino? 12. ¿Repiten ellos el diálogo?

B. Para expresar en español:

1. They sleep well; they slept well. 2. Thomas has a good time; he had a good time. 3. Jane asks for the book; she asked for the book. 4. My mother serves coffee; she served coffee. 5. The teacher repeats the question; he repeated the question. 6. Henry continues working there; he continued working there. 7. I do not drive my car downtown; I did not drive my car downtown. 8. I take a nap; we took a nap. 9. I obtained a job; my sister obtained a job also. 10. I ate lunch in the new restaurant; Mary ate lunch there yesterday.

5 Verbos que tienen formas irregulares en el imperfecto de indicativo

All verbs in Spanish have regular forms in the imperfect indicative tense except **ir, ser, ver.** Their forms are:

ir	**iba**	**ibas**	**iba**	**íbamos**	**ibais**	**iban**
ser	**era**	**eras**	**era**	**éramos**	**erais**	**eran**
ver	**veía**	**veías**	**veía**	**veíamos**	**veíais**	**veían**

---

[1] See Appendix D, pages 302–303, for verbs of these two classes used in the text.

EJERCICIOS

A. Repitan la frase; luego, repítanla otra vez, cambiando la forma del verbo al imperfecto de indicativo:

1. Yo no sé nada de particular. 2. Carlos siempre tiene mucha suerte. 3. Mi consejero no está en su oficina. 4. No queremos llegar tarde. 5. Van a la biblioteca todas las noches. 6. Vamos a la iglesia los domingos. 7. Es un día hermoso. 8. Las clases no son grandes. 9. Los vemos todos los días. 10. Yo los veo a menudo.

B. Para expresar en español:

1. Several of the classes which interested me were full. 2. It was nine o'clock, approximately, when Louise left (*pret.*) the residence hall. 3. Since her bicycle was new, she intended to buy herself a strong lock. 4. Philip said (*pret.*) that the bicycle that he had was very old.

6   Repaso de las formas del participio presente

Review the forms of the present participle in Appendix D, page 288. Some verbs which have irregular present participles are:

caer	**cayendo**	*falling*	oír	**oyendo**	*hearing*
creer	**creyendo**	*believing*	poder	**pudiendo**	*being able*
decir	**diciendo**	*saying, telling*	traer	**trayendo**	*bringing*
ir	**yendo**	*going*	venir	**viniendo**	*coming*
leer	**leyendo**	*reading*			

In stem-changing verbs, Class II and Class III, the stem vowel **e** becomes **i** and **o** becomes **u** in the present participle. Examples:

sentir	**sintiendo**	*feeling*	dormir	**durmiendo**	*sleeping*
pedir	**pidiendo**	*asking*	servir	**sirviendo**	*serving*

EJERCICIO

Repitan la frase; luego, repítanla otra vez, substituyendo el verbo con la forma correcta del presente de indicativo del verbo **estar** seguida del (*followed by the*) participio presente:

1. Mi padre lee el periódico. 2. Nosotros miramos el mapa. 3. Roberto aprende la lección. 4. María escribe una carta. 5. Los estudiantes oyen los discos. 6. Mi mamá duerme la siesta. 7. Carlos trae unas flores para Juanita. 8. Juan come con sus amigos.

Resumen de palabras y expresiones

a casa de (Ramón)   to (Raymond's)
afortunadamente   fortunately
alguna cosa   something, anything
ayer por la tarde (mañana)   yesterday
  afternoon (morning)
la **bicicleta**   bicycle
el **cambio**   change
el **candado**   lock
la **clase de español**   Spanish class
el **consejero**   counsellor, adviser
de la tarde   p.m., in the afternoon
desaparecer   to disappear
la **dificultad**   difficulty
el **director**   director, manager; editor (*of a
  newspaper*)
dormir (ue, u) la siesta   to take a nap
en seguida   at once, immediately
entrar (en + *obj.***)**   to enter, come (go) in
la **escuela superior**   high school
el **estadio**   stadium
(estar) en el centro   (to be) downtown
fuerte   strong
la **guitarra**   guitar
hacer un viaje (una excursión)   to take
  or make a trip (an excursion)
ir a la iglesia   to go to church
ir al centro   to go downtown
ir de compras   to go shopping
ir en autobús (avión, coche, taxi)   to go
  by bus (plane, car, taxi)

la **librería**   bookstore
el **libro de español**   Spanish book
lleno, -a   full, filled
más o menos   more or less,
  approximately
matricularse   to matriculate, register,
  enroll
nada de particular   nothing special
la **oficina de policía**   police department
  (station)
el **partido de fútbol**   football game
pasar por   to pass (go, come) by *or* along,
  drop by *or* in, stop by
pensar (ie) en (+ *obj.* or *inf.*)   to think of
  (about)
por fin   finally, at last
por la mañana (tarde)   in the morning
  (afternoon)
robar   to rob, steal
sacar (fotos)   to take (photos)
sacar la licencia   to get *or* obtain the
  license
la **sala de clase**   classroom
el **texto**   text, textbook
toda (la lección)   all the *or* the entire
  (lesson)
todos los días   every day
útil   useful
vamos a (cenar)   let's *or* let's go to (eat
  supper)

Repaso de las formas del futuro y del condicional de los verbos regulares ▪ Verbos que tienen formas irregulares en el futuro y en el condicional ▪ Formación de los tiempos compuestos ▪ Formas de mandato correspondientes a «usted, ustedes» ▪ Formas de mandato correspondientes a «tú»

REPASO TRES

Carmen consulta al profesor de español

Carmen ha ido al Departamento de Español para consultar al profesor Ramos. Habla con la secretaria, que está escribiendo a máquina.

Carmen. Buenos días, señorita Peña. ¿Podría usted decirme si el profesor Ramos ha venido esta mañana?

Srta. Peña. Sí, Carmen. Creo que está trabajando en su oficina. Siéntese usted, por favor. Voy a ver si puede recibirla. (*Al poco tiempo entra el profesor Ramos.*)

Sr. Ramos. ¡Hola, Carmen! ¿Quería verme?

Carmen. Sí, profesor. Tengo un problema. Han cambiado la hora del curso sobre la historia de México y no podré tomar el curso de gramática avanzada, como habíamos decidido.

Sr. Ramos. Pues, vamos a ver. (*Se dirige a la secretaria.*) Señorita Peña, ¿quiere usted traerme la lista de los cursos que ofreceremos el semestre que viene?

Srta. Peña. (*Después de buscar la lista en su fichero.*) Aquí la tiene usted.

Sr. Ramos. Gracias . . . Pues, se repetirá el curso de gramática avanzada durante el segundo semestre . . .

Carmen. ¿Podría tomar también algún curso sobre la literatura mexicana el semestre que viene?

Sr. Ramos. Si usted toma el curso de historia, estará muy bien preparada para tomar el curso sobre la novela mexicana.

Carmen. Entonces, ¿usted cree que no perderé nada si aplazo el curso de gramática?

Sr. Ramos. Al contrario. He oído comentarios muy favorables sobre el curso de historia.

Carmen. Pues, muchas gracias, profesor. Seguiré su consejo. Haré lo que usted me ha dicho.

Preparen un diálogo original, de unas diez líneas, para recitar en clase, empleando las frases y preguntas siguientes como elemento inicial:[1]

1. *María.* ¿Qué estás haciendo, Carmen? Luisa y yo vamos a ir al centro. ¿Por qué no vienes con nosotras?

    Carmen. ¿No ves que tengo que desempacar todas estas cajas?

2. *Enrique.* ¿Tiene un momento, señor Valdés? Quiero consultarlo sobre mi programa.

    Sr. Valdés. Siéntese, por favor. A ver, ¿qué le preocupa, Enrique?

PRONUNCIACIÓN

Intonation. The term intonation refers to the variations in pitch which occur in speech. Every language has its characteristic patterns of intonation. The intonation of Spanish is quite different from that of English.

The alternate rise and fall of the pitch depends upon the particular meaning of the sentence, the position of stressed syllables, and whether the sentence expresses command, affirmation, interrogation, exclamation, request, or other factors. In general, three meaningful levels of pitch can be distinguished in Spanish: one below the speaker's normal pitch (level 1), the speaker's normal tone (level 2), and a tone higher than the normal one (level 3). With respect to the use of these levels, the following basic principles should be observed:

A. At the beginning of a breath-group, the voice begins and continues in a relatively low pitch (level 1) as long as the first accented syllable is not reached.

B. When the first accented syllable of a breath-group is reached, the voice rises to the speaker's normal tone (level 2) and continues in the same pitch as long as the last accented syllable is not reached.

C. When the last accented syllable of the breath-group is reached, the voice falls or rises, depending on the following circumstances:

    1. At the end of a declarative statement, the voice falls to a pitch even lower than that of the initial unaccented syllable or syllables.
    2. At the end of an interrogative sentence, or of an incomplete sentence interrupted by a pause, the voice rises to a pitch above the normal tone (level 3).

---

[1] Review of dialogues on pages 2–4 and 12–14 will be helpful to the student in preparing the new dialogues.

D. In exclamations, and in questions which begin with an interrogative word, the voice begins in a pitch above the normal tone (level 3) and gradually falls in the following syllables as long as the final accented syllable is not reached; when the last accented syllable is reached, the voice falls to a pitch even lower than that of the initial unaccented syllable or syllables, as in the case of the end of a simple declarative sentence, unless special interest or courtesy is intended, in which case the voice rises to the normal tone or even higher.

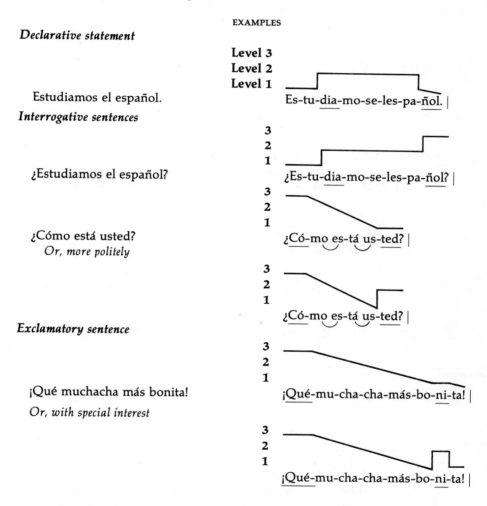

EXAMPLES

Declarative statement

Level 3
Level 2
Level 1

Estudiamos el español.

Es-tu-dia-mo-se-les-pa-ñol. |

Interrogative sentences

3
2
1

¿Estudiamos el español?

¿Es-tu-dia-mo-se-les-pa-ñol? |

3
2
1

¿Cómo está usted?
Or, more politely

¿Có-mo es-tá us-ted? |

3
2
1

¿Có-mo es-tá us-ted? |

Exclamatory sentence

3
2
1

¡Qué muchacha más bonita!
Or, with special interest

¡Qué-mu-cha-cha-más-bo-ni-ta! |

3
2
1

¡Qué-mu-cha-cha-más-bo-ni-ta! |

Write the second and third exchanges of the dialogue of this lesson, dividing them into breath-groups and syllables, and outline the intonation patterns. (Note that the comma before *Carmen* and *por favor* in the second exchange, and before *Carmen* in the third, does not represent a real pause and will not close the breath-group; consider, then, the entire expression in which these commas occur as one breath-group. Follow the same principle in all subsequent exercises of this type.)

PARA REPASAR

1 Repaso de las formas del futuro y del condicional de los verbos regulares

In Appendix D, page 288, review the forms of the future and conditional indicative tenses of regular verbs.

EJERCICIO

Repitan la frase; luego, al oír un sujeto nuevo, substitúyanlo en la frase, cambiando la forma del verbo cuando sea necesario:

1. *Inés* los llevará a casa.
   (*Yo, Tú, Mis hermanas, Marta y yo, Mi amiga*)
2. *Mis padres* no venderán el coche.
   (*Mi tío, Ella y yo, Tú, Uds., Yo*)
3. *Nosotros* asistiremos a la fiesta.
   (*Mis amigos, Ud., Tú, Yo, Tomás*)
4. *Ella* hablaría con otros estudiantes.
   (*Yo, Uds., Nosotros, Tú, José*)
5. *Yo* no comería hasta las seis.
   (*Nosotros, Las muchachas, Tú, Uds., Mi padre*)

2 Verbos que tienen formas irregulares en el futuro y en el condicional

Verbs irregular in the future and conditional indicative tenses are:

	Infinitive	Future	Conditional
1.	haber	habré, -ás, -á, etc.	habría, -ías, -ía, etc.
	poder	podré, -ás, -á, etc.	podría, -ías, -ía, etc.
	querer	querré, -ás, -á, etc.	querría, -ías, -ía, etc.
	saber	sabré, -ás, -á, etc.	sabría, -ías, -ía, etc.
2.	poner	pondré, -ás, -á, etc.	pondría, -ías, -ía, etc.
	salir	saldré, -ás, -á, etc.	saldría, -ías, -ía, etc.
	tener	tendré, -ás, -á, etc.	tendría, -ías, -ía, etc.
	valer	valdré, -ás, -á, etc.	valdría, -ías, -ía, etc.
	venir	vendré, -ás, -á, etc.	vendría, -ías, -ía, etc.
3.	decir	diré, -ás, -á, etc.	diría, -ías, -ía, etc.
	hacer	haré, -ás, -á, etc.	haría, -ías, -ía, etc.

The future and conditional tenses have the same stem, and the endings are the same as for regular verbs. Note that the irregularity is in the infinitive stem used: in group (1) the final vowel of the infinitive has been dropped, in (2) the final vowel of the infinitive has been dropped and the letter **d** inserted to facilitate pronunciation, and in (3) contracted stems are used.

EJERCICIOS

A. Formen frases completas empleando las palabras **Carlos dice que** como elemento inicial y cambiando el infinitivo en cursiva (*in italics*) a la forma correcta del futuro:

1. *tener* que trabajar el lunes.
2. *poder* ir a la librería.
3. *salir* de casa a las ocho.
4. *hacer* una excursión el domingo.
5. *poner* las cosas en el coche en seguida.
6. *haber* mucha gente en el teatro.
7. *saber* el diálogo pronto.
8. no *venir* a vernos mañana.
9. no *querer* acompañarnos al cine.
10. *valer* más esperar hasta mañana por la noche.

Repitan el ejercicio, empleando las palabras **Carlos dijo que** como elemento inicial y cambiando el infinitivo en cursiva a la forma correcta del condicional.

B. Para expresar en español:

1. Carmen says that she will go to the Spanish Department to consult Professor Ramos. 2. Carmen will ask the secretary whether he will receive her. 3. It will be necessary to arrive before nine o'clock. 4. At that hour Professor Ramos will be working (*progressive tense*) in his office. 5. Carmen will tell him that she has a problem. 6. Upon entering the office, Carmen says that she will not be able to take the course in advanced grammar. 7. (Professor Ramos turns to the secretary.) 8. "Will you bring me the list of courses that we shall offer next semester?" 9. "After looking at the list, he said that they would repeat the course the second semester." 10. Finally, Carmen decided that she would take the course on the Mexican novel.

3 Formación de los tiempos compuestos

The compound tenses are formed by using the appropriate form of the auxiliary verb **haber** with the past participle. In Appendix D, page 288, review the present perfect, pluperfect, preterit perfect, future perfect, and conditional perfect indicative tenses.

The following past participles are irregular:

abrir	**abierto** *opened*	hacer	**hecho** *done*
decir	**dicho** *said*	ir	**ido** *gone*
describir	**descrito** *described*	morir	**muerto** *died*
descubrir	**descubierto** *discovered*	poner	**puesto** *put, placed*
devolver	**devuelto** *given back*	romper	**roto** *broken*
envolver	**envuelto** *wrapped*	ver	**visto** *seen*
escribir	**escrito** *written*	volver	**vuelto** *returned*

Also note the written accent on the following forms: caer, **caído;** creer, **creído;** leer, **leído;** oír, **oído;** reír, **reído;** traer, **traído.**

EJERCICIOS

A. Para contestar negativamente en español, siguiendo los modelos.

MODELOS: ¿Cerraste la puerta?   No, todavía no he cerrado la puerta.
                    ¿Salió Ana de casa?   No, todavía no ha salido de casa.

1. ¿Abriste la ventana?
2. ¿Escribiste la carta?
3. ¿Recibiste la tarjeta?
4. ¿Envolvió Juan el paquete?
5. ¿Trajo Marta el vaso?
6. ¿Vieron Uds. la película?
7. ¿Fueron Uds. al cine?
8. ¿Oyeron Uds. la orquesta?
9. ¿Devolvieron ellos los libros?
10. ¿Hicieron ellas el trabajo?

B. Repitan la frase; luego, repítanla dos veces más, cambiando la forma del verbo al pluscuamperfecto (*pluperfect*) y al futuro perfecto de indicativo (y observando la posición del pronombre usado como objeto del verbo):

1. Yo le he devuelto el dinero. 2. Luisa no les ha dicho eso. 3. ¿Han vuelto ellos a casa? 4. —¿Quiénes los han visto? —Nosotros los hemos visto. 5. ¿Adónde has ido? 6. Carlos nos lo ha traído.

C. Lean la frase en español; luego, repítanla cuatro veces, cambiando la forma del verbo al imperfecto, al pretérito, al futuro y al pretérito perfecto (*present perfect*) de indicativo:

1. Yo busco a Tomás. 2. Ellos no traen nada. 3. Yo empiezo a leer el diálogo. 4. Él y yo abrimos las ventanas. 5. Marta se pone el sombrero. 6. ¿Vas tú a la oficina?

D. Para expresar en español:

1. "Where have you (*fam. sing.*) been?" 2. "I have been at (in) the bookstore." 3. Have you (*pl.*) written on the typewriter today? 4. We have not had time (in order) to go shopping. 5. The secretary has looked for the list in the

file.   6. I had seen it (*f.*) in the classroom.   7. John had heard very favorable comments about the courses.   8. Helen had already told me that.

4   Formas de mandato correspondientes a «usted, ustedes»

Infinitive	Stem	Singular	Plural
tomar	tom-	tome Ud.[1]	tomen Uds.[1]
comer	com-	coma Ud.	coman Uds.
abrir	abr-	abra Ud.	abran Uds.
traer	**traig-**	**traiga** Ud.	**traigan** Uds.
cerrar (ie)	**cierr-**	**cierre** Ud.	**cierren** Uds.
volver (ue)	**vuelv-**	**vuelva** Ud.	**vuelvan** Uds.
pedir (i)	**pid-**	**pida** Ud.	**pidan** Uds.
seguir (i)	**sig-**	**siga** Ud.	**sigan** Uds.

In Spanish, the stem for the formal command of all verbs, except the five which follow, is that of the first person singular present indicative. (In reality, the formal command forms are those of the third person singular and plural of the present subjunctive tense, which will be discussed later.) **Usted (Ud.)** and **ustedes (Uds.)** are usually expressed with the verb and are placed after it; in a series of commands, however, it is not necessary to repeat **usted** or **ustedes** with each verb:

Infinitive	1st Sing. Pres. Ind.	Singular Command	Plural Command
dar	**doy**	**dé** Ud.	**den** Uds.
estar	**estoy**	**esté** Ud.	**estén** Uds.
ir	**voy**	**vaya** Ud.	**vayan** Uds.
saber	**sé**	**sepa** Ud.	**sepan** Uds.
ser	**soy**	**sea** Ud.	**sean** Uds.

Remember that certain verbs ending in **-car, -gar, -zar** change **c** to **qu**, **g** to **gu**, and **z** to **c** before the endings **-e (-é), -en: busque(n)** Ud(s)., **llegue(n)** Ud(s)., **empiece(n)** Ud(s). Some infinitives of these types are:

acercarse   *to approach*
almorzar (ue)   *to take (eat) lunch*
buscar   *to look for*
comenzar (ie)   *to commence, begin, start*
desempacar   *to unpack*
empezar (ie)   *to begin*

entregar   *to hand (over)*
jugar (ue)   *to play (a game)*
llegar   *to arrive*
pagar   *to pay (for)*
practicar   *to practice*
sacar   *to take (out)*
tocar   *to play (music)*

---

[1] In writing, **usted** and **ustedes** may be abbreviated to **Ud.** and **Uds.**, or **Vd.** and **Vds.**

EJERCICIOS

A. Repitan la frase; luego, repítanla otra vez, cambiando el mandato al plural:

1. Pase Ud., por favor. 2. Espere Ud. unos minutos. 3. Aprenda Ud. el diálogo. 4. Escriba Ud. la composición. 5. Siéntese[1] Ud. ahora. 6. No le[1] permita Ud. entrar. 7. No siga Ud. cantando. 8. Tráigales Ud. refrescos. 9. Desempaque Ud. las maletas. 10. No juegue Ud. aquí.

B. Para contestar afirmativa y luego negativamente[2] en español, cambiando el verbo a la forma de mandato correspondiente a **usted** y **ustedes,** según los modelos.

MODELOS: ¿Abro la puerta?   Sí, abra Ud. la puerta.   No, no abra la puerta.
¿Abrimos los libros?   Sí, abran Uds. los libros.   No, no abran los libros.

1. ¿Entro en el cuarto?
2. ¿Traigo las cosas?
3. ¿Busco un regalo?
4. ¿Toco la guitarra?
5. ¿Cierro la ventana?

6. ¿Seguimos leyendo?
7. ¿Vamos al café?
8. ¿Empezamos a cantar?
9. ¿Ponemos las maletas aquí?
10. ¿Salimos a tomar café?

C. Para expresar en español de dos maneras (*in two ways*): primero, empleando la forma de mandato correspondiente a **Ud.,** y luego la forma correspondiente a **Uds.:**

1. Look at the map. 2. Learn the dialogue. 3. Repeat the sentence. 4. Leave before noon. 5. Don't arrive late. 6. Don't take the photos yet. 7. Don't continue singing tonight. 8. Don't go to the library, please.

5   Formas de mandato correspondientes a «tú»

Familiar singular commands are:

Affirmative	Negative	Affirmative	Negative
toma (tú)	no tomes (tú)	**vuelve** (tú)	no **vuelvas** (tú)
come (tú)	no comas (tú)	**pide** (tú)	no **pidas** (tú)
abre (tú)	no abras (tú)	busca (tú)	no **busques** (tú)

[1] For review of the position of object pronouns with respect to verbs used in commands, see Lección dos, pages 55–56.
[2] When two or more adverbs in **-mente** are used in a series, **-mente** is added only to the last one.

The affirmative familiar singular command has the same form as the third person singular of the present indicative in all verbs except the nine which follow. This form is often called the singular imperative. The subject pronoun **tú** is omitted except for emphasis.

The negative familiar singular command is the familiar second person singular of the present subjunctive tense; that is, add **-s** to the third person singular present subjunctive.

The nine verbs which have irregular familiar singular command forms are:

decir	**di**	no **digas**
hacer	**haz**	no **hagas**
ir	**ve**	no **vayas**
poner	**pon**	no **pongas**
salir	**sal**	no **salgas**
ser	**sé**	no **seas**
tener	**ten**	no **tengas**
valer	**val** (vale)	no **valgas**
venir	**ven**	no **vengas**

Note these examples of familiar singular commands of certain reflexive verbs:

levantarse	levántate (tú) *get up*	no te levantes *don't get up*
sentarse	**siénta**te (tú) *sit down*	no te **sientes** *don't sit down*
vestirse	**víste**te (tú) *get dressed*	no te **vistas** *don't get dressed*
ponerse	**pon**te (tú) *put on*	no te **pongas** *don't put on*
irse	**vete** (tú) *go away*	no te **vayas** *don't go away*

EJERCICIOS

A. Para contestar afirmativa y luego negativamente en español, cambiando el verbo a la forma de mandato correspondiente a **tú.**

MODELO: ¿Abro el libro?   Sí, abre el libro.   No, no abras el libro.

1. ¿Escribo la frase?
2. ¿Llevo las cajas?
3. ¿Salgo al patio ahora?
4. ¿Sirvo los refrescos?
5. ¿Me siento aquí?
6. ¿Me pongo los guantes?
7. ¿Me levanto de la silla?
8. ¿Me voy esta tarde?

B. Para expresar en español empleando la forma correspondiente a **tú**, primero afirmativa y luego negativamente:

1. Write the composition. 2. Come with the other students. 3. Do that tomorrow. 4. Return the books today. 5. Leave early. 6. Get up before eight o'clock. 7. Sit down near the table. 8. Put on your hat.

Resumen de palabras y expresiones

al contrario   on the contrary
al poco tiempo   after (in) a short time
antes de   *prep.* before
aplazar   to postpone
aquí la tiene usted   here it is
buenos días   good morning (day)
el **comentario**   comment, commentary
el **consejo**   advice
consultar   to consult
el **curso**   course
el **Departamento de Español**   Spanish Department
dirigirse a   to turn to, direct oneself to, address (*a person*)
dos veces   twice, two times
en clase   in class
escribir a máquina   to type(write), write on a (the) typewriter
favorable   favorable

el **fichero**   file, filing cabinet
la **gramática avanzada**   advanced grammar
la **historia**   history
la **lista**   list
la **literatura**   literature
mañana (por la noche)   tomorrow (night *or* evening)
(no) tener tiempo para + *inf.*   (not) to have time to
ofrecer   to offer
el **problema**   problem
¿qué le preocupa?   what are you worried (concerned) about?
¿quiere usted (traerme)?   will you (bring me)?
el **(semestre) que viene**   next (semester)
valer más   to be better
(vamos) a ver   let's see

Hermosos mosaicos adornan la fachada de varios edificios de la universidad de México.

Usos de «estar» y «ser» ▪ La construcción reflexiva para expresar el sujeto indefinido *one, they, you, we, people,* y para expresar la voz pasiva
▪ La «a» personal ▪ «Conocer» y «saber»

LECCIÓN PRIMERA

El programa de Carlos

Son las nueve de la mañana. Carlos está en la oficina de su consejero, el profesor Torres. La oficina está llena de estudiantes, que están esperando su turno para consultar al profesor. Es el turno de Carlos.

Sr. Torres. ¡Hola, Carlos! Tuve el gusto de conocerlo anoche en la residencia, ¿verdad?

Carlos. (*Está nervioso.*) Sí, señor. Y conoció a mi padre, también. La reunión fue muy útil.

Sr. Torres. (*Mirando los documentos de Carlos.*) Veo que su familia es de El[1] Paso.

Carlos. Sí, señor. Estudié en una de las escuelas superiores de la ciudad.

Sr. Torres. Y su padre es ingeniero . . . A ver, Carlos, ¿piensa usted prepararse para alguna carrera profesional?

Carlos. Después de graduarme quiero continuar mis estudios en la Escuela de Derecho o de Administración de Negocios.

Sr. Torres. En ese caso una buena preparación general sería la más apropiada. ¿En qué piensa especializarse?

Carlos. Prefiero esperar un poco antes de tomar una decisión definitiva.

Sr. Torres. Está bien. Como usted sabe, para graduarse es necesario tomar algunos cursos obligatorios.

---

[1] The contraction **del** (also **al**) is not used when the article is part of a proper name or part of a title when quoted.

Carlos. ¿Qué cursos obligatorios recomienda usted?

Sr. Torres. Pues, durante el primer año se toman generalmente cursos de historia y de biología o química.

Carlos. Lo malo es que esas clases siempre son muy grandes. Y ¿qué cursos de tipo electivo podría tomar?

Sr. Torres. En el caso de usted creo que el estudio de la psicología y de la ecología sería muy provechoso.

Carlos. Me interesan también los deportes, sobre todo, el fútbol de estilo *soccer.*

Sr. Torres. Se preparan las listas de esas clases en el Departamento de Educación Física. Usted debe pasar por allí esta tarde.

Carlos. Pues, muchas gracias, señor Torres. Estoy seguro de que el año va a ser muy interesante.

Preguntas sobre el diálogo: 1. ¿Por qué están los estudiantes en la oficina del profesor Torres? 2. ¿Dónde conoció el señor Torres al padre de Carlos? 3. ¿De dónde es la familia de Carlos? 4. ¿En qué escuela espera Carlos continuar sus estudios después de graduarse? 5. ¿En qué piensa especializarse Carlos? 6. ¿Qué cursos obligatorios se toman generalmente durante el primer año? 7. ¿Qué cursos de tipo electivo recomienda el señor Torres? 8. ¿Qué dice Carlos sobre los deportes? 9. ¿Dónde se preparan las listas de las clases de fútbol? 10. ¿De qué está seguro Carlos?

Preguntas para conversar: 1. ¿Cómo se llama el consejero de usted? 2. ¿Cuántas veces ha consultado usted a su consejero durante este semestre? 3. ¿De dónde es usted? 4. ¿Piensa usted prepararse para alguna carrera profesional? 5. ¿En qué piensa especializarse usted? 6. ¿Qué cursos obligatorios está tomando usted? 7. ¿Qué cursos de tipo electivo está tomando usted? 8. ¿Es necesario tomar algunos cursos de historia para graduarse de esta universidad? 9. ¿Qué deportes le interesan a usted? 10. ¿Se dan clases de fútbol de estilo *soccer* en esta universidad?

PRONUNCIACIÓN

A. Diphthongs. Review in Appendix A, page 275, the sounds of the diphthongs. A diphthong is a sequence of two vowels pronounced in one syllable. As the first element of a diphthong, unstressed **i** is pronounced like a weak English *y* in *yes,* and unstressed **u** is pronounced like *w* in *wet.* Pronounce after your teacher:

1. estudiante	iglesia	comienza	nadie	cambio
2. varios	cuarto	Suárez	nueve	Luisa

As the second element of a diphthong, unstressed **i** and **u** are glide sounds in the reverse direction: they start from the position of the preceding vowel and end in the position of Spanish **i** and **u,** respectively. Pronounce after your teacher:

3. baile	hay	traigo	seis	veinte
4. oigo	soy	muy[1]	autobús	a usted
5. restaurante	Europa	de usted	lo usamos	uso urgente

Remember that two adjacent strong vowels within a word do not combine in a single syllable, but form two separate syllables: **ve-o.** Likewise, when a weak vowel adjacent to a strong vowel has a written accent, it retains its syllabic value and forms a separate syllable: **dí-a.** An accent on a strong vowel merely indicates stress: **des-pués.** Pronounce after your teacher:

| 6. traen | ahora | leer | Dorotea | paseo |
| 7. país | librería | oímos | también | aprendió |

B. Review linking in Appendix A, pages 275–276, and pronounce as one breath-group:

¿Qué va a hacer?	Él no ha vuelto.	Está en su oficina.
¿Y usted?	Tiene otro oficio.	Me interesa el curso.
Tu amigo Luis.	Ganó un peso.	Es la una y cinco.
¿Diste un paseo?	Después de esta clase.	En esta universidad.

NOTAS GRAMATICALES

1 Usos de «estar» y «ser»

A. **Estar** is used:

1. To express location (*i.e.,* to indicate where the subject is), whether temporary or permanent:

Los jóvenes están en casa.   The young people are at home.
¿Dónde ha estado Carlos?   Where has Charles been?
Guadalajara está en México.   Guadalajara is in Mexico.

2. With an adjective to indicate the state or condition of the subject when the state or condition is relatively temporary, accidental, or variable:

¿Está caliente[2] el café?   Is the coffee hot?
Las muchachas han estado ocupadas.   The girls have been busy.
Yo sabía que él estaba nervioso.   I knew (that) he was nervous.

---

[1] In Spanish America, this word is usually pronounced with stress on the **u;** in Peninsular Spanish, on the other hand, the stress is commonly on the **y,** with **u** sounding like *w* in *wet.*
[2] Remember that in a question a predicate adjective normally follows the verb immediately.

3. With the present participle to stress that an action is (was, has been, etc.) in progress at a given moment:[1]

Están esperando su turno.   They are waiting for their turn.
¿Qué estás haciendo ahora?   What are you doing now?
Él estaba mirando los documentos.   He was looking at the papers.
Hemos estado leyendo la novela.   We have been reading the novel.

4. With the past participle to describe a state or condition resulting from a previous action (in this construction the past participle, which is used as an adjective rather than as a verb, agrees with the subject in gender and number):

Están sentados en el patio.   They are seated in the patio.
Los diálogos están bien escritos.   The dialogues are well written.
El almuerzo ya estaba preparado.   Lunch was already prepared.

NOTE: Certain verbs, like **encontrarse, hallarse, verse, quedar(se),** are often substituted for **estar:**

¿Dónde nos encontramos ahora?   Where are we now?
La puerta ya se encontraba (se hallaba) cerrada.   The door was already closed.
Ella quedó sorprendida al saber eso.   She was surprised upon knowing (to know) that.

B. **Ser** is used:

1. To establish an identity between the subject and a noun or pronoun, and, less commonly, with adverbs, infinitives, or clauses used as nouns:

Él es ingeniero y ella es escritora.   He is an engineer and she is a writer.
Soy yo; es ella.   It is I; it is she.
Aquí es donde viven.   Here is where they live.
Ver es creer.   Seeing is believing.
Lo malo es que esas clases son grandes.   What is bad is that those classes are large.

2. With an adjective to express an essential quality or characteristic of the subject that is relatively permanent; this includes adjectives of color, size, shape, nationality, and the like, and those adjectives which describe personal qualities, including the adjectives **joven, viejo, rico, pobre, feliz:**

Luis es mexicano.   Louis is a Mexican.
El año será interesante.   The year will be interesting.
Estas casas son grandes (blancas).   These houses are large (white).
No somos viejos (jóvenes).   We are not old (young).
Aquel hombre no es rico (pobre).   That man is not rich (poor).

---

[1]The progressive forms of **ir, salir, venir** are rarely used.

3. With the preposition **de** to show origin, possession, or material, and with the preposition **para** to indicate for whom or for what a thing is intended:

¿De dónde es Luis?   Where is Louis from?
¿Es de Roberto este cuaderno?   Is this notebook Robert's?
Estos relojes son de oro.   These watches are (of) gold.
¿Para quién es la revista?   For whom is the magazine?

4. In impersonal expressions:

Es necesario (mejor) tomar esos cursos.   It is necessary (better) to take those courses.
No es fácil recordar eso.   It is not easy to remember that.

5. To express time of day:

¿Qué hora es?   What time is it?
Es la una y media.   It is half past one.
Son las diez en punto.   It is ten o'clock sharp.

NOTE: The verb is always plural in expressing time of day, except when followed by **la una**, *one o'clock.*

6. With the past participle to express the passive voice:

El vestido fue hecho por Ana.   The dress was made by Ann.
Ella es estimada de todos.   She is esteemed by all.
Los niños fueron castigados.   The children were punished.

In expressing the passive voice (*i.e.,* when the subject of the verb is acted upon by a person or thing) by means of **ser** and the past participle, the latter agrees with the subject in gender and number. The agent *by* is usually expressed by **por; de** is used, however, when the action represents a mental or emotional act (second example).

When a person receives the action of the verb (second and third examples), the third person plural active construction is replacing the passive construction, particularly in modern usage:

Todos la estiman.   All esteem her (She is esteemed by all).
Castigaron a los niños.   They punished the children (The children were punished).

C. **Ser** and **estar** with certain adjectives:

The meaning of some adjectives varies according to whether they are used with **ser** or **estar**. In general, **ser** indicates the normal or natural quality of the adjective, while **estar** indicates a temporary or subjective idea, often with the value of *look, feel, taste,* etc. A few examples which show the contrasts are:

[handwritten margin notes: "inherint characteristic", "days of week", "material use", "nouns", "pt. of origin", "noun ↓", "passive - past participle followed with (by whom)", "location", "condition, state"]

With ser	With estar
Ana es buena. Ann is good. *(By nature)*	**Ana está buena.** Ann is well. *(In good health)*
Pepe es malo. Joe is bad. *(By nature)*	**Pepe está malo.** Joe is ill. *(In poor health)*
Él es enfermo. He is sickly. *(An invalid)*	**Él está enfermo.** He is sick. *(Temporary condition)*
Ella es bonita. She is pretty. *(Naturally pretty)*	**¡Qué bonita está ella hoy!** How pretty she is (looks) today! *(Appearance)*
La nieve es fría. Snow is cold. *(By nature)*	**El agua está fría.** The water is cold. *(Changeable, temporary condition)*
Dorotea es lista. Dorothy is clever. *(By nature)*	**Dorotea está lista.** Dorothy is ready. *(Temporary condition)*
Marta es joven. Martha is young. *(Age regarded as characteristic)*	**Marta está joven hoy.** Martha is (looks) young today. *(Appearance)*
¿Es casado o soltero? Is he married (a married man) or single (a bachelor)?	**Está casado con una norteamericana.** He is married to an American woman.

NOTE: In the last example, **casado** is considered a noun when used with **ser,** and an adjective, representing the result of an action (marriage), when used with **estar.**

EJERCICIOS

[handwritten margin note: "with par - ser", "sut - estar"]

A. Para contestar negativa y luego afirmativamente, según el modelo.

MODELO: ¿Es ella escritora?   No, ella no es escritora.
          ¿Profesora?   Sí, ella es profesora.

1. ¿Es ingeniero el padre de Luis? ¿Abogado?
2. ¿Vive aquí su amigo? ¿Allí?
3. ¿Son cortos los artículos? ¿Largos?
4. ¿Es de México aquel estudiante? ¿De la Argentina?
5. ¿Son nuevas las guitarras? ¿Viejas?
6. ¿Fue difícil el diálogo? ¿Fácil?
7. ¿Están abiertas las puertas? ¿Cerradas?
8. ¿Estaba contenta la muchacha? ¿Triste?
9. ¿Eran las dos cuando ella llegó? ¿Las doce?
10. ¿Era pequeña su escuela superior? ¿Grande?

B. Después de escuchar los dos grupos de palabras, combínenlos en una sola oración por medio de la forma correcta de **ser** o **estar** en el presente de indicativo:

1. Nuestros amigos _____ jóvenes. 2. Esta revista _____ para Roberto. 3. Mi tío no _____ listo todavía. 4. Uds. y yo _____ hablando en español. 5. Yo sé

que _____ necesario practicar.   6. Luis Sierra _____ de Colombia.   7. El joven _____ muy simpático.   8. Esta agua no _____ muy fría.   9. Aquella casa nueva _____ de piedra.   10. La hermana de Juan _____ muy enferma hoy.

C. Para contestar negativamente en español, según el modelo.

MODELO: ¿Trabajas ahora?   No, no estoy trabajando todavía.

1. ¿Miras los documentos?
2. ¿Prepara Carlos su lección?
3. ¿Escriben Uds. un resumen?
4. ¿Leen Uds. el artículo?
5. ¿Sirve Marta el café?
6. ¿Oye Luis la música?

D. Para completar con la forma correcta de **estar** o **ser** en el presente de indicativo, menos en 17 y 18:

1. ¿Qué _____ el tío de Juan? ¿ _____ médico?   2. Enrique _____ de la Argentina; _____ argentino.   3. Lima, que _____ una ciudad grande, _____ en el Perú.   4. Aunque aquella señora _____ rica, nunca _____ contenta.   5. —¿Qué hora _____? —Creo que _____ las cinco y media.   6. Los Andes, que _____ montañas muy altas, siempre _____ cubiertos de nieve. 7. La novia de Carlos _____ rubia; se dice que _____ muy simpática.   8. El profesor Valdés no _____ en su oficina hoy porque _____ enfermo. 9. ¿Cómo _____ tú? ¿ _____ muy cansado?   10. No _____ difícil aprender el diálogo porque _____ bastante corto.   11. ¿Cuál _____ la fecha de hoy? Y, ¿ _____ martes o miércoles?   12. —¿Qué _____ haciendo tú en este momento? —Yo _____ escuchando un disco.   13. _____ mejor decir que nosotros no _____ ni ricos ni pobres.   14. ¿Para quién _____ estas cartas que _____ escritas en portugués? 15. Aquellos niños que _____ sentados en el patio _____ muy corteses.   16. Hoy _____ un día muy hermoso; por eso mi mamá _____ trabajando en su jardín.   17. Las ventanas _____ (*pres.*) abiertas. ¿Por quién _____ (*pret.*) abiertas?   18. Este edificio _____ (*pret.*) construido por el señor Gómez. _____ (*pres.*) bien construido.

2 La construcción reflexiva para expresar el sujeto indefinido *one, they, you, we, people,* y para expresar la voz pasiva

A. To express an indefinite subject, corresponding to English *one, they, people, we, you* (indefinite), Spanish uses **se** with the third person singular of the verb:

Se dice que él es médico.   They say (People say, One says, We say, It is said) that he is a doctor.

No se puede entrar.   One (People, You) cannot enter.

Se trabaja mucho aquí.   One works (People, You work) hard here.

With a reflexive verb, and occasionally with other verbs, **uno** is used:

Uno se levanta tarde los domingos.   One gets up late on Sundays.
No se (Uno no) puede hacer eso.   One cannot do that (That cannot be done).

As in English, the third person plural may be used to indicate an indefinite subject:

Dicen que el señor Valdés saldrá pronto.   They say (It is said) that Mr. Valdés will leave soon.

B. If the subject of a passive sentence is a thing, and the doer of the action is not expressed, **se** is used to substitute for the passive voice. In this case, the verb is in the third person singular or plural, depending on whether the subject is singular or plural. The reflexive verb normally precedes the subject in this construction:

Allí se habla español.   Spanish is spoken there.
Se cierran las tiendas a las cinco.   The stores are closed at five o'clock.
Se escribieron los artículos ayer.   The articles were written yesterday.
Se han publicado algunos en el periódico.   Some have been published in the newspaper.

When the subject is singular, as in **Allí se habla español,** the construction may be considered as an indefinite subject, or as a passive sentence: *People (They) speak Spanish there,* or *Spanish is spoken there.*

EJERCICIOS

A. Después de escuchar cada frase, repitan la frase, cambiándola a la construcción reflexiva, según los modelos.

MODELOS: Cierran la puerta a las seis.   Se cierra la puerta a las seis.
Aquí no compran libros.   Aquí no se compran libros.

1. En el Brasil hablan portugués. 2. Preparan las listas en la oficina. 3. No venden zapatos en la librería. 4. No conocen muy bien la música hispanoamericana. 5. Cantan muchas canciones populares. 6. Ven un avión grande en el aeropuerto. 7. Necesitan mucho dinero para viajar. 8. No abren los edificios hasta las nueve. 9. Durante el primer año toman generalmente cursos de historia. 10. Estudian español en la mayor parte de las universidades. 11. Abren la biblioteca a las ocho. 12. Publican el periódico en Buenos Aires.

B. Para expresar en español, usando **se** o **uno** como sujeto indefinido:

1. They say that it is going to rain. 2. How do they do that in Spain? 3. People know that Carmen is in Mexico. 4. We cannot do that easily. 5. One enters through this door. 6. One dresses slowly at times.

3   La «a» personal

When the direct object of the verb is a definite person (or persons), or a personified object, the personal or distinctive **a** (not translated in English) regularly introduces the object, except after **tener:**

> **Encontré a Juanito en el jardín.**   I found Johnny in the garden.
> **Usted conoció a mi padre.**   You met my father.
> **Temen a la muerte.**   They fear death.
>
> BUT: **Tengo diez primos.**   I have ten cousins.

The personal **a** is also used when the direct object is **quien(es)**, *whom*, **¿quién(es)?** *whom?* or one of the indefinites or negatives[1] **alguien** and **nadie**, and **alguno, -a,** and **ninguno, -a,** when the last two refer to persons:

> **¿Has visto a alguien?**   Have you seen anyone?
> **No he llamado a ninguno de ellos.**   I haven't called any (one) of them.

The distinctive **a** may also be used before a geographical proper name, unless the name is preceded by the definite article, although in current usage **a** is being omitted more and more in such constructions:

> **Visitaron (a) México.**   They visited Mexico.
> **Desean ver el Cuzco.**   They want to see Cuzco.

Because of the flexible word order in Spanish, the distinctive **a** is required occasionally to avoid ambiguity when both the subject and the direct object refer to things:

> **La paz sigue a la guerra.**   Peace follows war.

EJERCICIO

Lean en español, supliendo la **a** personal cuando se necesite (*it is needed*):

1. Juan esperó _____ Bárbara. 2. ¿Han visto Uds. _____ sus tíos? 3. ¿ _____ quién llamaste? 4. Luis conoce bien _____ Bogotá. 5. Yo conocí _____ la señora Sierra. 6. No he ayudado _____ nadie hoy. 7. Él quería visitar _____ la Argentina. 8. Ana tiene _____ muchos amigos allí. 9. ¿Acompañó Ud. _____ alguien ayer? 10. Él y yo saludamos _____ la profesora.

---

[1] See Lección cuatro, pages 93–95, for discussion of the indefinites and negatives.

4   «Conocer» y «saber»

Conocer means *to know* in the sense of *to be acquainted with someone, to know* (*be familiar with*) *something, to meet* (for the first time):

> **Yo conozco a la señorita.**   I know the young lady.
> **El profesor conoce bien la ciudad.**   The instructor knows the city well.

Saber means *to know* in the sense of *to have knowledge of, know facts;* followed by an infinitive it means *to know how to, can* (mental ability):

> **Ya sé quién[1] es.**   I already know who he is.
> **Sabíamos que Pepe había llegado.**   We knew that Joe had arrived.
> **Luis sabe tocar la guitarra.**   Louis knows how to (can) play the guitar.

EJERCICIO

Para leer en español, completando las frases con la forma correcta de **conocer** o **saber:**

1. Yo _____ que Luis es español. 2. Voy a preguntarle si _____ a Marta. 3. Nosotros _____ a Miguel Valdés anoche. 4. ¿ _____ Ud. dónde vive él? 5. ¿ _____ tú si nuestro profesor _____ bien el arte mexicano? 6. Los estudiantes _____ hablar español. 7. Todo el mundo _____ que yo no _____ bien el país. 8. Ana no ha _____ a mi amiga María.

RESUMEN

A. Usos de los verbos **estar** y **ser.** Lean en español, supliendo la forma correcta del verbo que se necesite:

1. Mi mamá _____ enferma hoy. 2. Esta comida _____ (*tastes*) muy rica. 3. ¿ _____ rico su amigo mexicano? 4. ¿Qué _____ tu padre? 5. Mi hermano quiere _____ abogado. 6. Nuestra hermana _____ contenta. 7. ¿De dónde _____ tú? 8. La puerta _____ (*pret.*) abierta por mí. 9. La puerta todavía _____ abierta. 10. ¿ _____ joven tu tía? 11. Yo _____ (*pres. perf.*) leyendo el libro. 12. _____ las nueve y cuarto.

---

[1] Note that an accent mark is written on interrogative words when used in indirect questions as well as in direct questions.

B. Usos de la construcción reflexiva y de la voz pasiva. Para expresar en español:

1. How does one say that in Spanish?
2. People believe that John is from Puerto Rico.
3. Books are not sold in the library.
4. One can learn this lesson rapidly.
5. The letters are written in Spanish.
6. One sits down in order to rest.
7. Margaret made these blouses.
8. The blouses were made by Margaret.
9. The blouses are well made.
10. John wrote the letter.
11. The letter was written by John.
12. The letter is written.

C. Usos de la **a** personal y de los verbos **conocer** y **saber**. Para expresar en español:

1. Whom did you (*fam. sing.*) call?
2. Paul and I saw Louis Morales.
3. Have you (*pl.*) helped Jane this afternoon?
4. We know John's parents well.
5. I know that they left last night.
6. Do you (*pl.*) know anyone in Spain?

Resumen de palabras y expresiones

la **Administración de Negocios** Business Administration
apropiado, -a appropriate, fitting
la **biología** biology
la **carrera** career
el **caso** case
castigar to punish
de la mañana a.m., in the morning
definitivo, -a definite
el **documento** document, paper
la **ecología** ecology
la **Educación Física** Physical Education
electivo, -a elective
en este (ese) momento at this (that) moment
en punto sharp (*time*)
la **Escuela de Derecho** Law School
especializarse to specialize, major
está bien all right, that's fine
estar seguro, -a de que to be sure that
el **estudio** study
graduarse to graduate
la mayor parte de the greater part of, most (of)

lo malo what is bad, the bad thing (part)
obligatorio, -a obligatory, required
por eso therefore, because of that, for that reason, that's why
por medio de *prep.* by means of
la **preparación** (*pl.* **preparaciones**) preparation
prepararse para to prepare oneself for
profesional professional
el **programa** program, schedule
provechoso, -a advantageous, beneficial
la **psicología** psychology
publicar to publish
la **química** chemistry
la **reunión** (*pl.* **reuniones**) meeting
sobre todo above all, especially
el **tipo** type
todo el mundo everybody
tomar una decisión to make a decision
trabajar mucho to work hard
el **turno** turn

Completa.

Lectura 1

Observaciones sobre el sistema educativo en Hispanoamérica

Por muchos motivos hay que[1] considerar la educación como el medio más eficaz para transformar y mejorar la sociedad. En vista de[2] la importancia que tienen los problemas de la educación, sería conveniente[3] examinar algunos aspectos del sistema educativo en los países hispanoamericanos.

A diferencia del[4] sistema desarrollado[5] en los Estados Unidos, en Hispanoamérica la administración de la enseñanza[6] de cada país está centralizada en un ministerio del gobierno. En este ministerio se establecen los programas de estudio[7] en todos los niveles[8] de la enseñanza, desde la primaria y la secundaria hasta[9] la universitaria.

La escuela primaria cubre un período de seis a ocho años. Al terminarla, los alumnos que desean prepararse para los cursos universitarios pasan a las escuelas secundarias, llamadas liceos en algunos países y colegios nacionales o institutos en otros. En estos centros docentes[10] los estudios duran de cinco a seis años. Al graduarse, los alumnos reciben el título de bachiller,[11] que los capacita para ingresar en[12] una universidad. En México los que aspiran a ingresar en la universidad tienen que asistir durante dos años

[1]**hay que,** *one must.*   [2]**En vista de,** *In view of.*   [3]**conveniente,** *useful, desirable.*   [4]**A diferencia de,** *Unlike.*   [5]**desarrollar,** *to develop.*   [6]**enseñanza,** *education, instruction.*   [7]**programas de estudio,** *curricula (also see* **plan de estudios** *in the fifth paragraph).*   [8]**en todos los niveles,** *at all levels.*   [9]**desde . . . hasta,** *from . . . (up) to.*   [10]**docentes,** *educational.*   [11]**título de bachiller,** *bachelor's degree.*   [12]**que los capacita para ingresar en,** *which qualifies them to enter.*

47

Alumnos de la academia de San Jorge, San Juan, Puerto Rico.

más a una escuela preparatoria, que equivale, aproximadamente, a un *junior college* en los Estados Unidos.

La universidad hispanoamericana consta de[13] una serie de facultades (o escuelas) y el estudiante ingresa directamente en una de ellas. Las principales son de Medicina, Derecho,[14] Filosofía y Letras,[15] Ciencias Sociales y Políticas, Ciencias Físico-Químicas, Ingeniería, Arquitectura y Pedagogía.

La finalidad[16] específica de la universidad hispanoamericana es la formación profesional, es decir,[17] la capacitación[18] de los estudiantes para el ejercicio de la profesión elegida. Cada facultad tiene su reglamento y plan de estudios, fijados por el ministerio. Como en el bachillerato, casi ninguna de las asignaturas[19] es de tipo electivo. La duración del plan de estudios varía de una facultad a otra, pero generalmente se exigen de cinco a siete años de estudios. Al aprobar[20] los exámenes correspondientes a su facultad, el estudiante recibe el título de licenciado.[21]

Después de recibir el título de licenciado, el estudiante tiene la opción de continuar sus estudios para el doctorado, el último grado que confieren las universidades hispanoamericanas. Para obtenerlo se exigen normalmente un año de estudios avanzados y la preparación de una tesis doctoral. El grado de *Master of Arts*, que se confiere en las universidades de los Estados Unidos, el Canadá y el Reino Unido, no existe en Suramérica. El grado de licenciado, descrito arriba, es su equivalente aproximado.

Como en los Estados Unidos, en Suramérica tanto los estudiantes como los educadores[22] están tratando de transformar y modernizar los programas de estudio en todos los niveles y de hacerlos asequibles[23] a sectores más amplios de la población.

---

[13]**consta de,** *consists of.*   [14]**Derecho,** *Law.*   [15]**Letras,** *Letters.*   [16]**finalidad,** *end, purpose.*   [17]**es decir,** *that is (to say).*   [18]**capacitación,** *training*   [19]**asignaturas,** *subjects* (of study).   [20]**Al aprobar,** *Upon passing.*   [21]**licenciado,** *licentiate* (holder of a licentiate or master's degree).   [22]**tanto . . . educadores,** *students as well as educators,* or *both students and educators.*   [23]**asequibles,** *accessible, available.*

Estudiantes esperan la llegada del profesor, universidad de Barcelona, España.

Todos comprenden también que, además de favorecer las universidades, es necesario aumentar el número de escuelas de artes y oficios[24] y de institutos tecnológicos y científicos si se quiere crear un personal capacitado para competir en el mundo moderno.

EJERCICIO

Usando como guía las preguntas siguientes, escriban un breve ensayo (de unas 150 palabras) sobre la educación en Hispanoamérica:

1. ¿En qué aspecto importante difiere la administración de la enseñanza en los países hispanoamericanos del sistema desarrollado en los Estados Unidos?
2. ¿Dónde se establecen los programas de estudio en todos los niveles de la enseñanza en Hispanoamérica?
3. ¿Cuántos años duran los estudios en la escuela primaria? ¿En la escuela secundaria?
4. ¿Qué nombres dan a las escuelas secundarias?
5. ¿Cuál es el título que capacita al estudiante para ingresar en la universidad?
6. ¿Cuál es la finalidad específica de la universidad hispanoamericana?
7. ¿Cuáles son algunas de las facultades de las universidades hispanoamericanas?
8. ¿Qué título recibe el estudiante al aprobar los exámenes correspondientes a su facultad?
9. ¿Cuál es el último grado que confieren las universidades hispanoamericanas?
10. ¿Qué están tratando de hacer tanto los estudiantes como los educadores en Hispanoamérica?

---

[24]**artes y oficios,** *arts and crafts.*

Los pronombres personales ▪ Usos de los pronombres personales que designan el sujeto ▪ Colocación del pronombre como objeto del verbo ▪ Las formas preposicionales y la construcción redundante ▪ Los pronombres y verbos reflexivos ▪ Colocación respectiva de dos pronombres, uno como objeto directo y otro como objeto indirecto ▪ Repaso de los números cardinales

LECCIÓN DOS

¿Qué hizo usted durante el verano?

La profesora de español habla con los seis o siete estudiantes que se encuentran en la sala de clase. Los otros estudiantes tardan en presentarse porque han ido a una conferencia que ha dado el rector.

Sra. Cruz. Acérquense ustedes, por favor. Como los otros estudiantes van a llegar tarde, podemos charlar un poco antes de comenzar la lección.

Jaime. Sra. Cruz, ¿por qué no nos cuenta usted lo que hizo durante el verano?

Sra. Cruz. ¿No se lo he contado ya? Pasé los meses de julio y agosto en México, en la ciudad de Oaxaca. Me divertí mucho. Y usted, Jaime, ¿dónde pasó las vacaciones?

Jaime. Las pasé en la sierra, trabajando como consejero en un campamento de muchachos. No puedo quejarme. Me gustó mucho el trabajo.

Sra. Cruz. Me alegro de saberlo. ¿Qué va a hacer con el dinero que ha ganado?

Jaime. Cuento con él para pagar los gastos de este año. Solicité una beca, pero no me la concedieron.

Sra. Cruz. Creerían[1] que se había hecho rico. Y usted, María, ¿qué hizo durante las vacaciones?

---

[1] **Creerían,** *They probably believed.* For the use of the conditional to express probability, see page 132.

Tomando baños de sol en una playa de la Costa del Sol, España.

María. Con una amiga hice un viaje muy interesante por el suroeste de nuestro país.

Sra. Cruz. ¿Qué sitios visitaron ustedes?

María. Visitamos muchos sitios en los estados de Nuevo México, Arizona y California.

Sra. Cruz. Como ustedes saben, en esos estados muchos ríos, ciudades y montañas tienen nombres españoles.

María. Sí, y millones de personas de habla española, muchas de ellas de origen mexicano, viven en ellos, también.

(Diez o doce estudiantes entran en la sala.)

Sra. Cruz. Bueno, me parece que ya podemos comenzar la lección de hoy. Otro día hablaremos más de sus vacaciones.

Preparen un diálogo original, de unas diez líneas, para recitar en clase, empleando las frases y preguntas siguientes como elemento inicial:

1. *Ramón.* ¿Qué cursos va a tomar tu amigo Luis?

   Jaime. Me dice que piensa tomar dos cursos obligatorios y uno de tipo electivo.

2. *Inés.* ¿Dónde pasaste las vacaciones, José?

   José. Las pasé aquí, trabajando en una estación de gasolina.

PRONUNCIACIÓN

Intonation. Review the section on intonation, pages 24–25, paying special attention to the remarks on interrogative sentences and exclamations. A few additional observations follow:

A. The intonation pattern used to express special interest in an exclamatory sentence may also be used in questions (especially in those beginning with an interrogative word) and in declarative sentences. The voice rises above the normal tone when the last accented syllable is reached (level 3), and falls below the normal tone in the following syllable (or within the accented syllable, if no unstressed syllable follows). In a declarative sentence this pattern may be used to give special emphasis to any word of the breath-group. Examples:

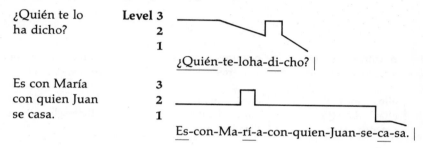

¿Quién te lo ha dicho?

Level 3
2
1

¿Quién-te-loha-di-cho? |

Es con María con quien Juan se casa.

3
2
1

Es-con-Ma-rí-a-con-quien-Juan-se-ca-sa. |

B. The pattern used in exclamations, and in questions which begin with an interrogative word, is typical of commands and requests. The latter differ in that the intervals between accented and unaccented syllables are less than in commands; furthermore, in requests the entire breath-group is usually uttered on a higher tone. Examples:

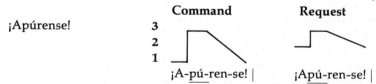

Command   **Request**

¡Apúrense!

3
2
1

¡A-pú-ren-se! | ¡Apú-ren-se! |

C. If an interrogative sentence consists of two breath-groups, the first group ends below the normal tone. Example:

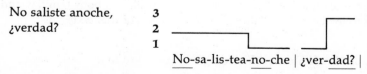

No saliste anoche, ¿verdad?

3
2
1

No-sa-lis-tea-no-che | ¿ver-dad? |

Write the interrogative sentences of the dialogue of this lesson, dividing them into breath-groups and syllables, and outline the intonation patterns.

NOTAS GRAMATICALES

1 Los pronombres personales

	Singular	
Subject of Verb	*Object of Preposition*	*Reflexive Object of Preposition*
1. **yo** I	**mí** me	**mí** me, myself
2. **tú** you	**ti** you	**ti** you, yourself
3. { **él** he **ella** she **usted** you	{ **él** him, it (*m.*) **ella** her, it (*f.*) **usted** you	**sí** himself, herself, yourself, itself

	Plural	
1. **nosotros, -as** we	**nosotros, -as** us	**nosotros, -as** us, ourselves
2. **vosotros, -as** you	**vosotros, -as** you	**vosotros, -as** you, yourselves
3. { **ellos** they **ellas** they (*f.*) **ustedes** you	{ **ellos** them **ellas** them (*f.*) **ustedes** you	**sí** themselves, yourselves

2 Usos de los pronombres personales que designan el sujeto

The subject pronouns, except the formal forms for *you* (**usted** and **ustedes,** which may be abbreviated to **Ud.** and **Uds.,** or **Vd.** and **Vds.,** in writing), are omitted unless needed for clearness or emphasis, or when two are combined as the subject. **Usted** and **ustedes,** which require the third person of the verb in Spanish, are regularly expressed, although excessive repetition should be avoided. The English subjects *it* and *they,* referring to things, are rarely expressed in Spanish, and the impersonal subject *it* is always omitted.

In general, the familiar forms **tú** and **vosotros, -as,** are used when the given name would be used in English (in speaking to children, relatives, or close friends). In most of Spanish America **ustedes** is used for the plural of *you,* both familiar and formal (this practice is followed in the dialogues and exercises of this text):

> **Vamos al café ahora.**   We are going (Let's go) to the café now.
> **Ella lee un libro y él escribe una carta.**   She reads a book, and he writes a letter.
> **Él y ella están en la biblioteca.**   He and she are in the library.
> **Ellas son felices.**   They (*f.*) are happy.
> **Usted habla bien el español.**   You speak Spanish well.
> **Tú hablas mejor que él.**   You speak better than he.

	Singular	
Direct Object of Verb	*Indirect Object of Verb*	*Reflexive Object of Verb*
me me	**me** (to) me	**me** (to) myself
te you	**te** (to) you	**te** (to) yourself
⎧ **lo, le**[1] him		
⎪ **lo** it (*m.*)		**se** ⎰ (to) himself, itself
⎨ **la** her, it (*f.*)	**le (se)** ⎰ (to) him, it	**se** ⎨ (to) herself, itself
⎪ **lo, le** you (*m.*)	⎨ (to) her, it	⎱ (to) yourself
⎪ **la** you (*f.*)	⎱ (to) you	
⎩ **lo** it (*neuter*)		

	Plural	
nos us	**nos** (to) us	**nos** (to) ourselves
os you	**os** (to) you	**os** (to) yourselves
⎧ **los, les**[2] them		
⎪ **las** them (*f.*)	**les (se)** ⎰ (to) them	**se** ⎰ (to) themselves
⎨ **los, les**[2] you	⎱ (to) you	**se** ⎱ (to) yourselves
⎩ **las** you (*f.*)		

3   Colocación del pronombre como objeto del verbo

A. All object pronouns (direct, indirect, and reflexive) are regularly placed immediately before the verb, including the auxiliary verb **haber** in the compound tenses (three major exceptions are explained in B, C, D, below):

Nos enviaron una tarjeta.   They sent us a card.
Ana no me llamó anoche.   Ann didn't call me last night.
Los he visto en la calle.   I have seen them in the street.

B. Object pronouns are placed after, and are attached to, affirmative commands. (In commands the formal **usted(es)** is regularly expressed, but the familiar **tú** is used only for emphasis.) Note that an accent must be written on the stressed syllable of a verb of more than one syllable when a pronoun is added:

Tráigalos usted en seguida.   Bring them at once.
Tómalo (tú), por favor.   Take it, please.
BUT: **Dame el periódico, por favor.**   Give me the newspaper, please.

---

[1] In Spanish America **lo** is more frequently used than **le**, meaning *him, you* (formal m.).
[2] In Spain the form **les** is often used instead of **los** as direct object referring to masculine persons.

In negative commands, however, object pronouns precede the verb and are placed between the negative and the verb:

No les escriba usted hoy.   Do not write to them today.
No me digas eso.   Don't tell me that.
No te pongas el vestido nuevo.   Don't put on the new dress.

C. Object pronouns are usually attached to an infinitive:

Empecé a leerlo.   I began to read it.
Vamos a sentarnos ahora.   We are going to (Let's) sit down now.

However, object pronouns may precede conjugated forms of certain verbs and verbal expressions, such as **ir a, querer, poder, saber,** followed by an infinitive:

Lo voy a hacer *or* **Voy a hacerlo.**   I am going to do it.
La quieren ver *or* **Quieren verla.**   They want to see her (it).
Usted se puede sentar *or* **Usted puede sentarse.**   You may (can) sit down.
Se va a hacer (*or* **Va a hacerse**) **rico, Carlos.**   You are going to become rich, Charles.

D. Object pronouns are attached to the present participle, except in the progressive forms of the tenses, in which case they may be attached to the participle or placed before the auxiliary. An accent must be written over the stressed syllable of the participle when a pronoun is attached:

Dándome la carta, Juan salió.   Giving me the letter, John left.
Están leyéndola *or* **La están leyendo.**   They are reading it.

EJERCICIOS

A. Repitan cada frase y luego substituyan la frase en cursiva con el pronombre correspondiente, según el modelo.

MODELO: Jaime solicitó *una beca.*   Jaime solicitó una beca.
Jaime la solicitó.

1. ¿Dónde pasó Ud. *las vacaciones?*
2. Visitamos *a nuestros amigos.*
3. Mi hermano compró *la bicicleta.*
4. No he practicado mucho *el español.*
5. ¿No ha hecho Ud. *el trabajo?*
6. No pronuncian bien *los nombres.*

B. Para contestar empleando formas de mandato afirmativas y negativas, substituyendo el substantivo con el pronombre correspondiente.

MODELO: ¿Hago *el trabajo?*   Sí, hágalo Ud.   No, no lo haga Ud.

1. ¿Traigo *el disco* ahora?
2. ¿Compro *las flores?*
3. ¿Escribo *la composición?*
4. ¿Aprendo *los diálogos?*
5. ¿Cierro *el libro?*
6. ¿Lavo *el coche* hoy?

C. Después de escuchar cada frase, repítanla dos veces, substituyendo el substantivo con el pronombre correspondiente.

MODELO: Estoy leyendo *el libro*.   Estoy leyéndolo. Lo estoy leyendo.

1. Estoy contando *el dinero*.
2. Están trayendo *las sillas*.
3. Estaban estudiando *la lección*.
4. Yo estaba visitando *a María*.
5. Uds. no están mirando *el mapa*.
6. No estás sirviendo *los refrescos*.

D. Después de escuchar cada frase, repítanla dos veces, substituyendo el substantivo con el pronombre correspondiente.

MODELO: Voy a hacer *el viaje*.   Voy a hacerlo. Lo voy a hacer.

1. ¿Vas a pasar *el verano* allí?
2. Puedo traer *las revistas*.
3. No quieren dejar *las guitarras* aquí.
4. No deseamos aprender *la canción*.

E. Para contestar negativamente, según el modelo.

MODELO: ¿Estás leyendo *el libro*?   No, no estoy leyéndolo, pero voy a leerlo pronto.

1. ¿Estás solicitando *la beca*?
2. ¿Estás trayendo *las revistas*?
3. ¿Están Uds. escribiendo *la carta*?
4. ¿Están Uds. escuchando *los discos*?

4   Las formas preposicionales y la construcción redundante

A. The prepositional forms are used only as objects of prepositions. They are the same as the subject pronouns, except for **mí** and **ti**:

Corrían hacia mí.   They were running toward me.
Charlaré con él (ella).   I shall chat with him (her).

When used with **con**, the forms **mí, ti**, and the reflexive **sí** (see section 5, A, page 58) become **conmigo, contigo, consigo**, respectively:

No van conmigo (contigo).   They aren't going with me (with you).

B. The prepositional phrases **a mí, a ti, a él**, etc., are used in addition to the direct or indirect object pronoun for emphasis:

Yo la vi a ella, pero no a Juan.   I saw her, but not John.
A mí me gusta el cuadro.   I like the picture.

Since the indirect objects **le** and **les** have several meanings, the prepositional forms are often added for clearness. They are frequently added for courtesy when the direct object pronouns meaning *you* (formal) are used:

Yo le di a ella las flores.   I gave her the flowers.
Mucho gusto en conocerlo (-la) a Ud.   (I'm very) pleased to meet (know) you.

C. When a noun is expressed as the indirect object of the verb in Spanish, the corresponding indirect object pronoun is normally added. With forms of **gustar**, the prepositional form must be used:

> **Le dimos a Felipe el dinero.**   We gave Philip the money.
> **A Carlos le gusta (Le gusta a Carlos) la casa.**   Charles likes the house.

The prepositional form must also be used when the verb is understood:

> **Les enseñé el reloj a ellos, pero no a ella.**   I showed them the watch, but not her.

The prepositional form would also be used to express a <u>direct</u> object pronoun when the verb is understood: **¿A quién viste? ¿A él?** *Whom did you see? Him?*

EJERCICIO

Repitan cada frase; luego, substituyan el substantivo con el pronombre correspondiente, según el modelo.

> MODELO: Corrieron hasta *la esquina.*   Corrieron hasta la esquina.
> Corrieron hasta ella.

1. Fueron al río con *Ricardo.* 2. Charle Ud. un poco con *Marta.* 3. Estos regalos son para *mis padres.* 4. No hablen Uds. más de *las muchachas.* 5. Cuento con *el dinero.* 6. El coche está enfrente de *esa casa.* 7. Roberto corre por *esas calles.* 8. En *esos estados* hay varios parques.

5   Los pronombres y verbos reflexivos

A. Reflexive pronouns, which are used when the subject acts upon itself, may be direct or indirect objects:

> **Ricardo se sentó.**   Richard sat down.
> **Voy a lavarme la cara.**   I'm going to wash my face.
> **Levántense ustedes.**   Get up.
> **Estamos desayunándonos.**   We are eating breakfast.

The pronouns **mí, ti, nosotros, -as, vosotros, -as,** and **sí** (third person singular and plural) may be used reflexively: **para mí,** *for myself;* **para sí,** *for himself, herself, yourself* (formal), *itself, themselves* (m. and f.), *yourselves;* **Ella se lo llevó consigo,** *She took it with her(self).*

B. Reflexive verbs are much more frequent in Spanish than in English. A few verbs are always used reflexively in Spanish, while others may also be used as transitive or

memorize

intransitive verbs, although usually with different meanings. Certain verbs and expressions which are regularly reflexive in Spanish are:

atreverse (a) *to dare (to)*	jactarse (de) *to boast (of)*
darse cuenta de *to realize*	quejarse (de) *to complain (of)*

Many intransitive verbs in English (that is, verbs that cannot take a direct object) are expressed in Spanish by using the reflexive pronoun with a transitive verb. Note the following verbs:

acercar *to bring . . . near*	acercarse (a) *to approach, draw near (to)*
acostar (ue) *to put to bed*	acostarse (ue) *to go to bed*
despertar (ie) *to awaken (somebody)*	despertarse (ie) *to wake up (oneself)*
divertir (ie, i) *to amuse*	divertirse (ie, i) *to have a good time*
lavar *to wash (something)*	lavarse *to wash (oneself)*
levantar *to raise, lift (up)*	levantarse *to get up, rise*
mudar *to change*	mudarse (de) *to change (one's cloth-ing, lodging, etc.)*
sentar (ie) *to seat*	sentarse (ie) *to sit down*

With certain verbs the reflexive translates *to become, get,* or *to be* plus an adjective. A few examples are:

alegrar *to make glad*	alegrarse (de) *to be glad (of, to)*
cansar *to tire (someone)*	cansarse *to become (get) tired*
vestir (i, i) *to dress (someone)*	vestirse (i, i) *to dress (oneself), get dressed*

Other common verbs whose meaning is changed when used reflexively are:

dormir (ue, u) *to sleep*	dormirse (ue, u) *to fall asleep*
hacer *to do, make*	hacerse *to become*
hallar *to find*	hallarse *to be found, be*
llamar *to call*	llamarse *to call oneself, be named*
poner *to put, place*	ponerse *to put on (oneself); (+ adj.) to become*

See Appendix E, pages 304–306, for other verbs of these types.

EJERCICIOS

A. Repitan cada frase; luego al oír el sujeto nuevo, cambien la frase según el modelo.

MODELO: Yo me dormí en seguida.   Yo me dormí en seguida.
              (*José*)   José se durmió en seguida.

1. *Ana* se puso los guantes.   (*Ana y yo*)
2. *Yo* voy a sentarme cerca de ella.   (*Ricardo*)
3. *La niña* se vistió despacio.   (*Los niños*)

4. *Enrique* se divirtió mucho ayer. (*Yo*)
5. *Jorge* está lavándose las manos. (*Tú*)
6. *Juan y José* se cansaron de eso. (*Luis y yo*)
7. *Pablo* se alegró de verlos. (*Pablo y Carlos*)
8. *Miguel y yo* nos mudamos de ropa hace media hora. (*Yo*)
9. *Nosotros* no nos quejamos del profesor. (*Roberto*)
10. *Tú* no tardaste en tomar la decisión. (*Uds.*)

B. Para contestar con un mandato afirmativo, empleando la forma correspondiente a **Ud.** en 1–3 y la forma correspondiente a **Uds.** en 4–6; luego, expresen el mandato negativamente:

1. ¿Me levanto ahora?
2. ¿Me pongo el abrigo?
3. ¿Me voy en este momento?

4. ¿Nos sentamos aquí?
5. ¿Nos acercamos al coche?
6. ¿Nos quedamos en casa?

6 Colocación respectiva de dos pronombres, uno como objeto directo y otro como objeto indirecto

When two object pronouns are used together, the indirect object pronoun always precedes the direct. When both are in the third person, the indirect (**le, les**) becomes **se.** Since **se** may mean *to him, to her, to you* (formal), *to it, to them,* the prepositional forms are often required in addition to **se** for clarity. A reflexive pronoun precedes any other object pronoun:

Carlos nos lo vendió.   Charles sold it to us.
Lléveselo usted a ellos.   Take it to them.
Marta empezó a leérmela.   Martha began to read it to me.
No se lo escribas (tú) a ella.   Don't write it to her.
Dándomelos, Pablo salió.   Giving them to me, Paul left.
Luisa se lo puso.   Louise put it on.

Remember that an accent mark must be written on the stressed syllable of the verb when two object pronouns are attached to an infinitive, an affirmative command form, or a present participle.

EJERCICIOS

A. Lean en español; luego, contesten las preguntas afirmativamente, substituyendo los substantivos en cursiva con los pronombres correspondientes, según los modelos.

MODELOS: ¿Le dio Juan *las cosas* a Marta?   Sí, Juan se las dio a ella.
             ¿Se lavó José *la cara*?   Sí, José se la lavó.

1. ¿Le llevaste *el dinero a Felipe?*
2. ¿Le escribiste *la carta a Luis?*
3. ¿Está explicándoles Juan *los problemas?*
4. ¿Se están poniendo ellos *los zapatos?*
5. ¿Se están lavando Uds. *las manos?*
6. ¿Vas a leerles *el libro a los niños?*

B. Repitan cada frase; luego, substituyan los substantivos en cursiva con los pronombres correspondientes:

1. Envíele Ud. *la tarjeta a su amiga.*
2. No le vendan Uds. *a Ana el coche.*
3. Pónganse Uds. *el abrigo.*
4. Concédanle Uds. *la beca al estudiante.*
5. No te quites *esa camisa.*
6. No le devuelvas *a Luis el regalo.*

7   Repaso de los números cardinales

A. Después de repasar los números cardinales y sus usos (Appendix C, pages 284–285), lean en español:

1. 18 muchachas. 2. 21 países. 3. 51 universidades. 4. 100 páginas. 5. 116 discos. 6. 200 preguntas. 7. 365 días. 8. 500 casas. 9. 1,000 empleados. 10. 1,000,000 de personas. 11. 5,000,000 de dólares. 12. 150,000 hombres.

B. Repasen el uso de los números para expresar fechas y los nombres de los meses (Appendix C, page 286); luego, lean en español:

1. January 1, 1979. 2. May 2, 1972. 3. October 12, 1492. 4. September 29, 1547. 5. July 4, 1775. 6. February 22, 1789. 7. December 10, 1810. 8. November 11, 1812. 9. April 15, 1817. 10. March 31, 1827. 11. June 29, 1903. 12. August 14, 1809.

RESUMEN

A. Repitan cada frase; luego, substituyan el substantivo en cursiva con el pronombre correspondiente, colocándolo (*placing it*) correctamente:

1. Ellos comenzaron *el trabajo.* 2. Carlos visitó *a su tío.* 3. María compró *la bicicleta.* 4. Marta no hizo *los vestidos.* 5. Luis no leyó *las revistas.* 6. Traiga Ud. *las cintas.* 7. Llevan Uds. *sus cuadernos.* 8. Sirvan Uds. *los refrescos.* 9. No despierten Uds. *a Luisa.* 10. No pierdan Uds. *el autobús.*

11. Estamos terminando *las composiciones*. 12. Él y ella están leyendo *la novela*. 13. Mi mamá está visitando *a sus padres*. 14. Estaban practicando *español*. 15. Vamos a leer *la lección*. 16. Desean llamar *a sus amigos*. 17. No querían lavar *el coche*. 18. Podían aprender *los diálogos*.

B. Repitan cada frase; luego, substituyan los substantivos en cursiva con los pronombres correspondientes:

1. Juan le envió *una tarjeta a Ana*. 2. Léales Ud. *la carta a los niños*. 3. No le vendas *el coche a Pablo*. 4. Ella está poniéndose *el vestido*. 5. Pónganse Uds. *los zapatos*. 6. No te pongas *el sombrero*. 7. Tengo que lavarme *las manos*. 8. Él ya se ha lavado *la cara*.

9. Los niños jugaban en *el parque*. 10. Marta está cerca de *sus padres*. 11. Ellos se quejaron de *las películas*. 12. Están sentados detrás de *su papá*.

C. Para expresar en español, usando las formas correspondientes a **Ud.** para los mandatos:

1. Martha and he practice with me.
2. He and I work more than they.
3. We saw Barbara; we saw her.
4. I found my gloves; I found them.
5. They took the course; they took it.
6. I bought the cards; I bought them.
7. Take them this magazine, please.
8. Mary likes this picture.
9. Do not give Ann the flowers today.
10. Do not show them (*f.*) to her.
11. Give it (*m.*) to him, not to us.
12. Jane amused the children; she amused them.
13. Robert's mother awakened him; Robert woke up early.
14. We know that Richard became a doctor.

Resumen de palabras y expresiones

alegrarse de   to be glad to (of)
apurarse   to hurry (up)
la **beca**   scholarship
el **campamento de muchachos**   boys' camp
casarse (con + *obj.***)**   to marry, get married (to)
conceder   to grant, give
la **conferencia**   lecture; conference
contar (ue) con   to count on
de habla española   Spanish-speaking
detrás de   *prep.*   behind
enfrente de   *prep.*   in front of
la **esquina**   corner (*street*)

el **gasto**   cost, expense
hace (media hora)   (a half hour) ago
hacerse (rico, -a)   to become (rich)
(me) parece que   (I) think *or* believe that, it seems to (me) that
mucho gusto en conocerlo (-la)   (I'm very) glad *or* pleased to meet *or* know you
el **origen** (*pl.* **orígenes**)   origin
quejarse (de)   to complain (of)
el **rector**   rector, president
solicitar   to solicit, apply for
tardar en   to be late (long) in

La ciudad de Caracas (Venezuela) en 1838 según una litografía antigua.

Lectura 2

La presencia hispánica en los Estados Unidos

Entre los muchos cambios que han ocurrido en la sociedad norteamericana durante los últimos treinta años, hay uno de interés especial. Se trata del[1] aumento extraordinario del número de hispanoparlantes en nuestro país. Si incluimos los habitantes del Estado Libre Asociado[2] de Puerto Rico, se calcula que unos dieciocho millones de personas en los Estados Unidos tienen el español como lengua materna. La población de habla española en los Estados Unidos sólo la[3] exceden cuatro naciones hispánicas: México, España, la Argentina y Colombia.

Aunque hay personas de habla española en todos los estados de nuestro país, la mayoría se ha concentrado en tres grandes zonas: Nueva York y sus alrededores, la Florida y los estados del suroeste.

En Nueva York la gran mayoría de los hispanos[4] son de origen puertorriqueño, aunque la ciudad también ha atraído personas de todo el mundo hispánico. La inmigración de puertorriqueños se aceleró notablemente a partir de[5] la segunda guerra mundial, y en tiempos más recientes grupos de cubanos, colombianos y mexicanos también se han establecido en la gran metrópoli. Se calcula que unos dos millones de personas de habla española residen en la zona citada.

---

[1] **tratarse de,** *to be a question of.* [2] **Estado Libre Asociado,** *Commonwealth (Associated Free State).* [3] When the noun object precedes the verb, the corresponding object pronoun must be used with the verb. [4]**hispanos,** *persons of Hispanic origin.* [5] **a partir de,** *beginning with.*

En la Florida la población hispanoparlante es predominantemente de origen cubano. Durante los últimos veinte años casi un millón de exiliados políticos han llegado al territorio norteamericano. En su mayoría[6] estos inmigrantes son de la clase media y de cierta preparación profesional y han logrado establecerse en nuestro país sin grandes dificultades. Se cree que hoy día un millón y medio de hispanos residen en la Florida.

Más de la mitad de los hispanoparlantes de nuestro país residen en los cinco estados del suroeste: California, Arizona, Nuevo México, Colorado y Texas. Hasta 1810 estas tierras formaban la frontera septentrional[7] del imperio español en América. Pertenecieron a México desde ese año hasta 1848, cuando, por el tratado de Guadalupe Hidalgo, pasaron a ser[8] territorio de los Estados Unidos.

Éstas son las tierras en que el aumento de la población de ascendencia hispánica ha sido más rápido y donde mejor se conserva la influencia española.

Los españoles exploraron las costas de California y las tierras al norte de México en la primera mitad del siglo XVI. Durante los años 1540–1542, Francisco Vásquez de Coronado llegó a la región que hoy se conoce como Kansas y soldados de su expedición descubrieron el Gran Cañón del Río Colorado. En 1598 Juan de Oñate estableció la primera capital de la provincia de Nuevo México en San Juan de los Caballeros, cerca del pueblo indio de San Juan.

Se fundaron diversas misiones y colonias en Arizona y Texas en los siglos XVII y XVIII, y en California en el siglo XVIII. Las actividades misioneras del célebre padre Kino, en Arizona, se llevaron a cabo[9] en la última parte del siglo XVII, y las de Fray Junípero Serra, en California, durante los últimos años del siglo siguiente.

La misión y el presidio[10] fueron los instrumentos esenciales utilizados en la colonización española. Se establecían en lugares fértiles y estratégicos y muchos de ellos han dado origen a ciudades hoy prósperas y populosas, como San Francisco, San Diego, Los Ángeles, El Paso y San Antonio.

También es importante recordar que tanto la agricultura como la ganadería[11] se desarrollaron en el suroeste después de la llegada de los españoles. Se introdujeron nuevos cultivos[12] y la introducción de los animales domésticos llegó a[13] transformar totalmente la economía de estas regiones.

Es notable el vigor con que se han conservado las costumbres y la cultura hispánica en algunas regiones del suroeste. En California, en el norte de Nuevo México y en el sur de Colorado se cantan coplas y romances[14] de origen español y circulan refranes, adivinanzas[15] y cuentos populares del mismo origen.

En las fiestas religiosas y populares es igualmente clara la influencia española. La arquitectura del suroeste refleja la influencia del estilo español, combinado en Nuevo México, por ejemplo,[16] con elementos de las culturas indígenas. Como es sabido, muchas palabras españolas han pasado al inglés por el contacto de las dos culturas en el suroeste.

Aunque las tierras del suroeste siempre han atraído inmigrantes de México, esta corriente ha aumentado considerablemente durante el siglo actual.[17] En California, por ejemplo, había menos de veinte mil personas de habla española en 1900. Hoy día se

---

[6] **En su mayoría,** *For the most part.*   [7] **septentrional,** *northern.*   [8] **pasaron a ser,** *(they) became.*   [9] **se llevaron a cabo,** *were carried out.*   [10] **presidio,** *garrison of soldiers; fort.*   [11] **ganadería,** *livestock raising.*   [12] **cultivos,** *crops.*   [13] **llegó a,** *came to, went so far as to.*   [14] **coplas y romances,** *popular songs and ballads.*   [15] **adivinanzas,** *riddles.*   [16] **por ejemplo,** *for example.*   [17] **actual,** *present.*

Trabajadores de origen mexicano recogiendo fresas en California.

calcula que hay más de cinco millones de hispanoparlantes en el estado. La situación desfavorable en que se encuentran muchos de los inmigrantes recientes ha producido problemas graves, que sólo podrán resolverse eliminando obstáculos y preparando el terreno[18] para una más efectiva cooperación y una más fecunda[19] coexistencia de las dos culturas.

EJERCICIO

Escriban diez preguntas sobre puntos tratados en esta Lectura para que las contesten los otros estudiantes de la clase.

---

[18] **preparando el terreno,** *paving the way.*   [19] **fecunda,** *fruitful.*

Usos del pretérito de indicativo ▪ Usos del imperfecto de indicativo ▪ Verbos con significados especiales en el pretérito ▪ La construcción reflexiva para traducir *each other, one another* ▪ Observaciones sobre el uso de algunos verbos

people - generally use imperfect

LECCIÓN TRES

Una llamada telefónica

Luisa y Elena son compañeras de cuarto. Las dos se han distinguido en los deportes. Luisa está estudiando. Llega Elena, que regresa[1] de las pistas de tenis.

Elena. ¡Hola, Luisa! ¿Qué hay de nuevo? *whats new*
Luisa. Te llamaron a eso de las tres del Departamento de Educación Física.
Elena. ¿De veras? ¿Preguntaste por qué me llamaban? *really*
Luisa. Era la secretaria. Preguntó por ti, pero no quiso decirme nada más.
Elena. Llamaré ahora mismo. (*Marca el número en el teléfono.*) 497-1647[2] . . . ¡La línea está ocupada! (*Cuelga el auricular. Al poco rato vuelve a levantar el auricular y marca el número otra vez.*)
Secretaria. ¡Bueno![3]
Elena. Aquí habla Elena Smith. Me dice mi compañera de cuarto que querían hablar conmigo.

---

[1] In Spanish America **regresar,** *to return, come back,* is widely used along with **volver,** which is more common in Spain.   [2] Read: **cuatro nueve siete-uno seis cuatro siete.**   [3] Several Spanish expressions are used for the telephone greeting *Hello:* **Diga,** or **Dígame** (Spain); **Bueno** (Mexico); **Hola** (Argentina); **Aló** (in many other countries).

Secretaria.   Sí, señorita. Tengo el gusto de informarle que le han concedido la beca atlética que usted había pedido. ¿Podrá usted pasar mañana por la oficina del director?

Elena.   Con mucho gusto. Y mil gracias por la noticia . . . Sí, nos veremos a las once. Adiós. (*Cuelga el auricular.*) Luisa, me han concedido la beca atlética.

Luisa.   Pues, no me sorprende. Cuando supe que habías ganado el campeonato de tenis, sabía que no podían negártela.

Elena.   ¡Pues, debemos felicitarnos! Hemos recibido las primeras becas atléticas que se conceden a muchachas de esta universidad.

Luisa.   ¡Ya era hora de dar a las mujeres las mismas oportunidades que a los hombres!

Preguntas sobre el diálogo: 1. ¿En qué se han distinguido las estudiantes que hablan en este diálogo?   2. ¿De dónde regresa Elena?   3. ¿Qué noticia le da Luisa a Elena?   4. ¿Qué decide hacer Elena?   5. ¿Por qué cuelga Elena el auricular después de marcar el número?   6. ¿Por qué había llamado la secretaria a Elena?   7. ¿Adónde tiene que ir Elena al día siguiente?   8. ¿Qué dice Luisa cuando Elena le da la noticia?   9. Según Elena, ¿por qué deben felicitarse?   10. ¿Qué dice Luisa sobre las oportunidades que deben darse a las mujeres?

Preguntas para conversar: 1. ¿Cuáles son algunas expresiones que se emplean en español al contestar el teléfono?   2. ¿Tiene Ud. un teléfono en su cuarto?   3. ¿Dónde hay un teléfono público cerca de aquí?   4. ¿Cuál es el número de teléfono de sus padres?   5. ¿Cuántas veces por semana habla Ud. por teléfono con sus padres?   6. ¿En qué deportes hay equipos de muchachas en esta universidad?   7. ¿Cuántas becas atléticas se dan a muchachos en esta universidad?   8. ¿Cuántas becas atléticas se dan a muchachas en esta universidad?   9. ¿Cree Ud. que se debe dar a los equipos de muchachas la misma importancia que a los equipos de muchachos?   10. ¿Cuántas veces ha ido Ud. a partidos en que toman parte equipos de muchachas?

PRONUNCIACIÓN

The sounds of **r** and **rr**. Single **r**, except when initial in a word and when after **l, n,** or **s,** is a voiced, alveolar, single trill, that is, it is pronounced with a single tap produced by the tip of the tongue against the gums of the upper teeth. The sound is much like *dd* in *eddy* pronounced rapidly. Pronounce after your teacher:

1. perderé	verano	Carlos	verdad	preparar
eres	suroeste	cuarto	verbo	favor
parece	creerían	forma	sirve	abrir

When initial in a word, when after **l, n,** or **s,** and when doubled, the sound is a multiple trill, the tip of the tongue striking the gums in a series of very rapid vibrations. Pronounce after your teacher:

2. rato	recitar	rico	río	robar
repaso	rector	alrededor	Enrique	Israel
regular	irregular	carrera	sierra	correspondiente

3. El perro de San Roque
no tiene rabo
porque Ramón Ramírez
se lo ha cortado.

4. Erre con erre cigarro,
erre con erre barril,
rápidos corren los carros
del ferrocarril.

NOTAS GRAMATICALES

1 Usos del pretérito de indicativo

The preterit tense, sometimes called the past definite, is a narrative tense. It expresses a single past action or state, the beginning or end of a past action, or a series of acts when viewed as a complete unit in the past, regardless of the length of time involved. Duration is often defined by an adverb or adverbial expression; for example, **nunca** regularly requires the preterit:

Te llamé hace unos minutos.   I called you a few minutes ago.
Pablo hizo tres viajes a México el año pasado.   Paul made three trips to Mexico last year.
Los moros vivieron en España casi ocho siglos.   The Moors lived in Spain almost eight centuries.
Empecé a tocar unos discos.   I began to play some records.
Él nunca creyó lo que le dije.   He never believed what I told him.

interruptor

2 Usos del imperfecto de indicativo

A. General use of the imperfect tense   *weather & time*

The imperfect indicative tense, frequently called the past descriptive, describes past actions, scenes, or conditions which were continuing for an indefinite time in the past. The speaker transfers himself mentally to a point of time in the past and views the action or situation as though it were taking place before him. There is no reference to the beginning or end of the action or situation described:

Era un día frío del mes de febrero. El mar ofrecía un color azul obscuro. La madre y su hijo iban tristes y silenciosos por la playa. Cuando se hallaban a mitad del camino más o menos, vieron a lo lejos dos personas que venían hacia ellos.	It was a cold day in the month of February. The sea was a dark blue color. The mother and her son were going along the beach sad and silent. When they were more or less half way, they saw in the distance two persons who were coming toward them.

B. Specific uses of the imperfect tense

1. To describe what was happening at a certain time:

    Marta leía (estaba leyendo) y María escribía (estaba escribiendo).
    Martha was reading and Mary was writing.

2. To indicate that an action was customary or habitual, or indefinitely repeated, equivalent to English *used to, would,*[1] *was (were) accustomed to* plus an infinitive, and often to *was (were)* plus the present participle:

    Iban a la iglesia todos los domingos.   They went (used to go, would go) to church every Sunday.

3. To describe the background or setting in which an action took place or to indicate that an action was in progress when something happened (the preterit indicates what happened under the particular circumstances described):

    Juan estudiaba cuando yo regresé de la biblioteca.   John was studying when I returned from the library.
    Llovía mucho cuando Ana volvió a casa.   It was raining hard when Ann returned home.

4. To describe a mental, emotional, or physical state in the past; thus, Spanish verbs used for English *believe, know, wish, feel, be able,* etc., are often in the imperfect rather than in the preterit (see section 3, below):

    Yo creía que estabas enferma.   I believed that you were ill.
    Ella quería ir al cine con él.   She wanted to go to the movie with him.

---

[1] Do not confuse *would* meaning a habitual action with *would* used as a conditional: **¿Podría (yo) hablar con él?** *Could I (Would I be able to) talk with him?* (See Lección seis, page 132.)

5. To express indirect discourse in the past:

   Carlos dijo que quería hablar contigo.   Charles said he wanted to talk with you.
   Ana me preguntó si yo podía ir con ella.   Ann asked me if (whether) I could go with her.

6. To express time of day in the past:

   —¿Qué hora era cuando saliste? —Eran las ocho.   "What time was it when you went out?" "It was eight o'clock."

3 Verbos con significados (*meanings*) especiales en el pretérito

Certain common verbs, such as **saber, conocer, tener, querer, poder,** often have special meanings when used in the preterit. In general, the imperfect tense indicates existing desire, ability, etc., while the preterit indicates that the act was or was not accomplished. Contrastive examples are:

Sabíamos que Pablo estaba en Chile.   We knew that Paul was in Chile. (*Mental state*)
Supimos anoche que él estaba allí.   We found out (learned) last night that he was there.

Yo conocía[1] bien a Marta.   I knew Martha well.
Yo la conocí el año pasado.   I met her (made her acquaintance) last year.

Tomás quería llamar a Inés.   Thomas wanted to call Inez.
Tomás quiso llamarla.   Thomas tried to call her.

Ella no quería quedarse en casa.   She didn't want (was not willing) to stay at home.
Ella no quiso quedarse allí.   She refused to (would not) stay there.

Ana tenía una carta cuando la vi.   Ann had a letter when I saw her.
Ana tuvo tres cartas esta mañana.   Ann received (got) three letters this morning.

Le dije que yo podía buscar el libro.   I told him that I could look for the book (*i.e.,* I was able to look, capable of looking, for the book).
Lo busqué pero no pude hallarlo.   I looked for it but couldn't find it (*i.e.,* I did not succeed in finding it).

---

[1] **Conocer** may be used in all tenses to mean *to recognize.*

EJERCICIOS

A. Para contestar afirmativamente, empleando la forma del pretérito de indicativo, según el modelo.

MODELO:　¿Ha abierto Juan la puerta?　Sí, Juan abrió la puerta.

1. ¿Ha regresado Elena de las pistas de tenis?
2. ¿Ha hablado Elena con su amigo?
3. ¿Has marcado el número de teléfono otra vez?
4. ¿Le has preguntado a Ana por un diccionario?
5. ¿Ha podido hallarlo Miguel en casa?
6. ¿Les han traído ellos regalos a las muchachas?
7. ¿Ha venido Carolina al concierto?
8. ¿Han ido Uds. a la oficina del director?
9. ¿Le han concedido a Elena la beca atlética?
10. ¿Ha ganado nuestro equipo el campeonato de tenis?

B. Repitan cada frase; luego, cambien el tiempo del verbo al imperfecto de indicativo:

1. Ella quiere charlar un rato contigo.　2. Yo estoy seguro de eso.　3. Dorotea necesita el diccionario de español.　4. Son las diez de la noche.　5. Pablo y yo no sabemos eso.　6. Vamos a la biblioteca todos los días.　7. Se encuentran allí a menudo.　8. ¿Puedes hablar con Ana María a veces?　9. Hay varias personas en la calle.　10. Hacemos planes para la fiesta.

C. Repitan cada frase; luego, cambien el primer verbo al pretérito y el segundo al imperfecto de indicativo:

1. Carlos dice que quiere cenar con Miguel.
2. Él me pregunta si yo voy a la biblioteca con él.
3. Cuando marca el número, la línea está ocupada.
4. ¿Ves a la muchacha que piensa tocar los discos?
5. Elena nos escribe que puede visitarnos pronto.
6. Yo veo que hay muchos estudiantes en el teatro.

D. Lean cada frase en español, supliendo la forma correcta del pretérito o del imperfecto de indicativo de cada infinitivo en cursiva:

1. Juan no *hablar* por teléfono cuando yo *entrar* en su cuarto.
2. Él *estudiar* su lección cuando yo *abrir* la puerta.
3. Juan me *decir* que *querer* enseñarme una composición que había escrito.
4. Él me *preguntar* si yo *tener* tiempo para leerla.
5. Al leerla, yo *ver* que *estar* bien escrita y que *ser* muy interesante.
6. Mientras yo *estar* leyéndola, Tomás *llamar*.

7. Juan *levantar* el auricular y *contestar* en español.
8. Los dos *charlar* unos minutos y luego Juan *colgar* el auricular.
9. Su amigo *querer* saber si Juan *poder* ir al teatro el sábado.
10. Al poco rato yo *mirar* el reloj; *ser* las ocho y yo *tener* que irme en seguida.

4 La construcción reflexiva para traducir *each other, one another*

The plural reflexive pronouns **nos, os, se** may express a mutual or reciprocal action (one subject acting upon another):

Debemos felicitarnos.   We must congratulate each other *or* We must congratulate ourselves.

Nos vemos en el partido de fútbol.   We see (We'll see, We'll be seeing) each other at the football game.

Nos escribíamos a menudo.   We wrote to each other often.

Se saludan todos los días.   They greet one another every day.

The redundant construction **uno (-a) a otro (-a), el uno al otro, unos a otros (unas a otras),** etc., may be added for clarity or emphasis. With prepositions other than **a,** the redundant form is added regularly:

Se burlan uno de otro.   They make fun of each other (one another).

Ellos se gritaron el uno al otro.   They shouted to each other (one another).

EJERCICIO

Para contestar afirmativamente en español:

1. ¿Se escriben Uds. a menudo?
2. ¿Se miraron ellos tristemente?
3. ¿Van a ayudarse uno a otro?
4. ¿Se verán Uds. mañana?
5. ¿Se quejaban uno de otro?
6. ¿Se saludaron Ana y Pablo?

5 Observaciones sobre el uso de algunos verbos

A. **Preguntar** and **pedir**

Preguntar means *to ask* (a question); **preguntar por** means *to ask for (about), inquire about:*

Él me preguntó si yo quería ir.   He asked me if (whether) I wanted to go.

Te llamé para preguntar por el libro.   I called you to ask about the book.

Pedir means *to ask* (a favor), *ask for* (something), *to request* (something of someone). Later the use of **pedir**, *to ask* or *request someone to do something*, will be discussed:

>   **Le pedí a Miguel el diccionario.**   I asked Michael for the dictionary.
>   **Ellas no nos pidieron nada.**   They didn't ask us for anything.

With both these verbs (also with **decir** and a few other verbs), the person of whom something is asked is the indirect object. The neuter pronoun **lo** is used to complete the sentence if a direct object is not expressed:

>   **—¿Pueden ir también? —Se lo preguntaré (a ellos).**   "Can they go too?" "I shall ask them (*lit.*, ask it of them)."
>   **—¿Le dijo Ud. eso a Felipe? —Sí, se lo dije.**   "Did you tell Philip that?" "Yes, I told him."

B. **Tomar, llevar,** and other verbs meaning *to take*

Tomar means *to take* in the sense of *to take* (in one's hand), *to take* (meals, food, beverages, etc.):

>   **José, toma el libro, por favor.**   Joseph, take the book, please.
>   **¿Tomas café?**   Do you take (drink) coffee?
>   **Tomaron el avión de las dos.**   They took the two-o'clock plane.

Llevar means *to take* (*along*), *carry* (to some place):

>   **Tomás llevó a su novia al baile.**   Thomas took his girl friend to the dance.
>   **Yo tomé la maleta en la mano y la llevé al coche.**   I took the suitcase in my hand and took (carried) it to the car.

Llevarse means *to take* (*carry*) *away* (often *with oneself*):

>   **Ella compró una blusa y se la llevó.**   She bought a blouse and took it with her.

Quitar means *to take away* (*off*), *remove from;* **quitarse** means *to take off* (from oneself):

>   **Ella quitó el libro de la mesa.**   She took (removed) the book from the table.
>   **Ellos se quitaron los zapatos.**   They took off their shoes.

Sacar means *to take out, take* (photos), *get* (a license):

>   **Ella sacó muchas cosas de la cartera.**   She took many things from her purse.
>   **Yo saqué varias fotos en el parque.**   I took several photos in the park.
>   **Jaime sacó la licencia.**   James got the license.

A few idiomatic expressions which include other uses of the English verb *to take* are:

>   **almorzar (ue)**   to take (eat) lunch
>   **dar un paseo (una vuelta)**   to take a walk *or* stroll
>   **desayunarse**   to take (eat) breakfast

despedirse (i, i) (de)   to take leave (of)
dormir (ue, u) la siesta   to take a nap
hacer un viaje (una excursión)   to take a trip (excursion)
tardar (mucho) en   to take (very) long to, be (very) long in, delay (long) in
tener lugar   to take place, occur

C. **Gustar** and **querer (a)**

The English verb *to like*, usually referring to things, is regularly expressed in Spanish by **gustar**, meaning *to please, be pleasing (to)*. The English subject (*I, he, you*, etc.) becomes the indirect object in Spanish, and the English object becomes the subject of the Spanish verb; *e.g.*, instead of *She likes the hat*, turn the sentence into *The hat is pleasing to her*: **Le gusta a ella el sombrero.** This means that normally only the third person singular and plural forms of **gustar** are used. English *it* and *them* are not expressed, and the Spanish subject, when expressed, usually follows the verb:

Me (Nos) gusta la foto.   I (We) like the photo.
¿No le gusta a Ud.?   Don't you like it?
Le gustaban a ella los regalos.   She liked the gifts.

Remember that when a noun is the indirect object of **gustar**, the indirect object pronoun must also be used (see Lección dos, page 58):

A Carlos le gustan (Le gustan a Carlos) los discos.   Charles likes the records.

Querer (a) means *to like, love, feel affection for*, a person:

Queremos mucho a Juanita.   We like Jane very much (We are very fond of Jane).
Felipe y Ana se quieren mucho.   Philip and Ann love each other a great deal.

EJERCICIOS

A. Para contestar afirmativamente en oraciones completas:

1. ¿Cuándo diste un paseo? ¿Anoche?
2. ¿Cuándo dormiste la siesta? ¿Ayer por la tarde?
3. ¿Qué autobús tomó Ud.? ¿El autobús de las dos?
4. ¿Adónde llevó Jorge a María? ¿Al cine?
5. ¿Cuándo hizo Ud. una excursión? ¿El sábado?
6. ¿Qué se quitó Ud.? ¿El abrigo?
7. ¿Quién se lavó la cara? ¿Usted?
8. ¿Quiénes se desayunaron temprano? ¿Ustedes?
9. ¿Adónde llevaron ellos las cosas? ¿A casa?
10. ¿Cuál de ellas tardó mucho en llegar? ¿Luisa?

B. Repitan cada oración; luego, substituyan la frase entre paréntesis:

1. Me gusta *la canción.* (las canciones)
2. Nos gustan *estos estilos.* (este estilo)
3. A Luisa le gustan mucho *los vestidos rojos.* (el vestido verde)
4. ¿Le gusta a Ud. *aquella casa amarilla?* (aquellas casas blancas)
5. ¿Te gusta *ese cuadro pequeño?* (esos cuadros grandes)
6. No les gusta *la revista mexicana.* (las revistas mexicanas)

C. Para contestar negativamente en oraciones completas:

1. ¿A quién le pidió Ud. el diccionario? ¿A Inés?
2. ¿A quién le preguntó Ud. por el curso? ¿A Miguel?
3. ¿De quién se despidieron Uds.? ¿Del profesor Díaz?
4. ¿Dónde sacaron Uds. muchas fotos? ¿En el parque?
5. ¿A quién quiere Roberto? ¿A Carolina?
6. ¿Quiénes se quieren mucho? ¿Marta y Jorge?

RESUMEN

A. Lean en español, cambiando cada infinitivo en cursiva a la forma correcta del pretérito o del imperfecto de indicativo:

1. *Ser* las nueve cuando yo *volver* del aeropuerto. 2. Cuando yo *ver* a María, la *invitar* a almorzar conmigo. 3. Pablo le *preguntar* a Carolina si ella *poder* ir al cine con él. 4. Miguel *marcar* el número de María, pero ella no *estar* en casa. 5. Él *querer* hablar con ella acerca de un artículo que él *estar* preparando. 6. Al poco rato él *ir* al café, pero no *poder* hallarla. 7. Los estudiantes *charlar* cuando el profesor *entrar* en la sala de clase. 8. Ellos *saber* que él *ir* a darles un examen. 9. Jorge *andar* despacio por la calle cuando yo lo *ver*. 10. Yo le *decir* que *querer* devolverle su libro de español.

B. Usos del verbo *to take*. Para expresar en español:

1. Thomas took Martha to the dance. 2. Did Paul take the ten-o'clock bus? 3. Will you (*pl.*) take a trip to Mexico? 4. Why didn't he take a walk with her? 5. I believe (that) he took a nap. 6. I took several photos in the park. 7. He took off his hat; he took it off. 8. He took the watch in his hand.

C. Usos del pronombre reflexivo **se** y de los verbos **gustar** y **querer.** Para expresar en español:

1. We see each other every day. 2. Raymond and I help each other. 3. They were making fun of each other. 4. Do you visit one another often? 5. I like this gold watch. 6. Do you (*fam. sing.*) like it? 7. We like George's guitar. 8. They do not like this picture. 9. Mary likes to write articles. 10. Do you (*pl.*) like to talk on the telephone? 11. Charles likes Helen very much. 12. I know that the two love each other.

Resumen de palabras y expresiones

a eso de   at about (*time*)
ahora mismo   right now, right away
al día siguiente   (on) the next (following) day
al poco rato   after a short while
atlético, -a   athletic
el **auricular**   receiver (*telephone*)
el **avión de las dos**   the two-o'clock plane
¡bueno!   hello! (*telephone*)
el **campeonato**   championship
colgar (ue)   to hang (up)
el **concierto**   concert
de la noche   p.m., in the evening
de veras   really, truly
el **diccionario**   dictionary
distinguirse   to distinguish oneself, become distinguished; to shine
habla (Elena)   this is (Helen), (Helen) is speaking
hablar por teléfono   to talk by (on the) telephone
felicitar   to congratulate
la **importancia**   importance
informar   to inform, tell

la **línea**   line
la **llamada**   call
marcar el número   to dial the number
mil gracias   many (a thousand) thanks, thanks loads
las **mismas (oportunidades) que**   the same (opportunities) as
negar (ie)   to deny, refuse
no me sorprende   it doesn't surprise me, I'm not surprised
la **noticia**   news (item), notice, information; *pl.* news, information
la **pista (de tenis)**   (tennis) court
por semana   per (each) week
preguntar por   to ask for (about), inquire about
público, -a   public
¿qué hay de nuevo?   what's new?
regresar   to return, come back
el **sábado por la noche**   Saturday night
telefónico, -a   telephone (*adj.*)
volver (ue) a (levantar)   (to lift *or* take up) again
¡ya era hora!   it was about time!

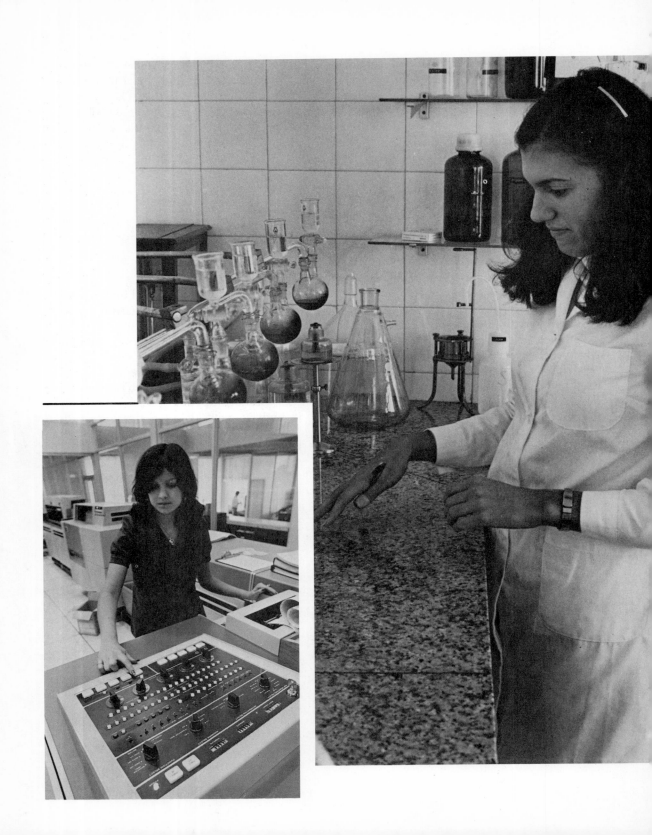

Lectura 3

La liberación de la mujer

La lucha por la liberación de la mujer sigue siendo[1] uno de los movimientos más importantes de nuestro tiempo. Además, va creciendo en complejidad, pues abarca, al parecer,[2] casi todos los aspectos de la existencia feminina. También es claro que las reformas y mejoras deseadas no son las mismas en todas partes.[3] En las naciones más avanzadas, las marchas y manifestaciones de las feministas han traído como resultado varios adelantos importantes, pero en otras partes,[4] sobre todo en las naciones subdesarrolladas, la situación de la mujer todavía deja mucho que desear.[5]

Como sería imposible tratar del asunto[6] adecuadamente en unos cuantos[7] párrafos, nos limitaremos a hacer algunas observaciones sobre el progreso del movimiento en estos últimos años.[8] Para concluir trataremos de comparar brevemente la posición de la mujer en las dos Américas—la anglosajona y la hispánica.

La participación de la mujer en la vida económica y política de las naciones va aumentando día a día.[9] Tanto en el hemisferio occidental como en Europa, las mujeres trabajan al lado de[10] los hombres en el comercio y la industria y hay numerosos ejemplos

---

[1] **sigue siendo,** *continues to be.* [2] **va creciendo . . . al parecer,** *it continues to increase (is gradually increasing) in complexity, since it apparently embraces (includes).* [3] **en todas partes,** *everywhere.* [4] **en otras partes,** *elsewhere, in other places.* [5] **deja mucho que desear,** *leaves much to be desired.* [6] **tratar del asunto,** *to deal with the subject.* [7] **unos cuantos,** *a few.* [8] **en estos últimos años,** *recently, (in) the last few years.* [9] **día a día,** *day by day.* [10] **al lado de,** *beside, at the side of.*

de mujeres que ocupan puestos importantes en el gobierno. Algo más lenta, en cambio,[11] ha sido la conquista de derechos igualitarios en los campos del matrimonio y la vida doméstica.

Desde hace varios años una mujer preside[12] el partido conservador en el Reino Unido. En Francia e Italia, como también en los Estados Unidos, varias mujeres han ocupado puestos ministeriales.

Varias naciones han promulgado leyes para mejorar la posición de la mujer en el campo industrial y comercial. Un ejemplo importante es la ley que garantiza la igualdad de pago por el mismo trabajo, sin hacer caso del[13] sexo de la persona interesada. Pero a pesar de [14] estas leyes, las mujeres todavía encuentran obstáculos al buscar trabajo. Con frecuencia se ven obligadas a aceptar puestos poco remunerativos y muchas veces figuran entre los primeros que pierden el empleo en tiempos difíciles.

En cuanto a[15] los asuntos financieros, varios países han aprobado leyes que establecen la igualdad ante la ley de los dos esposos.[16] Una mujer casada, por ejemplo, tiene el derecho de abrir una cuenta en un banco sin el consentimiento de su esposo.

Según las feministas, los problemas más graves se encuentran en la esfera de la vida doméstica. Para lograr la verdadera igualdad y hacer más llevadera[17] la vida diaria de la mujer casada, habrá que conseguir[18] muchas mejoras más, entre ellas la multiplicación de las guarderías infantiles,[19] el escalonar[20] las horas de trabajo, y una colaboración más activa del marido en las labores domésticas.

Si comparamos brevemente la posición de la mujer en nuestro país y en el mundo hispano, encontramos un contraste notable. En los Estados Unidos las mujeres están esforzándose por poner en práctica[21] los derechos que han conseguido, mientras que en Hispanoamérica y en España están luchando por conseguirlos.

¿Qué factores han contribuido a crear este contraste? Además de diversos factores económicos y sociales, cuya influencia es evidente, los más importantes, sin duda,[22] son el desarrollo más rápido de las ideas democráticas y la educación más liberal de la mujer en nuestro país. Como los gobiernos del mundo han descubierto, la democracia moderna trae consigo la reclamación de derechos igualitarios para la mujer, y, desgraciadamente,[23] por tradición, la educación de la mujer hispana ha sido más conservadora que la de la mujer norteamericana.

Sin embargo,[24] es indudable que las costumbres y formas de vida van cambiando rápidamente en todo el mundo hispánico. Las jóvenes estudian y viajan más, aprenden a trabajar fuera de casa[25] y, en general, están al tanto de[26] lo que pasa en los demás países del mundo. Además, con los grandes cambios que se realizan modernamente en la sociedad, hay más oportunidades para las generaciones jóvenes.

---

[11] **en cambio,** *on the other hand.*   [12] **Desde . . . preside,** *For several years a woman has presided over (dominated).*   [13] **sin hacer caso de,** *without taking into account.*   [14] **a pesar de,** *despite, in spite of.*   [15] **En cuanto a,** *As for, Concerning.*   [16] **los dos esposos,** *the husband and wife* (lit., *the two spouses*).   [17] **llevadera,** *bearable, tolerable.*   [18] **habrá que conseguir,** *it will be necessary to obtain (attain).*   [19] **guarderías infantiles,** *day nurseries.*   [20] **el escalonar,** *staggering.*   [21] **están . . . práctica,** *are making an effort to put into practice.*   [22] **sin duda,** *doubtless.*   [23] **desgraciadamente,** *unfortunately.*   [24] **Sin embargo,** *Nevertheless.*   [25] **fuera de casa,** *outside (of) the house.*   [26] **están al tanto de,** *they are aware (informed) of.*

Dos estudiantes preparan el programa de un ordenador en la universidad de Guadalajara, México.

En fin,[27] la mujer feminista está convencida de que para cumplir sus obligaciones como es debido[28] y alcanzar la plenitud[29] de su vida, necesita cultura e independencia, además de gozar de[30] los mismos derechos y los mismos deberes[31] que los hombres. Está segura de que viviremos en un mundo mejor si tiene éxito[32] en su misión.

EJERCICIO

Empleando como elemento inicial las preguntas y oraciones siguientes, preparen un breve diálogo, de unas quince líneas, sobre la posición de la mujer en la sociedad norteamericana o hispana:

Alicia. ¡Hola, Jorge! Me dicen que vuelves a Lima la semana que viene. ¿Qué te ha interesado más durante tu visita en nuestro país?

Jorge. Pues, no es difícil contestar a tu pregunta—la posición de la mujer en la sociedad norteamericana.

---

[27] **En fin,** *In short.*   [28] **como es debido,** *as is only right.*   [29] **alcanzar la plenitud,** *to attain the fullness (abundance).*   [30] **además de gozar de,** *besides (in addition to) enjoying.*   [31] **deberes,** *duties, obligations.*   [32] **si tiene éxito,** *if she is successful.*

LECCIÓN CUATRO

La comida del "Día Internacional"

Para celebrar el Día Internacional la Casa Española va a preparar una comida especial, con baile y música. Se ha reunido[1] la Junta Directiva para organizar la fiesta. Elena es la presidenta y Ramón es el secretario.

Elena. Como ya saben todos, acostumbramos celebrar el Día Internacional con una comida especial. ¿Qué sugieren ustedes para el menú?

Carlos. Como plato principal no hay nada más apropiado que la paella valenciana.

Luisa. Yo preferiría algo diferente, como el mole de guajolote, por ejemplo.

Juan. (*Es puertorriqueño.*) Otra posibilidad sería un asopao de pollo.

Elena. Alguien tendría que cortar y adobar la carne con horas de anticipación. ¿Queremos pasar el día en la cocina?

Juan. Elena tiene razón. Retiro mi propuesta.

Luisa. Yo también voto por la paella.

Ramón. Para comenzar podríamos servir unas empanaditas de queso o un gazpacho andaluz.

Luisa. ¡Oh, sí! A todos les gustan las empanaditas.

Carlos. Y con los entremeses, cebiche y una ensalada de aguacate.

---

[1] For forms of **reunir(se),** see Appendix D, page 300, footnote 1.

Ramón. Bueno, lo he apuntado todo.[1] Sólo falta el postre.

Luisa. Sin duda alguna, el flan es el postre más típico.

Elena. Pues, ya tenemos el menú. Va a ser un banquete. Alguien tendrá que buscar las recetas . . . Además, ¿quién va a cocinar?

Carlos. Pues, nadie mejor que la presidenta para ser la cocinera.

Elena. Bueno . . . como último recurso y con la ayuda de todos. Cualquiera de nosotros lo podría hacer.

Juan. Yo me encargo de buscar las recetas.

Ramón. El conjunto de mariachis, "Los Tapatíos,"[2] se ha ofrecido a tocar durante la comida. ¿Necesitamos alguna orquesta más para el baile?

Carlos. Tenemos muchos discos de música hispanoamericana. Alguno de nosotros podrá encargarse de ponerlos.

Elena. Bueno, creo que queda todo resuelto. Ramón mandará las invitaciones a los huéspedes de honor, ¿verdad?

Ramón. Sí, a la señora Valdés y al profesor Navarro. Y Luisa ha prometido decorar las mesas.

Elena. Pues, ya son las doce. Muchas gracias a todos. Hasta la vista.

Otros. Hasta luego, Elena.

Preparen una conversación por teléfono, de unas diez líneas, para recitar en clase, empleando las frases y preguntas siguientes como elemento inicial:

1.   *José.* ¿Eres tú, Ana? Te llamo para preguntarte si quieres jugar al tenis esta tarde.

     Ana. No se lo cuentes a nadie, pero voy a encontrar a alguien muy especial en el aeropuerto a las tres.

2.   *Ramón.* ¡Hola, María! ¿Te gustaría venir a cenar en la Casa Española el sábado por la noche?

     María. Con mucho gusto. ¿A qué hora comienza la comida?

PRONUNCIACIÓN

A. Spanish **p, t, c (qu, k).** In pronouncing these consonants, recall that the Spanish sounds are pure stops, not aspirated stops as in English. To avoid the aspiration, or puff of air, that often follows the English sounds (p^hen, t^hen, c^han), the breath must be held back during the articulation of the sound. The aspiration of the English sound is especially objectionable before **r** and before unstressed **i** and **u** in diphthongs; avoid t^h**iene,** t^h**res.** In the case of **t,** remember also that the Spanish sound is dental, that is, the tip of the tongue touches the back of the upper teeth, not the ridge above the teeth, as in English. Pronounce after your teacher:

---

[1] When **todo,** *everything,* is the direct object of a verb, the direct object pronoun **lo** is also used.   [2] The word **tapatío, -a** is associated with Guadalajara, capital of the Mexican state of Jalisco. The **jarabe tapatío,** national *Hat Dance* of Mexico, is normally played by the **mariachis,** an orchestra consisting almost entirely of string instruments.

1. patio	pregunta	profesor	mapa	puse
2. tú	admitir	está	tengo	Tomás
3. canto	caso	saco	cuento	busqué
pequeño	aquí	quise	kilómetro	kilogramo
4. tiempo	tiene	quiero	puede	entrego

B. Review the observations on Spanish intonation, Repaso tres, pages 24–25 and Lección dos, page 53; then read in Spanish, noting carefully the intonation patterns and the division into breath-groups. Why have certain syllables been underlined?

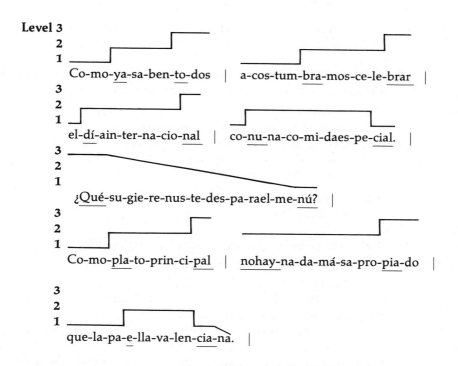

NOTAS GRAMATICALES

1 Usos del artículo definido

The definite article **el** (*pl.* **los**) or **la** (*pl.* **las**) is used in Spanish, as in English, to denote a specific noun. In addition, the definite article in Spanish has a number of other important functions.

A few of the special uses in Spanish are:

1. With abstract nouns and with nouns used in a general sense, indicating a whole class:

   A todos les gustan los entremeses.   All like appetizers.
   Tengo mucho interés en el arte mexicano.   I have much interest in Mexican art.
   La vida en el Perú es interesante.   Life in Peru is interesting.

2. With titles (except before **don, doña, san, santo, santa**) when speaking about, but not directly to, a person:

   El profesor Navarro acepta nuestra invitación.   Professor Navarro accepts our invitation.

   BUT: **Buenos días, señora Valdés.**   Good morning, Mrs. Valdés.
   Don Carlos López me llamó.   Don Carlos López called me.

3. With days of the week and seasons of the year, except after **ser,** and with dates, meals, hours of the day, and modified expressions of time:

   Saldrán el domingo.   They will leave (on) Sunday.
   Ana regresó el quince de mayo.   Ann returned (on) May 15.
   Llegarán tarde para el almuerzo.   They will arrive (be) late for lunch.
   Ya son las doce.   It is already twelve o'clock.
   Vi al señor Ortiz la semana pasada.   I saw Mr. Ortiz last week.

   BUT: **Hoy es jueves.**   Today is Thursday.
   Es otoño.   It is autumn.

4. With parts of the body, articles of clothing, and other things closely associated with a person, in place of the possessive adjective when the reference is clear:

   Juanita se lavó las manos.   Jane washed her hands.
   Nos quitamos los guantes.   We took off our gloves.
   He perdido el reloj.   I have lost my watch.
   Ella tiene el pelo rubio.   She has blond hair (Her hair is blond).

5. With the name of a language, except after **de** and **en** or immediately after **hablar** (and often after verbs such as **aprender, comprender, escribir, estudiar, leer, practicar, saber**):

   El español no es fácil.   Spanish is not easy.
   Ana habla bien[1] el francés.   Ann speaks French well.

---

[1] When any word other than the subject pronoun comes between forms of **hablar** and the other verbs given in this subsection and the name of a language, the article is used.

BUT: **Éste es un libro de español.**   This is a Spanish book.
La carta está escrita en inglés.   The letter is written in English.
¿Habla Ud. portugués?   Do you speak Portuguese?
¿Estudiamos inglés y español.   We study English and Spanish.

6. With nouns of rate, weight, and measure (English regularly uses the indefinite article):

Cuestan cuarenta dólares el par.   They cost forty dollars a pair.
Pagué noventa centavos la docena.   I paid ninety cents a dozen.

7. With names of rivers and mountains, with proper names and names of places when modified, and with the names of certain countries and cities:

El Amazonas está en el Brasil.   The Amazon (River) is in Brazil.
Conocemos la España moderna.   We know modern Spain.

Some commonly used names of countries and cities which are preceded by the definite article in conservative literary usage (but which are often used without the article in journalistic and colloquial use) are:

(el) Canadá	**(el)** Brasil	**(el)** Perú	**(el)** Callao
(los) Estados Unidos	**(el)** Ecuador	**(el)** Paraguay	**(el)** Cuzco
(la) Argentina	**(la)** Florida	**(el)** Uruguay	**(la)** Habana

The article is seldom omitted in the case of **El Salvador,** which means *The Savior.*

8. In certain set phrases:

a (en) la escuela   to (at, in) school
a la iglesia   to church
al poco rato   in a short while

NOTE: Special use of the definite article **el.** Feminine nouns which begin with stressed **a-** or **ha-** require **el** in the singular, instead of **la,** when the article immediately precedes: **el agua,** *the water,* **el hambre,** *hunger;* but **las aguas,** *the waters,* **la altura,** *the height.*

Recall the two contractions in Spanish of the masculine singular definite article: **a + el = al; de + el = del.** Examples: **Vamos al cine,** *We are going (Let's go) to the movie;* **Entro en el cuarto del muchacho,** *I enter the boy's room.*

2   Usos del artículo indefinido

The indefinite article **un** (*m.*), **una** (*f.*), *a, an,* is regularly repeated before each noun:

Ana tiene un reloj y una pulsera.   Ann has a watch and a bracelet.

The plural form **unos, unas** means *some, any, a few, several, about* (in the sense of *approximately*). Normally *some* and *any* are expressed in Spanish only when emphasized:

> **Podríamos servir unas empanaditas de queso.**   We could serve some cheese turnovers.
> **El señor Ortega tiene unos sesenta años.** Mr. Ortega is about sixty years old.

> BUT: **¿Tiene Ud. dinero?**   Do you have any (some) money?
> **No tenemos que tomar notas.**   We don't have to take (any) notes.

In Spanish the indefinite article is omitted in certain cases in which it is regularly used in English:

1. After **ser,** with an unmodified noun of profession, occupation, religion, nationality, rank, or political affiliation, or in answer to the English *What is (he)?*

> **La madre de Juanita es escritora.**   Jane's mother is a writer.
> **—¿Qué es él? —Es abogado.**   "What is he?" "He is a lawyer."

The indefinite article is used, however, when a person's identity is stressed, and when these nouns are modified:

> **—¿Quién es ella? —Es una profesora.**   "Who is she?" "She is a teacher."
> **Ella es una buena profesora.**   She is a good teacher.

2. Often before nouns, particularly in interrogative and negative sentences, after prepositions, and after certain verbs (such as **tener** and **buscar**), when the numerical concept of *a, an (one)* is not emphasized:

> **¿Busca Ud. receta ahora?**   Are you looking for a recipe now?
> **Pepe salió sin sombrero.**   Joe went out without a hat.
> **Marta no tiene coche.**   Martha doesn't have a car (has no) car.
> **. . . como último recurso.**   . . . as a last resort.

3. With adjectives such as **otro, -a,** *another,* **tal,** *such a,* **cien(to),** *a (one) hundred,* **mil,** *a (one) thousand,* **cierto, -a,** *a certain,* **medio, -a,** *a half,* and with **¡qué!** *what a!* in exclamations:

> **Tráigame Ud. otro vaso de leche.**   Bring me another glass of milk.
> **Cierta muchacha me dijo eso.**   A certain girl told me that.
> **¡Qué hombre!**   What a man!

EJERCICIO

Lean en español, supliendo el artículo—definido o indefinido—cuando sea necesario:

1. Buenos días, _____ señor López. _El_ señor Díaz no ha llegado todavía.
2. Hoy es _____ miércoles. Siempre tengo tres clases _el_ miércoles.
3. Ellos hablan _____ español. Dicen que _el_ español es difícil.
4. Piensan ir a _____ España. Quieren conocer bien _la_ España moderna.

5. El tío de Ana es _____ médico. Es _____ médico distinguido.
6. —¿Qué es _el_ don Carlos? —Creo que es _____ abogado.
7. —¿Quién es _el_ doña Inés? —Se dice que es _____ profesora.
8. Felipe no tiene _un_ reloj. Vamos a regalarle _____ reloj de oro.
9. —¿Busca Ud. _____ disco hoy? —Sí, busco _____ disco hecho en España.
10. A ella le gustan _las_ rosas. Su novio le manda _____ flores cada semana.
11. María habla bien _el_ portugués. No habla _____ francés.
12. Carlos siempre toma _el_ café aquí. No le gusta _____ café frío.

3   El género (gender) y el número de los substantivos

A. Nouns referring to male beings, most nouns ending in **-o**, days of the week, the names of languages, certain nouns ending in **-ma, -pa, -ta**, and infinitives used as nouns, are masculine:

   el jueves Thursday   **el español** Spanish   **el mapa** map

   BUT: **la mano** hand
         la radio[1] radio (*as a means of communication*)
         la foto (*abbreviation of* **fotografía**) photo

Nouns referring to female beings and most nouns ending in **-a** (except those ending in **-ma, -pa, -ta**) or in **-(c)ión, -dad, -tad, -tud, -umbre, -ie** are feminine:

   la invitación invitation   **la reunión** meeting   **la verdad** truth

   BUT: **el día** day   **el avión** (air)plane   **el programa** program

Some nouns ending in **-a**, particularly in **-ista**, are either masculine or feminine: **el (la) artista**, *artist* (man or woman). The gender of other nouns must be learned by observation:

   el plan plan   **el postre** dessert   **el té** tea   **la leche** milk

Many nouns ending in **-o**, particularly those of relationship, have a corresponding feminine form ending in **-a: el hijo**, *son*, **la hija**, *daughter*.

B. In general, to form the plural of nouns, add **-s** to those ending in an unaccented vowel and **-es** to those ending in a consonant, including **y**. Most nouns ending in an unstressed syllable ending in **-s** and most family names do not change in the plural: **el (los) parabrisas**, *windshield(s)*, **el (los) tocadiscos**, *record player(s)*, **el (los) lunes**, *Monday(s)*; **Gómez** (family name), **los Gómez**, *the Gómez family*. **Los señores Gómez** means *Mr. and Mrs. Gómez*.

---

[1] **El radio**, *radio, radio set*, is gradually being used more widely, especially in Spanish America, than **la radio**, *radio*, as a network or means of communication.

Singular	Plural
la cocinera cook (*f*.)	**las cocineras** cooks
el jardín garden	**los jardines** gardens
el joven young man	**los jóvenes** young men
el examen examination	**los exámenes** examinations

Note that the accent is not written on the plural **jardines** and that it is added on the plurals **jóvenes** and **exámenes** to keep the stress on the same syllable as in the singular. Nouns ending in **-z** change the **z** to **c** before **-es,** and those ending in **-ión** drop the accent in the plural: **el lápiz, los lápices; la reunión, las reuniones.**

Certain nouns denoting rank or relationship may be used in the masculine plural to refer to individuals of both sexes: **los reyes,** *the kings, the king(s) and queen(s);* **los hermanos,** *the brothers, the brother(s) and sister(s).*

EJERCICIOS

A. Repitan cada oración; luego, repítanla otra vez, cambiando los substantivos al plural y haciendo los otros cambios necesarios.

MODELO: El amigo de ella trae su libro.   El amigo de ella trae su libro.
Los amigos de ellas traen sus libros.

1. La niña deja el lápiz en su cuarto. 2. El artista le explica el cuadro al estudiante. 3. La mujer siempre pasa por la calle el domingo. 4. La profesora de francés no sabe la canción. 5. La muchacha habla del plan para la próxima reunión. 6. El joven no puede aceptar mi invitación. 7. El huésped de honor hablará sobre un problema social. 8. La estudiante mira la foto del parque nacional.

B. Para contestar negativamente:

1. ¿Quieren Uds. paella como plato principal?
2. ¿Comes cebiche a veces?
3. ¿Es artista la señora Valdés?
4. ¿Es escritora tu mamá?
5. ¿Trabajas todo el día en casa?
6. ¿Tiene jardín la Casa Española?
7. ¿Necesitan orquesta para el baile?
8. ¿Vas a mandar invitaciones para el almuerzo?

C. Después de oír el substantivo, repítanlo empleando el artículo definido; luego, repitan la frase en el plural.

MODELO: mapa   el mapa, los mapas

1. hijo 2. cocinera 3. parque 4. mano 5. autobús 6. universidad 7. mes 8. ciudad 9. viaje 10. jardín 11. librería 12. país 13. carne 14. avión 15. noche 16. viernes 17. flor 18. vez 19. agua 20. examen

4 Usos de las palabras indefinidas y negativas

Pronouns	
algo something, anything	**nada** nothing, (not) . . . anything
alguien someone, somebody, anybody, anyone	**nadie** no one, nobody, (not) . . . anybody (anyone)

Pronoun or Adjective	
alguno, -a some(one), any; (*pl.*) some	**ninguno, -a** no, no one, none, (not) . . . any (anybody)
cualquier(a) any *or* anyone (at all)	

Adverbs	
siempre always	**nunca** / **jamás** } never, (not) . . . ever
también also, too	**tampoco** neither, (not *or* nor) . . . either

Conjunctions	
o or	**ni** nor, (not) . . . or
o . . . o either . . . or	**ni . . . ni** neither . . . nor, (not) . . . either . . . or

---

A. Simple negation is expressed by placing **no** immediately before the verb (or the auxiliary in the compound tenses and in the progressive forms of the tenses).

If negatives such as **nada, nadie,** etc., follow the verb, **no** or some other negative word must precede the verb; if they precede the verb or stand alone, **no** is not used. If a negative precedes the verb, all the expressions in the Spanish sentence are negative, rather than indefinite as in English. After **que,** *than,* the negatives are used:

Miguel quiere algo.   Michael wants something.
No tiene nada *or* **Nada tiene.**   He has nothing (He doesn't have anything).
Él nunca (jamás) trajo nada.   He never brought anything.
Ana salió sin decir nada.   Ann left without saying anything.
No lo hice tampoco *or* **Tampoco lo hice.**   I didn't do it either (Neither did I do it).
—¿Qué sabes? —Nada de particular.   "What do you know?" "Nothing special."
Carlota lee más que nadie (nunca).   Charlotte reads more than anyone (ever).
No me gusta ni el café ni el té.   I don't like either coffee or tea (I like neither coffee nor tea).
Ni Pablo ni Luis pueden[1] cocinar.   Neither Paul nor Louis can cook.

---

[1]Singular nouns connected by **o** or **ni** which precede the verb normally take a plural verb.

If the verb is not expressed, **no** usually follows the word it negates: **Yo no,** *Not I;* **todavía no,** *not yet.*

B. The pronouns **alguien** and **nadie** refer only to persons, unknown or not mentioned before, and the personal **a** is required when they are used as objects of the verb:

> **¿Vio Ud. a alguien?**   Did you see anyone?
> **Nadie me llamó a mí, ni yo llamé a nadie.**   No one called me, nor did I call anybody.

C. **Alguno** and **ninguno,** used as adjectives or pronouns, refer to *someone* or *none* of a group of persons or things already thought of or mentioned. The plural **algunos, -as,** means *some, any, several.* Before a masculine singular noun **alguno** is shortened to **algún,** and **ninguno** to **ningún. Ninguno, -a** is normally used only in the singular:

> **Alguno de nosotros podrá encargarse de ponerlos.**   Someone of us will be able to take charge of putting them on.
> **Ninguna de ellas debe saber eso.**   None of them should know that.
> **¿Conoces a algunas de las señoritas?**   Do you know any (some) of the young ladies?
> **Nos reuniremos allí algún día.**   We shall meet there some day.
> **Ningún hombre haría eso.**   No man would do that.

D. Both **nunca** and **jamás** mean *never,* but in a question **jamás** means *ever* and a negative answer is expected. When neither an affirmative nor negative answer is implied, **alguna vez,** *ever, sometime, (at) any time,* is used:

> **Tomás nunca (jamás) toma mucho.**   Thomas never takes (eats) much.
> **—¿Has visto jamás tal cosa? —No, nunca.**   "Have you ever seen such a thing?" "No, never."
> **¿Ha estado Ud. alguna vez en Puerto Rico?**   Have you ever (at any time) been in Puerto Rico?

E. The plural **algunos, -as** means *some, several, a few;* **unos, -as,** with the same meanings, is more indefinite and expresses indifference as to the exact number. In some cases **unos, -as** corresponds to *a pair of, two;* its place is taken by **algunos, -as** with a **de**-phrase:

> **Hay algunos discos sobre la mesa.**   There are some records on the table.
> **Tendré que buscar algunas recetas.**   I shall have to look for some recipes.
> **Unos (Algunos) niños están en el jardín.**   Some children are in the garden.
> **Algunos de ellos van a querer refrescos.**   Some of them are going to want refreshments.

Remember that unemphatic *some* and *any* are not regularly expressed in Spanish:

¿Quieres queso para el almuerzo?   Do you want some (any) cheese for lunch?

An emphatic way to express *any (at all)* is to place **alguno, -a** after the noun:

Sin duda alguna . . .   Without any doubt (at all) . . .

F. **Cualquiera** (*pl.* **cualesquiera**), which may drop the final **a** before a noun, means *any, anyone* in the sense of *any at all, just any*:

Cualquier(a) persona puede decorar la mesa.   Any person (at all) can decorate the table.
Cualquiera de nosotros lo podría hacer.   Anyone of us could do it.

G. **Algo** and **nada** are sometimes used as adverbs, meaning *somewhat, rather*, and *(not) at all*, respectively:

A menudo Pepe llega algo tarde.   Often Joe arrives rather late.
Ese libro no es nada interesante.   That book isn't at all interesting.

EJERCICIOS

A. Repitan la frase; luego, cámbienla a la forma negativa.

MODELO: Ramón tiene algo.   Ramón tiene algo.   Ramón no tiene nada.

1. Juan le dio algo a Elena. 2. Hay algo más apropiado que el asopao. 3. Alguien tendrá que preparar el flan. 4. Veo algo sobre la mesa. 5. Hemos visto a alguien en la sala. 6. Hay alguien en la cocina. 7. Alguno de los muchachos ha buscado unas recetas. 8. Algún muchacho comprará el pollo. 9. Han invitado a alguno de los profesores. 10. ¿Viene alguna de tus amigas? 11. ¿Siempre dices algo a alguien? 12. Alguna de las niñas está gritando. 13. Han visto a Juan o a Pablo. 14. La novela es algo larga.

B. Para contestar negativamente:

1. ¿Llamó alguien anoche?
2. ¿Se desayunó contigo alguno de ellos?
3. ¿Va a ayudarnos algún estudiante?
4. ¿Has comprado alguna cosa esta mañana?
5. ¿Han estado Uds. jamás en la ciudad de México?
6. ¿Siempre toma Ud. mucho para el almuerzo?
7. ¿Fueron Uds. al cine con alguien anoche?
8. ¿Sugieres algo diferente?
9. ¿Buscó Ud. a alguna de las estudiantes?
10. ¿Quieres hablar de los planes con alguien?

C. Para completar empleando el equivalente de las palabras inglesas *some* o *any* cuando sea necesario:

1. ___Un___ día pasaré por tu casa.   2. ___algunos___ estudiantes fueron a la Casa Española.   3. ¿Compró Ud. ___unos___ zapatos en esta zapatería?   4. Esta noche queremos preparar _____ empanaditas.   5. ___algunas___ de las jóvenes puede traer el postre.   6. Mi mamá va a servir _____ flan esta noche.   7. ¿Hay _____ aguacates en la cocina?   8. No conozco _____ orquesta más popular.   9. Mi hermano pondrá ___algunos___ discos hispanoamericanos.   10. ¿Tienen Uds. _____ planes para la próxima reunión?

RESUMEN

A. Lean en español, supliendo el artículo indefinido cuando sea necesario:

1. Luis no tiene _____ reloj.
2. ¿Desea Ud. _____ ensalada para el almuerzo?
3. Mi tío no necesita _____ coche más grande.
4. Dicen que aquella mujer es _____ puertorriqueña.
5. —¿Qué es ella? —Es _____ profesora de español.
6. ¿Buscan Uds. _____ receta para la paella?
7. Marta no quiere _____ cartera nueva.
8. —¿Quién es él? —Es _____ médico.
9. Hoy tengo que comprar _____ cuaderno y ___(no una)___ otra pluma.
10. Nunca oí tal _____ cosa.

B. Usos del artículo definido. Para expresar en español:

1. We go to church on Sundays.
2. Ann, wash (*fam.*) your hands.
3. All like (small) turnovers.
4. Professor Navarro will leave for Argentina next month.
5. Today is Wednesday, isn't it?
6. The water was not cold (hot).
7. ¿Do you (*pl.*) like cheese?
8. The guest of honor will talk about Mexican food.

C. Usos de las palabras indefinidas y negativas. Para contestar negativamente en español:

1. ¿Tiene Ramón algo en la mano?
2. ¿Invitó Ana a alguien a almorzar?
3. ¿Vio Luis a alguien en el centro?
4. ¿Perdió el reloj alguna muchacha?
5. ¿Lo encontró alguno de los niños?
6. ¿Siempre compran Uds. algo aquí?
7. ¿Ha estado Ud. alguna vez en México?
8. ¿Puede venir algún muchacho?

D. Para escribir en español:

1. Some students are organizing (*progressive*) a fiesta to celebrate International Day.
2. They are accustomed to celebrate it in the Spanish House.   3. Helen, the
president, asks what (*qué*) they suggest for the menu.   4. Charles says that there isn't
anything more appropriate than *paella*.   5. John, who is a Puerto Rican, prefers
chicken *asopao*.   6. Helen replies that no one wants to spend all day in the kitchen.
7. Therefore, John says that Helen is right and that he withdraws his proposal.
8. Finally, they vote for *paella*, cheese turnovers, avocado salad, and *flan*.   9. Raymond will send the invitations to the guests of honor.   10. An orchestra has offered to
play during the meal.   11. Afterwards, they will play some Spanish-American
records for dancing (*para el baile*).   12. Someone of the boys will take charge of putting
them on.

Baile folklórico, Bogotá, Colombia.

Resumen de palabras y expresiones

acostumbrar   to be accustomed to, be in the habit of

adobar   to prepare; to pickle

el **aguacate**   avocado

alguna orquesta más   another (an additional) orchestra

andaluz, -uza   Andalusian

apuntar   to note, take note of

el **asopao de pollo**   *dish of chicken, rice, vegetables, and herbs.*

el **banquete**   banquet

la **carne**   meat

el **cebiche**   seviche (*pickled fish*)

cocinar   to cook

la **cocinera**   cook (*f.*)

con horas de anticipación   hours in advance (ahead of time)

el **conjunto**   group

decorar   to decorate

la **empanadita**   small turnover

encargarse de   to take charge of, undertake

la **ensalada**   salad

el **entremés** (*pl.* **entremeses**)   appetizer, side dish

faltar   to lack, be lacking

el **flan**   flan (*a custard*)

el **gazpacho**   cold vegetable soup

el **guajolote**   turkey (*Mex.*)

hasta luego   (I'll) see you later, until later

hasta la vista   so long, until (I'll see you) later

el **huésped de honor**   guest of honor

internacional   international

la **Junta Directiva**   governing board (committee), officers

el **mariachi**   *member of Mexican popular orchestra*

el **menú**   menu

el **mole**   mole (*a sauce*)

ofrecerse a   to offer to

organizar   to organize

la **paella**   *rice dish, containing meat, vegetables, and shellfish*

para el almuerzo   for lunch

el **plato**   plate, dish, course (*at meals*)

el **pollo**   chicken

por ejemplo   for example

la **posibilidad**   possibility

el **postre**   dessert

la **presidenta**   president (*f.*)

principal   principal, main

la **propuesta**   proposal, proposition

puertorriqueño, -a (*also noun*)   Puerto Rican

el **queso**   cheese

el **radio**   radio, radio set

la **radio**   radio (*communication*)

la **receta**   recipe

el **recurso**   recourse, resort, resource

resuelto, -a   resolved, settled, decided

retirar   to withdraw, retire

reunirse   to meet, gather

el **secretario**   secretary (*m.*)

sugerir (ie, i)   to suggest

tener razón   to be right

todo el día   all day, the whole (entire) day

valenciano, -a   Valencian, of Valencia (*Spain*)

votar (por)   to vote (for)

Grupo de estudiantes en un café al aire libre en Macuto, Venezuela.

Lectura 4

Observaciones sobre las comidas hispanoamericanas

Las comidas constituyen una parte esencial de la cultura de los pueblos. En los siguientes párrafos trataremos de dar una idea de algunas comidas típicas de los países al sur del Río Grande.

Las comidas hispanoamericanas reflejan, en general, los cultivos y las condiciones de vida de las diversas regiones. En México y en la América Central, por ejemplo, el maíz[1] ha sido durante siglos la base de la alimentación.[2] No es una sorpresa, por lo tanto,[3] encontrar que de harina de maíz se hacen las tortillas mexicanas, que se necesitan para preparar las enchiladas, tostadas y tacos tan conocidos en el suroeste de nuestro país.

La enchilada es una tortilla de harina de maíz, enrollada,[4] que se rellena de[5] queso o carne y se cuece en el horno. La tostada es una tortilla tostada que se cubre de[6] frijoles refritos, y se aedereza[7] con lechuga, tomate, cebolla y queso. Se prepara el taco doblando[8] la tortilla tostada y rellenando el interior de carne picada; se cuece en el horno y al servirse se cubre de lechuga, tomate y queso rallado.[9] Como condimento no falta la salsa de chile (un pimiento, o ají, como se llama en América, muy picante).

Otros platos típicos de las mismas regiones son el tamal, los chiles rellenos y el mole de guajolote (el nombre que dan al pavo en México). El tamal cambia con las localidades.

---

[1] To facilitate preparation of this Lectura, see the glossary on page 103 for meanings of words and expressions used here and, with a few exceptions, not elsewhere in the text.   [2] **alimentación,** *nutrition.*   [3] **por lo tanto,** *therefore.*   [4] **enrollada,** *rolled.*   [5] **rellenar,** *to fill, stuff;* **rellenarse de,** *to be filled (stuffed) with.*   [6] **se cubre de,** *is covered with.*   [7] **se aedereza,** *is garnished.*   [8] **doblando,** *by folding.*   [9] **rallado,** *grated.*

En México es una especie de empanada de harina de maíz que se rellena de pescado o carne y se envuelve en hojas de plátano o de la mazorca del maíz; se cuece al vapor[10] o en el horno. La hayaca de Venezuela y la humita del Perú, Chile y la Argentina son variedades del tamal, con ingredientes diferentes. Los chiles rellenos contienen carne picada de vaca o de cerdo, aderezada con almendras, pasas y un poco de chocolate.

El mole es la salsa con que se preparan en México los guisados de carne, como el guajolote, por ejemplo. Es famoso el mole poblano. Se prepara con tomate, cebolla, canela, chile y chocolate, entre otros ingredientes.

En las regiones marítimas de Hispanoamérica los pescados y los mariscos son una parte importante de las comidas. Un plato muy popular es el escabeche. Se prepara macerando[11] el pescado frito en una salsa de vinagre, aceite, ají, cebolla y pimienta; se sirve frío. Entre los mariscos son corrientes los cangrejos, langostas, langostinos, calamares, almejas y ostiones (el nombre que se da en América a las ostras).

En los países en que abunda el ganado vacuno,[12] como en la Argentina y el Uruguay, la carne asada es el plato favorito. Los biftecs de estas regiones, asados al horno o en parrillas,[13] como en el caso de la famosa parrillada argentina, son de primera calidad.

Otros platos hispanoamericanos, como el arroz con pollo y la paella, son de origen español. Suelen variar un poco según la localidad.

Los postres, en general, parecen seguir modelos españoles. Como en España, los más corrientes son el arroz con leche y el flan. Populares también en Hispanoamérica son las deliciosas conservas de frutas. En México y la América Central una clase de dulce en pasta, hecho de frutas, se llama ate; en forma de jalea, se llama cajeta. Son famosas las cajetas de Celaya (Guanajuato, México).

EJERCICIO

Traduzcan al español las frases siguientes, tratando de imitar las construcciones y fraseología del texto:

1. We would need many paragraphs to describe the typical foods of all the Spanish-American countries.
2. Persons who live in the Southwest are well acquainted with several Mexican dishes, such as the enchilada, the taco, and the tostada.
3. The enchilada is a rolled corn cake which contains meat or cheese; as seasoning, chili sauce is used.
4. There are different types of tamales according to the ingredients they contain.
5. In Mexico, the tamale is a kind of small pie which is filled with fish or meat, and is wrapped in corn husks.
6. Stuffed peppers are prepared with ground pork or beef, garnished with almonds, raisins, and chocolate.
7. In the maritime regions many kinds of fish and shellfish are served; stuffed crab is a very popular dish.
8. To prepare pickled fish one steeps fried fish in a sauce made of vinegar, olive oil, chili, onion, and (black) pepper.

---

[10] **al vapor,** *in steam, steamed.*   [11] **macerar,** *to steep, soak.*   [12] **ganado vacuno,** *cattle.*   [13] **parrillas,** *grills.*

9. In countries in which cattle abound, roast meat is a favorite food, as in the case of the Argentine *parrillada*.
10. We have always liked the desserts which are common in Spain, like rice pudding, custard, and fruit preserves.

Glosario

el **aceite**   olive oil
el **ají**   chili, pepper (*vegetable*)
la **almeja**   clam
la **almendra**   almond
el **arroz (con leche)**   rice (pudding)
   arroz con pollo   rice with chicken
   asado, -a   roast(ed)
el **ate**   preserve
el **biftec**   (beef)steak
la **cajeta**   *kind of jelly*
el **calamar**   squid
la **canela**   cinnamon
el **cangrejo**   crab
la **carne**   meat
   carne asada   roast, roasted meat
   carne de cerdo   pork
   carne de vaca   beef
   carne picada   ground meat
la **cebolla**   onion
   cocer (ue)   to cook
el **condimento**   condiment, seasoning
las **conservas**   preserves
el **chile**   chili, pepper
   salsa de chile   chili sauce
el **dulce**   sweet; candy
la **empanada**   *small meat* (or *fish*) *pie*
la **enchilada**   corn cake with chili
el **escabeche**   pickled fish
los **frijoles (refritos)**   (refried) kidney beans
   frito, -a   fried
las **frutas**   fruit
   conservas de frutas   fruit preserves
el **guisado**   stew
la **harina**   flour
   harina de maíz   cornmeal
la **hayaca**   tamale (*Venezuela*)
el **horno**   oven
   al horno   in an oven

la **humita**   tamale (*South America*)
el **ingrediente**   ingredient
la **jalea**   jelly
la **langosta**   lobster
el **langostino**   prawn, crawfish
el **maíz**   maize, corn
el **marisco**   shellfish; *pl.* seafood, shellfish
la **mazorca**   ear (*of corn*)
   hojas de la mazorca del maíz   corn husks
el **mole**   *a sauce*
   mole poblano   *sauce in the style of Puebla* (*Mexico*)
el **ostión** (*pl.* **ostiones**)   oyster
la **ostra**   oyster
la **parrillada**   barbecued beef
la **pasa**   raisin
la **pasta**   paste (*confection*)
   dulce en pasta   *a fruit paste* (*in form of a bar*)
el **pavo**   turkey (*Spain*)
el **pescado**   fish
   picado, -a   minced, chopped, ground
   picante   hot, highly seasoned
la **pimienta**   black pepper
el **pimiento**   pepper (*vegetable*)
el **plátano**   plantain, banana
   hojas de plátano   banana leaves
   rallado,-a   grated
   relleno, -a   stuffed, filled
la **salsa**   sauce
el **taco**   *a rolled corn cake*
el **tamal**   tamale
la **tostada**   toasted corn cake
   tostar (ue)   to toast
el **vinagre**   vinegar

Uso del infinitivo después de una preposición ▪ Verbos seguidos del infinitivo sin preposición ▪ Verbos que necesitan preposición ante un infinitivo ▪ Expresiones con «hacer», «haber» y «tener» ▪ Palabras interrogativas y exclamaciones

LECCIÓN CINCO

Mente sana en cuerpo sano[1]

Pepe y Luis son aficionados a los deportes, aunque no sobresalen en ninguno. Al vestirse en el gimnasio, después de jugar al tenis, hablan de los deportes en que piensan participar.

Pepe. ¡Qué bien juegas al tenis, Luis! ¿No podrías formar parte del equipo universitario?

Luis. Hay muchos jugadores mejores que yo en esta universidad. Y, además, no sé si me gustaría tener que practicar tantas horas todos los días.

Pepe. ¿Qué deporte vas a escoger el semestre que viene?

Luis. Tal vez el fútbol de estilo *soccer*. Me gusta el béisbol, también. Es difícil decidir entre los dos. Y tú, Pepe, ¿vas a continuar con el atletismo?

Pepe. Creo que sí. Como sabes, me gustan las carreras de vallas y el salto de altura.

Luis. Lo más agradable es estar al aire libre cuando hace mucho sol.

Pepe. ¿Te acuerdas de Carlos Arrillaga, que vivió en nuestra residencia el año pasado?

Luis. ¡Cómo no! . . . El capitán del equipo de baloncesto.

Pepe. Pues, acabo de recibir una carta de él. Ha pasado un año fantástico en España jugando a su deporte favorito.

Luis. ¿No aspiraba a formar parte de algún equipo profesional en los Estados Unidos?

---
[1] **Mente sana en cuerpo sano,** *A healthy mind in a healthy body.*

Pepe. Sí, pero al parecer ningún equipo se interesó por él y aceptó la invitación de un club español.

Luis. Y, ¿qué tal lo pasó?

Pepe. Pues, tuvo mucho éxito. Además de ganar mucho dinero, se distinguió como el mejor jugador de su equipo. Terminó la temporada con un promedio de treinta puntos el partido.

Luis. ¡Hombre! Tenemos que felicitarlo. ¿Qué planes tiene?

Pepe. Ya tiene muchas ganas de volver, pues ahora está en contacto con dos o tres equipos profesionales.

Luis. ¡Cuánto me alegro! Dale recuerdos míos, Pepe.

Pepe. Gracias. Le dará mucho gusto saber de ti. Bueno, tengo que darme prisa. Hasta la vista, Luis.

Preguntas sobre el diálogo: 1. ¿Dónde se encuentran Pepe y Luis? 2. ¿Qué le dice Pepe a Luis? 3. ¿Qué contesta Luis? 4. ¿Qué deporte va a escoger Luis el semestre que viene? 5. ¿Qué deporte va a escoger Pepe? 6. ¿Dónde ha pasado Carlos Arrillaga un año fantástico? 7. ¿Qué ha estado haciendo en España? 8. ¿Por qué no pudo jugar al baloncesto en los Estados Unidos? 9. ¿Qué planes tiene Carlos ahora? 10. ¿Qué le dará mucho gusto a Carlos?

Preguntas para conversar: 1. ¿Qué deporte le gusta más a Ud., el fútbol americano o el fútbol de estilo *soccer*? 2. ¿Qué deporte es más popular en este país, el fútbol americano o el fútbol de estilo *soccer*? 3. ¿Cuáles son algunos países en que es muy popular el fútbol de estilo *soccer*? 4. ¿Jugó Ud. al fútbol americano en la escuela superior? 5. ¿Forma Ud. parte de algún equipo universitario? 6. ¿En qué deportes tiene un equipo la residencia en que Ud. vive? 7. ¿En qué deportes ha sobresalido la residencia en que Ud. vive? 8. ¿En qué deportes ha tenido esta universidad equipos excelentes? 9. ¿En qué deportes han sobresalido los equipos de muchachas en esta universidad?

PRONUNCIACIÓN

The sounds of Spanish **g (gu)** and **j (x)**. At the beginning of a breath-group or after **n**, Spanish **g** (written **gu** before **e** or **i**) is a voiced velar stop, like a weak English *g* in *go*. In all other cases, except before **e** or **i** in the groups **ge, gi,** Spanish **g** is a voiced velar continuant, that is, the breath is allowed to pass between the back of the tongue and the palate. (The diaeresis is used over **u** in the combinations **güe** and **güi** when the **u** is pronounced: **vergüenza.**) Pronounce after your teacher:

1. ganamos	graduarse	guitarra	lengua
distinguido	ninguno	con gusto	un gazpacho
2. jugando	luego	agradable	alguien
aguacate	la guitarra	es grande	me gusta

Spanish **g** before **e** and **i,** and **j** in all positions, have no English equivalent. They are pronounced approximately like a strongly exaggerated *h* in *halt* (rather like the rasping German *ch* in *Buch*). Remember that the letter **x** in the words **México, mexicano,** and **Texas,** spelled **Méjico, mejicano,** and **Tejas** in Spain, is pronounced like Spanish **j.** Note also that the consonant **j** is silent in **reloj,** but is pronounced in the plural **relojes.** Pronounce after your teacher:

3. jamón   jalea   mejor   junta
   escoger   ecología   la Argentina   generalmente

4. Tengo un gato algo glotón.   Gané un reloj de pulsera.
   Ningún jugador se quejó.   El viaje de Jorge a México.

NOTAS GRAMATICALES

1 Uso del infinitivo después de una preposición

In Spanish the infinitive is used after a preposition; in English the present participle is often used. **Al** plus an infinitive is the Spanish equivalent of English *Upon* (*On*) plus the present participle, or occasionally of a clause beginning with *When*. The infinitive may have a subject (which follows the infinitive), an object, or both:

Ricardo salió sin decir nada.   Richard left without saying anything.
Al saberlo yo, le escribí.   Upon finding it out (When I found it out), I wrote to him.
Además de ganar mucho dinero, . . .   Besides earning a lot of money, . . .

2 Verbos seguidos del infinitivo sin preposición

A. Verbs that do not require a preposition before an infinitive

A few of the many verbs which do not require a preposition before an infinitive when there is no change in subject are: **acostumbrar, deber, decidir, desear, esperar, necesitar, pensar (ie)** (when it means *to intend, plan*), **poder, preferir (ie, i), prometer, querer, saber, sentir (ie, i)** (*to be sorry, regret*), **temer:**

Hablan de los deportes en que piensan participar.   They talk about the sports in which they intend to participate.
Siento no poder ir con Uds.   I'm sorry I cannot go (I am sorry not to be able to go) with you.

The infinitive follows impersonal expressions without a preposition:

Es difícil escoger entre los dos.   It is difficult to choose between the two.

See Appendix E, pages 304–306, for a more complete list of verbs of the types mentioned in this section and in section 3, which follows.

B. Some special uses of the infinitive

1. After **oír** and **ver,** the infinitive is regularly used in Spanish, while the present participle is often used in English. Note the word order in the first example:

Oigo entrar a Margarita.   I hear Margaret coming in (enter).
Los vimos salir.   We saw them leave (leaving).

2. **Dejar, hacer, mandar,** and **permitir** are usually followed by the infinitive when the subject of the verb which follows is a pronoun. (Some exceptions to this usage will be discussed later.)

Déjeme (Permítame) Ud. llamarlo.   Let me (Permit me to) call him.
Le mandé escribir un artículo.   I ordered him to (had him) write an article.

While usage varies, with **dejar** and **hacer** personal objects are usually direct; with other verbs they are usually indirect.

Often the infinitive is translated by the passive voice, especially when its subject is not expressed and its object is a thing:

Mandé (Hice) poner las cosas en el coche.   I ordered *or* had the things put in the car.
Lo mandó llamar el profesor.   The teacher had him called (sent for him).
Hice escribir la carta.   I had the letter written.

3   Verbos que necesitan preposición ante un infinitivo

A. Verbs which take **a** before an infinitive

All verbs expressing motion or movement to a place, the verbs meaning *to begin,* and certain others such as **atreverse,** *to dare,* **aprender,** *to learn,* **enseñar,** *to teach, show,* **ayudar,** *to help, aid,* and **obligar,** *to oblige,* require **a** before an infinitive. The last three verbs have the subject of the infinitive expressed:

Fueron (Corrieron) a ver el coche.   They went (ran) to see the car.
Él aprendió (empezó) a cantar la canción.   He learned (began) to sing the song.
Él me enseñó (ayudó) a hacer el trabajo.   He taught (helped) me to do the work.

Volver a plus an infinitive means (to do) again:

Vuelvan Uds. a reunirse.   Meet again.

B. Verbs which take **de** before an infinitive

Three common verbs which require **de** are **acordarse (ue) (de),** to remember (to), **alegrarse (de),** to be glad (to), and **olvidarse (de),** to forget (to). (Recall that **olvidar** plus an infinitive also means to forget [to].)

Nos alegramos de verte.   We are glad to see you.
Juan se olvidó de llamar a Juanita.   John forgot to call Jane.

Dejar de plus an infinitive means to stop, fail to. **Tratar de** means to try to, and **tratarse de** means to be a question of. **Acabar de** in the present and imperfect means have just, had just, respectively:

Dejaron de tocar la guitarra.   They stopped playing the guitar.
No dejes de escribirnos.   Don't fail to write us.
No se trata de aprender eso.   It is not a question of learning that.
Ramón acaba (acababa) de entrar.   Raymond has (had) just entered.

Some verbs followed by an adjective or noun require **de** before an infinitive as well as before a noun or noun clause:

Estamos seguros de que Miguel nos ayudará.   We are sure that Michael will help us.
Estamos seguros de poder ayudarlos.   We are sure of being able to help them.
Los muchachos están cansados de trabajar.   The boys are tired of working.
Tengo miedo de esperar aquí.   I'm afraid to wait here.

C. Verbs which take **en** before an infinitive

Common verbs are: **consentir (ie, i) en,** to consent to, agree to, **insistir en,** to insist on, **pensar (ie) en,** to think of, **tardar en,** to delay in, take long to:

Pepe tardaba en aparecer.   It was taking Joe long to appear (Joe delayed in appearing).

EJERCICIOS

A. Repitan la frase; luego, cámbienla a una forma de mandato con **Ud.** o **Uds.** como sujeto:

1. Elena nos enseña a preparar la paella.
2. Ana comienza a leer la novela.
3. Luisa aprende a tocar la canción española.
4. No dejan de practicar el béisbol.
5. María la ayuda a decorar la mesa.
6. No se olvidan de felicitar a Carlos.
7. No tratan de jugar al tenis hoy.
8. No tardan mucho en vestirse.

B. Lean en español, supliendo la preposición correcta cuando sea necesario:

1. Los dos son aficionados _de_ los deportes.   2. Pepe va _a_ participar _con_ las carreras de vallas. 3. Tardaron una hora _a_ terminar el partido.
4. ¿Te acuerdas _a_ Tomás Molina? 5. Acabo _a_ recibir una tarjeta de él.
6. No dejen Uds. _de_ ir al gimnasio hoy. 7. ¿Se olvidaron Uds. _de_ traer
las cintas?   8. Ana insiste _en_ quedarse aquí un rato.   9. Mi hermana no
consentirá _a_ asistir a la reunión. 10. Esperamos _____ divertirnos mucho.
11. Estamos seguros _de_ que Luis jugará bien.   12. ¿Sabe Ud. si Tomás
prefiere _____ tocar otros discos? 13. No se trata _de_ pasar mucho tiempo
allí. 14. Carlos tiene muchas ganas _de_ volver a este país. 15. Mi hermano no
puede _____ darse prisa. 16. Nos alegramos _de_ saber eso.

4   Expresiones con «hacer», «haber» y «tener»[1]

A. **Hacer** is used impersonally with certain nouns in Spanish in speaking of the state of
the weather and the temperature, while *to be* is used in English:

¿Qué tiempo hace hoy?   What kind of weather is it today?
Hace buen (mal) tiempo.   It is good (bad) weather.
Hizo (mucho) calor ayer.   It was (very) warm yesterday.
Hará (mucho) fresco mañana.   It will be (very) cool tomorrow.
Ha hecho (mucho) frío.   It has been (very) cold.
Hacía (mucho) viento.   It was (very) windy.
Hace mucho sol hoy.   It is very sunny (The sun is shining brightly) today.

Since **calor, fresco, frío, viento, sol** are all nouns in these expressions, they are
modified by the adjective **mucho,** not by the adverb **muy.**

B. **Haber,** used impersonally, also applies to certain natural phenomena, especially
those that are seen:

Hay mucho sol.   It is very sunny.
Hay luna esta noche.   The moon is shining (It is moonlight) tonight.
Hay pocas nubes en el cielo.   There are few clouds in the sky.
Había mucho lodo (polvo).   It was very muddy (dusty).
Había niebla (neblina).   It was foggy (misty).

C. In speaking of a person, or anything living, **tener** is used with certain nouns:

Juan tiene (mucho) frío.   John is *or* feels (very) cold.
Tenemos (mucho) calor.   We are *or* feel (very) warm.

---

[1] New words and expressions used in this section are not repeated in the **Resumen de palabras y expresiones.**

Compare the use of **estar** or **ser** with an adjective when referring to a changeable or inherent quality:

> **Está nublado (despejado).**   It is cloudy (clear).
> **El agua estaba muy fría.**   The water was very cold.
> **El hielo es frío.**   Ice is cold.

Other common idiomatic expressions with **tener** are:

> **tener cuidado**   to be careful
> **tener éxito**   to be successful
> **tener hambre**   to be hungry
> **tener miedo**   to be afraid, frightened
> **tener prisa**   to be in a hurry
> **tener razón**   to be right
> **no tener razón**   to be wrong
> **tener sed**   to be thirsty
> **tener sueño**   to be sleepy
> **tener suerte**   to be lucky, fortunate
> **tener vergüenza**   to be ashamed

With all the above nouns, **mucho, -a,** translates English *very, (very) much.* **Mucha** is used with the feminine nouns **hambre, prisa, razón, sed, suerte, vergüenza.**

Some additional expressions with **tener** are:

> **¿Cuántos años tienes (tiene Ud.)?**   How old are you?
> **Tengo dieciocho años.**   I am eighteen (years old).
> **¿Qué tiene Carlos?**   What is the matter (What's wrong) with Charles?
> **Tienen (muchas) ganas de ir a casa.**   They desire *or* wish (very much) *or* They are (very) eager to go home.
> **Aquí tiene Ud. (el libro).**   Here is (the book). (*Handing someone something.*)
> **Pablo tenía la culpa.**   Paul was at fault (to blame).
> **Tenemos que darnos prisa.**   We have to (must) hurry (up).
> **Tienen muchos deseos de jugar.**   They are very eager (wish very much) to play.

NOTE: **Tener prisa** means *to be in a hurry,* while **darse prisa** means *to hurry (up).*

EJERCICIOS

A. Para contestar en español:

1. ¿Qué tiempo hace hoy? 2. ¿Qué tiempo hizo ayer? 3. ¿Qué tiempo ha hecho esta semana? 4. ¿En qué estación del año hace más calor? 5. ¿En cuál de las estaciones hace más frío? 6. ¿Qué tiempo hace en el otoño? 7. ¿Dónde hace frío todo el año? 8. ¿Qué tomamos cuando hace mucho calor?

9. ¿Hay sol hoy? 10. ¿Habrá luna esta noche? 11. ¿Hay mucho polvo ahora? 12. ¿Cuándo hay lodo? 13. ¿Hay niebla aquí a veces?

14. ¿Tiene Ud. frío en este momento? *[No tengo]* 15. ¿Qué hace Ud. cuando tiene hambre? *[tomo comida]*
16. ¿Qué toma Ud. cuando tiene mucha sed? *[tomo mucha agua]* 17. ¿Tiene Ud. sueño en clase a veces? *[Si tengo]*
18. ¿Tiene Ud. miedo de los animales? *[No, no tengo]* 19. ¿Tiene Ud. ganas de ir al cine esta noche? *[No, no tengo]*
20. ¿Cuántos años tiene Ud.? *[tengo diez y ocho anos]*

B. Para expresar en español:

1. Are you (*pl.*) very sleepy? 2. The boys are in a hurry. 3. What's the matter with Paul? 4. How old is your (*fam. sing.*) sister? 5. Here is the football; take (*fam. sing.*) it. 6. We are not at fault. 7. I am hungry and thirsty. 8. He isn't very eager to study. 9. Hurry up (*pl.*); it is late. 10. The children are not afraid. 11. It has been cloudy today. 12. There are no clouds in the sky. 13. Be (*pl.*) very careful. 14. Arthur is right. 15. It has been very cool today.

5 Palabras interrogativas y exclamaciones

A. Interrogative words

1. **¿Quién?** (*pl.* **¿Quiénes?**) *Who? Whom?* refers only to persons; it requires the personal (or distinctive) **a** when used as the object of a verb:

    ¿Quién llamó?   Who called?
    ¿A quiénes vio Ud. anoche?   Whom did you see last night?

    Whose? can only be expressed by **¿De quién(es)?** and the verb **ser:**

    ¿De quién es esta cinta?   Whose tape is this?

    All interrogatives bear the written accent in both direct and indirect questions:

    No sé quién gritaba.   I don't know who was shouting.

2. **¿Qué?** *What? Which?* is both a pronoun and an adjective; as an adjective it may mean *Which?* For a definition, **¿Qué?** is used with **ser:**

    ¿Qué le enviaste a Marta?   What did you send (to) Martha?
    ¿Qué cuadro le gusta a Ud.?   Which picture do you like?
    ¿Qué es un examen?   What is an examination?
    —¿Qué es Roberto? —Es abogado.   "What is Robert?" "He is a lawyer."

3. **¿Cuál?** (*pl.* **¿Cuáles?**) *Which one (ones)? What?* asks for a selection, and is regularly used only as a pronoun. With **ser,** use **¿Cuál(es)?** for *What?* unless a definition or identification is asked for:

    ¿Cuál de los cuadros le gusta a Ud. más?   Which (one) of the pictures do you like best?
    ¿Cuál es la capital de Chile?   What (*i.e.,* Which city) is the capital of Chile?

4. Other interrogative words are:

   ¿cómo? how? (in what way?)
   ¿cuándo? when?
   ¿cuánto, -a? how much?
   ¿cuántos, -as? how many?
   ¿dónde? where?
   ¿adónde? where? (*with verbs of motion*)
   ¿por dónde se va . . . ? how (*i.e.*, by what route) does one go . . . ?
   ¿para qué? why? (for what purpose?)
   ¿por qué? why? (for what reason?)
   ¿qué clase de . . . ? what kind of . . . ?
   ¿qué tal . . . ? how . . . ?

   ¿Cuántas personas hay aquí? How many persons are there here?
   ¿Adónde iban ellos? Where were they going?
   ¿Cómo se puede hacer eso? How can one do that?
   ¿Cómo te gusta el café? ¿Con azúcar? How do you like your coffee? With sugar?

The last sentence refers to one's taste. *How do you like?* in the sense of *What do you think of?* is expressed by **¿Qué le (te) parece(n) . . . ?**

   —**¿Qué te parece esta cafetera?** —**Me gusta mucho.** "How do you like this coffeepot?" "I like it very much."

B. Exclamations

1. **¡Qué** + *a noun!* means *What a (an) . . . !* When an adjective follows the noun, either **más** or **tan** must precede the adjective:

   ¡Qué lástima (sorpresa)! What a pity (surprise)!
   ¡Qué obra más (tan) interesante! What an interesting work!

When the adjective precedes the noun, **más** or **tan** is omitted; before plural nouns **¡qué!** means *what!*

   ¡Qué buena idea! What a good idea!
   ¡Qué hermosas flores! What beautiful flowers!

¡Qué + *an adjective or adverb!* means *how!*

   ¡Qué guapo es! How handsome he is!
   ¡Qué bien jugaron todos! How well all played!
   ¡Qué suerte has tenido! How lucky (fortunate) you have been!

NOTE: In the last example, **suerte** is a noun in Spanish, but an adjective in English; the expression means literally: *What luck you have had!*

2. All interrogatives may be used in exclamations if the sense permits:

   ¡Quién haría eso! Who would do that!
   ¡Cuántas flores tiene ella! How many flowers she has!

With verbs, **¡cuánto!** means *how* . . . !

¡Cuánto me alegro de saber eso!   How glad I am to know that!
¡Cuánto lo sentimos!   How we regret it (sorry we are)!

EJERCICIOS

A. Para leer en español supliendo **¿qué?** o **¿cuál(es)?**:

1. ¿ _Qué_ pasó en el partido? 2. ¿A _qué_ hora terminó? 3. ¿_cuáles_ jugadores jugaron mejor? 4. ¿_cuál_ de ellos se gradúan este año? 5. ¿ _qué_ otro deporte le gusta a Ud.? 6. ¿ _qué_ clases tiene Ud. hoy? 7. Allí vienen dos jóvenes extranjeros. ¿ _qué_ es Luis Sierra? 8. ¿ _qué_ es el señor Martínez, abogado o médico? 9. ¿A _cuál_ de los cafés prefieres ir? 10. ¿ _cuál_ de tus amigos te acompañan?

B. Escuchen cada frase; luego, cámbienla a una exclamación, usando **¡que!** o **¡cuánto!**

MODELOS: Las flores son hermosas.   ¡Qué hermosas son las flores!
La noche es muy bonita.   ¡Qué noche más (tan) bonita!
Siento mucho no saberlo.   ¡Cuánto siento no saberlo!

1. La tarde es mala.   *Que mala es la tarde*
2. Juan tiene suerte.   *Que suerte que tiene*
3. Hace buen tiempo.   *Que buen tiempo*
4. Luis es guapo.   *Que guapo es Luis*
5. Es una sorpresa muy agradable.   *es una sorpresa*
6. Doña María es simpática.   *Que ... es*

7. Juegas bien al tenis.   *Que*
8. El jardín es bonito.   *es el ... Que*
9. La muchacha está triste.   *Cuánto*
10. Me alegro de estar aquí.   *Cuánto*
11. Ha pasado un año fantástico.
12. Nos divertimos allí.   *Que ... Cuánto*

RESUMEN

A. Usos de los infinitivos. Para expresar en español:

1. After playing tennis, we begin to talk about sports.   2. Louis doesn't know whether he would like to have to practice many hours.   3. Joe could become a member of a university team.   4. It is difficult to choose between tennis and football, "soccer" style.   5. Joe has just received a letter from Charles, who has played basketball with a professional team in Spain.   6. Besides earning a great deal of money, he was very successful.   7. He is very eager to return home, since he is in contact with some professional teams.   8. Upon seeing him, we have to congratulate him.   9. I forgot to write to Mary.   10. We heard Martha play the Mexican song.   11. John had us wait a while.   12. Let me (*formal sing.*) practice with you, please.

13. Joe insists on participating in some sport. 14. Since Thomas is the best player on the team, don't (*formal sing.*) fail to talk with him. 15. After getting dressed, shall we go to take some refreshments?

B. Para leer en español, supliendo la forma correcta de **estar, haber, hacer, ser** o **tener.** Usen el tiempo presente si no se indica otro tiempo:

1. ¿Qué tiempo _hace_ hoy? 2. _hace_ fresco y mucho viento. 3. Nosotros _hace_ mucho calor en este edificio. 4. No _ha hecho_ (*pres. perf.*) mucho frío aquí este otoño. 5. A veces _hace_ mucho polvo. 6. No _hay_ (*future*) luna esta noche. 7. _tiene_ (*fam. sing. command*) mucho cuidado y no _tiene_ miedo. 8. Ud. _tiene_ razón; parece que él siempre _tiene_ mucho frío. 9. _hacía_ (*imp.*) niebla cuando salimos de casa. 10. El hielo _hace_ frío, pero a menudo el agua _hace_ caliente.

C. Usos de las palabras interrogativas y las exclamaciones. Para expresar en español:

1. Whom did Charlotte call this morning?
2. Which (ones) of the boys are going to the game?
3. Who are the best players on the team?
4. How fortunate our team is! How well all play!
5. How glad I am to see you (*pl.*)! What a surprise!
6. What a beautiful day! What pleasure it gives me to be outdoors!
7. Why don't you (*fam. sing.*) want to play tennis with me today?
8. How pretty Betty is! What beautiful hair she has!

Practicando el baloncesto en un parque público de Tegucigalpa, Honduras.

Resumen de palabras y expresiones

acordarse (ue) (de + *obj.*)   to remember, recall

además de *prep.*   besides, in addition to

al aire libre   in the open air, outdoors

al parecer   apparently

aspirar a   to aspire to

el **atletismo**   athletics, track (and field sports)

el **baloncesto**   basketball

el **capitán**   captain

las **carreras de vallas**   hurdles

¡cómo no!   of course! certainly!

creer que sí (no)   to believe so (not)

¡cuánto me alegro (de)!   how glad I am (to)!

el **cuerpo**   body

dale recuerdos míos   give him my regards

dar mucho gusto a   to please a lot, give much pleasure to

darse prisa   to hurry (up)

en contacto con   in contact (touch) with

fantástico, -a   fantastic

favorito, -a   favorite

formar parte de   to be a member of, form a part of

la **gana**   desire

el **gimnasio**   gym(nasium)

¡hombre!   man (alive)! upon my word!

interesarse por (en)   to be interested in

lo más agradable   the most pleasant thing

la **mente**   mind

participar en   to participate (take part) in

el **promedio**   average

pues *conj.*   since, for, because

¿qué tal lo pasó?   how did he (she, you) fare (do)?

el **salto de altura**   high jump

sano, -a   healthy, sound

ser aficionado, -a a   to be fond of

sobresalir   to excel

tal vez   perhaps

la **temporada**   season

treinta puntos el partido   thirty points a (per) game

Estudiantes universitarios jugando al fútbol en Chapala, México.

Lectura 5

El triunfo del fútbol de estilo *soccer*

Para los aficionados a los deportes[1] el suceso[2] más notable de estos últimos años[3] ha sido la aceptación entusiasta, de parte del público norteamericano, del fútbol de estilo *soccer*. Tradicionalmente, el fútbol «americano», el béisbol y el básquetbol (o baloncesto) han sido los deportes de máxima atracción popular en nuestro país. Pues ahora los deportistas norteamericanos han descubierto lo que ya sabían millones de personas en otras partes del mundo, esto es,[4] que el balompié, o fútbol de estilo *soccer*, puede ser un deporte tan artístico y tan emocionante como cualquier otro.

Entre todos los deportes que se practican en los países hispanoamericanos, el balompié es el que suscita[5] el mayor interés y el mayor apasionamiento.[6] Es uno de los pocos deportes que se practican en casi todas las naciones del mundo y más de 143 países lo tienen como su deporte nacional. Se calcula que más de doscientos millones de personas observan por televisión los partidos que se celebran para conseguir el campeonato mundial.

En Rusia hay dos millones de futbolistas, entre aficionados[7] y profesionales. En Francia hay un millón doscientos mil balompedistas; en el pequeño Chile hay medio

---

[1] **los aficionados a los deportes,** *sports fans.* [2] **suceso,** *happening.* [3] **de estos últimos años,** *of recent years.* [4] **esto es,** *this (that) is.* [5] **suscita,** *arouses.* [6] **apasionamiento,** *enthusiasm.* [7] **aficionados,** *amateurs.*

millón. En los alrededores de Londres hay todas las semanas unos ochocientos partidos de carácter más o menos oficial. Hasta en el África más primitiva se juega al *soccer*.

En Hispanoamérica, México, Chile, la Argentina y el Uruguay han tenido equipos excelentes. Los equipos uruguayos, que han ganado tres campeonatos mundiales en este deporte, gozan de extraordinario prestigio y tienen muchos admiradores. El Estadio Centenario, en Montevideo, tiene una capacidad para más de ochenta mil personas. En los grandes torneos sus amplias instalaciones se ven colmadas[8] de enormes masas de espectadores, atraídos por la importancia de los conjuntos[9] que intervienen en los partidos.

Dos factores parecen haber contribuido a estimular el interés del público norteamericano en este deporte. En primer lugar,[10] la North American Soccer League (la NASL)[11] ha invitado a formar parte de nuestros equipos profesionales a algunos de los mejores jugadores del mundo—entre ellos el brasileño Pelé,[12] el símbolo de excelencia y maestría en el deporte. Y luego, para dar mayor rapidez y movimiento al juego, se ha atrevido a modificar algunas de las reglas.

Entre las innovaciones introducidas por la NASL, hay tres de especial importancia. La más interesante, tal vez, es el *shootout*, utilizado para decidir el ganador de los partidos que terminan en empate.[13] Si los equipos siguen empatados después de dos períodos adicionales, se concede a un jugador de cada lado cinco oportunidades de chutar[14] contra la portería contraria.

En otra de las innovaciones se ha liberalizado la regla del *offside*, ampliando el terreno en que los jugadores pueden maniobrar sin incurrir en falta.[15] Por último,[16] para que los equipos traten de mantenerse siempre en la ofensiva, en la clasificación de los equipos, se agregan puntos adicionales[17] según el número de goles marcados.

Gracias a las modificaciones descritas y a la participación de varios jugadores de fama internacional, el éxito del deporte ha sido fenomenal. Más de setenta mil espectadores han asistido a partidos en que ha intervenido el equipo "Cosmos" de Nueva York y una concurrencia de veinte o treinta mil personas no es rara en los partidos entre equipos de cierto prestigio.

Hay que añadir que el balompié parece ser el deporte que va ganando partidarios más rápidamente en las escuelas y universidades de nuestro país. Se calcula que se juega en unas tres mil escuelas secundarias y en la mayoría de las universidades. Lo más notable es que va ganando popularidad entre los muchachos y las muchachas de las escuelas primarias. Si continúa creciendo el interés actual, el éxito del deporte está asegurado.

EJERCICIO

Usando como guía las preguntas siguientes, escriban un breve ensayo (de unas 160 palabras) sobre el triunfo del fútbol de estilo *soccer* en los Estados Unidos:

1. ¿Cuáles han sido los deportes de máxima atracción popular en nuestro país?
2. ¿Qué han descubierto los deportistas norteamericanos en estos últimos años?

---

[8] **se ven colmadas de,** *are crowded (filled) with.*   [9] **conjuntos,** *teams.*   [10] **En primer lugar,** *In the first place..*   [11] See Appendix A, page 270, for the Spanish alphabet.   [12] Pelé has now retired again (from the Cosmos team) and returned to Brazil.   [13] **en empate,** *in a tie.*   [14] **chutar,** *to kick.*   [15] **sin incurrir en falta,** *without incurring a penalty.*   [16] **Por último,** *Finally.*   [17] **se agregan puntos adicionales,** *bonus points are added.*

3. ¿Cuál es el deporte que suscita el mayor interés en los países hispanoamericanos?
4. ¿Qué naciones hispanoamericanas han tenido equipos excelentes en este deporte?
5. ¿A quiénes ha invitado la NASL a formar parte de nuestros equipos profesionales?
6. ¿Qué más se ha atrevido a hacer la NASL?
7. ¿Cuál es la finalidad del *shootout?* ¿Cuándo se utiliza?
8. ¿Qué otra regla se ha modificado?
9. ¿Cuántos espectadores, aproximadamente, han asistido a los partidos entre conjuntos de cierto prestigio?
10. ¿En qué otros sectores de la población va ganando partidarios el balompié?

Las formas, la concordancia y la colocación de los adjetivos ▪ El tiempo futuro ▪ El tiempo condicional ▪ El futuro y el condicional para expresar probabilidad

LECCIÓN SEIS

Una "sala de clase" ideal

Los estudiantes de las clases de ecología harán su excursión anual durante el próximo fin de semana. Pasarán dos días en "La Serranía," un lugar remoto que la Universidad ha reservado para ese fin. Carlos habla con Luisa, quien hizo la excursión el año pasado.

Carlos. ¿Es cierto que no irás a La Serranía este fin de semana? El profesor ha dicho que es una parte valiosa del curso.

Luisa. Este año no voy a ir. Hice la excursión el año pasado, y aunque me gustaría repetirla, tengo que estudiar para un examen.

Carlos. Todos dicen que es un lugar ideal para la protección de los[1] animales y plantas que necesitan un ambiente remoto y aislado.

Luisa. Es verdad. Por su flora y su fauna será uno de los lugares más hermosos y pintorescos del estado.

Carlos. Nos interesarán especialmente los pájaros y las plantas que han desaparecido en otras regiones.

Luisa. La Serranía podría describirse como una espléndida sala de clase. Se han hecho numerosos estudios de la geología, la botánica, la zoología y la ecología del lugar.

---

[1]Note that the masculine plural **los** is used to modify the masculine noun **animales** and the feminine **plantas**.

Una granja en Costa Rica, pequeño país esencialmente agrícola de la América Central.

Carlos. ¿Qué animales salvajes se encuentran en La Serranía?

Luisa. Pues, abundan los conejos y los venados, y a veces se ve algún oso o puma.

Carlos. ¿Se permite la caza de esos animales?

Luisa. En el caso de los animales que están en peligro de desaparecer, como los osos y los pumas, está prohibido cazarlos.

Carlos. ¿Habrá mucha nieve en esta estación del año?

Luisa. En las regiones más elevadas, sí. Pero no sé si habrá tiempo para recorrer todo el lugar.

Carlos. En todo caso parece preferible no llevar mi coche. No me gusta conducir cuando hay nieve y hielo en la carretera.

Luisa. Además, en algunos trechos el camino está en muy malas condiciones. Será más cómodo ir en el autobús de la universidad.

Carlos. Pues, mil gracias por tus informes, Luisa. Ya[1] te daré cuenta de todo.

Luisa. Hasta luego, Carlos. ¡Diviértete mucho!

Preparen un diálogo original, de unas diez líneas, para recitar en clase, empleando las frases y preguntas siguientes como elemento inicial:

1. *María.* ¿Dónde estará Ricardo? El autobús sale a las seis, ¿verdad?

   Jorge. Cuando estábamos para salir, lo mandó llamar el director. Como ya era tarde, decidí no esperarlo más.

2. *Marta.* ¿Has visto la foto que aparece en la primera plana del periódico?

   José. Será una broma. Pero, ¿tú crees que merece tanto espacio en la primera plana?

---

[1]**Ya** sometimes means *soon, later, in due time,* and occasionally, as in this case, it is used for emphasis without an English equivalent.

PRONUNCIACIÓN

Review the observations on Spanish intonation, Repaso tres, pages 24–25, and Lección dos, page 53; then write the first two exchanges of the dialogue of this lesson, dividing them into breath-groups and syllables, and outline the intonation patterns. Read the exchanges, paying close attention to the intonation patterns.

NOTAS GRAMATICALES

1 Las formas, la concordancia (*agreement*) y la colocación de los adjetivos

A. Forms and agreement of adjectives

An adjective, which limits or describes a noun, must agree with the noun in gender and number, whether the adjective modifies the noun directly or is in the predicate. An adjective which modifies two or more singular nouns is put in the plural; if one noun is masculine and the other feminine, the adjective is regularly masculine plural. (The adjective should stand nearest the masculine noun.) Adjectives form their plurals in the same way as nouns (see Lección cuatro, pages 91–92).

The feminine singular of adjectives ending in **-o** is formed by changing final **-o** to **-a.** Adjectives of nationality that end in a consonant and adjectives that end in **-án, -ón, -or** (except the comparatives **mejor, peor, mayor, menor,** and such words as **interior, exterior, superior,** and a few others which are comparatives in Latin) add **-a** for the feminine. Other adjectives have the same form for the masculine and feminine:

Singular		Plural	
Masculine	*Feminine*	*Masculine*	*Feminine*
nuevo	nueva	nuevos	nuevas
mexicano	mexicana	mexicanos	mexicanas
español	española	españoles	españolas
francés	francesa	franceses	francesas
hablador[1]	habladora	habladores	habladoras
mayor	mayor	mayores	mayores
feliz	feliz	felices	felices
joven	joven	jóvenes	jóvenes
cortés	cortés	corteses	corteses

---

[1] **hablador, -ora,** *talkative.*

Note the addition of the written accent: **joven-jóvenes;** the dropping of the accent: **cortés-corteses** and **francés-francesa, franceses, francesas;** and the change in spelling: **feliz-felices.**

B. Position of adjectives

Limiting adjectives (articles, unstressed possessives, demonstratives, numerals, indefinites, and other adjectives which show quantity) usually precede the noun.

Adjectives which distinguish or differentiate a noun from others of the same class (adjectives of color, size, shape, nationality, adjectives modified by adverbs, past participles used as adjectives, and the like) regularly follow the noun:

veinte estudiantes españoles   twenty Spanish students
algunas muchachas mexicanas   some Mexican girls
un lugar ideal   an ideal place
una pluma y un lápiz rojos   a red pen and pencil
un niño muy feliz   a very happy little boy
muchas cosas interesantes   many interesting things

When two or more adjectives modify a noun, each occupies its normal position; if they follow the noun, the last two are regularly connected by **y.** Two or more singular adjectives may modify a plural noun:

el distinguido autor mexicano   the distinguished Mexican author
un ambiente remoto y aislado   a remote and isolated (*or* a remote, isolated) environment
las literaturas española y mexicana   Spanish and Mexican literatures

Certain common adjectives (**bueno, mejor, mayor, malo, peor,** and less frequently **pequeño, joven, viejo,** and a few others) often precede the noun, but they may follow the noun to place more emphasis on the adjective than on the noun:

una buena muchacha *or* **una muchacha buena**   a good girl
un joven poeta *or* **un poeta joven**   a young poet

Certain adjectives have a different meaning when they precede or follow a noun. In addition to **grande** (see C, 2, which follows), other examples are:

un traje nuevo   a new suit (*brand-new*)
un nuevo estudiante extranjero   a new foreign student (*another student*)

el hombre pobre   the poor man (*not rich*)
el pobre hombre   the poor man (*a man to be pitied*)

un amigo viejo   an old friend (*elderly*)
un viejo amigo   an old friend (*of long standing*)

él mismo   he himself
el mismo día   the same day

Descriptive adjectives may also precede the noun when they are used figuratively or when they express a quality that is generally known or is not essential to the recognition of the noun. In such cases there is no desire to single out or to differentiate. Also, when a certain quality has been established with reference to the noun, the adjective often precedes the noun.

Whenever an adjective is changed from its normal position, the speaker or writer gives a subjective or personal interpretation of the noun. An adjective placed before the noun loses much of its force and expresses its quality as belonging to the noun as a matter of course. When it follows, it indicates a distinguishing quality and it assumes the chief importance. In English this result is attained by a slight pause and the stress of voice:

un magnífico (famoso) cuadro mexicano   a magnificent (famous) Mexican picture
los altos Andes   the high Andes
la blanca nieve   white snow

C. Shortened forms of adjectives

1. A few adjectives drop the final **-o** when they precede a masculine singular noun: **bueno, malo, uno, primero, tercero, postrero** (*last*), **alguno, ninguno. Alguno** and **ninguno** become **algún** and **ningún,** respectively:

el primer mes   the first month   **ningún jugador**   no player
algún estudiante   some student   **un buen coche**   a good car

BUT: **los primeros días**   the first days
       una buena idea   a good idea

2. Three common adjectives drop the last syllable under certain conditions:

a. **Grande** becomes **gran** before either a masculine or feminine singular noun, and usually means *great*:

un gran equipo   a great team   **una gran sorpresa**   a great surprise

BUT: **dos grandes hombres**   two great men
       esas grandes mujeres   those great women

When **grande** follows the noun, it regularly means *large, big*:

un país grande   a large country
estos coches grandes   these large cars

b. **Santo** (not **Santa**) becomes **San** before names of all masculine saints except those beginning with **Do-** or **To-:**

             San Pablo   St. Paul   **San Francisco**   St. Francis
BUT: **Santo Tomás**   St. Thomas   **Santa María**   St. Mary
       Santo Domingo   St. Dominic   **Santa Inés**   St. Agnes

c. **Ciento** becomes **cien** before all nouns, including **millones,** and before the adjective **mil,** but it is not shortened before numerals smaller than one hundred:

> **cien teléfonos**   100 telephones
> **cien muchachas**   100 girls
> **cien mil personas**   100,000 persons
> **ciento cincuenta hombres**   150 men

D. Use of prepositional phrases instead of adjectives

In Spanish a noun is rarely used as an adjective; instead, a prepositional phrase beginning with **de** or **para** is normally used. Such constructions may be considered compound nouns:

> **la Escuela de Derecho**   the Law School
> **el fin de semana**   the weekend
> **el partido (equipo) de fútbol**   the football game (team)
> **el reloj de pulsera**   the wristwatch
> **la residencia de estudiantes**   the student dormitory
> **el salto de altura**   the high jump
> **una casa de piedra**   a stone house
> **un programa de televisión**   a TV program
> **estas tazas para café**   these coffee cups
> **un vaso para agua**   a water glass

EJERCICIOS

A. Repitan cada frase; luego, al oír un nuevo substantivo, formen otra frase haciendo los cambios necesarios.

MODELO: Es una canción mexicana.   Es una canción mexicana.
                canciones   Son canciones (*or* unas
                                    canciones) mexicanas.

1. Es un traje bonito.
   corbata
   sombreros
   blusas

2. Mi amigo es español.
   Mi amiga
   Los jugadores
   Las señoritas

3. ¿Es hablador el hombre?
   mujer?
   estudiantes?
   muchachas?

4. Es un día hermoso.
   noche
   árboles
   rosas

B. Repitan cada frase; luego, cámbienla al singular:

1. sus buenos amigos   2. nuestras buenas amigas   3. aquellos malos caminos
4. aquellas niñas muy buenas   5. otras revistas españolas   6. nuestros hermanos
menores   7. los primeros días buenos   8. esas grandes oportunidades   9. algunos
jugadores mexicanos   10. aquellos grandes profesores   11. estos pobres muchachos
12. los nuevos estudiantes   13. unos compañeros de cuarto   14. estas tazas para té
15. aquellos programas de televisión   16. unos lugares pintorescos

C. Para contestar afirmativamente, según los modelos.

MODELOS: ¿Es rojo el vestido?   Sí, es un vestido rojo.
           ¿Son blancas las camisas? Sí, son camisas blancas.

1. ¿Es buena la carretera?   6. ¿Son remotos los lugares?
2. ¿Es valioso el curso?   7. ¿Son cómodos los autobuses?
3. ¿Es elevada la montaña?   8. ¿Son bonitas las plantas?
4. ¿Es larga la excursión?   9. ¿Son malos los caminos?
5. ¿Es pintoresca la región?   10. ¿Son hermosos los pájaros?

2   El tiempo futuro

A. Meaning

In general, the future tense in Spanish corresponds to the English future tense,
translated by *shall* or *will*:

¿Habrá espacio para las fotos?   Will there be space for the photos?
¿Dónde pondremos el artículo?   Where shall we put the article?

B. Substitutes for the future

1. The present indicative tense is often substituted for the future (particularly if an
   expression of time is included) to make the statement more vivid, to imply greater
   certainty that the action will take place, and in questions, when immediate future
   time is involved:

   El partido empezará a las dos.   The game will begin at two.
   El partido empieza a las dos.   The game begins at two.
   Vuelvo en seguida.   I'll return at once (be right back).
   ¿Escuchamos un disco ahora?   Shall we listen to a record now?

2. **Ir a** plus an infinitive is used in the present indicative tense to refer to the near future. (The imperfect **iba a, ibas a,** etc., is similarly used to replace the conditional, especially in Spanish America.)

> **Van a regresar a la ciudad mañana.**   They are going to return to the city tomorrow.
> **Carlos dijo que iba a venir hoy.**   Charles said that he would (was going to) come today.

3. **Haber de** plus an infinitive, which denotes what *is*, or *is supposed*, *to* (happen), is sometimes the equivalent of the future tense, often with a sense of obligation. (In the imperfect, this expression may be used to represent the conditional.)

> **Ha de aparecer en la primera plana.**   It is to appear on the first page.
> **¿Qué he de hacer?**   What am I to do (shall I do)? (What am I supposed to do?)
> **Yo sabía que el hombre no había de pagar (= pagaría).**   I knew that the man wouldn't pay.

4. In **si**-clauses the present indicative tense is normally used in Spanish, as in English, even though the action is to be completed in the future:

> **Si Roberto regresa mañana, me llamará.**   If Robert returns tomorrow, he will call me.

NOTE: Do not confuse the use of **querer** plus an infinitive in asking a favor, which corresponds to English *will, be willing to,* with the true future. Similarly, **no querer** plus an infinitive may express *be unwilling to, will not:*

> **¿Quiere Ud. abrir la ventana?**   Will you open the window?
> **¿Quieres ir al cine conmigo?**   Will you (Are you willing to) go to the movie with me?
> **Ellos no quieren quedarse.**   They won't (are unwilling to) stay.

The future must be used, however, in cases such as:

> **¿Estarás en casa esta noche?**   Will you be at home tonight?

3   El tiempo condicional

A. Meaning

The conditional tense expresses a future action from the standpoint of the past and is translated in English by *should* or *would.* (Its use in conditional sentences will be discussed in Lección nueve.)

> **Luis dijo que saldría pronto.**   Louis said that he would leave soon.

Remember that English *would* (*used to*) is often used to express repeated action in the past, in which case the imperfect indicative tense is used, as explained in Lección tres:

A veces dábamos paseos por el campo.   At times we would take walks in the country.

In the preterit, **no querer** plus an infinitive may express *would not* (*refused to*), *was unwilling to*:

Ricardo no quiso decir nada de los informes.   Richard would not (refused to) say anything about the information.

B. The conditional may be used to express a polite or softened future statement:

Me gustaría acompañarlos.   I should like to accompany them.
¿No sería bastante reservar espacio en la última página del periódico?   Wouldn't it be sufficient to reserve space on the last page of the newspaper?

EJERCICIOS

A. Repitan cada frase; luego, empiecen la frase con **Luis dice que,** cambiando el verbo en cursiva al futuro:

1. *Puede* escribir un artículo.
2. *Hay* espacio para las fotos.
3. *Tiene* que poner una noticia.
4. *Sale* después de vestirse.
5. Les *gusta* el postre.
6. No lo *han* llamado.

B. Repitan cada frase; luego, al oír otra forma del verbo, formen una nueva frase, según el modelo.

MODELO: Yo *sé* que Juan lo hará.   Yo sé que Juan lo hará.
   (*sabía*)   Yo sabía que Juan lo haría.

1. Yo *creo* que Carlos irá a La Serranía. (*creía*)
2. Juan y yo *sabemos* que habrá hielo en la carretera. (*sabíamos*)
3. Luis *dice* que le interesarán especialmente los pájaros. (*dijo*)
4. *Creemos* que los estudiantes verán algunos osos o pumas. (*Creíamos*)
5. *Saben* que encontrarán venados también. (*Sabían*)
6. Mi amigo *está* seguro de que será un lugar pintoresco. (*estaba*)

C. Repitan la frase; luego, repítanla empleando el futuro, según los modelos.

MODELOS: Van a salir mañana.   Van a salir mañana. Saldrán mañana.
   Ana ha de cantar hoy.   Ana ha de cantar hoy. Ana cantará hoy.

1. He de poner algunas noticias en el periódico.
2. Hemos de tener un artículo sobre la excursión.

3. Ha de aparecer en la primera plana.
4. ¿Qué van a decir ellos de las otras páginas?
5. Va a ser mucho más cómodo trabajar en mi cuarto.
6. ¿Cuáles de las muchachas van a preparar la comida?

D. Después de oír la pregunta, contéstenla empleando formas de mandato afirmativas y negativas con **Ud.** como sujeto, y substituyendo el substantivo con el pronombre correspondiente.

MODELO: ¿Pongo *el artículo* aquí?   Sí, póngalo Ud. allí.
    No, no lo ponga Ud. allí.

1. ¿Espero más *a Ricardo?*
2. ¿Tomo *el autobús* en la esquina?
3. ¿Describo *las regiones* ahora?
4. ¿Empiezo a escribir *la noticia?*
5. ¿Hago *el trabajo* esta tarde?
6. ¿Busco *las fotos* esta noche?

4 El futuro y el condicional para expresar probabilidad

The future tense is often used to indicate probability, supposition, or conjecture concerning an action or state in the present time:

¿Dónde estará Ricardo?   I wonder where Richard is. (Where do you suppose Richard is?)
Estará en casa.   He is probably (must be) at home.
¿Adónde irán?   Where can they be going? (I wonder where they are going.)
Será una broma.   It must be (probably is) a joke.

Similarly, the conditional tense indicates probability or conjecture with reference to the past:

¿Quién escribiría la carta?   Who probably (do you suppose) wrote the letter?
¿Sería Luis?   Do you suppose it was Louis? (I wonder if it was Louis.)
Serían las dos cuando regresaron.   It was probably two o'clock when they returned.

Probability or conjecture may also be expressed by the future perfect tense and occasionally by the conditional perfect:

¿Adónde habrá ido Carlos?   Where can Charles have gone? (Where has Charles probably gone? Where do you suppose Charles has gone?)
¿Habrá terminado el artículo?   Do you suppose he has finished the article?
¿Qué habría hecho Pepe?   What could Joe have done?

EJERCICIOS

A. Repitan cada frase; luego, cambien el verbo al futuro para expresar probabilidad:

1. ¿Quién es aquel hombre?
2. ¿Dónde está la cocinera?
3. ¿Adónde van los niños?
4. ¿Quién tiene el periódico?
5. Los muchachos están cazando.
6. Hay mucha gente en la fiesta.

Cambien el verbo al condicional:

7. ¿Qué hora era?
8. Eran las diez y media de la mañana.
9. ¿Adónde iban Juan y Ana?
10. ¿Dónde estaban los dos el domingo pasado?

B. Para expresar en español:

1. What time can it be? 2. Paul probably has many friends there. 3. Do you suppose Jane is ill? 4. I wonder who has the photos. 5. The students have probably written the news items. 6. Who do you suppose called Richard? 7. Where did the boys probably go? 8. Arthur probably returned home early.

RESUMEN

A. Repitan cada frase; luego, al oír un nuevo substantivo, formen otra frase haciendo los cambios necesarios:

1. un día hermoso (noche)
2. un pueblo español (ciudad)
3. aquel niño cortés (niños)
4. su hermano mayor (hermanas)
5. mi amigo feliz (amigas)
6. el equipo portugués (equipos)
7. un hombre hablador (mujer)
8. ese camino largo (calles)

B. Repaso de palabras y expresiones. Para expresar en español:

1. The students of our ecology class will make an excursion next weekend. 2. We shall go to a remote and isolated place which the University has reserved for that purpose. 3. The teacher has told us that the excursion will be a valuable part of the course. 4. People say that it is an ideal place for the protection of the animals and plants which need an isolated environment. 5. It must be one of the most picturesque places in the state. 6. The birds and the plants which have disappeared from many other regions will interest me especially.[1] 7. Many rabbits and deer are found there, and at times one can see a bear or a cougar. 8. It is forbidden to hunt

[1] Place the long subject after the verb (see the Dialogue, page 122, lines 9–10).

(the) animals which are in danger of disappearing.   9. In some stretches the road is in very bad condition, since there is ice and snow in the mountains.   10. We are sure that it will be more comfortable to go on the university bus.

C. Para contestar en español, cambiando el verbo al tiempo correspondiente para expresar probabilidad, según los modelos.

MODELO: ¿Qué hora es? ¿Las ocho?   Sí, serán las ocho.

1. ¿Qué tiene Pepe? ¿Un pájaro?
2. ¿Adónde van? ¿Al partido?
3. ¿Quién es? ¿Tomás?
4. ¿Quién viene? ¿Carmen?

MODELO: ¿Ha ido Pablo al cine?   Sí, creo que Pablo habrá ido al cine.

5. ¿Ha llegado Carlos al centro?
6. ¿Han puesto las fotos allí?
7. ¿Ha terminado Ana el artículo?
8. ¿Ya han vuelto los jóvenes?

MODELO: ¿Fue Luis a jugar?   Sí, creo que iría a jugar.

9. ¿Eran españolas las muchachas?
10. ¿Estuvieron en casa anoche?
11. ¿Recorrió José la región?
12. ¿Salieron para cazar?

Resumen de palabras y expresiones

abundar   to abound, be abundant
aislado, -a   isolated
el **ambiente**   environment, atmosphere
anual   annual
el **autobús de la universidad**   the university bus
la **botánica**   botany
la **broma**   joke
la **carretera**   highway, road
la **caza**   hunting
cazar   to hunt
la **condición** (*pl.* condiciones)   condition
el **conejo**   rabbit
darle cuenta a uno de   to give one an account of
describir   to describe; *reflex.* to be described

elevado, -a   high, lofty
en muy malas condiciones   in very bad condition
en todo caso   in any case
es verdad   it is true, that's right
el **espacio**   space
esperar más   to wait longer
espléndido, -a   splendid
estar para   to be about to
la **fauna**   fauna (*animals of a region*)
el **fin**   end, purpose
el **fin de semana**   weekend
la **flora**   flora (*plants of an area*)
la **geología**   geology
los **informes**   information
lo mandó llamar   (he) had him called, (he) sent for him

merecer to merit, deserve
numeroso, -a numerous
el oso bear
el pájaro bird
el peligro
pintoresco, -a picturesque
la plana page (*printing*)
la planta plant
preferible preferable
prohibido, -a forbidden, prohibited
la protección protection

el puma puma, cougar
recorrer to go (travel) over
la región (*pl.* regiones) region
remoto, -a remote
salvaje savage, wild
La Serranía sierra, mountainous country
el trecho stretch
valioso, -a valuable
el venado deer
la zoología zoology

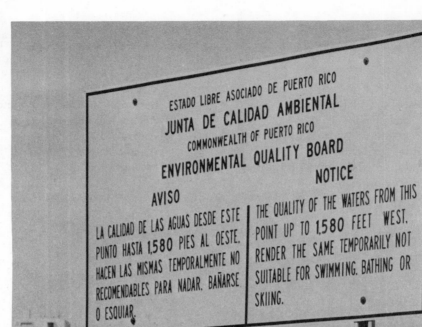

ESTADO LIBRE ASOCIADO DE PUERTO RICO
JUNTA DE CALIDAD AMBIENTAL
COMMONWEALTH OF PUERTO RICO
ENVIRONMENTAL QUALITY BOARD

AVISO

LA CALIDAD DE LAS AGUAS DESDE ESTE
PUNTO HASTA 1,580 PIES AL OESTE,
HACEN LAS MISMAS TEMPORALMENTE NO
RECOMENDABLES PARA NADAR, BAÑARSE
O ESQUIAR.

NOTICE

THE QUALITY OF THE WATERS FROM THIS
POINT UP TO 1,580 FEET WEST,
RENDER THE SAME TEMPORARILY NOT
SUITABLE FOR SWIMMING, BATHING OR
SKIING.

ensuciar la ciudad es tirar su dinero

Lectura 6

El hombre y su medio ambiente[1]

Una de las ironías más grandes de nuestro tiempo es que, con todos los avances de la ciencia moderna, la humanidad corre el riesgo de desaparecer, no sólo por un acto de locura, sino por la negligencia o despreocupación del hombre, es decir, por su imprudente desatención hacia las condiciones especiales en que vive en relación con[2] su medio ambiente. Como ha dicho un historiador inglés, ha llegado la hora de unirnos contra el enemigo común, que no es otro que la humanidad misma.

En muchos países se han acelerado los programas para impedir o moderar el constante deterioro del medio ambiente, que se observa sobre todo en las zonas urbanas e industrializadas. En los Estados Unidos, por orden del gobierno federal, se están haciendo estudios y planes[3] para lograr la misma finalidad. Estos estudios tratarán de informar al público de la necesidad de conservar el medio ambiente y de los peligros que nos esperan si desatendemos sus recomendaciones.

La destrucción del ambiente es evidente en todas partes y se podrían citar numerosos ejemplos para ilustrarla. El hombre ha tenido que alterar[4] el paisaje no sólo para la construcción de casas y carreteras, sino para la creación de fábricas y establecimientos industriales y comerciales. Con el crecimiento de las ciudades, la multiplicación de

---

[1] **medio ambiente,** *environment.* (See line 13, below, and page 138, line 2 for the use of **el ambiente** and **el medio** for *environment.*)   [2] **en relación con,** *in relation to.*   [3] **se están haciendo estudios y planes,** *studies and plans are being made.*   [4] **alterar,** *to disturb, upset.*

chimeneas y automóviles y el empleo general de productos químicos, la destrucción del medio continúa a pasos agigantados.[5]

Los programas para la conservación del ambiente tienen muchos postulados *assumption* comunes. Para poder llevarlos a cabo tendremos que adoptar un sistema de vida más disciplinado y más sujeto a reglamentos y restricciones gubernamentales que el actual. Pero la recompensa lo justificará todo. Tendremos aire más puro que respirar, ríos y costas libres de contaminación, agua potable en abundancia, una manera más eficaz de utilizar o deshacernos de los desperdicios[6]. . . .

En el caso del agua, por ejemplo, habrá que racionarla y, también, descubrir métodos que nos permitan usarla varias veces. Habrá programas especiales para la limpieza de las calles y para los servicios de alcantarillado.[7] Se utilizarán de una manera más eficaz el agua de las lluvias, como también las aguas de las inundaciones. Los glaciares, los hielos del Ártico y del Antártico, así como los mares, serán fuentes inagotables de este elemento. Se tomarán medidas *measure* para que los ríos y las bahías no se obstruyan con sedimentos.

Según otras recomendaciones, al sacar la basura tendremos que separar los desperdicios servibles de los no-servibles. Para reducir el consumo de papel, habrá que aceptar nuestras compras sin envoltura.[8]

Una de las consecuencias más graves de la destrucción de la naturaleza ha sido el peligro que representa para los animales y plantas de la tierra. Hasta el siglo XX la caza de animales para obtener pieles o para la alimentación del hombre representaba el peligro mayor. Hoy día, en cambio, la expansión de la civilización constituye la amenaza más seria, tanto en los Estados Unidos como en el resto del mundo.

El crecimiento de las ciudades, la construcción de represas para la producción de energía eléctrica, el empleo de productos químicos en la agricultura y en la industria, la explotación de los bosques y el aumento de las actividades de recreo—que lleva a millones de personas a regiones antes remotas y deshabitadas—ejercen una presión excesiva sobre la flora y fauna de los países.

Los proyectos para proteger la flora y fauna silvestres han avanzado notablemente en nuestro país desde que se aprobaron las primeras leyes para protegerlas hace más de un siglo. La ley promulgada en 1973 para proteger las especies de animales y plantas que están en peligro de desaparecer se considera como la medida más eficaz que se haya tomado[9] respecto de la ecología en la historia de la humanidad.

Recientemente las organizaciones interesadas en la conservación del ambiente han fijado su atención no sólo en la protección de especies individuales sino también en la conservación, en su estado natural, de regiones enteras. La técnica que emplean es la de establecer "sistemas ecológicos": las autoridades prohiben la entrada del público en ciertas regiones para que éstas puedan subsistir y desarrollarse en su estado natural, sin la intervención del hombre.

---

[5] **a pasos agigantados,** *at a gigantic (an extraordinary) pace.*   [6] **deshacerse de los desperdicios,** *to get rid of waste products.*   [7] **servicios de alcantarillado,** *sewerage services.*   [8] **sin envoltura,** *unwrapped.*   [9] **como . . . se haya tomado,** *as the most effective measure that has been taken.* (Note that the subjunctive may be used after a relative preceded by a superlative to modify the force of the superlative or to suggest that the statement is only an opinion. Also see Lección ocho, pages 165–166, for a discussion of the subjunctive in adjective clauses.)

A pesar de estos avances, la mayoría de los partidarios de la conservación están convencidos de que ninguna de las medidas recomendadas logrará detener la destrucción del medio ambiente hasta que el hombre decida dejar de contaminar el aire, el agua y la tierra y de malgastar sus recursos. Básicamente, el destino de la flora y fauna está íntimamente unido con el del hombre.

EJERCICIO

Escriban diez preguntas sobre puntos tratados en esta Lectura para que las contesten los otros estudiantes de la clase.

Teoría del modo subjuntivo ▪ Las formas del presente de subjuntivo ▪ El subjuntivo en cláusulas substantivas ▪ Otras formas de mandato

LECCIÓN SIETE

Cambios en la universidad

La Asociación de Estudiantes recomienda que se estudie la posibilidad de que los estudiantes participen más activamente en el gobierno de la universidad y que se haga una evaluación anual del profesorado. El Rector ha aprobado las recomendaciones y pide que se formen comisiones para estudiarlas. En la residencia en que viven Miguel y Carmen se celebra una reunión para tratar del asunto.

Director. El Rector desea que le mandemos nuestras recomendaciones sobre la composición de las comisiones que han de hacer los dos estudios. ¿Quién tiene alguna sugerencia? ¿Miguel?

Miguel. En el caso de la participación estudiantil, me parece que la comisión de estudio debe constar únicamente de estudiantes.

Carmen. Apoyo la observación de Miguel. Los estudiantes no aceptarían un informe hecho por los profesores.

Juan. Pero los profesores podrían contribuir mucho con su propia experiencia. La colaboración de un par de profesores de la Facultad de Derecho sería muy valiosa.

Miguel. Pues propongo que recomendemos que la mitad de los miembros de la comisión sean estudiantes, y que el resto sean profesores, preferiblemente de la Facultad de Derecho.

Carmen. Apoyo la moción (propuesta).

140

Director. Si están en favor, digan que sí.

Todos. Sí.

Director. El voto parece unánime. Y ¿qué sugieren respecto de la comisión que ha de evaluar el profesorado?

Carmen. Si queremos ejercer alguna influencia sobre las decisiones académicas, creo que los estudiantes deben formar la mayoría en esa comisión.

Miguel. Pero en ese caso hay el peligro de que la evaluación degenere en un concurso de popularidad.

Juan. Yo estoy de acuerdo con Miguel. Además, es cierto que la evaluación de los colegas de un profesor vale más que la[1] de los estudiantes.

Carmen. El argumento de Juan me parece convincente. Propongo que la comisión conste en su mayoría de profesores, pero que incluya una representación numerosa de estudiantes.

Miguel. Apoyo la propuesta.

Director. ¿Están de acuerdo todos?

Todos. Sí.

Director. Pues se mandarán al Rector las dos recomendaciones. Supongo que se someterá todo a la votación de los estudiantes dentro de unos días.

Preguntas sobre el diálogo: 1. Además de recomendar que se haga una evaluación anual del profesorado, ¿qué recomienda la Asociación de Estudiantes? 2. ¿Quién ha aprobado las recomendaciones? 3. Según el Director de la Residencia, ¿qué desea el Rector? 4. ¿Cuál es la opinión de Miguel respecto de la comisión que ha de estudiar la participación estudiantil? 5. Según Carmen, ¿qué no aceptarían los estudiantes? 6. ¿Qué dice Juan acerca de la colaboración de los profesores? 7. ¿Por qué cree Carmen que los estudiantes deben formar la mayoría en la comisión que ha de evaluar el profesorado? 8. Según Miguel, ¿en qué podría degenerar la evaluación? 9. Según Juan, ¿cuál vale más, la opinión de los colegas de un profesor o la de los estudiantes? 10. ¿Cuál es la propuesta de Carmen?

Preguntas para conversar: 1. ¿Ejerce la Asociación de Estudiantes alguna influencia sobre las decisiones académicas en esta universidad? 2. ¿Sabe Ud. si hay estudiantes en alguna comisión académica? 3. ¿Sabe Ud. si los estudiantes participan activamente en la administración de algún Departamento? 4. En su opinión, ¿quiénes deben participar más activamente en el gobierno de la universidad, los profesores o los estudiantes? 5. ¿Quiénes se interesan más en el gobierno de la universidad, los profesores o los estudiantes? 6. ¿Cree Ud. que sería útil hacer una evaluación anual de los profesores de esta universidad? 8. ¿Sabe Ud. si los profesores participan en alguna evaluación del profesorado? 9. En la opinión de Ud., ¿cuál valdría más, la opinión de los colegas de un profesor o la opinión de los estudiantes? 10. Si se hace una evaluación, ¿deben publicarse los resultados?

---

[1] See Lección 10, page 196, for the use of **la.**

PRONUNCIACIÓN

A. The sounds of **s.** Spanish **s** is a voiceless, alveolar continuant, somewhat like the English hissed *s* in *sent*. Before voiced **b, d, g, l, ll, m, n, r, v, y,** however, Spanish **s** becomes voiced, and is pronounced like English *s* in *rose*. Pronounce after your teacher:

1. desayuno   José   residencia   visitar   has estado
2. antes de   buenos días   es grande   las listas   las muchachas

B. The sounds of **x.** Historically **x** is equivalent to English *ks*, and it is pronounced this way sometimes in affected pronunciation. In normal usage, however, it is pronounced the following ways:

1. Before a consonant it is pronounced *s*: **expresar (es-pre-sar).**
2. Between vowels it is pronounced *gs*: **examinar (eg-sa-mi-nar).**
3. In a few words, **x** may be pronounced *s*, even between vowels, as in **exacto (e-sac-to)** and **auxilio (au-si-lio)** and in words built on these words. Pronounce after your teacher:

excelente   excursión   explicar   exposición
extenso   extranjero   extraordinario   exactamente
auxiliar   examen   existe   éxito

C. Silent consonants. A few consonants are dropped in Spanish pronunciation:

1. As stated earlier, the consonant **j** is silent in **reloj,** but is pronounced in the plural **relojes.**
2. The consonant **p** is silent in **septiembre.**
3. The consonant **t** is silent in **istmo.**
4. Spanish **d** tends to fall in the ending **-ado,** and final **d** is regularly dropped, in familiar speech, in the word **usted.**
5. The letter **h** is silent in modern Spanish: **ahora.**

NOTAS GRAMATICALES

1 Teoría del modo (*mood*) subjuntivo

The word *subjunctive* means *subjoined*, and except for its use in main clauses to express commands, the subjunctive mood is regularly used in subordinate or dependent clauses.

The indicative mood expresses *facts*, makes *assertions*, states *certainties*, or asks direct questions. In general, the subjunctive is dependent upon an *attitude*, a *wish*, a *feeling*, or some *uncertainty* in the mind of the speaker, expressed or implied in the main clause. The reference in the dependent clause is to an unaccomplished act or state.

In the case of a dependent clause, the student must observe whether the idea expressed in the principal clause is one which requires the subjunctive in Spanish, and then whether the subject of the dependent clause is *different* from that of the main verb. If this is true in both cases, the subjunctive will generally be used.

The subjunctive is more widely used in English than many persons realize because its forms differ from the indicative mood only in the third person singular and in some irregular verbs. In this and later lessons the subjunctive will be discussed according to its use in noun, adjective, and adverbial clauses. In the examples which follow, note, in the noun clauses, the various English equivalents of the Spanish subjunctive forms: English present tense, the future, use of the modal auxiliary *may*, and the infinitive:

Yo no creo que Ana esté aquí.	I do not believe (that) Ann is (will be) here.
Esperamos que Uds. lo hagan.	We hope (that) you may (will) do it.
Yo no quiero que Juan venga.	I do not wish that John come (I don't want John to come).

2   Las formas del presente de subjuntivo

Recall that in the present subjunctive tense the endings of **-ar** verbs begin with **e**, while those of **-er** and **-ir** verbs begin with **a**:

tomar:	tome	tomes	tome	tomemos	toméis	tomen
comer:	coma	comas	coma	comamos	comáis	coman
abrir:	abra	abras	abra	abramos	abráis	abran

In earlier lessons we have used the third person singular and plural and the second person singular forms of the present subjunctive in commands. See Repaso tres, pages 29–31, for uses of these forms, and Appendix D, pages 289–303, for the present subjunctive forms of all types of verbs. Remember that the stem of the present subjunctive of all but six verbs **(dar, estar, haber, ir, saber, ser)** is formed by dropping the ending **-o** of the first person singular of the present indicative.

EJERCICIO

Para contestar afirmativamente, empleando una forma de mandato con **Ud.** o **Uds.** como sujeto.

MODELOS: ¿Busco el libro?   Sí, búsquelo Ud.
                   ¿Le pedimos algo?   Sí, pídanle Uds. algo.

1. ¿Apruebo la recomendación?	6. ¿Vamos a la reunión?
2. ¿Hago la evaluación?	7. ¿Empezamos a las ocho?
3. ¿Apoyo la propuesta?	8. ¿Nos sentamos aquí?
4. ¿Acepto las sugerencias?	9. ¿Incluimos a los profesores?
5. ¿Recomiendo un estudio?	10. ¿Servimos refrescos?

3 El subjuntivo en cláusulas substantivas

The subjunctive is regularly used in a noun clause (*i.e.*, a clause used as the subject or object of a verb) when the verb in the main clause expresses or implies ideas of the speaker such as those of *wish, advice, request, command, permission, approval, cause, suggestion, preference, proposal, recommendation, insistence,* and the like, as well as their negatives. Remember that in English the infinitive is most commonly used after such verbs, but in Spanish a noun clause, usually introduced by **que,** is regularly used if the subject of the dependent clause is *different* from that of the main clause:

Carmen quiere hacer el estudio.   Carmen wants to make the study. (*Subjects the same*)

Ella quiere que los estudiantes hagan el estudio.   She wants the students to make the study. (*Subjects different*)

José prefiere tratar del asunto.   Joseph prefers to deal with the matter. (*Subjects the same*)

José prefiere que el profesorado trate del asunto.   Joseph prefers that the faculty deal with the matter. (*Subjects different*)

Proponen que se haga una evaluación anual.   They propose that an annual evaluation be made.

With certain verbs, *e.g.*, **decir, pedir, aconsejar,** and others which require the indirect object of a person, the subject of the infinitive in English is expressed as the indirect object of the main verb and understood as the subject of the subjunctive verb in the dependent clause. In the case of a sentence like *Ask him to go*, think of it as, *Ask of (to) him that he go*:

Pídales Ud. a ellos que celebren una reunión.   Ask them to hold a meeting.

Alguien les aconseja que formen comisiones.   Someone advises them to form committees.

El Rector les permitirá a los estudiantes que hagan el estudio.   The Rector will permit the students to make (let the students make) the study.

Recomendaré que se estudie el asunto.   I shall recommend that the matter be studied.

In Lección seis we found that **dejar, hacer, mandar,** and **permitir** are usually followed by the infinitive when the subject of a dependent verb is a pronoun. The subjunctive is also used after these verbs, particularly when the dependent verb has a noun subject (third example, above). One also says: **Permitiremos que celebren una reunión,** *We shall permit that they hold a meeting.*

EJERCICIOS

A. Repitan la oración; luego, al oír la frase con la conjunción (*conjunction*) **que,** formen una nueva oración, según el modelo.

MODELO: Prefiero hacer eso.   Prefiero hacer eso.
(que Ud.)   Prefiero que Ud. haga eso.

1. Quiero asistir a la reunión. (que Uds.)
2. El Rector prefiere evaluar el profesorado. (que una comisión)
3. Él desea formar las comisiones. (que la Asociación)
4. Miguel insiste en hacer el estudio. (en que los estudiantes)
5. Ellos desean mandarle al Rector sus recomendaciones. (que los profesores)
6. ¿Prefieren Uds. aprobar las evaluaciones? (que yo)
7. Juan no quiere apoyar la moción. (que Carmen)
8. ¿Insiste Ud. en pedir su colaboración? (en que el Rector)

B. Después de oír una frase, oirán una oración incompleta; formen una nueva oración introducida por la oración incompleta, según el modelo.

MODELO: formar una comisión. (Dígales Ud. que)   Dígales Ud. que formen una
comisión.

1. aceptar el informe de la comisión. (El Rector quiere que nosotros)
2. celebrar la reunión en la residencia. (Yo sugiero que los estudiantes)
3. constar de varios profesores. (Ellos proponen que la comisión)
4. no olvidarse de la evaluación anual. (Les diré que)
5. aprobar las recomendaciones. (Preferimos que la Asociación)
6. reunirse a las ocho. (Les aconsejo a los miembros que)

4   El subjuntivo en cláusulas substantivas (continuación)

The subjunctive is used in noun clauses dependent upon verbs or expressions of emotion or feeling, such as *joy, sorrow, fear, hope, pity, surprise,* and the like, as well as their opposites, provided that there is a change in subject from that of the main verb. Some common expressions of emotion are:

alegrarse (de que) to be glad (that)	**sentir (ie, i)** to regret, be sorry
esperar to hope	**ser lástima** to be a pity (too bad)
estar contento, -a (de que) to be happy (that)	**sorprender** to surprise
hay el peligro (de que) there is the danger (that)	**temer** to fear
	tener miedo (de que) to be afraid (that)

Me alegro de verte.   I am glad to see you. (*Subjects the same*)

¡Cuánto me alegro de que vayas a la reunión! How glad I am that you will go (are going) to the meeting! (*Subjects different*)

Siento no poder quedarme.   I'm sorry I cannot (I'm sorry not to be able to) stay.

Sienten que no podamos esperar más.   They are sorry (that) we cannot wait longer.

Tenemos miedo de que ellos no ejerzan[1] mucha influencia.   We are afraid that they will (may) not exert much influence.

Me sorprende (Es lástima) que la mayoría no apoye la propuesta.   It surprises me *or* I am surprised (It is a pity) that the majority doesn't support the proposal.

EJERCICIO

Repitan la oración; luego, al oír la frase con la conjunción **que**, úsenla para formar una nueva oración, siguiendo el modelo.

MODELO: Espero apoyar la moción.   Espero apoyar la moción.
           (que tú)   Espero que tú apoyes la moción.

1. Me alegro de poder ir a la reunión contigo. (de que Elena)
2. Temen someter la propuesta a la votación. (que la Facultad de Derecho)
3. Es lástima no contribuir más con su experiencia. (que los profesores)
4. Esperamos proponer varias recomendaciones. (que la Asociación)
5. ¿Sienten Uds. no formar parte de la comisión? (que el Rector)
6. Hay el peligro de no incluir a los estudiantes. (de que las comisiones)
7. El Rector está contento de saber los resultados. (de que los estudiantes)
8. Nos sorprende no tener más sugerencias. (que el profesorado)

5 El subjuntivo en cláusulas substantivas (continuación)

The subjunctive is used in noun clauses after expressions of *doubt, uncertainty, belief expressed negatively*, and *denial*. Common verbs of this type are:

dudar to doubt	**no creer** not to believe
negar (ie) to deny	**no estar seguro, -a de que** not to be sure that

Creemos que tomarán buenas decisiones.   We believe (think) they will make good decisions. (*Certainty*)

No creo que todos digan que sí.   I don't believe that all will say yes. (*Uncertainty*)

---

[1] For forms of **ejercer**, see those of **vencer**, Appendix D, page 298.

Dudo que haya mejores sugerencias.　I doubt that there are (will be) better suggestions.

Niegan que toda la comisión conste de profesores.　They deny that the whole committee is (will be) composed of professors.

No estamos seguros de que la mayoría esté en favor.　We are not sure that the majority is (will be) in favor.

Note that **creer** and **estar seguro, -a de que** express certainty and are followed by the indicative in a clause, while **no creer que** and **no estar seguro, -a de que** express uncertainty or doubt and require the subjunctive in a clause.

When **creer** is used in questions, the speaker may imply doubt of the action in the dependent clause, in which case the subjunctive is used. If no implication of doubt is made, the indicative is used. **No creer que** in a question implies certainty:

¿Cree Ud. que el voto sea unánime?　Do you believe (that) the vote will be unanimous? (*Doubt in the mind of the speaker*)

¿Creen que todos estarán de acuerdo?　Do they believe (that) all will agree? (*The speaker has no opinion*)

¿No crees que la colaboración de los profesores será valiosa?　Don't you believe (that) the collaboration of the professors will be valuable?

EJERCICIO

Para expresar en español:

1. I believe that the Rector will recommend a study of student participation in university government. 2. Carmen believes that the students should form the majority of the members of the committee. 3. She doesn't believe that the students will accept decisions made by the professors alone. 4. We are sure that several committees are to be formed. 5. The students are not sure that a meeting to deal with the matter will be held at once. 6. Do you (*formal sing.*) believe that they will send their proposals to the Rector? (*Certainty implied*) 7. We doubt that there is danger that the evaluation of the teaching staff will degenerate into a popularity contest. 8. Do you (*formal sing.*) believe that the evaluation of (the) colleagues of a professor is worth more than that of (the) students? (Explain your use of the indicative or the subjunctive mood in this sentence.)

6　El subjuntivo en cláusulas substantivas (fin)

Impersonal expressions that contain ideas of *possibility, necessity, uncertainty, probability, strangeness, doubt,* and the like, require the subjunctive in the dependent clause provided that a subject is mentioned. Impersonal expressions of fact and certainty, such as **Es cierto (verdad, evidente),** *It is certain (true, evident),* require the indicative; when no subject is expressed, the infinitive is used:

Será preciso (mejor) esperar un rato.   It will be necessary (better) to wait a while.

Es posible (probable) que ellos contribuyan mucho.   It is possible (probable) that they will contribute a lot.

Puede (ser) que Ana esté en favor.   It may be that Ann is (will, may) be in favor.

No es cierto (verdad) que todos aprueben la moción.   It isn't certain (true) that all will approve the motion.

Hay el peligro de que el Rector no apoye la recomendación.   There is the danger that the Rector will not support the recommendation.

Some common impersonal expressions which often require the subjunctive are:

basta	it is sufficient (enough)	**es mejor**	it is better
conviene	it is fitting (advisable)	**es necesario**	it is necessary
es bueno	it is well	**es posible**	it is possible
es difícil	it is difficult	**es preciso**	it is necessary
es dudoso	it is doubtful	**es probable**	it is probable
es extraño	it is strange	**es urgente**	it is urgent
es fácil	it is easy	**hay el peligro**	there is the danger
es importante	it is important	**importa**	it is important, it matters
es imposible	it is impossible	**más vale (vale más)**	it is better
es lástima	it is a pity (too bad)	**puede (ser)**	it may be

These expressions really fall under sections 3, 4, and 5, pages 145–148, but they are treated separately for convenience and clarity.

The infinitive *may* be used after most impersonal expressions if the subject of the dependent verb is a *personal pronoun*, not a noun. In this case the subject of the dependent verb is the indirect object of the main verb:

Me (Les) es mejor esperar.   It is better for me (them) to wait.

BUT: **Es extraño que Ana no esté aquí todavía.**   It is strange for Ann not to be (that Ann is not) here yet.

EJERCICIOS

A. Repitan cada oración; luego, formen una nueva oración empleando el infinitivo, como en el modelo.

MODELO: Vale más que se reúnan hoy.   Vale más que se reúnan hoy.
Vale más reunirse hoy.

1. Es preciso que busquemos un lugar más hermoso. 2. Importa que Ud. contribuya algo con su experiencia. 3. Es posible que ejerzan alguna influencia. 4. No basta que Ud. apoye la moción. 5. Será mejor que estemos de acuerdo. 6. Conviene que hagamos planes para el estudio. 7. Es lástima que no puedan incluir más estudiantes. 8. No es fácil que sugieran eso. 9. No es preciso que mandemos las recomendaciones hoy. 10. Es bueno que Uds. traten del asunto esta tarde.

B. Repitan la frase; luego, al oír una expresión impersonal, formen otra frase cambiando la original, según los modelos.

MODELOS: Juan podrá verlos.   Juan podrá verlos.
          (Es posible que)   Es posible que Juan pueda verlos.
          (Es cierto)   Es cierto que Juan podrá verlos.

1. Los estudiantes no hacen otros planes. (Es urgente que)
2. El Rector aprobará las propuestas. (Es probable que)
3. No aceptarán la sugerencia de Juan. (Será mejor que)
4. Muchos estudiantes no asistirán a la reunión. (Es extraño que)
5. Uds. recomendarán una evaluación. (Será necesario que)
6. La mayoría participará en las decisiones. (Importa que)
7. Miguel propondrá la participación de más estudiantes. (Es cierto que)
8. Se mandarán los resultados al Rector. (No es posible que)

7   Otras formas de mandato

A. The first person plural of the present subjunctive, and sometimes **vamos a** plus the infinitive, expresses commands equal to *let's* or *let us* plus a verb. **A ver** is regularly used for *Let's see.*

Remember that object pronouns are attached to affirmative commands and to infinitives, but they precede the verb in negative commands:

Llamemos a Elena.   Let's call Helen.
Abrámosla.
Vamos a abrirla. } Let's open it.
No los dejemos allí.   Let's not leave them there.

NOTE: **Vamos** is used for the affirmative *Let's* (*Let us*) *go.* The subjunctive **No vayamos** must be used for *Let's not go;* **No vayamos todavía,** *Let's not go yet.* **No vamos a casa** can only mean *We are not going home.*

When the reflexive **nos** is added to this command form, the final **-s** is dropped from the verb:

Vámonos.   Let's be going (Let's go).
Quedémonos (Vamos a quedarnos) un rato.   Let's stay a while.
No nos sentemos.   Let's not sit down.

B. **Que,** equivalent to the English *have, let, may, I wish,* or *I hope,* introduces indirect commands, except in the first person. In such cases, object pronouns precede the verb, and a noun or pronoun subject often follows the verb. This construction is really a clause dependent upon a verb of *wishing, hoping, permitting,* etc., with the main verb understood, but not expressed:

Que los traiga Juan.   Have (Let, May) John bring them.
Que esté él aquí a las seis.   Let him be here at six.

Que descanses. May (I hope) you rest.

¡Que te diviertas mucho! May you (I want you to, I hope you) have a very good time!

Remember that when *let* means *allow* or *permit*, it is translated by **dejar** or **permitir**: **Déjele (Permítale) usted a Pablo que vaya a la reunión,** *Let Paul (Allow* or *Permit Paul to) go to the meeting.*

EJERCICIOS

A. Para contestar dos veces, primero afirmativa, y luego negativamente, según los modelos.

MODELO: ¿Escribimos la frase? Sí escribámosla. No, no la escribamos.

1. ¿Llevamos las maletas?
2. ¿Seguimos la carretera?
3. ¿Buscamos a Elena?
4. ¿Devolvemos las bicicletas?

MODELO: ¿Nos acostamos? Sí, acostémonos. No, no nos acostemos.

5. ¿Nos levantamos?
6. ¿Nos sentamos?
7. ¿Nos vamos?
8. ¿Nos vestimos?

B. Después de oír un mandato, formen otra frase de mandato precedida de la frase **Yo no puedo** o **Nosotros no podemos,** siguiendo los modelos.

MODELOS: Lleve Ud. la comida.   Yo no puedo, que la lleve él.
          Cierren Uds. las ventanas. Nosotros no podemos, que las cierren ellos.

1. Traiga Ud. los paquetes.
2. Sirva Ud. el café.
3. Pague Ud. la cuenta.
4. Siéntese Ud.
5. Escojan Uds. el sitio.
6. Toquen Uds. los discos.
7. Váyanse Uds.
8. Acérquense Uds.

RESUMEN

A. Repitan la oración; luego, al oír el comienzo (*beginning*) de otra oración, complétenla, según los modelos.

MODELOS: Juan está en favor.   Juan está en favor.
          (Creo que)   Creo que Juan está en favor.
          (No creo que)   No creo que Juan esté en favor.

1. La Asociación hará un estudio importante. (Yo estoy seguro de que)
2. Harán una evaluación del profesorado. (No estamos seguros de que)

3. Se formará una comisión de estudiantes. (Creemos que)
4. Los profesores pueden contribuir mucho con su experiencia. (¿No crees que . . . ?)
5. La comisión constará en su mayoría de estudiantes. (Juan niega que) *deny*
6. Todos apoyarán la propuesta del Rector. (Yo dudo que)
7. Se someterá todo a la votación de los estudiantes. (¿Creen Uds. que . . . ?)
8. Habrá mejores sugerencias. (Todos creen que)

B. Usos del subjuntivo en cláusulas substantivas. Para expresar en español:

1. The Association of Students suggests that student participation in university government be studied. 2. The Rector recommends that committees be formed to study the suggestions. 3. Some of the students propose that a meeting be held to deal with the matter. 4. The Rector asks that the students send him their recommendations on the composition of the committee. 5. Michael believes that the students themselves must make the study. 6. Carmen doubts that all the students will support Michael's observations. 7. John is sure that the collaboration of the professors of the Law School would be very valuable. 8. Then Michael proposes that (the) half of the members of the committee be students, and that the rest be professors. 9. Carmen believes that if the students want to exert some influence on the academic decisions, they must form the majority on the committee which is to evaluate the teaching staff. 10. Finally, she proposes that the committee be composed for the most part of professors, but that it include a large representation of students.

C. Para contestar afirmativamente, usando la forma de mandato con **usted:**

1. ¿Empiezo a hacer el estudio?
2. ¿Sigo formando la comisión?
3. ¿Le llevo algo a Carolina?
4. ¿Busco a los estudiantes?
5. ¿Me siento a la derecha?
6. ¿Me quedo aquí hasta la una?
7. ¿Me acerco al señor Díaz?
8. ¿Les digo que vuelvan hoy?

D. Otras formas de mandato. Para expresar en español:

1. Have John wash the car.
2. May you (*fam. sing.*) be happy!
3. Have Jane wait a few moments.
4. May you (*pl.*) have a good time tonight!
5. Let's send him the results (*two ways*).
6. Let's sit down now (*two ways*).
7. Let's not go to the meeting until eight o'clock.
8. Let's not stay longer.

Resumen de palabras y expresiones

activamente actively
el **acuerdo** accord, agreement
la **administración** administration
apoyar to support, second, back
aprobar (ue) to approve
el **argumento** argument
la **asociación** (*pl.* **asociaciones**) association
el **asunto** matter, subject
la **colaboración** collaboration
el (la) **colega** colleague
la **comisión** (*pl.* **comisiones**) committee, commission
la **comisión de estudio** study committee
el **concurso** contest, competition
el **concurso de popularidad** popularity contest
constar de to be composed of, consist of
contribuir to contribute
convincente convincing
¿cuál valdría más? which would be better?
decir que sí (no) to say yes (no)
degenerar to degenerate
dentro de *prep.* in, inside, within
ejercer to exert
en su mayoría in its majority, for the most part
estar de acuerdo to agree, be in agreement
estar en favor to be in favor
estudiantil student (*adj.*)
la **evaluación** (*pl.* **evaluaciones**) evaluation

evaluar (*like* **continuar**) to evaluate
la **Facultad de Derecho** Law School
el **gobierno** government, control, management
incluir to include
la **influencia** influence
el **informe** report
la **mayoría** majority
el **miembro** member
la **mitad** half
la **moción** (*pl.* **mociones**) motion
la **opinión** (*pl.* **opiniones**) opinion
la **participación** participation
la **popularidad** popularity
preferiblemente preferably
el **profesorado** faculty, teaching staff
propio, -a (one's) own
proponer (*like* **poner**) to propose
la **recomendación** (*pl.* **recomendaciones**) recommendation
respecto de *prep.* with respect to, concerning
el **resto** rest
el **resultado** result
someter to submit
la **sugerencia** (*pl.* **sugerencias**) suggestion
tratar de + *obj.* to deal with, treat of
unánime unanimous
únicamente only
un par de a pair (couple) of
la **votación** vote, voting
el **voto** vote

+ creer = I
− creer = S
? creer = S
−? creer I

Lectura 7

La función política de la universidad

¿Tiene la universidad una función política? Se trata de una de las cuestiones más debatidas de nuestro tiempo. Una breve comparación de la universidad norteamericana con la hispanoamericana parece indicar que no hay una sola contestación, válida para todos los países y para todas las circunstancias.

En los Estados Unidos la universidad—sea del estado, del municipio o particular[1]— siempre ha defendido su autonomía frente al[2] gobierno. El principio que se invoca para justificar tal autonomía es significativo: el estado debe abstenerse de[3] intervenir en la organización técnica de la universidad, y la universidad, por su parte,[4] debe observar una completa abstención frente a las cuestiones políticas del estado.

Esto no quiere decir[5] que la universidad deba quedar al margen de[6] la vida nacional. Lo que se quiere es que la universidad sea apolítica, es decir, que sea un centro académico y científico donde se puedan estudiar los problemas de la nación objetivamente, sin partidarismo ni proselitismo de ninguna clase.[7]

Para muchos hispanoamericanos, en cambio, la idea de una universidad apolítica es ilusoria. En su opinión, la universidad, que en Hispanoamérica es un organismo del estado, además de los fines reconocidos por todos—la formación profesional, la

---

[1]**sea . . . particular,** *whether it be a state, municipal, or private institution.*   [2]**frente a,** *in the face (presence) of.*
[3]**abstenerse de,** *refrain (abstain) from.*   [4]**por su parte,** *on its part.*   [5]**no quiere decir,** *doesn't mean.*   [6]**al margen de,** *on the fringe of.*   [7]**sin partidarismo . . . clase,** *without partisanship or proselitism of any kind.*

organización de la investigación científica y la difusión de la cultura—, tiene una función social de la mayor importancia: la de poner la cultura al servicio de[8] la nación. Si los estudiantes han de ser los hombres de mañana y los futuros profesionales, la universidad tiene la obligación de asumir la alta misión política de formar ciudadanos aptos,[9] conscientes de sus derechos y responsabilidades y capaces de enfrentarse con éxito con[10] los problemas nacionales. La universidad debe formar en primer lugar al ciudadano y, partiendo de allí,[11] formará al profesional.

Esta orientación política de la universidad hispanoamericana explica la participación activa de los estudiantes y profesores en la vida nacional. Como en todas partes, las preocupaciones inmediatas son la defensa de la autonomía de la institución, la libertad de cátedra[12] y la reforma y democratización de los sistemas académicos; pero en Hispanoamérica las energías están orientadas también hacia la identificación y resolución de los problemas nacionales.

Durante estos últimos años se han realizado algunos cambios importantes en las universidades de los Estados Unidos. Antes de la década de los 60,[13] por ejemplo, las reformas universitarias eran iniciadas generalmente por los profesores y las universidades se esforzaban por mantenerse libres de la intervención del gobierno. A partir de la década citada, en cambio, la influencia de los estudiantes ha aumentado notablemente y la intervención del gobierno va creciendo cada vez más.[14]

Gracias a las leyes que eliminan la discriminación, ha habido un aumento considerable en el número de representantes de las minorías en las universidades, tanto entre los profesores como entre los estudiantes. Los centros de enseñanza tienen que dar a las muchachas las mismas oportunidades en los deportes que a los muchachos y están obligados a tomar las medidas necesarias para permitir que todo estudiante capacitado, aunque tenga algún impedimento físico, como la ceguera, pueda inscribirse en el curso que le interese. Otra ley de interés concede a los estudiantes el derecho de estar al tanto de toda la documentación y correspondencia que la universidad posea acerca de ellos.

En muchas universidades los estudiantes eligen representantes suyos para servir en diversas comisiones administrativas, tales como la de admisiones y la de becas y ayuda financiera. En algunas hay estudiantes no sólo en las comisiones académicas que seleccionan y evalúan los cursos y los profesores, sino hasta en la Junta de Síndicos.[15] En varias universidades prestigiosas, los estudiantes tienen el derecho de organizar cursos sobre materias que ellos creen que han sido desatendidas.

Como es sabido, los estudiantes han participado en los movimientos de protesta contra la guerra y en favor de la conservación del medio ambiente. Continúan sus protestas, con algún éxito, contra ciertas investigaciones científicas y actividades industriales que consideran nocivas para la humanidad.

Es indudable que las generaciones jóvenes tienen un papel[16] importante en la mejora de la sociedad y que su influencia—principalmente por medio de las universidades—irá creciendo cada vez más en el futuro.

---

[8] **al servicio de,** *in the service of.*   [9] **ciudadanos aptos,** *competent citizens.*   [10] **capaces de enfrentarse con éxito con,** *capable of successfully facing (coping with).*   [11] **partiendo de allí,** *beginning there.*   [12] **libertad de cátedra,** *academic freedom.*   [13] **de los 60,** *of the 60's.*   [14] **va creciendo cada vez más,** *is increasing more and more.*   [15] **Junta de Síndicos,** *Board of Trustees.*   [16] **papel,** *role.*

EJERCICIO

Escriban una carta, de unas 150 palabras, a algún miembro de su familia sobre un tema relacionado con la Lectura 7. Pueden utilizar las fórmulas siguientes:

San Antonio, Texas
20 de enero de 19_____

Querida hermana (mamá):

    Como te conté en mi carta anterior, formo parte de una nueva comisión, nombrada por el decano, para tratar de los asuntos estudiantiles. _____

_____

Un abrazo de tu hermano (hijo),

_____

El pretérito perfecto de subjuntivo ▪ Las cláusulas adjetivas y los pronombres relativos ▪ El subjuntivo en cláusulas adjetivas ▪ Usos especiales del objeto indirecto

LECCIÓN OCHO

Buscan un médico que hable español

Cuando Luis vuelve de su clase de Física, encuentra que Felipe, su compañero de cuarto, está sentado en el borde de su cama, rodeado de varios amigos. Al acercarse más, observa que Felipe, que está pálido, tiene el pie derecho muy hinchado.

Luis. Pero, ¿qué ha pasado? ¿Qué hacen todos aquí?

Carlos. ¿No te han dicho lo que ha pasado? Parece que tendremos que llevar a Felipe a la clínica.

Luis. ¿Otra vez? ¡Dudo que haya conocido a nadie[1] más propenso a los accidentes!

Carlos. Tropezó con el borde de la acera jugando al baloncesto y se dio un golpe tremendo al caer al suelo.

Luis. ¿Te duele mucho el pie, Felipe?

Felipe. Pude levantarme y entrar en la residencia, pero ahora me duele tanto que no puedo andar.

Carlos. Es posible que se haya torcido el tobillo.

Luis. Esperemos que no se haya roto algún hueso . . . Supongo que no tiene fiebre.

---

[1]The negative **nadie**, *anyone*, is used because of the negation implied in the preceding clause.

158

374

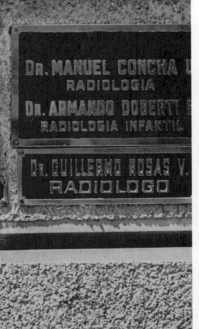

Dr. MANUEL CONCHA
RADIOLOGIA
Dr. ARMANDO DOBERTI
RADIOLOGIA INFANTIL

Dr. GUILLERMO ROSAS V.
RADIOLOGO

PISO DEP. 12

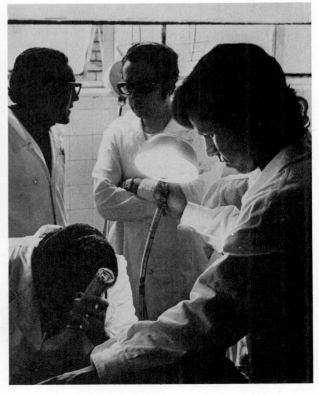

Carlos. Solamente un poquito. Le tomé la temperatura y no tiene más que medio grado.

Enrique. Nos preguntó Felipe si conocemos a algún médico que hable español.

Luis. El médico con quien hablamos en el Club Hispano es puertorriqueño. Trabaja en la clínica de la universidad.

Carlos. Es el edificio en cuyo piso bajo se encuentra la farmacia, ¿verdad?

Luis. Sí. ¿Hay alguien que pueda llevarlo a ver al médico?

Enrique. Yo no lo puedo llevar porque tengo clase. Que lo lleve José.

José. Yo lo puedo llevar. ¿Cómo se llama el médico?

Luis. Si no me equivoco, es de apellido Solís. Debemos llamarlo antes de ir a su oficina.

Carlos. Yo lo haré en seguida. Así sabremos si puede recibirlo pronto.

Enrique. Espero que no sea más que una torcedura.

Carlos. Si es una fractura, tendremos que llamar a los padres de Felipe, los cuales viven en San Antonio.

Luis. Ya veremos. De todos modos habrá que hacer lo que diga el médico.

Preparen un diálogo original, de unas doce líneas, para recitar en clase, empleando las frases y preguntas siguientes como elemento inicial:

1. *Luisa.* ¿Has llamado a tus padres, María? ¿Puedes ir a la sierra con nosotros?

   María. Acabo de hablar con ellos. No tienen otros planes. Tendré mucho gusto en aceptar tu invitación.

2. *José.* ¿Qué te pasa, Ramón? Estás muy pálido. ¿No te sientes bien?

   Ramón. No, José; creo que tengo un resfriado. Me duele la garganta y tengo dolor de cabeza.

PRONUNCIACIÓN

Intonation. Review the observations on Spanish intonation, Repaso tres, pages 24–25, and Lección dos, page 153. In a series or enumeration, which may consist of three or more members (nouns, adjectives, phrases or clauses), each member of the series constitutes a separate breath-group. The intonation pattern varies depending on the position of the series in the sentence.

a. If the series begins the sentence, all the breath-groups end with a slight fall of the voice except the last group, in which the voice rises to a pitch above the normal tone (level 3).

b. If the series occurs at the end of a sentence, the last two groups follow the pattern of the contrasting rise and fall of a declarative sentence of two members, but the preceding groups all end with a fall of the voice slightly below the normal tone. If the series is left incomplete (that is, if the last two members are not connected by the conjunction **y**), all the groups will end with a slight fall in the voice. Practice the following examples:

Series at the beginning:

Los lunes, los martes y los jueves ceno en casa.
Level 3

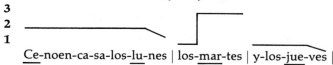

Los-<u>lu</u>-nes | los-<u>mar</u>-tes | y-los-<u>jue</u>-ves | ce-noen-<u>ca</u>-sa |

Series at end:

Ceno en casa los lunes, los martes y los jueves.

<u>Ce</u>-noen-ca-sa-los-<u>lu</u>-nes | los-<u>mar</u>-tes | y-los-<u>jue</u>-ves |

Incomplete series, at end:

Su novia es guapa, rica, elegante . . .

Su-<u>no</u>-viaes-<u>gua</u>-pa | <u>ri</u>-ca | e-le-<u>gan</u>-te |

NOTAS GRAMATICALES

1 El pretérito perfecto (*present perfect*) de subjuntivo

The present perfect subjunctive tense is formed by the present subjunctive of **haber** with the past participle. After verbs in the main clause which require the subjunctive in the dependent clause, Spanish uses the present perfect subjunctive tense to translate English *have* (*has*) plus the past participle:

	Singular		*Plural*
haya		**hayamos**	
hayas	} tomado, comido, vivido	**hayáis**	} tomado, comido, vivido
haya		**hayan**	

Dudo que haya conocido a nadie más propenso a los accidentes.   I doubt that I have known anyone more prone to accidents.

Esperemos que no se haya roto algún hueso.   Let's hope that he hasn't broken a (some) bone.

Es posible que Felipe se haya torcido el tobillo.   It's possible that Philip has sprained his ankle.

EJERCICIO

Repitan cada frase; luego, al oír el comienzo de otra frase, completen la nueva frase, según los modelos.

MODELOS: Ana está aquí.   Ana está aquí.
           Dudo que   Dudo que Ana esté aquí.

           Ana estuvo aquí.   Ana estuvo aquí.
           Dudo que   Dudo que Ana haya estado aquí.

1. Felipe no se siente bien.   Es lástima que *Felipe no se sienta bien*
   Felipe no se sentía bien.   Es lástima que *Felipe no haya sentido*
2. No es más que una torcedura.   Espero que *no esté más que un*
   No fue más que una torcedura.   Espero que *no haya estado mas que*
3. Ramón tiene dolor de cabeza.   No creo que *Ramon tenga dolor de*
   Ramón tenía dolor de cabeza.   No creo que *Ramon haya tenido dolor*
4. Tú lo puedes llevar a la clínica.   Me alegro de que *tu lo pueda llevar a*
   Tú lo pudiste llevar a la clínica.   Me alegro de que *tu lo hayas puesto llevar*
5. Uds. conocen al médico.   Arturo duda que *Uds conocan al medico*
   Uds. conocieron al médico.   Arturo duda que *Uds hayan conocido al*
6. El joven tiene una fractura.   Sentimos que *El joven haya tenido una*
   El joven tenía una fractura.   Sentimos que *el joven tenga una fractur*
7. El muchacho tropieza con el borde de la acera.   Tengo miedo de que
   El muchacho tropezó con el borde de la acera.   Tengo miedo de que
8. Ellos pueden ir a la sierra.   No estamos seguros de que *Ellos puedan ir a*
   Ellos pudieron ir a la sierra.   No estamos seguros de que *Ellos hayan puesto*

2   Las cláusulas adjetivas y los pronombres relativos

An adjective clause modifies a noun or pronoun and is introduced by a relative pronoun. In the sentence *I know a boy who can help us*, the adjective clause *who can help us* modifies *boy*. *Who* is a relative pronoun, and *boy* is the antecedent of the adjective clause.

A. Simple relative pronouns

1. **Que,** *that, which, who,* and, *whom,* when used as direct object of a verb, is invariable and refers to persons or things. Used as the object of a preposition, **que** refers normally to things and only occasionally to persons. The relative pronoun is

sometimes omitted in English when used as the object of a verb, but not in Spanish:

la casa de campo que él compró   the country house (that) he bought
los amigos que se acercan   the friends who are approaching
la farmacia de que hablan   the pharmacy about which they are talking
los jóvenes que vimos   the young men (whom) we saw

2. **Quien** (*pl.* **quienes**), *who, whom,* refers only to persons. It is used mainly as the object of a preposition, always meaning *whom,* and sometimes instead of **que** when the relative pronoun *who* is separated from the antecedent by a comma. The personal **a** is required when **quien(es)** is the direct object of a verb:

el médico con quien hablamos   the doctor with whom we talked
el señor Díaz, quien me llamó anoche, quiere . . .   Mr. Díaz, who called me last night, wishes . . .
las muchachas a quienes vimos ayer   the girls (whom) we saw yesterday

In the last sentence **que** may replace **a quienes,** and in conversation it is more widely used.

3. **El cual (la cual, los cuales, las cuales),** *that, which, who, whom,* is used to clarify which one of two possible antecedents the clause modifies, and after prepositions such as **sin, por,** and those of more than one syllable. Be sure that the long relative agrees with its antecedent. (These long relatives are much more widely used in literary style than in everyday conversation.)

la hermana de Carlos, la cual se ha torcido el tobillo, . . .   Charles' sister, who has sprained her ankle, . . .
el coche cerca del cual (del que) están jugando   the car near which they are playing
los padres de Felipe, los cuales viven en . . .   Philip's parents, who live in . . .

El que (la que, los que, las que) may be substituted for forms of **el cual,** particularly after prepositions, as in the second example.

4. **Lo cual** (sometimes **lo que**), *which (fact),* a neuter form, is used to refer back to an idea, statement, or situation, but not to a specific noun:

Felipe está pálido, lo cual me parece extraño.   Philip is pale, which (fact) seems strange to me.

B. Compound relative pronouns

1. **El (la) que,** *he (she) who, the one who (that, which),* and **los (las) que,** *those* or *the ones who (that, which),* may refer to persons or things. These forms are often called

compound relatives because the definite article (which originated from the Latin demonstrative) serves as the antecedent of the **que**-clause. (Do *not* use forms of **el cual** in this construction.)

> **Juan pregunta por el que no está aquí.**   John asks about the one who is not here.
> **Estas muchachas y las que están en la acera . . .**   These girls and the ones (those) who are on the sidewalk . . .
> **Los que se reúnen aquí . . .**   Those who meet here . . .

Quien (*pl.* **quienes**), which refers only to persons, sometimes means *he (those) who, the one(s) who*, particularly in proverbs:

> **Quien mucho duerme, poco aprende.**   He who sleeps much, learns little.

2. **Lo que**, *what, that which*, a neuter form, refers only to an idea or statement:

> **¿No te han dicho lo que ha pasado?**   Haven't they told you what has happened?
> **Yo sé lo que Uds. quieren hacer.**   I know what you want to do.

3. **Cuyo, -a, -os, -as**, *whose, of whom, of which*, is a relative possessive adjective. It agrees in gender and number with the noun it modifies.

> **el edificio en cuyo piso bajo**   the building on the first floor of which (on whose first floor)
> **la mujer cuyos hijos**   the woman whose children (the children of whom)

Remember that **¿De quién(es)?** expresses *Whose?* in a question: **¿De quién es esta casa?** *Whose house is this?* (lit., *Of whom is this house?*)

EJERCICIOS

A. Después de oír las dos frases, combínenlas, usando el pronombre relativo **que,** según el modelo.

MODELO: Ella tenía un libro. Era nuevo.   El libro que ella tenía era nuevo.

1. Ana compró un vestido. Es muy bonito. *El vestido que Ana compró*
2. Juanita sirvió unos refrescos. Eran excelentes. *Los refrescos que Juanita*
3. Vimos a la estudiante. Estaba sentada en el sofá. *La estudiante que vimos*
4. Conocimos al hombre ayer. Es médico. *El hombre que conocimos es med*
5. Invité a varios jóvenes. Son estudiantes. *Los jovenes que invité son*

Combinen las dos frases de las dos maneras, usando el pronombre relativo **quien (quienes),** según el modelo.

MODELO: Vimos al joven. Es mexicano.   Vimos al joven, quien es mexicano.
El joven a quien vimos es mexicano.

6. Saludé al médico. Es puertorriqueño.
7. Hablamos con la muchacha. Es estudiante de esta universidad.
8. Charlamos con aquellos señores. Trabajan en esta tienda.
9. Llamé a aquella niña. Está jugando en el patio.
10. Anoche conocimos a aquella señorita. Es profesora de inglés.

Combinen las dos frases, usando **el cual** o una de sus formas, según el modelo.

MODELO: La madre de Carlos vive en Los   La madre de Carlos, la cual vive en
Ángeles. Vendrá a visitarlo   Los Ángeles, vendrá a visitarlo
pronto.   pronto.

11. Los amigos de Marta estudian en la biblioteca. Tienen un examen mañana.
12. La hermana de Miguel viaja por España. Me ha enviado una tarjeta.
13. La tía de Inés ha escrito libros sobre México. Vive en San Antonio.
14. Las hijas de la señora Díaz corren hacia el parque. Son muy simpáticas.

B. Lean en español, supliendo el pronombre relativo:

1. La casa de campo _que_ compraron es hermosa.   2. La residencia en _que_ vivo es nueva.   3. El niño _a quien_ (two ways) vieron Uds. es mi hermanito.   4. El señor Navarro, _quien_ (two ways) es argentino, dio la conferencia.   5. El edificio de _que_ hablan es muy grande.   6. Las señoras con _a quienes_ charla mi mamá son mexicanas.   7. Me gusta la casa cerca de _la que_ juegan los muchachos.   8. Los amigos de Juan, _que_ se reúnen aquí, son estudiantes de esta universidad.   9. ¿Hiciste _que_ dijo el médico?   10. Los jóvenes no han vuelto, _lo cual_ nos parece extraño.   11. Ese argumento y _el que_ propone Luis son interesantes.   12. Esta tarjeta y _la que_ recibí la semana pasada son de mis padres.   13. Mi tío construyó este edificio y _el que_ está en la esquina.   14. _el que_ busca, halla.

el cual — only w/ prepos.

3 El subjuntivo en cláusulas adjetivas

When the antecedent of an adjective clause is *indefinite* or *negative*, that is, when the adjective clause refers back to someone or something that is uncertain, unknown, indefinite, or nonexistent, the subjunctive is used in it. In general, if *any*, *whatever*, or *whoever* can be applied to the antecedent, the subjunctive is required. The idea of futurity is often involved.

The indicative is used, however, when the antecedent refers back to someone or something that is certain or definite. This includes an action that occurs as a general rule:

¿**Hay alguien que pueda llevarlo a ver al médico?**   Is there anyone who can take him to see the doctor?

¿**Tiene Marta un amigo que haya estado en México?**   Does Martha have a friend who has been in Mexico?

Queremos una casa que sea más grande.   We want a (any) house that is larger.

Habrá que hacer lo que diga el médico.   It will be necessary to do what(ever) the doctor says (may say).

No hay nadie que haya jugado mejor.   There is no one who has played better.

Ana no ve nada que le guste.   Ann doesn't see anything (sees nothing) that she likes.

BUT: **Ana encuentra algo que le gusta mucho.**   Ann finds something that she likes a great deal.

Yo siempre hago lo que me piden.   I always do what (that which) they ask of me.

Luis tiene un tío rico que vive en San Francisco.   Louis has a rich uncle who lives in San Francisco.

In adjective clauses the personal **a** is omitted when a noun does not refer to a specific person (first example below). It is used, however, before the pronouns **alguien** and **nadie,** and before forms of **alguno** and **ninguno** when the latter refer to a person and are used as direct objects:

Necesito un hombre que me ayude mañana.   I need a man who will (may) help me tomorrow.

No conozco a nadie que diga eso.   I don't know anyone who says (will say) that.

¿**Conoce Ud. a algún médico que hable español?**   Do you know a (any) doctor who speaks Spanish?

EJERCICIOS

A. Repitan cada frase; luego, al oír el comienzo de otra frase, completen la nueva frase, según el modelo.

MODELO: Tengo un traje que me gusta.   Tengo un traje que me gusta.
    (Quiero un traje)   Quiero un traje que me guste.

1. Buscamos al joven que habla bien el español. (Buscamos un joven)
2. Tienen una casa que tiene ocho cuartos. (Necesitan una casa)
3. Cerca de aquí hay un lugar que es más hermoso. (Cerca de aquí no hay ningún lugar)
4. Deseamos reunirnos en el café donde sirven comidas mexicanas. (Deseamos reunirnos en algún café)

5. Quiero encontrar a la señorita que ha vivido en México. (Quiero encontrar una
señorita)
haya

6. Espero ver al estudiante que ha estado en la clínica. (Espero ver un estudiante)
ya

B. Para expresar en español:

1. I see some of the young men who meet here every day.   2. We believe that there
is someone who can take Philip to the doctor's office right away.   3. We are looking
for a student who doesn't have a class.   4. Do you (*formal sing.*) know a doctor who
speaks Spanish well? 5. If I am not mistaken, the surname of the man I met is Solís.
6. At any rate it will be necessary to do whatever the doctor may say. 7. Is there any
boy who wants to go to the drugstore now? 8. We do not see anyone who has time
(in order) to do it at this moment. 9. Mr. Martínez needs a woman who can work in
his new store. 10. He prefers a person who has had experience in the United States.

Yo veo a algunos

4   Usos especiales del objeto indirecto

A. If an action is performed on one person by another, the corresponding indirect object
pronoun is used with the verb. This construction most often involves parts of the
body, articles of clothing, or things closely related to the person. Note that the
definite article replaces the possessive adjective:

Le tomé la temperatura.   I took his temperature (*lit.*, I took to him the
temperature).
La madre les lavó las manos.   The mother washed their hands.

Remember that the reflexive pronoun is used when the subject acts upon itself:

Mi madre se tomó la temperatura.   My mother took her (own) temperature.
Juanito se lavó las manos.   Johnny washed his hands.

B. The verb **doler,** *to ache, hurt,* has as its subject a noun expressing a part of the body,
and the person is the indirect object:

Me (Le) duele la cabeza.   My (Her, His) head aches (I have [She, He has] a
headache).
A ella le duele (Le duele a ella) la garganta.   Her throat aches (hurts).
¿Te duele mucho el pie?   Does your foot hurt (ache) much?

Note that **Tengo dolor de cabeza** has the same meaning as **Me duele la cabeza:** *I have a
headache.* Also note: **Él tiene el pie hinchado,** *His foot is swollen, He has a swollen foot.*

EJERCICIO

Repitan la frase; luego, al oír un nuevo sujeto, formen otra frase, según el modelo.

MODELO: Ana se tomó la temperatura.   Ana se tomó la temperatura.
(Mi hermana)   Mi hermana le tomó la temperatura a Ana.

yo me le   a Juaneza

1. Juanito se lavó las manos. (Yo)
2. Pablo se quitó los zapatos. (Ellos)
3. Ana se compró un reloj. (Su papá)
4. Marta se puso la ropa. (Su mamá)
5. Juan se sirvió café. (Carolina)
6. Luisa se cortó la mano. (Yo no)

RESUMEN

A. Repitan cada pregunta; luego, contéstenla negativamente, haciendo los cambios necesarios en la cláusula adjetiva.

MODELO: ¿Ve Ud. algo que sea mejor?   ¿Ve Ud. algo que sea mejor?
No, no veo nada que sea mejor.

1. ¿Ve Ud. a alguien que pueda llevarlo a la clínica? *nadie*
2. ¿Hay alguien que tenga un resfriado hoy? *nadie*
3. ¿Conoce Ud. a algún médico que sea de Puerto Rico? *ningún*
4. ¿Ves algo que Marta pueda comprar? *nada*
5. ¿Hay alguna cosa aquí que le guste a él? *ninguna*
6. ¿Hay alguien que conozca a aquel señor? *nadie*
7. ¿Has visto a alguien que se haya roto el pie? *no nadie*
8. ¿Hay alguna estudiante que sea más inteligente que Carlota? *ninguna*

B. Usos de los pronombres relativos. Para expresar en español:

1. The young lady whom (*two ways*) we met yesterday is from Colombia. 2. John's sister, who has just arrived, is studying at another university. 3. We can see the building on whose first floor the lawyer has his office. 4. Ask (*fam. sing.*) George what he did with the book of which we were talking. 5. Our cousins have not returned yet, which (*fact*) surprises me. 6. These women and the one who is near the car are friends of my mother. 7. It can be said that those who (*two ways*) practice much, learn rapidly. 8. These two articles and the one which Helen read are well written.

C. Usos del objeto indirecto. Para expresar en español:

1. The children washed their hands. *se lavaron las*
2. Their mother washed their hands. *Las lavo las manos a ellos*
3. The doctor took her temperature. *le tomó la   a ella*
4. Did he take his temperature? *se tomó la*
5. Did Jane put on her new hat? *doler de cabeza*
6. I put her hat on her.
7. Ann didn't take off her shoes.
8. Her sister took her shoes off her.
9. My head aches (*two ways*). *Medida la cabeza*
10. Does your (*fam. sing.*) throat hurt? *tienes dolor de garganta me duele de garganta*

D. Repaso. Repitan cada oración; luego, repítanla otra vez, cambiando el verbo al pretérito de indicativo:

1. Carolina va a la sierra con algunos amigos. 2. José y yo no podemos acompañarlos. 3. El señor Díaz hace un viaje a México. 4. Los jóvenes nos traen varios regalos. 5. Carlos se sienta en el borde de la cama. 6. Felipe no duerme la siesta. 7. Los muchachos nunca me piden nada. 8. Oyen cantar a María. 9. Roberto sigue leyendo la novela. 10. ¿Qué te dicen tus amigos? 11. ¿Cuáles de los estudiantes vienen a la reunión? 12. ¿Es fácil aprender el diálogo? 13. No tropiezo con el borde de la acera. 14. Mi amiga se pone el vestido nuevo. 15. Arturo no se acuerda de eso. 16. Todos se divierten mucho en la excursión. 17. Mi papá conduce el coche al aeropuerto. 18. Nuestro tío construye una casa de campo. 19. El estudiante se da un golpe tremendo. 20. María no quiere dar un paseo con Pablo. 21. Yo llego a la universidad a las nueve. 22. Me equivoco; él no sabe nada de particular. 23. Bárbara tiene que escribir una carta a un amigo mexicano. 24. Roberto y Carolina andan despacio por la calle. 25. Ella y yo volvemos a casa a las cinco de la tarde.

Resumen de palabras y expresiones

el **accidente** accident
la **acera** sidewalk
acercarse más to draw nearer, approach (come closer)
el **apellido** surname, last name
el **borde** edge, border
la **clínica** clinic, hospital
de todos modos at any rate, by all means
el **dolor** ache, pain
el **dolor de cabeza** headache
elegante elegant
equivocarse to be mistaken
la **farmacia** pharmacy, drugstore
la **fiebre** fever
la **Física** Physics
la **fractura** fracture
la **garganta** throat
el **golpe** blow
el **grado** degree
habrá que + *inf.* it will be necessary to + *inf.*
hinchado, -a swollen
hispano, -a Hispanic, Spanish
el **hueso** bone

inteligente intelligent
el **modo** manner, way, means
no . . . más que only
pálido, -a pale
el **pie** foot
el **piso bajo** lower (first) floor
propenso, -a prone, disposed
¿qué (te) pasa? what's the matter with (you)?
rodeado, -a de surrounded by
sentirse (i,i) bien to feel well
el **sofá** sofa
el **suelo** ground
la **temperatura** temperature
tener mucho gusto en + *inf.* to be very glad to + *inf.*, have much pleasure in + *pres. part.*
el **tobillo** ankle
la **torcedura** sprain
torcer (ue) to twist, turn, sprain
tremendo, -a tremendous, terrible
tropezar (ie) con to stumble (strike) against
un poquito a little (tiny) bit

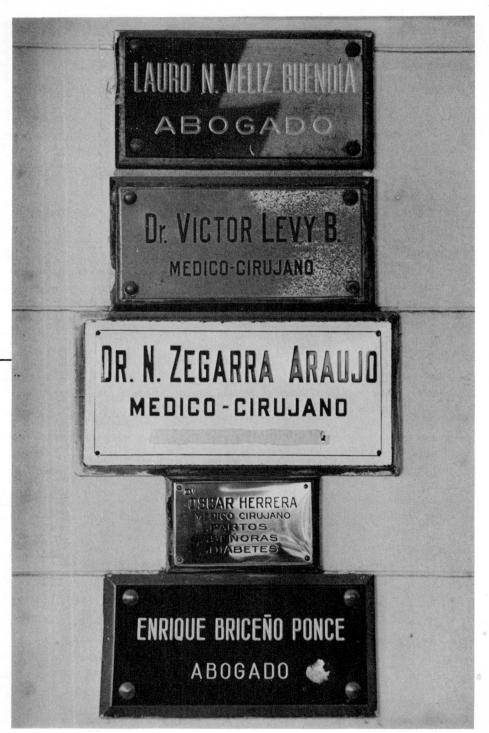

Lectura 8

Las carreras profesionales que atraen al estudiante

¿Cuáles son las carreras profesionales que atraen más a los estudiantes universitarios? ¿Hay diferencias respecto de este punto entre los estudiantes hispanoamericanos y los norteamericanos?

Al considerar las profesiones que prefieren los estudiantes hispanoamericanos, hay que tener en cuenta[1] la influencia de diversos factores sociales y económicos. En los países subdesarrollados, por el elevado coste de las instalaciones que se necesitan para la preparación de profesionales en las carreras técnicas y científicas, como las de medicina o ingeniería, el número de estudiantes que pueden prepararse para dichas profesiones es muy limitado. Las universidades, por lo tanto, tienden a favorecer las disciplinas en que las instalaciones son menos costosas, como en el caso del derecho, la pedagogía, las humanidades y las ciencias sociales.

La generalización citada parece válida para Hispanoamérica. Una minoría selecta escoge las profesiones de médico, de arquitecto y las diversas ramas de ingeniería—las que tienen mayor consideración social y brindan mayores entradas—, aunque tenga que efectuar sus estudios en el extranjero.[2] Grandes masas de estudiantes, en cambio, se acumulan en las facultades de derecho y de las ciencias sociales, y, según algunos críticos, se da un énfasis excesivo a las humanidades. (¡Se ha dicho que hasta la edad de veintidós años todo estudiante hispanoamericano aspira a ser poeta o novelista!)

---

[1]**tener en cuenta,** *bear in mind (take into account).*   [2]**efectuar . . . extranjero,** *to carry on its studies abroad.*

Las preferencias de los estudiantes graduados que vienen a las universidades norteamericanas para continuar sus estudios parecen confirmar estas observaciones. La mayor parte de ellos vienen a ampliar sus estudios de medicina, ingeniería y agricultura.

No debe olvidarse, además, otra diferencia muy importante: en Hispanoamérica, por razones sociales y económicas, sólo una pequeña minoría de los estudiantes—el uno por ciento,[3] aproximadamente—continúa sus estudios en la universidad.

En los Estados Unidos casi todos los años se realizan encuestas[4] sobre las preferencias de los estudiantes respecto de las carreras profesionales. En una de estas encuestas, por ejemplo, se pide a individuos de unas trescientas localidades que indiquen cuál de una lista de nueve profesiones consideran la mejor para un joven de hoy. Las nueve profesiones son las de médico, abogado, ingeniero, profesor, industrial o comerciante, dentista, funcionario del gobierno, banquero y clérigo.

Será de interés comparar las respuestas recibidas en distintas fechas de adultos de menos de treinta años de edad. Es evidente que se han realizado cambios radicales en la sociedad norteamericana durante estos últimos años, sobre todo en la manera de pensar[5] de los jóvenes. ¿Se reflejan estos cambios en las ideas de la juventud respecto de las carreras preferidas?

En encuestas realizadas en 1962 y 1973, una cuarta parte de los interrogados opinaron que la medicina era la mejor profesión para un joven. (El público en general favorecía la medicina aún más: el 23 por 100[6] le dio el primer lugar en 1962 y el 28 por 100 en 1973.) Pues los datos más recientes muestran un cambio notable: de los estudiantes que ingresaron en las universidades en 1976, sólo el 16 por 100 indicaron que deseaban estudiar la medicina.

Es general la impresión de que las universidades producen un número excesivo de abogados. A pesar de esta impresión, ha habido un aumento considerable en el interés por los estudios de derecho: el 8 por 100 los escogió en 1962 y el 20 por 100 en encuestas más recientes. No parece difícil explicar este aumento. Los estudios de derecho no sólo preparan al estudiante para una carrera lucrativa como abogado, sino que también constituyen una base excelente para una carrera en el gobierno o en los negocios. Para algunos estudiantes la abogacía[7] ofrece también un instrumento útil para combatir los abusos e injusticias de la sociedad.

Otras carreras que han atraído a muchos jóvenes son las de ingeniero y de profesor. El interés por ellas ha disminuido un poco durante los últimos años. El 17 por 100 escogió la profesión de ingeniero en 1962, y el 14 por 100 en 1973 y 1976. La profesión de maestro fue la preferida del 18 por 100 en 1962 y del 14 por 100 en las encuestas más recientes.

Se observa un aumento considerable en el porcentaje de jóvenes que desean prepararse para una carrera en los negocios. Sólo el 3 por 100 la escogió en 1962, mientras que el 9 por 100 la eligió en 1973. Hoy día su popularidad continúa creciendo.

La atracción de la carrera de dentista ha aumentado un poco: desde el 5 por 100 en 1962 hasta el 6 por 100 en las encuestas más recientes. La popularidad de los puestos en el gobierno no ha variado apreciablemente: el 7 por 100 los eligió en 1962 y el 6 por 100

---

[3] **el uno por ciento,** *one per cent.*   [4] **se realizan encuestas,** *polls are made (carried out, taken).*   [5] **la manera de pensar,** *the way of thinking.*   [6] **el 23 por 100,** *23 per cent.* (Read: **el veintitrés por ciento.**)   [7] **abogacía,** *legal profession.*

en las últimas encuestas. No ha habido cambio en el porcentaje de jóvenes que desean ser banqueros: el 2 por 100 en varias encuestas.

Los resultados respecto de la última profesión de la lista parece indicar un descenso del idealismo en nuestra sociedad actual. Mientras que el 4 por 100 escogió la carrera de clérigo en 1962, sólo el 1 por 100 la eligió en una encuesta reciente.

EJERCICIO

Traduzcan al español las frases siguientes, tratando de imitar las construcciones y fraseología del texto:

1. What professional career would you recommend to a young man who is planning to start his university studies next year?
2. Are the professions which Spanish American students prefer the same as those preferred by North American students?
3. Some critics have said that in some Spanish American countries an excessive emphasis has been given to the Humanities.
4. Most graduate students who come to North American universities plan to broaden their studies in (de) medicine, engineering, or agriculture.
5. In the United States polls have been made to discover which of nine professions is considered the best for a young person of today.
6. According to recent polls, the two most popular professional careers among North American students seem to be medicine and law.
7. The study of law not only prepares the student for a lucrative career as a lawyer, but also offers a useful instrument for combatting the abuses and injustices of society.
8. Do the polls show that the interest in the teaching profession has diminished in recent years?
9. A noteworthy increase has been observed in the percentage of young people who wish to prepare themselves for a career in business.
10. The drastic (radical) changes which have occurred in North American society during the last twenty years do not seem to be reflected in the ideas of young people concerning their professional careers.

Formas del imperfecto de subjuntivo ▪ El pluscuamperfecto de subjuntivo ▪ Usos de los tiempos del subjuntivo ▪ El subjuntivo en cláusulas adverbiales ▪ El subjuntivo en frases condicionales

LECCIÓN NUEVE

La conservación de la energía

Los estudiantes de la residencia en que viven Diana y Jorge han organizado un concurso para reducir el consumo de gas y de electricidad en las residencias universitarias. Diana y Jorge dirigen el concurso. Son las nueve de la noche. Jorge llama a la puerta del cuarto de Diana.

Jorge. ¿Se puede?

Diana. Pasa, Jorge. No pensé que volvieras tan pronto. ¿Cuántas residencias pudiste visitar hoy?

Jorge. Cuatro más. Sólo faltan tres. No ha habido problemas. Todo el mundo quiere participar en el concurso.

Diana. Antes de que vinieras, llamó el director del periódico. Quería noticias sobre el progreso del concurso.

Jorge. ¿Qué le contaste?

Diana. Que hasta ahora seis residencias están participando.

Jorge. Si vuelve a llamar, dile que el año pasado la reducción media en el consumo de energía en las residencias fue del once por ciento.

Diana. Sí, y que esperamos economizar aún más este año.

Jorge. También debes explicarle algunas de las técnicas que recomendamos, tales como la eliminación de algunas lámparas y el empleo de bombillas de menor vatiaje.

Diana. Dices bien . . . Y lo que es aún más eficaz, bajar los termóstatos a 67 grados y emplear en la ducha un aparato para reducir el consumo de agua.

Jorge. Muy bien . . . Pues, aquí te traigo algunos folletos más para que los distribuyas cuando tengas tiempo.

Diana. Podré hacerlo mañana cuando vaya a clase.

Jorge. Es lástima que comenzáramos el concurso tan tarde. Si hubiésemos comenzado en el otoño, habríamos economizado ya una cantidad considerable.

Diana. Según un artículo que acabo de leer, se ha conseguido una reducción del 58 por ciento en una universidad del sur del país.

Jorge. Pero esas cifras son excepcionales. No olvidemos que las condiciones no son iguales en todas partes.

Diana. Tienes razón. Estoy segura de que si viviéramos en el sur, podríamos alcanzar esas cifras fácilmente.

Jorge. Bueno, Diana. Parece que todo marcha bien. Hasta mañana.

Diana. Hasta mañana, Jorge. Y gracias por los folletos.

Preguntas sobre el diálogo: 1. ¿Cuál es el tema del diálogo de esta lección? 2. ¿Quiénes han organizado el concurso para reducir el consumo de gas y de electricidad? 3. ¿Cuántas residencias ha visitado Jorge hoy? 4. ¿Por qué había llamado el director del periódico? 5. ¿Qué le había contado Diana? 6. ¿Cuál fue la reducción media en el consumo de energía el año pasado? 7. ¿Cuáles son algunas técnicas que recomiendan los estudiantes para reducir el consumo de energía? 8. ¿Cuándo podrá Diana distribuir los folletos que le ha traído Jorge? 9. Según el artículo que ha leído Diana, ¿qué se había conseguido en una universidad del sur del país? 10. ¿De qué está segura Diana?

Preguntas para conversar: 1. ¿Por qué es importante la conservación de la energía? 2. ¿Qué han hecho los estudiantes de esta universidad para reducir el consumo de energía? 3. ¿Qué técnicas recomienda Ud. para reducir el consumo de electricidad? 4. ¿Qué técnicas recomienda Ud. para reducir el consumo de gas? 5. ¿Sería posible organizar un concurso para reducir el consumo de energía en la residencia en que vive Ud.? 6. ¿Quiénes podrían dirigir un concurso de ese tipo? 7. ¿Cómo despertaría Ud. el interés de los estudiantes? 8. ¿En qué clase de concursos ha participado Ud.? 9. ¿En qué clase de concursos han participado los estudiantes en épocas pasadas? 10. ¿En qué ocasiones han servido los estudiantes de modelo para la nación en general?

PRONUNCIACIÓN

The pronunciation of **y**, *and*. Recall that within a breath-group the conjunction **y** (phonetically an unstressed **i**) combines with a preceding vowel or consonant or with a following vowel to form one syllable. The principles that govern the pronunciation of **y** are the following:

1. When initial in a breath-group before a consonant, or when between consonants, it is pronounced like the Spanish vowel **i**: **Y se marchó (Y-se-mar-chó), tres y tres (tre-s y-tres).**

2. When initial in a breath-group before a vowel, or when between vowels, it is pronounced like Spanish **y**: **¿y usted? (¿y us-ted?), éste y aquél (és-te-y a-quél).**

3. Between **d, s,** or **z** and a vowel within a breath-group, it is also pronounced like Spanish **y**: **usted y ella (us-ted-y e-lla), éstos y aquéllos (és-tos-y a-qué-llos).**

4. Between **l, n** or **r** and a vowel within a breath-group, it is pronounced as the first element of a diphthong, with the preceding consonant, the **y**, and the following vowel in a single syllable: **aquél y éste (a-qué-l y és-te), hablan y escriben (ha-bla-n y es-cri-ben), entrar y esperar (en-tra-r y es-pe-rar).**

5. Between a vowel and a consonant, it forms a diphthong with the vowel that precedes it: **Marta y Juan (Mar-ta y-Juan).**

Apply the above principles in the following exercises:

1. Write the following phrases and sentences, dividing them into syllables and underlining the stressed syllables:

Son las tres y cuarto.	Y se fue.
Es rica y elegante.	Y escribe bien.
Son blancos y amarillos.	¿Van Carlos y Arturo?
El español y el francés.	Treinta y seis.

2. Read the following phrases and sentences as single breath-groups:

Lean y traduzcan esta frase.	Iremos Carlos y yo.
Saben leer y escribir.	Sabe inglés y español.
Es fácil y agradable.	Miren y escuchen.
Blanco y negro.	Usted y Arturo van.

NOTAS GRAMATICALES

1 Formas del imperfecto de subjuntivo

The imperfect subjunctive tense in Spanish has two forms, often referred to as the **-ra** and **-se** forms, and the same two sets of endings are used for the three conjugations. To form the imperfect subjunctive of *all* verbs, regular and irregular, drop **-ron** of the third person plural preterit indicative and add **-ra, -ras, -ra, -ramos, -rais, -ran** or **-se, -ses, -se, -semos, -seis, -sen.** Only the first person plural form has a written accent. Remember that the **-er** and **-ir** verbs have the same endings in all tenses except in the present indicative. The two imperfect subjunctive tenses are interchangeable in Spanish, except in conditional sentences (section 5 of this lesson) and in softened statements (Lección diez, page 200):

tomar:	tomara	tomaras	tomara	tomáramos	tomarais	tomaran
	tomase	tomases	tomase	tomásemos	tomaseis	tomasen
comer:	comiera	comieras	comiera	comiéramos	comierais	comieran
vivir:	viviese	vivieses	viviese	viviésemos	vivieseis	viviesen

See Appendix D, pages 293–303, for the imperfect subjunctive forms of irregular and stem-changing verbs. For easy reference, the infinitive, the third person plural preterit, and the first person singular imperfect subjunctive forms of some common irregular verbs are listed here:

Inf.	3rd Pl. Pret.	Imp. Subj.
andar	anduvieron	anduviera, -se
caer	cayeron	cayera, -se
conducir	condujeron	condujera, -se
construir	construyeron	construyera, -se
creer	creyeron	creyera, -se
dar	dieron	diera, -se
decir	dijeron	dijera, -se
estar	estuvieron	estuviera, -se
haber	hubieron[1]	hubiera, -se
hacer	hicieron	hiciera, -se
ir	fueron	fuera, -se
oír	oyeron	oyera, -se
poder	pudieron	pudiera, -se
poner	pusieron	pusiera, -se
querer	quisieron	quisiera, -se
saber	supieron	supiera, -se
ser	fueron	fuera, -se
tener	tuvieron	tuviera, -se
traer	trajeron	trajera, -se
ver	vieron	viera, -se

Stem-changing verbs, Class I (which end in **-ar** and **-er**), have no stem change in the imperfect subjunctive. In Class II verbs (**sentir, dormir**), the stem vowel **e** becomes **i**, and **o** becomes **u**, in the third person singular and plural of the preterit and in the entire imperfect subjunctive. In Class III verbs (**pedir, reír**), the stem vowel **e** becomes **i** in the same forms:

---

[1] See page 238 for the preterit forms of **haber.**

sentir (ie, i)	**sintieron**	**sintiera, -se**
dormir (ue, u)	**durmieron**	**durmiera, -se**
pedir (i, i)	**pidieron**	**pidiera, -se**
reír (i, i)	**rieron**	**riera, -se**

2 El pluscuamperfecto de subjuntivo

The pluperfect subjunctive is formed by using either the **-ra** or **-se** imperfect subjunctive form of **haber** plus the past participle:

hubiera	**hubiese**
hubieras	**hubieses**
hubiera	**hubiese**
hubiéramos	**hubiésemos**
hubierais	**hubieseis**
hubieran	**hubiesen**

} tomado, comido, vivido

Yo sentía mucho que él ya hubiera (hubiese) comido.   I was very sorry that he had already eaten.

3 Usos de los tiempos del subjuntivo

When the main verb in a sentence which requires the subjunctive in a dependent clause is in the present, future, or present perfect tense, or is a command, the verb in the dependent clause is regularly in the present or present perfect subjunctive tense:

Quiero que veas el folleto.   I want you to see the pamphlet.
Le diré (he dicho) que vuelva pronto.   I shall tell (have told) him to return soon.
Pídales Ud. que bajen el termóstato.   Ask them to lower the thermostat.
Es posible que podamos economizar más.   It is possible that we can economize more.

When the main verb is in the preterit, imperfect, conditional, or pluperfect tense, the verb in the dependent clause is usually in the imperfect subjunctive, unless the English past perfect tense is used in the dependent clause, in which case the pluperfect subjunctive is used in Spanish:

Les pedí (pedía) que bajaran la temperatura.   I asked (was asking) them to lower the temperature.

Yo no pensé que volvieras tan pronto.   I didn't believe (that) you would return so soon.

No había nadie que pudiese ayudarnos.   There was no one who could help us.

Yo dudaría que Ana hubiese ido a la reunión.   I would doubt that Ann had gone to the meeting.

Contrary to the above statements, the imperfect subjunctive may follow the present, future, or present perfect tense when, as in English, the action of the dependent clause took place in the past:

Es lástima que comenzáramos el concurso tan tarde.   It's too bad we began the contest so late.

EJERCICIOS

A. Lean en español, supliendo la forma correcta del verbo entre paréntesis; cuando sea necesario el imperfecto de subjuntivo, usen las dos formas:

1. Diana insiste en que yo (dirigir) el concurso. 2. Ella insistió en que otros estudiantes (participar) en él también. 3. Quiero que tú les (explicar) algunas de las técnicas. 4. Jorge quería que yo (traer) algunos folletos. 5. Me alegro de que Juan (poder) distribuir algunos de ellos mañana. 6. Le pedí a Diana que (venir) temprano a la reunión. 7. No creemos que todo el mundo (economizar) más en el consumo de energía. 8. Tratábamos de presentar una propuesta que (despertar) el interés de los estudiantes.

B. Repitan cada oración; luego, al oír una nueva frase inicial, completen la oración, haciendo los cambios necesarios:

1. Pepe no quiere que Jorge distribuya los folletos. (Pepe no quería)
2. Les aconsejaré que organicen el concurso pronto. (Les aconsejé)
3. Les pediré que lo hagan mañana. (Yo les pediría)
4. ¿Buscan Uds. a alguien que dirija el concurso? (¿Buscaban Uds. a alguien . . .)
5. Es posible que Diana escriba un artículo para el periódico. (Era posible)
6. No hay nadie que tenga mejores ideas que Marta. (No había nadie)
7. No creemos que todo el mundo participe en los planes. (No creíamos)
8. Será mejor que Uds. busquen bombillas de menor vatiaje. (Sería mejor)

4   El subjuntivo en cláusulas adverbiales

An adverbial clause, which modifies a verb and indicates *time, purpose, concession, condition, result, negative result,* and the like, is introduced by a conjunction, often a compound with **que** as the last element. If the action has taken place or is an accepted fact, the indicative mood is used; if the action may take place but has not actually been accomplished, the subjunctive is normally used in the clause.

A. Time clauses

The subjunctive is used after conjunctions of time if the action in the dependent clause has not been completed at the time indicated by the main clause, that is, when the time referred to in the clause is <u>indefinite</u> and <u>future</u>, and therefore uncertain, from the standpoint of the time expressed in the main clause. **Antes (de) que,** *before,* always requires the subjunctive, since the action indicated in the clause cannot have taken place.

When the time clause expresses an accomplished fact in the present or past, or a customary occurrence, the indicative is used.

Common conjunctions which introduce time clauses are:

antes (de) que before	**en cuanto** as soon as
así que as soon as	**hasta que** until
cuando when	**luego que** as soon as
después (de) que after	**mientras (que)** while, as long as

Yo esperé hasta que regresó Felipe.   I waited until Philip returned.

Cuando yo veo a Juan, lo saludo.   When I see John, I greet him.

En cuanto yo lo vea, lo saludaré.   As soon as I see him, I shall greet him.

Podré distribuir los folletos mañana cuando vaya a clase.   I can (shall be able to) distribute the pamphlets tomorrow when I go to class.

Antes de que vinieras, llamó el director del periódico.   Before you came, the editor of the newspaper called.

Ana quería leer hasta que Pablo la llamase.   Ann wanted to read until Paul called (should call) her.

B. Concessive and result clauses

Aunque, *although, even though, even if,* is followed by the subjunctive mood unless the speaker wishes to express a statement as a certainty or is indicating an accomplished fact, in both of which cases the indicative mood is used:

Aunque sea tarde, he venido a la reunión.   Even though it may be late, I have come to the meeting.

Aunque es tarde, he venido a la reunión.   Although it is late, I have come to the meeting. (*Certainty implied*)

Aunque yo estaba cansado, les expliqué el programa.   Although I was tired, I explained the program to them. (*A fact*)

Two other conjunctions, **de manera que** and **de modo que,** both meaning *so that,* may express result, in which case they are followed by the indicative mood. They may also express purpose, in which case the subjunctive is used. Compare the following sentences (also see C, which follows):

> **Juan habló de manera (modo) que lo entendimos.**   John spoke so that (in such a way that) we understood (did understand) him.
> **Juan, hable Ud. de manera (modo) que lo entendamos.**   John, speak so that we may understand you. (*No certainty that we will*)

C. Purpose, proviso, conditional, negative result clauses

Certain conjunctions denoting *purpose, proviso, condition, negative result,* and the like, always require the subjunctive because they cannot introduce a statement of fact. By their very meaning, they indicate that the action in the clause is uncertain, or that the action may not, or did not, actually take place. In addition to **de manera que** and **de modo que**, *so that* (see B above), some other conjunctions of these types are:

a fin de que	in order that	**para que**	in order that
a menos que	unless	**siempre que**	provided that
con tal (de) que	provided that	**sin que**	without

> **¿Por qué no me llamaste para que te ayudara?**   Why didn't you call me in order that I might help you?
> **Prometo acompañarte con tal que yo consiga el dinero.**   I promise to go with you provided that I get (obtain) the money.
> **Los niños salieron sin que los oyera su mamá.**   The children went out without their mother hearing them.

EJERCICIOS

A. Para leer en español, supliendo la forma correcta del verbo entre paréntesis:

1. Siempre empieza la clase en cuanto (entrar) el profesor.
2. Eran las diez de la noche cuando Roberto (regresar) a su cuarto.
3. Vamos a enseñarles el folleto en cuanto (llegar) ellos.
4. Compré el tocadiscos aunque me (costar) demasiado.
5. Aunque (llover) esta noche, tendremos que ir al teatro.
6. Dijeron que se irían mañana aunque (hacer) mal tiempo.
7. Quédense Uds. en casa hasta que (volver) yo de la tienda.
8. No llegarán a tiempo a menos que (darse) prisa.
9. Hable Ud. de modo que lo (oír) bien todos los estudiantes.
10. Traeré los folletos para que Ud. los (distribuir).
11. Jorge me los trajo para que yo (poder) leerlos.
12. Tráigame Ud. café con tal que (estar) caliente.
13. Ya habíamos cenado antes de que ellos (haber) vuelto a casa.
14. Juan no podrá ir con Uds. sin que yo le (dar) el dinero.
15. María no ganará mucho mientras que (trabajar) en esta tienda.

[handwritten margin notes: "conditional requires subjunc."; "subjunctive or preterite"]

B. Repitan cada pregunta; luego, contéstenla afirmativamente, agregando (*adding*) una cláusula introducida por la frase **aunque Pablo,** según el modelo.

MODELO: ¿Hará Ud. el viaje?   ¿Hará Ud. el viaje? Sí, aunque Pablo lo haga también.

1. ¿Escogerá Ud. la maleta?
2. ¿Buscará Ud. el periódico?
3. ¿Pedirá Ud. la beca?

4. ¿Mirará Ud. los pájaros?
5. ¿Explicará Ud. el problema?
6. ¿Seguirá Ud. su consejo?

C. Para expresar en español:

1. Some students intend to organize a contest to reduce the consumption of gas and electricity. 2. It seems that everybody wants to participate in the contest. 3. We want all (the) students to economize more than last year. 4. Before Diane came, the editor of the newspaper called. 5. He was hoping that she could give him information on the progress of the contest. 6. Most of us did not believe that she would arrive so soon. 7. George brought some pamphlets in order that we might distribute them as soon as we had time. 8. Diane said that she would do it when she went to class.

5   El subjuntivo en frases condicionales

In earlier lessons we have used simple conditions in which the present indicative is used in the English *if*-clause and the same tense in the Spanish **si**-clause (see Lección seis, page 130):

Si Juan está en su cuarto,	**está escuchando discos.**
If John is in his room,	he is listening to records.
Si ellos tienen dinero,	**comprarán el coche.**
If they have (the) money,	they will buy the car.

Simple conditions are also expressed in past time:

Si Ana recibió (ha recibido) el cheque,	**compró la cámara.**
If Ann received (has received) the check,	she bought the camera.

In a **si**-clause which implies that a statement is contrary to fact (*i.e.*, not true) in the present, Spanish uses either form of the imperfect subjunctive. A contrary-to-fact sentence may also be expressed in the past, in which case the pluperfect subjunctive is used in the **si**-clause (see the second example which follows).

The conclusion or main clause of a contrary-to-fact condition is usually expressed by the conditional (or conditional perfect), as in English. (In reading you will also find the **-ra** form of the imperfect or pluperfect subjunctive in the main, or result, clause; in the exercises of this text only the conditional or conditional perfect will be used.)

Si yo tuviera (tuviese) dinero,	**compraría el coche.**
If I had (the) money (*but I don't*),	I would buy the car.
Si Pablo hubiese (hubiera) venido,	**me habría llamado.**
If Paul had come (*but he didn't*),	he would have called me.

Como si, *as if,* also expresses a contrary-to-fact condition, in which case the conclusion, or main clause, is understood:

¡Gastas el dinero como si fueras millonario!   You spend money as if you were a millionaire!

Similarly, either form of the imperfect subjunctive is used in the si-clause to express a condition that <u>may</u> (<u>might</u>) not be fulfilled in the future. Whenever the English sentence has *should* or *were to* in the *if*-clause, the imperfect subjunctive is used in Spanish:

Si fuésemos (fuéramos) allá,	**dirigiríamos el concurso.**
If we should (were to) go there,	we would manage the contest.
Si vinieran (viniesen) mañana,	**asistirían a la reunión.**
If they should (were to) come tomorrow,	they would attend the meeting.

NOTE: The future and conditional indicative and the present subjunctive tenses are not used after **si** meaning *if*. When **si** means *whether*, the indicative must be used: **No sé si podrán venir,** *I do not know whether they will be able to come.*

EJERCICIOS

A. Repitan cada frase; luego, al oír otra cláusula con **si,** completen la frase:

1. Si Carlos tiene dinero, comprará un traje.
   Si Carlos tuviera dinero,
   Si Carlos hubiera tenido dinero,
2. Si Diana ve a Marta, le dará el folleto.
   Si Diana viese a Marta,
   Si Diana hubiese visto a Marta,
3. Si vamos juntos, nos divertiremos.
   Si fuéramos juntos,
   Si hubiéramos ido juntos,

B. Repitan la frase; luego, cambien la forma de los verbos, según el modelo.

MODELO: Si tengo tiempo, iré al cine.   Si tengo tiempo, iré al cine.
                                                              Si yo tuviera tiempo, iría al cine.

1. Si José vuelve a casa, nos llamará.
2. Si María está en su cuarto, escribirá la composición.

3. Si vamos a México, sacaremos muchas fotografías.
4. Si no es tarde, charlaré con Ud. un rato.

MODELO: Si vienen, los veré.   Si vienen, los veré.

Si viniesen, yo los vería.

5. Si tengo tiempo, llamaré al director del periódico.
6. Si bajamos el termóstato, reduciremos el consumo de gas.
7. Si traen los folletos, podremos distribuirlos mañana.
8. Si seguimos trabajando, tendremos éxito en el concurso.

MODELO: Si han venido, lo habrán visto.   Si han venido, lo habrán visto.

Si hubieran venido, lo habrían visto.

9. Si han empleado bombillas de menor vatiaje, habrán economizado mucho.
10. Si han leído el artículo, habrán visto las recomendaciones.

RESUMEN

A. Repitan cada frase; luego, al oír una nueva conjunción, substitúyanla en la frase:

1. *En cuanto* yo tenga tiempo, voy a escoger una cámara. (*Cuando*)
2. *Después que* llegue Miguel, organizaremos el concurso. (*Antes de que*) — always subjunctive
3. No podré acompañarte *a menos que* él me preste el dinero. (*sin que*)
4. Todos se reunirán aquí *con tal que* vengan los otros jóvenes. (*después que*)
5. Yo traje la foto *para que* Ud. la viera. (*de modo que*)
6. Decidieron ir a la sierra *aunque* lloviese. (*a menos que*)
7. Ellos querían quedarse aquí *hasta que* llegase el médico. (*aunque*)
8. Se lo di a Luisa *de manera que* ella pudiera comprar un regalo. (*para que*)

B. Lean en español; luego, repitan cada frase, comenzando con las palabras entre paréntesis y cambiando el verbo de la cláusula subordinada a la forma del imperfecto de subjuntivo que termina en **-ra**:

1. Queremos que ellos *participen* en el concurso. (Queríamos)
2. Yo no creo que Felipe *haya* podido hacer el viaje. (Yo no creía)
3. Pídale Ud. al señor Díaz que *vaya* a la clínica. (Jorge le pidió)
4. No será posible que *vuelvan* antes del mes de mayo. (No sería)
5. No vemos a nadie que *tenga* un resfriado. (No vimos)
6. ¿Hay alguien que *conozca* a aquel señor? (¿Había alguien . . . ?)
7. Ella dice que saldrá en cuanto *venga* el profesor. (Ella dijo que saldría)
8. Yo lo llamaré para que te *ayude* a escoger una maleta. (Yo lo llamé)
9. Creen que él irá a verlos aunque *sea* tarde. (Creían que él iría)
10. Ana quiere esperar hasta que *lleguen* sus amigas. (Ana quería esperar)

C. Usos del subjuntivo en frases condicionales. Para expresar en español:

1. If Robert has the money, he will buy a camera. 2. If Robert were to go to Mexico, he would take many photographs. 3. If he had had time, he would have shown us the camera. 4. If Charles arrives before six o'clock, we shall eat supper downtown. 5. If he should come earlier, we would look at some pamphlets on Mexico. 6. If I had seen a good bracelet, I would have bought it. 7. Raymond talks as if he had a cold. 8. I know that if he stayed at home, he was ill.

D. Repaso de algunas expresiones usadas en las Lecciones siete, ocho y nueve. Para expresar en español:

1. Ann washed his face.
2. I was mistaken.
3. John broke his hand.
4. What's the matter with him?
5. I stumbled against the edge of the sidewalk.
6. Jane doesn't feel well.
7. She has a headache.
8. His ankle is swollen.
9. My foot hurts.
10. Everybody says yes.
11. At any rate.
12. Diane and George are in agreement.
13. Ann serves as secretary.
14. Joe is right.

Resumen de palabras y expresiones

alcanzar   to reach, attain
el **aparato**   apparatus
bajar   to lower
la **bombilla**   bulb (*light*)
la **cámara**   camera
la **cantidad**   quantity
la **cifra**   figure
conseguir (i, i)   to get, obtain, attain; to bring about
la **conservación**   conservation
considerable   considerable
el **consumo**   consumption
decir bien   to be right
despertar (ie)   to awaken, arouse
dirigir   to direct, manage
distribuir   to distribute
la **ducha**   shower (*bath*)
economizar   to economize
eficaz   effective

la **electricidad**   electricity
la **eliminación**   elimination
el **empleo**   use, employment
en (por) todas partes   everywhere
la **energía**   energy
la **época**   epoch, period
excepcional   exceptional
el **folleto**   pamphlet, folder
el **gas**   gas
gastar   to spend (*money*), waste, use (up)
gracias por   thanks (thank you) for
ha habido   there has (have) been
hasta mañana   until (see you) tomorrow
igual   equal, uniform, the same
la **lámpara**   lamp, light
marchar   to go, proceed, come along
medio, -a   average
el **millonario**   millionaire
la **nación** (*pl.* **naciones**)   nation

por ciento   per cent
el **progreso**   progress
la **reducción**   reduction
reducir   to reduce
¿se puede?   may (I) come in?

según *prep.*   according to
servir (i,i) de   to serve as
la **técnica**   technique
el **termóstato**   thermostat
el **vatiaje**   wattage

Lectura 9

La crisis de la energía y el sistema educativo

La crisis de la energía es, sin duda, el problema más grave con que la humanidad tendrá que enfrentarse durante las próximas décadas. Cuando pensamos en ella, generalmente reparamos en lo que nos afecta más de cerca:[1] el alza del precio de la gasolina o del gas; la necesidad de reducir el consumo de energía en la calefacción y en el aire acondicionado; y el uso de bicicletas o de medios de transporte públicos en lugar de[2] coches particulares. En realidad, se trata de un problema mucho más complicado, con facetas que el público en general apenas parece comprender.

La crisis de la energía no es más que una parte del problema global de la utilización prudente o imprudente de los recursos de la naturaleza. Este problema presenta dos aspectos principales. En primer lugar, vamos descubriendo que nuestro planeta no puede continuar absorbiendo los desperdicios de las acciones del hombre; y luego es evidente que se van agotando[3] irremediablemente las fuentes más accesibles de gas y de petróleo—los combustibles que representan casi tres cuartas partes de la energía en que depende la economía de nuestro país.

Para algunos la solución consistiría sencillamente en la busca de nuevas fuentes de energía. Es cierto que hay otras formas de energía que podemos utilizar, tales como el carbón, la energía solar, la hidráulica, la nuclear y la del viento. Pero sería trágico pensar

---

[1] **reparamos . . . cerca,** *we notice what affects us most closely.*   [2] **en lugar de,** *instead of.*   [3] **se van agotando,** *(they) are gradually becoming exhausted (used up).*

que por resolver el problema podemos continuar malgastando los recursos de la naturaleza como hemos hecho hasta ahora. Al contrario, la solución exigirá no sólo una tecnología nueva, sino otro sistema de valores y nuevas formas de vida. Será necesario cambiar nuestra actitud respecto de los recursos de la tierra y aprender a cooperar unos con otros, como también con las demás naciones del mundo.

En la busca de una solución las escuelas y universidades tendrán un papel de la mayor importancia. En primer lugar, los centros de enseñanza de nuestro país son importantes consumidores de energía. Según cálculos oficiales, las escuelas de la nación consumen el 11 por 100 de los combustibles utilizados en el país y casi la mitad de la energía es perdida por la construcción defectuosa de los edificios escolares. Renovando el 30 por 100 de las ochenta mil escuelas primarias y secundarias, se ahorrarían más de veinticinco millones de barriles de petróleo al año.[4]

Pero es claro que las escuelas y universidades son algo más que establecimientos que consumen enormes cantidades de energía. Su responsabilidad mayor será la de preparar los técnicos y científicos capacitados para conducirnos hacia una sociedad más consciente de sus obligaciones. Si el uso más abundante de carbón va a ser una de las soluciones interinas, necesitaremos profesionales instruidos en las nuevas técnicas mineras. Al mismo tiempo habrá que preparar a los especialistas en el campo de la conservación necesarios para velar por los intereses del público. Las esperanzas representadas por la energía solar, la nuclear y la del viento necesitarán también personal capaz de realizarlas.

Además de reducir el consumo de energía en sus establecimientos y de preparar a los profesionales en los campos de la energía y de la conservación del ambiente, los centros de enseñanza tienen otra responsabilidad esencial: la de instruirnos a todos[5] sobre las verdaderas dimensiones de la crisis de la energía. Tienen que convencer a nuestra sociedad de que es necesario cambiar nuestros hábitos y forma de vida si deseamos asegurar nuestra supervivencia en la tierra.

Según una encuesta reciente, sólo la mitad de los norteamericanos saben que tenemos que importar petróleo para satisfacer las necesidades de nuestra sociedad actual. ¿Cuántas personas saben que aunque constituimos sólo el 6% (seis por ciento) de la población del mundo, consumimos cerca del 33% de la energía que la tierra suministra?

Además, tenemos que comprender que la mayoría de los problemas del hombre están íntimamente relacionados unos con otros. Como hemos visto, la crisis de la energía tiene facetas sociales además de las físicas y biológicas. Así como la sociedad está en evolución constante, la solución de la crisis de la energía tendrá que ser flexible y dinámica, para poder ajustarse a las necesidades del momento, las cuales nunca serán las mismas.

Básicamente, pues, la crisis de la energía, la conservación del medio ambiente y nuestro sistema educativo están ligados entre sí con lazos inseparables.[6]

---

[4] **al año,** *yearly, each year.*   [5] **la de instruirnos a todos,** *that of informing (advising) all of us.*   [6] **están . . . inseparables,** *(they) are bound together with inseparable ties.*

EJERCICIO

Usando como guía las preguntas siguientes, escriban un breve ensayo (de unas 175 palabras) sobre la crisis de la energía:

1. Al pensar en la crisis de la energía, ¿en qué reparamos generalmente?
2. ¿Qué vamos descubriendo respecto de los desperdicios de las acciones del hombre?
3. ¿Qué se van agotando irremediablemente?
4. ¿Qué otras formas de energía podemos utilizar?
5. ¿Por qué sería trágico pensar que la solución de la crisis consistiría sencillamente en la busca de nuevas fuentes de energía?
6. ¿Qué exigirá la solución de la crisis de la energía?
7. ¿Son importantes consumidores de energía los centros docentes de nuestro país?
8. Al enfrentarse con el problema de la energía, ¿cuál es la responsabilidad mayor de las escuelas y universidades?
9. ¿Qué otra responsabilidad esencial tienen los centros docentes?
10. ¿Por qué puede decirse que la solución de la crisis de la energía tendrá que ser flexible y dinámica?

Repaso de los adjetivos y pronombres demostrativos ▪ Los adjetivos posesivos ▪ Los pronombres posesivos ▪ Otros usos del subjuntivo ▪ Usos de los adjetivos como substantivos ▪ Los diminutivos

LECCIÓN DIEZ

Un regalo de cumpleaños excepcional

Como Ramón es aficionado a la música, sus padres le han dicho que quieren regalarle un equipo estereofónico para su cumpleaños. Acompañado de su amigo Tomás, Ramón entra en una tienda donde venden equipos estereofónicos. Se acerca un dependiente.

Dependiente. Buenos días, señores. ¿En qué puedo servirles?

Ramón. Me interesan los equipos estereofónicos que ustedes anuncian en el periódico. ¿Quiere enseñarme algunos, por favor?

Dependiente. Entren ustedes en el departamento a la izquierda, por favor. Allí pueden comparar las distintas marcas que recomendamos. (*Entran en el departamento y el dependiente pone un disco en el plato de uno de los equipos.*)

Ramón. Este equipo tiene precio especial, ¿verdad?

Dependiente. Sí, hoy lo damos en ciento sesenta dólares. Comprando los componentes por separado, el precio sería mucho más elevado.

Ramón. (*Dirigiéndose a Tomás.*) El tono es maravilloso. Me recuerda el tuyo.

Tomás. (*Al dependiente.*) Nos gustaría comparar varias marcas. ¿Podríamos escuchar aquel equipo, por favor?

Dependiente. ¡Cómo no! (*Pone un disco y lo escuchan un rato.*)

Ramón. No me gusta tanto como el otro.

Tomás. Ni a mí tampoco.[1]

---

[1]**Ni a mí tampoco,** *Neither do I.* Remember that the prepositional form must be used when the verb (**gustar** here) is understood.

Escaparates de una tienda en que se venden discos y equipos de sonido en Bogotá, Colombia.

Dependiente.	Como ustedes pueden ver, tenemos equipos de muchas marcas. (*Señalando otro*) El receptor y la bocina de éste son de mejor calidad. El volumen y los tonos graves y agudos pueden ajustarse tanto para la música popular como para la clásica. Voy a poner un disco.
Tomás.	(*A Ramón.*) Los receptores de esa marca son excelentes. Un amigo mío tiene uno y está encantado con él.
Ramón.	(*Al dependiente, después de escuchar unos momentos.*) Este último me parece el mejor. ¿Cuánto cuesta?
Dependiente.	Trescientos ochenta dólares.
Ramón.	¡Dios mío!
Dependiente.	A ese precio es una ganga.
Ramón.	Tal vez tenga usted razón; pero antes de decidirme quisiera consultarlo con mis padres. ¡Ojalá me lo regalen!
Dependiente.	Como usted quiera,[1] pero no debiera esperar mucho. Es un equipo muy popular.

Preparen un diálogo original, de unas doce líneas, para recitar en clase, empleando las frases y preguntas siguientes como elemento inicial:

1. *Luisa.* Pienso comprar bombillas de menor vatiaje para nuestro cuarto cuando vaya al centro esta tarde, Elena.

   Elena. Como estudiamos mucho de noche, no sé si debiéramos cambiar todas las bombillas.

2. *Tomás.* ¿Consultaste a tus padres sobre el equipo estereofónico que nos enseñaron esta tarde, Ramón?

   Ramón. Sí. Me dicen que compre el que me guste, con tal que sea de buena calidad.

---

[1] Note the use of the subjunctive here after the conjunction **como,** *as,* expressing indefiniteness.

PRONUNCIACIÓN

Review the observations on Spanish intonation (Repaso tres, pages 24–25, Lección dos, page 53, and Lección ocho, pages 160–161); then read the first four exchanges of the dialogue of this lesson, paying close attention to the intonation patterns.

NOTAS GRAMATICALES

1 Repaso de los adjetivos y pronombres demostrativos

A. A demonstrative adjective agrees in gender and number with the noun it modifies, and, in Spanish, is repeated before nouns in a series. **Este** points out persons or things near the speaker; **ese,** persons or things near to, or associated with, the person addressed; **aquel,** persons or things distant from the speaker or person addressed, or unrelated to either. (Do not confuse the demonstrative, which points out the noun to which it refers, with the relative pronoun **que,** *that, which, who, whom.*)

	Singular			Plural	
Masculine	*Feminine*		*Masculine*	*Feminine*	
este	**esta**	this	**estos**	**estas**	these
ese	**esa**	that (*nearby*)	**esos**	**esas**	those (*nearby*)
aquel	**aquella**	that (*distant*)	**aquellos**	**aquellas**	those (*distant*)

este hombre y esta mujer   this man and woman
esos discos que están cerca de Ud.   those records that are near you
aquella joven que está allí   that young lady who is there (*distant*)

B. The demonstrative pronouns are formed by placing an accent on the stressed syllable of the adjectives: **éste, ése, aquél,** etc. The use of the pronouns corresponds to that of the adjectives, except that singular forms often mean *this (one), that (one).* They may be used as subject or object of the verb, or they may stand alone.

There are three neuter pronouns (**esto,** *this,* **eso,** *that,* **aquello,** *that*) which are used when the antecedent is a statement, a general idea, or something which has not been identified. Since there are no neuter adjectives, an accent is not required on these three forms:

Me gustan ese equipo y éste.   I like that (stereo) system and this one.
¿Quiere Ud. que yo ponga éste o ése?   Do you want me to turn on this one or that one?

Este modelo y aquéllos son nuevos.   This model and those (*yonder*) are new.

¿Cuál de las marcas prefieres? ¿Ésta?   Which one of the brands do you prefer? This one?

¿Qué es esto?   What is this?

Eso no es muy interesante.   That isn't very interesting.

C. The demonstrative pronoun **éste** is used to indicate *the latter* (that is, the nearer), and **aquél,** *the former.* Contrary to English usage, in Spanish, when both are used, *the latter* always comes first:

Ana y Marta no vienen porque ésta no se siente bien.   Ann and Martha aren't coming because the latter doesn't feel well.

Ricardo y su hermana van de compras; ésta busca un radio y aquél, un tocadiscos.   Richard and his sister go shopping; the former is looking for a record player and the latter, a radio.

D. We found in Lección ocho that the Spanish definite article replaces the demonstrative before **que.** Similarly, it replaces the demonstrative before **de. El (la, los, las) de** means *that (those) of, the one(s) of (with, in)*; sometimes in English this construction is expressed by a possessive (first two examples):

mi radio y el de Felipe   my radio and Philip's (that of Philip)

estos discos y los de Ana   these records and Ann's (those of Ann)

las del pelo rubio   the ones (girls) with (the) blond hair

la del sombrero rojo   the one (girl) with (in) the red hat

The neuter article **lo** followed by **de** means *that (matter, affair) of:*

Lo de su amigo me interesa.   That (affair) of your friend interests me (I am interested in . . .).

EJERCICIOS

A. Para contestar afirmativamente, empleando el pronombre demostrativo correspondiente.

MODELOS: ¿Quiere Ud. este equipo?   Sí, quiero ése.
           ¿Es buena esta marca?   Sí, ésa es buena.

1. ¿Le gusta a Ud. este radio?
2. ¿Le interesan a Ud. estos receptores?
3. ¿Tiene buen tono esa marca?
4. ¿Podríamos mirar aquel televisor?
5. ¿Son caras esas cámaras?
6. ¿Son de buena calidad esas bocinas?
7. ¿Prefieres oír aquel tocadiscos?
8. ¿Escogerá Ud. esa maleta?

B. Para expresar en español:

1. This record and that one (*distant*) are new. 2. Those (*nearby*) stereo sets and these have a marvelous tone. 3. I prefer this small one (*m.*) to that one (*nearby*). 4. Shall I turn on this stereo set or that one (*distant*)? 5. Here are (**Aquí tiene Ud.**) two brands; this one has a small speaker, and that one (*nearby*), a larger one. 6. The clerk says it is a bargain, but I do not believe that. 7. John and Mary entered the store; the latter was looking for a television set. 8. Jane's dress and Helen's are very pretty. 9. Who is that (*distant*) boy, the one with red hair? 10. That girl (*distant*) and the one in the green hat are cousins of Paul.

2 Los adjetivos posesivos

Possessive adjectives agree in gender and number with the thing possessed (that is, with the noun modified), not with the possessor, as in English. The short, or unstressed, forms precede the nouns, and they are repeated before nouns in a series in Spanish:

Singular	*Plural*	
mi	mis	my
tu	tus	your (*fam.*)
su	sus	his, her, its, your (*formal*)
nuestro, -a	nuestros, -as	our
vuestro, -a	vuestros, -as	your (*fam.*)
su	sus	their, your

The long, or stressed, forms follow the noun. They are used for clearness and emphasis, after the verb **ser,** to translate *of mine, of his,* etc., in direct address, and in a few set phrases. These forms are:

Singular	*Plural*	
mío, mía	míos, mías	my, (of) mine
tuyo, tuya	tuyos, tuyas	your (*fam.*), (of) yours
suyo, suya	suyos, suyas	his, her, your (*formal*), its, (of) his, (of) hers, (of) yours, (of) its
nuestro, nuestra	nuestros, nuestras	our, (of) ours
vuestro, vuestra	vuestros, vuestras	your (*fam. pl.*), (of) yours
suyo, suya	suyos, suyas	their, your (*pl.*), (of) theirs, (of) yours

¿Traes tu cámara?   Are you bringing your camera?

Carlos, ¿son suyas estas cosas?   Charles, are these things yours?

Estos lápices son míos y ésos son tuyos.   These pencils are mine and those are yours.

Se han mudado de la casa suya al apartamento nuestro.   They have moved from their house to our apartment.

Ana tiene dos cintas mías.   Ann has two tapes of mine.

Diana y una amiga suya vienen pronto.   Diane and a friend of hers are coming soon.

Los dos jóvenes son buenos amigos míos (nuestros).   The two young men are good friends of mine (ours).

Querida (amiga) mía: My dear (friend):

¡Dios mío!   Heavens!

Since **su(s)** and **suyo (-a, -os, -as)** have several meanings, the forms **de él, de ella,** etc., may be substituted to make the meaning clear. (The prepositional form is not used for any long possessive other than **suyo, -a, -os, -as.**)

Me gusta su casa nueva.   I like his (her, your, their) new house.

Me gusta la casa de él (de ella, de usted).   I like his (her, your) house.

—¿Es de ellos este coche? —No, es de él.   "Is this car theirs?" "No, it is his."

EJERCICIOS

A. Repitan cada frase; luego, repítanla otra vez empleando una frase con una forma de **suyo,** según el modelo.

MODELO: Ramón y una amiga *de él*   Ramón y una amiga de él
                                        Ramón y una amiga suya

1. este equipo *de él*
2. ese radio *de ella*
3. aquellas cintas *de ellos*
4. esos discos *de usted*
5. aquel tocadiscos *de ellos*
6. esta cámara *de él*
7. esas películas *de ustedes*
8. varias fotografías *de ella*

B. Para contestar afirmativamente, según los modelos.

MODELOS: ¿Es nuestra esta cámara?   Sí, es nuestra (*or* es suya).
           ¿Son míos esos libros?   Sí, son suyos.
           ¿Son suyas esas compras?   Sí, son mías.

1. ¿Es nuestro aquel disco?
2. ¿Son míos estos dos folletos?
3. ¿Son suyas estas transparencias?
4. ¿Es suya esta bicicleta?
5. ¿Es nuestra aquella guitarra?
6. ¿Son nuestros aquellos cuadros?
7. ¿Es tuyo ese televisor?
8. ¿Son mías esas revistas?

3 Los pronombres posesivos

The possessive pronouns are formed by using the definite article with the long forms of the possessive adjectives. Remember that after **ser** the article is usually omitted:

el mío; la mía; los míos; las mías	mine
el tuyo; la tuya; los tuyos; las tuyas	yours (*fam.*)
el suyo; la suya; los suyos; las suyas	his, hers, its, yours (*formal*)
el nuestro; la nuestra; los nuestros; las nuestras	ours
el vuestro; la vuestra; los vuestros; las vuestras	yours (*fam.*)
el suyo; la suya; los suyos; las suyas	theirs, yours

mi radio; el mío, el nuestro my radio; mine, ours
nuestra casa; la mía, la nuestra our house; mine, ours
Ana, yo tengo los libros míos y los tuyos. Ann, I have *my* books and yours.
Señor López, ¿tiene usted los suyos? Mr. López, do you have yours?
Juan tiene la pluma suya y las mías. John has *his* pen and mine.

Since **el suyo (la suya, los suyos, las suyas)** may mean *his, hers, its, yours* (formal), *theirs*, these pronouns may be clarified by using **el (la) de él, el (la) de ella,** etc. The article agrees with the thing possessed:

Carlos mira el suyo. Charles looks at his (hers, yours, theirs).
El coche de ellos y el de ustedes están aquí. Their car and yours are here.
Nuestros padres y los de ella vienen. Our parents and hers are coming.

EJERCICIOS

A. Repitan cada frase; luego, repítanla otra vez, substituyendo el substantivo con el pronombre posesivo, o con la frase **el (la) de él (de ella,** etc.).

MODELOS: Él trae *su equipaje.*   Él trae su equipaje. Él trae el suyo.
   Tengo la *maleta de Juan.*   Tengo la maleta de Juan. Tengo la de él.

1. La hermana de Ana tiene *su blusa.*
2. Pablo y yo vamos a *nuestra casa.*
3. ¿Tiene ella *su pulsera?*
4. Pablo lleva *mis cámaras.*
5. El *jardín de mi mamá* es bonito.
6. Las *flores de Inés* son hermosas.
7. ¿Quieres ver *nuestras transparencias?*
8. Juan, no conduzcas *tu coche* hoy.

B. Para contestar afirmativamente, según los modelos.

MODELOS: ¿Tienes *tu cámara?*   Sí, tengo la mía.
            ¿Quieren ellos *sus fotos?* Sí, quieren las suyas.

1. ¿Ve Ud. *su coche?*
2. ¿Escuchan Uds. *su tocadiscos?*
3. ¿Traen Uds. *sus composiciones?*
4. ¿Buscas *tus guantes?*

5. ¿Mira Ana *su televisor?*
6. ¿Tiene Carlos *sus compras?*
7. ¿Desean ellas *sus regalos?*
8. ¿Lleva él *su maleta?*

C. Para expresar en español:

1. I want you (*formal sing.*) to bring your camera and mine. 2. Tell (*formal*) them to take their slides and yours to the meeting. 3. John doubts that his sister and mine will go to the movie. 4. Wait (*formal sing.*) a moment in order that I may give you her composition and his. 5. Let (*formal sing.*) me bring my small radio and hers tomorrow morning. 6. Whose records are these? Do you (*fam. sing.*) have mine?

4   Otros usos del subjuntivo

Uses of the subjunctive as the main verb in a sentence, other than in formal commands and in negative familiar commands (see Repaso tres, pages 29–31), are:

A. After **tal vez** and **quizá(s),** and less commonly **acaso,** all meaning *perhaps,* when doubt or uncertainty is implied:

Quizás él ha llegado.   Perhaps he has arrived. (*Certainty implied*)
Tal vez tenga Ud. razón.   Perhaps you may be right. (*Uncertainty implied*)

B. To make a statement or question milder or more polite (sometimes called a softened statement or question), the **-ra** imperfect subjunctive forms of **deber, querer,** and sometimes **poder,** are used:

Debo ayudar a mi mamá.   I must (ought to) help my mother. (*Strong obligation*)
Yo debiera llamarla.   I should call her. (*Milder obligation*)
Quiero ir al cine.   I want to go to the movie. (*Strong wish*)
Yo quisiera ir contigo.   I should like to go with you. (*More polite*)
¿Pudieras esperar un momento?   Could you wait a moment? (*Polite question*)

NOTE: Remember that the conditional of **gustar** also means *should (would) like* and may be used instead of **quisiera,** etc.: **Nos (Me) gustaría compararlos,** *We (I) should like to compare them.*

C. After **¡Ojalá!**, with or without **que,** *Would that! I wish that!* the present subjunctive is used in an exclamatory wish which refers to something which may happen in the future. The imperfect subjunctive is used to express a wish concerning something that is contrary to fact in the present, and the pluperfect subjunctive to express a wish concerning something that was contrary to fact in the past:

¡Ojalá (que) me lo regalen!   Would that they give it to me!
¡Ojalá que supiesen eso!   Would that they knew that!
¡Ojalá hubieran vuelto antes!   (How) I wish they had returned before!

When used alone, **¡Ojalá!** means *God grant it! I hope so!*

—**¿Viene Juan mañana?** —**¡Ojalá!**   "Is John coming tomorrow?" "I hope so!"

EJERCICIOS

A. Para contestar negativamente, agregando una frase introducida por **pero quisiera,** y substituyendo el objeto del verbo con el pronombre correspondiente.

MODELO: ¿Has oído el radio de él?   No, pero quisiera oírlo.

1. ¿Has llamado a tu hermana?
2. ¿Has comprado el televisor?
3. ¿Has oído mis discos?
4. ¿Has escuchado aquel equipo?

B. Para cambiar al imperfecto de subjuntivo, según los modelos.

MODELOS: Quiero usar la cámara.   Yo quisiera usar la cámara.
Quiero que tú saques la foto.   Yo quisiera que tú sacaras la foto.
Debo llamar a Carolina.   Yo debiera llamar a Carolina.

1. Quiero enseñarle este modelo ahora.
2. Queremos escuchar éste.
3. Quieren comprar el equipo grande.
4. ¿Quieres que yo ponga ése?
5. Queremos que Uds. oigan aquél.
6. Debo consultar eso con mi padre.
7. Debemos ayudar a Carlos.
8. No deben esperar mucho.

C. Para contestar con una oración introducida por **tal vez (quizás).**

MODELO: ¿Volverán ellos esta noche?   Tal vez (Quizás) vuelvan esta noche.

1. ¿Saldrá Juan mañana?
2. ¿Encontrarán una ganga allí?
3. ¿Les interesará el tocadiscos?
4. ¿Escogerán otra marca?

D. Para cambiar al presente de subjuntivo después de ¡Ojalá que!

MODELO: ¿Leerán la novela?   ¡Ojalá que lean la novela!

1. ¿Llegarán esta noche?   3. ¿Se divertirán en la fiesta?
2. ¿Podrá ella vistarnos?   4. ¿Buscará él otra casa?

Para cambiar al imperfecto y al pluscuamperfecto de subjuntivo después de ¡Ojalá que!, siguiendo los modelos.

MODELOS: No creen lo que él dijo.   ¡Ojalá que creyeran lo que él dijo!
            No han llegado a tiempo.   ¡Ojalá que hubieran llegado a tiempo!

5. No están en casa.   8. No van a Los Ángeles.
6. Ella no sabe la canción.   9. No han vuelto del viaje.
7. No pueden pasar por aquí.   10. Él no ha oído el equipo.

5 Usos de los adjetivos como substantivos

Many adjectives may be used with the definite article, demonstratives, numerals, and other limiting adjectives to form nouns. In this case the adjective agrees in gender and number with the noun understood. Remember that adjectives of nationality are also used as nouns: **Luis es mexicano,** *Louis is (a) Mexican.*

Este último me parece el mejor.   This last one seems to me (to be) the best (one) (*m.*).
No me gusta tanto como el otro.   I don't like it so much as the other one (*m.*).
Me trajeron el más pequeño.   They brought me the smaller (smallest) one (*m.*).
Una joven compró las blancas.   A young lady bought the white ones (*f.*).

EJERCICIO

Repitan cada frase; luego, repítanla otra vez, empleando el adjetivo como substantivo.

MODELO: ¿Te gusta la blusa roja?   ¿Te gusta la blusa roja?
                                       ¿Te gusta la roja?

1. La casa amarilla es del señor Díaz. 2. Me gusta este televisor grande. 3. Quieren buscar una casa más grande. 4. Prefiero ver unos zapatos negros. 5. Esta última blusa es muy bonita. 6. ¿Les gusta la música clásica? 7. ¿Cuánto cuesta la otra marca? 8. Miramos varios equipos nuevos. 9. Yo quisiera escuchar algunos discos españoles. 10. ¿Qué les parece a Uds. este radio pequeño?

6 Los diminutivos

In Spanish, diminutive endings are often used to express not only small size but also affection, pity, scorn, ridicule, and the like. The most common endings are: -ito, -a; -illo, -a; -(e)cito, -a; -(e)cillo, -a. Frequently, the use of these suffixes with nouns precludes the need for adjectives. For the choice of ending, rely upon observation. A final vowel is often dropped before adding the ending:

hermana	sister	**hermanita**	little sister
hermano	brother	**hermanito**	little brother
Juan	John	**Juanito**	Johnny
pueblo	town	**pueblecito**	small town, village
señora	lady, woman	**señorita**	young lady (woman)
ventana	window	**ventanilla**	ticket window

Applied to baptismal names, these endings indicate affection, with no implication of size: **Juanita,** *Jane;* **Anita,**[1] *Annie;* **Tomasito,** *Tommy.* Sometimes a change in spelling is necessary to preserve the sound of a consonant when a final vowel is dropped: **Diego,** *James,* and **Dieguito,** *Jimmie.* Similarly, note the change in spelling in the adverb **poco,** *little* (quantity), and **poquito,** *very little;* also, in the noun **taza,** *cup,* and **tacita,** *small (tiny) cup.*

EJERCICIO

Give the base word to which each diminutive suffix has been added:

casita	small house, cottage	**mesita**	small table, stand
cosilla	small thing, trifle	**momentito**	(short) moment
florecita	small (tiny) flower	**mujercita**	pleasant little woman
golpecito	slight blow, tap	**pequeñito, -a**	very small, tiny
hijito	(dear) son	**piedrecita**	small stone, pebble
hombrecito	nice little man	**pobrecito**	poor boy (man, thing)
jovencito	nice young fellow	**regalito**	small gift

---

[1] The diminutives given in the rest of this section are not listed in the end vocabulary unless they are used elsewhere in this text. Watch for similar and other uses of diminutives in reading.

RESUMEN

A. Repitan la frase; luego, repítanla otra vez, siguiendo el modelo.

MODELO: ` mi casa y la casa de Ana   mi casa y la casa de Ana
mi casa y la de Ana

1. estos jardines y el jardín de mi madre 2. estas mujeres y la mujer del vestido amarillo 3. este edificio y el edificio de piedra 4. esta señorita y la señorita del pelo negro 5. este radio y el radio de mi hermano 6. aquellos discos y los discos de música popular 7. este lugar y el lugar que visitó él 8. estas dos marcas y la marca que nos ha enseñado Ud. 9. estos modelos y los modelos que él me enseñó 10. aquel equipo estereofónico y los equipos que oímos ayer

B. Para completar, empleando el pronombre posesivo correspondiente, según los modelos.

MODELOS: Éstas son *mis cintas*.   Estas cintas son mías.
Marta tiene *su radio*.   Luis tiene el suyo.

1. Éste es *nuestro disco*. Este disco es _____ .
2. Éstos son *mis discos*. Estos discos son _____ .
3. Ésa es *mi revista*. Esa revista es _____ .
4. Ésas son *sus transparencias*. Esas transparencias son _____ .
5. Aquélla es *nuestra guitarra*. Aquella guitarra es _____ .
6. Aquél es *tu televisor*. Aquel televisor es _____ .
7. Juan conduce *su coche*. Marta conduce _____ .
8. Ellos escuchan *su radio*. Ud. escucha _____ .
9. Nosotros llevamos *nuestras cámaras*. Ana lleva _____ .
10. Yo vivo en *mi casa*. Nosotros vivimos en _____ .

C. Otros usos del subjuntivo y usos de los adjetivos como substantivos. Para expresar en español:

1. I should like to buy the large stereo set, not the small one.
2. You (*formal sing.*) ought to listen to this radio and the other one.
3. Which one of the brands do you (*formal sing.*) like, this one or the other one?
4. Would that they give me a new stereo set for my birthday!
5. Perhaps you (*formal sing.*) may prefer small sets to larger ones.
6. Do you (*fam. sing.*) like this last one (*m.*) or the first one?
7. Would you (*fam. sing.*) like to take Mary the yellow roses or the red ones?
8. I wish that (Would that) I had had enough money to buy the white ones (*f.*)!

D. Usos de los adjetivos y pronombres posesivos. Para expresar en español:

1. This stereo set reminds me of yours (*fam. sing.*).
2. They listen to their radio, and we listen to ours.

3. "Is this camera ours?" "Yes, it is ours, not hers."
4. These slides are mine, and those (*distant*) are his.
5. Mary and a cousin (*f.*) of hers want to buy a birthday gift for a friend of theirs.
6. Heavens! I have brought your (*fam. sing.*) purse, not mine.
7. This composition is not mine. Is it yours (*formal sing.*) (*two ways*)?
8. These pamphlets are ours, and that one (*nearby*) is yours (*fam. sing.*).

Resumen de palabras y expresiones

a la izquierda to (on) the left
acompañado, -a accompanied by
agudo, -a high(-pitched) (*tone*)
ajustarse to be adjusted
antes *adv.* before
la **bocina** speaker
la **calidad** quality
clásico, -a classic
comparar to compare
el **componente** component
de noche at night
decidirse to decide, make a decision
¡Dios mío! heavens! for heaven's sake!
distinto, -a different
¿en qué puedo servirle (s)? what can I do for you?
el **equipo** set, system

esperar mucho to wait long
estereofónico, -a stereo(phonic)
la **ganga** bargain
grave deep, low (*tone*)
lo damos en we are selling (offering) it for (at)
la **marca** brand, make, kind
me interesan los equipos I am interested in the sets, the sets interest me
el **plato** turntable
por separado separately
el **receptor** receiver
recordar (ue) a uno to remind one of
el **regalo de cumpleaños** birthday gift
tanto . . . como as (so) much . . . as
el **tono** tone
el **volumen** volume

Lectura 10

La exploración del espacio exterior

Los avances tecnológicos de los últimos años han hecho posibles las exploraciones del espacio exterior. Desde el lanzamiento del primer satélite artificial por la Unión Soviética, en 1957, asistimos a una emocionante «carrera del espacio» entre las dos mayores potencias industriales del mundo. No se trata de una simple rivalidad de prestigio científico, sino de una serie de investigaciones del espacio que ofrece una gran diversidad de aspectos.

El hecho más sensacional de esta competencia internacional tuvo lugar[1] el 21 de julio de 1969, cuando el hombre desembarcó por primera vez[2] en un cuerpo celeste y pudo regresar sano y salvo[3] a la tierra. Corresponde a nuestro país, con el éxito del vuelo Apolo 11, la realización de tan gloriosa hazaña.[4] Televisado por una cámara colocada sobre el módulo lunar, el acontecimiento fue observado por los telespectadores de todo el mundo. Los astronautas no sólo pusieron el pie en la luna, sino que caminaron sobre su superficie, recogieron muestras del suelo lunar e instalaron el equipo científico para varios experimentos.

Se había cumplido el compromiso contraído por el presidente Kennedy, en 1961, de situar a un norteamericano en la luna y devolverlo a la tierra antes de terminar la década.[5]

---

[1]**tuvo lugar,** *took place.*   [2]**por primera vez,** *for the first time.*   [3]**sano y salvo,** *safe and sound.*   [4]**Corresponde . . . hazaña,** *With the success of the Apollo 11 flight, the achievement of such a glorious deed (feat) belongs to our country.*   [5]**antes de terminar la década,** *before the end of the decade.*

El vuelo abrió una nueva época en la conquista del espacio y sentó[6] las bases para la futura exploración de los planetas por astronaves tripuladas.

Durante los mismos años los límites de la exploración planetaria a base de astronaves automáticas fueron extendidos por vuelos dirigidos hacia. Venus y Marte. Vuelos soviéticos de la serie *Venus* lograron lanzar cápsulas con equipo científico sobre Venus; de los datos que transmitieron se deducen las condiciones adversas del planeta. Astronaves del programa *Mariner*, lanzadas por los Estados Unidos hacia Marte, también realizaron su misión con éxito, transmitiendo fotografías del planeta y datos sobre la atmósfera marciana.

Más recientemente se han realizado los vuelos del programa *Viking* (Estados Unidos), de astronaves automáticas capaces de aterrizar en Marte. Han tenido por misión la exploración de la superficie y también recoger muestras de su suelo para investigar si hay vida en dicho planeta. Se sigue estudiando el proyecto *Marte* para el desembarco del hombre en el planeta. Para llevarlo a cabo se piensa utilizar[7] una astronave tripulada, propulsada por energía nuclear. Este proyecto podría realizarse a finales de la década de los 80.

Es importante señalar que el avance tecnológico que se ha logrado en estos proyectos espaciales también ha tenido su aplicación práctica en los más diversos campos. Los servicios de telecomunicación y los meteorológicos, a base de los correspondientes sistemas de satélites, se desarrollan normalmente. Los satélites meteorológicos van equipados con cámaras avanzadas para almacenar imágenes del tiempo global, y también con cámaras de transmisión automática de imágenes para la lectura directa por las estaciones terrestres.

La capacidad y utilidad de los satélites automáticos parece casi ilimitada. Suministran datos útiles para la navegación tanto de navíos como de aviones. Pueden usarse en la busca de minerales o de petróleo, como también para dar a conocer[8] las condiciones de las cosechas y de los bosques, o el grado de contaminación de los lagos, ríos y costas. Continúa el lanzamiento en órbita de observatorios solares, para ampliar nuestro conocimiento de la estructura del sol y estudiar la influencia solar sobre la tierra.

Hay que señalar también el efecto de la nueva tecnología sobre la medicina, como, por ejemplo, la aplicación a los enfermos de sensores, aparatos y mecanismos desarrollados para el vuelo espacial; sobre la industria, en lo que se refiere a nuevos materiales y procesos de fabricación desarrollados en la construcción de vehículos espaciales; y sobre la organización industrial, por la aplicación a la industria en general de los nuevos métodos y sistemas de organización que la complejidad de la industria aeroespacial ha obligado a emplear.[9]

A pesar de todos los avances mencionados, puede decirse que la «Edad espacial» todavía está en su infancia. El hombre apenas está recogiendo los primeros frutos de los vuelos a la luna y la exploración del espacio exterior. Si el hombre puede trasladarse a otros cuerpos celestes y transportar a ellos los medios necesarios para sostener la vida, es claro que las energías y la creatividad humanas ya no están ligadas a la tierra.

---

[6] **sentó,** *set, established.*   [7] **se piensa utilizar,** *they plan to make use of.*   [8] **dar a conocer,** *to make known.*   [9] **ha obligado a emplear,** *has forced into use.*

La imaginación más activa queda abrumada[10] ante los posibles proyectos futuros, tales como la construcción de grandes estaciones espaciales, la explotación minera de los planetas, la busca de planetas que puedan sostener nuestras formas de vida y hasta el cambiar el ambiente natural de alguno[11] para hacerlo habitable. En suma,[12] puede afirmarse que la exploración y la explotación del espacio exterior presentan uno de los mayores desafíos a la capacidad de la especie humana para cooperar por el bien común de la humanidad.

EJERCICIO

Escriban diez preguntas sobre puntos tratados en esta Lectura para que las contesten los otros estudiantes de la clase.

---

[10] **queda abrumada,** *is overwhelmed.*   [11] **hasta . . . alguno,** *even (the) changing the natural environment of one* (= planet).   [12] **En suma,** *In short, In a word.*

Comparación de los adjetivos y de los adverbios ▪ Comparaciones de igualdad ▪ «Hacer» en expresiones de tiempo ▪ La traducción de *must* ▪ Formas de mandato correspondientes a «vosotros, -as»

LECCIÓN ONCE

El concurso de pintura

Elena y Luis van a participar en el concurso de pintura que la Universidad organiza todos los años. Sus amigos Carmen y Ramón entran en el salón del Centro de Estudiantes donde hay que entregar las obras. Los cuatro estudiantes han pasado un año en la Universidad de Madrid y emplean formas peninsulares.

Carmen. (*Impaciente.*) ¿Qué hora es, Ramón?

Ramón. Deben de ser las siete y cuarto.

Carmen. Según las bases del concurso, había que colocar las obras en el salón antes de las siete y media. ¿Qué les habrá pasado?

Ramón. Mira, por allí vienen.[1] (*Llegan Elena y Luis con varios cuadros debajo del brazo.*)

Elena. Hola, ¿qué tal? ¿Hace tiempo que nos esperáis?

Carmen. Llegamos hace media hora. ¡Creíamos que no llegaríais nunca!

Luis. Pues, nunca he visto tantos coches . . . Pero falta más de un cuarto de hora, ¿verdad?

Elena. ¿Habéis escogido un buen sitio para los cuadros? ¿Qué os parece aquel rincón?

---

[1]**por allí vienen,** *there they come.*

Salón del Museo Picasso en Barcelona, España.

Carmen. ¿No se verían mejor en esta pared?

Luis. Sí, es verdad. La pared está muy bien iluminada.

Ramón Pues, ¡adelante! Ayudadme con los cuadros. (*Cuelgan las obras en la pared.*)

Luis. Pues, gracias a todos, hemos tardado menos de lo que yo pensaba.

Carmen. Debe de haber menos interés este año. No hay más que unos treinta cuadros en el salón.

Luis. Pero la calidad parece superior. La tarea del jurado va a ser más difícil.

Ramón. ¿Cuándo se reúne el jurado para otorgar los premios?

Luis. Esta noche a las diez. Consta de tres pintores distinguidos. Se anunciarán los ganadores mañana al inaugurarse la exposición de las obras presentadas.[2]

Carmen. Me gusta muchísimo el cuadro de la fuente, con la biblioteca al fondo. ¿No creéis que merece uno de los premios?

Luis. Sí, es hermosísimo. Es de Elena. Al clausurarse la exposición, tendrá que vendérmelo.

Elena. Pues, te lo vas a llevar . . . Es un regalo mío.

Luis. Sería un regalo espléndido . . . ; pero fijaos en la hora. No os olvidéis de que el concierto comienza a las ocho.

Elena. Es verdad. Recoged los papeles y dejadlo todo en orden. Tenemos que salir lo más pronto posible.

Ramón. Sí. No queremos perder la composición de Chávez.

Luis. ¡Claro que no! Es el representante más ilustre de la música mexicana de nuestros días. ¡Vamónos!

---

[2]**al inaugurarse . . . presentadas,** *when the exhibition of the works that have been entered (presented) opens (is opened).*

Preguntas sobre el diálogo: 1. ¿Quiénes van a participar en el concurso de pintura? 2. ¿Quiénes entran en el salón donde se va a celebrar el concurso? 3. ¿Dónde han estudiado durante un año los cuatro estudiantes? 4. ¿Por qué está impaciente Carmen? 5. ¿A qué hora llegan al salón Luis y Elena? 6. ¿Tardan mucho en colocar los cuadros? 7. ¿Por qué dice Luis que la tarea del jurado será más difícil que la del jurado del año pasado? 8. ¿Cuándo se reunirá el jurado para otorgar los premios? 9. ¿Qué dice Luis de uno de los cuadros de Elena? 10. ¿Por qué tienen que salir lo más pronto posible?

Preguntas para conversar: 1. ¿Se interesa Ud. o algún amigo suyo en la pintura? 2. ¿Sabe Ud. si se han organizado concursos de pintura en esta universidad? 3. ¿Tiene Ud. cuadros en su cuarto? ¿Qué representan? 4. ¿Piensa Ud. participar en algún concurso este año? 5. ¿Qué premios ha ganado Ud.? 6. ¿Cuántos cursos de música ha tomado Ud.? 7. ¿Pone o quita Ud. el radio cuando comienza a estudiar? 8. ¿Sabe Ud. si esta universidad tiene una orquesta sinfónica? 9. ¿Prefiere la mayor parte de los estudiantes la música sinfónica o la música popular? 10. ¿Se presentan conciertos de música popular en el teatro universitario?

NOTAS GRAMATICALES

1 Comparación de los adjetivos y de los adverbios

A. When one makes unequal comparisons in English, one says, for example, *tall, taller, tallest; expensive, more (less) expensive, most (least) expensive.* In Spanish, place **más,** *more, most,* or **menos,** *less, least,* before the adjective. The definite article is used when *the* is a part of the meaning, and the adjective must agree with the noun in gender and number: **el más alto, la más alta, los más altos, las más altas.** Sometimes the possessive adjective (**mi, tu,** etc.) replaces the definite article.

One can tell from the context when an adjective in Spanish has comparative or superlative force, that is, whether **más** means *more* or *most* and whether **menos** means *less* or *least.* Even though an adjective modified by **más** or **menos** usually follows the noun, in reading you will note exceptions to this practice (also see Lección cinco, pages 126–127). After a superlative, *in* is translated by **de.** *Than* is translated by **que** before a noun or pronoun. After **que,** *than,* the negatives **nadie, nunca, nada, ninguno, -a,** replace **alguien, siempre, algo, alguno, -a,** respectively:

La tarea va a ser más difícil.   The task is going to be more difficult.
Es un compositor más moderno que los otros.   He is a more modern composer than the others.
Es el representante más ilustre de la música mexicana de nuestros días.   He is the most famous representative of Mexican music in our time.
Ella habla más que nunca (nadie).   She talks more than ever (anyone).

Than is translated by **de** before a numeral or numerical expression in an affirmative sentence; if the sentence is negative, either **que** or **de** may be used, the preference being for **que.** Theoretically, **no . . . más que** means *only* and **no . . . más de** means *not . . . more than:*

Falta más de un cuarto de hora.   More than a quarter of an hour is left (remains).
No necesito más que cinco dólares.   I need only five dollars.
No necesito más de cinco dólares.   I do not need more than five dollars. (*Five at the most*)

When *than* is followed by an inflected verb form, it is expressed by **de** + the definite article + **que,** that is, by **del que, de la que, de los que, de las que,** really meaning *than the one(s) who (which, that),* if the point of comparison is a noun which is the object of the first verb and is elliptically omitted in the second member:

Él tiene más flores de las que vende.   He has more flowers than he sells.
Hace más frío hoy del que hizo ayer.   It is colder today that it was yesterday.
Yo escribo más cartas de las que recibo.   I write more letters than I receive.

When *than* is followed by an inflected verb form, but the second member is elliptical in such a way that the verb of the first member must be repeated in order to complete the idea, **que** is replaced by **de lo que.** (In such sentences the verb which follows **de lo que** often expresses a mental state.)

Diana es más bonita de lo que crees.   Diane is prettier than (what) you believe (she is).
Hemos tardado menos (tiempo) de lo que yo pensaba.   We have taken less time than I thought (we would take).
La exposición es más interesante de lo que yo esperaba.   The exhibition is more interesting than I expected (it to be).

B. The comparative of adverbs is also regularly formed by placing **más** or **menos** before the adverb. The article is not used in the superlative, except that the neuter form **lo** is used when an expression of possibility follows:

Los autobuses pasan más rápidamente que nunca.   The buses pass more rapidly (faster) than ever.
Tenemos que salir lo más pronto posible.   We must (have to) leave the soonest possible (as soon as possible).

C. Six adjectives and four adverbs, most of which have already been used in this text, are compared irregularly:

Adjectives	
bueno good	**(el) mejor** (the) better, best
malo bad	**(el) peor** (the) worse, worst
grande large	{ **(el) más grande** (the) larger, largest
	{ **(el) mayor** (the) greater, older, greatest, oldest
pequeño small	{ **(el) más pequeño** (the) smaller, smallest
	{ **(el) menor** (the) smaller, younger, smallest, youngest
mucho(s) much (many)	**más** more, most
poco(s) little (few)	**menos** less, fewer

Mejor and **peor** precede the noun, just as **bueno, -a,** and **malo, -a,** regularly precede it, except when emphasized. Used with the definite article, the forms are:

el mejor (peor)   **los mejores (peores)**
la mejor (peor)   **las mejores (peores)**

Se otorgarán premios para las mejores pinturas.   Prizes will be awarded for the best paintings.
Debe de haber menos interés este año.   There must be (probably is) less interest this year.

Grande and **pequeño, -a,** have regular forms which refer to size, while the irregular forms **mayor** (*m.* and *f.*) and **menor** (*m.* and *f.*) usually refer to persons and mean *older* and *younger,* respectively:

Estos cuadros son más grandes que ésos.   These pictures are larger than those.
Mi hermano mayor ha colocado su obra en el salón.   My older brother has placed his work in the lounge.
Most (of), The greater part of, is translated by **La mayor parte de;** the verb normally agrees with the noun following this expression: **La mayor parte de los estudiantes van a los conciertos,** *Most (of the) students go to the concerts.*

Adverbs	
bien well	**mejor** better, best
mal bad, badly	**peor** worse, worst
mucho much	**más** more, most
poco little	**menos** less, least

La exposición ha sido menos interesante este año.   The exhibition has been less interesting this year.
¿No se verían mejor en esta pared?   Wouldn't they be seen better on this wall?

D. A high degree of quality, without any element of comparison (sometimes called the absolute superlative), is expressed by the use of **muy** before the adjective or adverb, or by adding the ending **-ísimo (-a, -os, -as)** to the adjective. When **-ísimo** is added, a final vowel is dropped. **Muchísimo,** rather than **muy mucho,** is used for the adjective or adverb *very much (many)*:

> **Elena es muy hermosa (hermosísima).**   Helen is very beautiful.
> **Éste es un sitio lindísimo.**   This is a very pretty place.
> **Me gusta muchísimo el cuadro.**   I like the picture very much.

EJERCICIOS

A. Completen las frases con la forma comparativa del adjetivo o del adverbio.

MODELO: Este concierto es bueno,   Este concierto es bueno,
pero el otro fue _____ .   pero el otro fue mejor.

1. Este edificio es grande, pero aquél es _____ . 2. Esta música popular es buena, pero la clásica es _____ . 3. Esta obra es larga, pero la última fue _____ . 4. Aquella casa blanca es pequeña, pero la amarilla es _____ . 5. Aquellas calles son cortas, pero ésta es _____ . 6. Yo estoy cansado, pero mi mamá está _____ . 7. José tiene dos años más que Pablo; éste es el _____ . 8. Marta tiene un año menos que Ana; aquélla es la _____ . 9. Carolina toca bien, pero su hermana toca _____ . 10. Juan baila mal, pero Miguel baila _____ . 11. A mí me interesa mucho la pintura, pero a él le interesa _____ . 12. Ellos tienen poco tiempo, pero yo tengo _____ .

B. Para contestar afirmativamente, siguiendo los modelos.

MODELOS: ¿Es grande el parque?   Sí, es más grande que éste.
¿Son difíciles las frases?   Sí, son más difíciles que éstas.

1. ¿Son hermosas las flores?   4. ¿Es mala la novela?
2. ¿Es larga la carretera?   5. ¿Está contenta la muchacha?
3. ¿Es bueno el cuadro?   6. ¿Es popular la música?

MODELO: ¿Es bonita la casa?   Sí, es la casa más bonita de todas.

7. ¿Es grande el cuadro?   9. ¿Es ilustre el pintor?
8. ¿Es bonita la fuente?   10. ¿Es interesante la obra?

MODELO: ¿Es hermosa Carolina?   Sí, es muy hermosa; es hermosísima.

11. ¿Son altos los árboles?   13. ¿Son famosas las obras?
12. ¿Es guapo su novio?   14. ¿Es valioso el premio?

C. Lean en español, supliendo la palabra o frase equivalente a *than*:

1. Creo que hay más _____ mil estudiantes en el teatro. 2. Este concierto es mejor _____ el último. 3. Hay más fuentes en México _____ tenemos en este

país. 4. Pablo tiene más amigos en la ciudad _____ tú crees. 5. Marta ha escrito más composiciones _____ me imaginaba. 6. Hoy ella tocará más números _____ tocó la semana pasada. 7. Esta música es más popular _____ yo esperaba. 8. No te olvides de que este compositor es más moderno _____ el otro.

2 Comparaciones de igualdad (*equality*)

Tan + an adjective or adverb + **como** means *as (so) . . . as*. **Tan** used without **como** means *so*, sometimes *as*:

> **Este cuadro es tan lindo como ése.**   This picture is as pretty as that one.
> **¿Por qué está ella tan contenta?**   Why is she so happy?

Before an adjective **tan** is used instead of **tal** to mean *such (a)*:

> **¡Es una exposición tan excelente!**   It is such an excellent exhibition!
> **Nunca he colgado obras tan interesantes.**   I have never hung such interesting works.

> BUT: **¿Has visto jamás tal cosa?**   Have you ever seen such a thing?

Tanto, -a, (-os, -as) + a noun + **como** means *as (so) much (many) . . . as*. **Tanto** is also used as a pronoun or adverb, with or without **como,** meaning *as (so) much (many) (. . . as)*:

> **No hay tantas exposiciones como antes.**   There aren't so many exhibitions as before.
> **Nunca he visto tantos coches.**   I have never seen so many cars.
> **Dígales Ud. a los estudiantes que no estudien tanto.**   Tell the students not to study so much.
> **Nos gusta la segunda pintura tanto como la primera.**   We like the second picture as much as the first.

EJERCICIOS

A. Repitan cada oración; luego, al oír un substantivo o un adjetivo, substitúyanlo en la oración original, haciendo los cambios necesarios:

1. Esta casa no es tan *vieja* como aquélla.
   (*nuevo, pequeño, grande, cómodo, bonito*)
2. Este año no hay tantos *concursos* como antes.
   (*pinturas, cuadros, estudiantes, obras, exposiciones*)
3. Ella recibe muchas *revistas,* pero yo no recibo *tantas.*
   (*periódicos, dinero, cartas, invitaciones, regalos*)

B. Oirán una frase y luego una o más palabras. Formen una frase nueva empleando **tan . . . como,** según el modelo.

MODELO: Luis está ocupado. (Carlos)   Luis está tan ocupado como Carlos.

1. La fuente es muy hermosa. (la otra)
2. Las composiciones son magníficas. (las de Chávez)
3. Esta exposición es espléndida. (la de obras mexicanas)
4. Las estudiantes estaban contentas. (la profesora)
5. El primer concierto fue maravilloso. (el segundo)
6. Estos cuadros son excelentes. (los que están en el salón)

Formen frases nuevas empleando **no . . . tanto, -a (-os, -as) . . . como,** según el modelo.

MODELO: Yo toco muchos discos.   Yo no toco tantos discos como Luisa.

7. Ramón cuelga muchas pinturas.
8. Elena lleva varios cuadros debajo del brazo.
9. Carmen pasa mucho tiempo organizando el concurso.
10. Marta ha colocado muchas obras en el salón.
11. El joven ha ganado muchos premios.
12. Nosotros hemos asistido a muchas exposiciones.

3   «Hacer» en expresiones de tiempo

A. In Spanish, **hace** followed by a period of time (**minuto, hora, día, mes,** etc.) plus **que** and a verb in the present tense, or a present tense plus **desde hace** followed by a period of time, indicates that an action began in the past and that it is still going on in the present. When **desde hace** is used, the word order in Spanish is the same as in English. Note that in English the present perfect tense is used:

Hace una hora que estoy aquí *or* **Estoy aquí desde hace una hora.**   I have been here for an hour (*lit.,* It makes an hour that I am here).

¿Cuánto tiempo hace que trabajan aquí?   How long have they been working (*lit.,* How long does it make that they work) here?

Hace varios días que Ricardo busca un radio.   Richard has been looking for a radio for several days (For several days Richard has been looking for a radio).

¿Hace tiempo que nos esperáis?   Have you been waiting for us long (a long time)?

Hace mucho tiempo que no te veo.   I haven't seen you for a long time (It is a long time since I have seen you).

Hacía followed by a period of time plus **que** and a verb in the imperfect tense, or the imperfect tense plus **desde hacía** followed by a period of time, indicates that an action had been going on for a certain length of time and was still continuing when something else happened. The pluperfect tense is used in English:

> **Hacía un mes que yo vivía allí cuando la conocí** or **Yo vivía allí desde hacía un mes cuando la conocí.**   I had been living there (for) a month when I met her (*lit.*, It made a month that I was living there . . .).
>
> **Hacía tiempo que (yo) no os veía.**   I had not seen you for a long time.

NOTE: If the verb of the main clause is negative, the present perfect and pluperfect tenses may be used, as in English. The following alternate constructions, then, are often used: **Hace tiempo que no te he visto, Hacía tiempo que yo no os había visto.**

B. When **hace** is followed by a period of time after a verb in a past tense, it regularly means *ago, since*. If the **hace**-clause comes first in the sentence, **que** usually (although not always) introduces the main clause:

> **Llegamos hace media hora** or **Hace media hora que llegamos.**   We arrived a half hour ago or It is a half hour since we arrived.
>
> **Nos vimos hace dos semanas.**   We saw each other two weeks ago.

EJERCICIOS

A. Después de oír una oración, oirán una expresión de tiempo; combinen los dos elementos en una nueva oración, siguiendo el modelo.

MODELO: Miro la televisión.   Hace una hora que miro la televisión.
            (Hace una hora)

1. Están en México. (Hace tres semanas)
2. Estudio español. (Hace más de un año)
3. Estamos en el salón. (Hace una hora y media)
4. No te veo en la biblioteca. (Hace tiempo) (*two ways*)
5. No vamos al teatro. (Hace un mes) (*two ways*)
6. Estoy esperando a Marta. (Hace quince minutos)

B. Después de oír una pregunta, oirán una expresión de tiempo; úsenla para contestar la pregunta, según los modelos.

MODELO: ¿Cuánto tiempo hace que lees?   Leo desde hace una hora.
            (una hora)

1. ¿Cuánto tiempo hace que vives aquí? (seis meses)
2. ¿Cuánto tiempo hace que conoce Ud. a María? (un mes y medio)
3. ¿Cuánto tiempo hace que tocas la guitarra? (cuatro años)
4. ¿Cuánto tiempo hace que ella habla por teléfono? (veinte minutos)

MODELO: ¿Cuándo salió ella?   Ella salió hace media hora.
           (hace media hora)   Hace media hora que ella
                                  salió.

5. ¿Cuándo escogiste el sitio? (hace tiempo)
6. ¿Cuándo fueron Uds. a la exposición? (hace varios días)
7. ¿Cuándo organizaron el concurso? (hace un mes)
8. ¿Cuándo viste a Carlota? (hace una semana)
9. ¿Cuándo colgaron las pinturas? (hace treinta minutos)
10. ¿Cuándo llegaste al salón? (hace un cuarto de hora)

C. Para expresar en español:

1. The students organized the painting competition six months ago. 2. Carmen and Raymond entered the lounge of the Student Center almost a half hour ago. 3. When Helen and Louis arrived, they asked: "Have you (*fam. pl.*) been waiting for us (for) a long time?" 4. "Yes," answered Raymond, "we have been here for more than twenty minutes." 5. He also said that they began to hang the pictures a few moments before. 6. The University has been holding an exhibition of paintings for many years.

4   La traducción de *must*

When *must* = *to have to*, expressing a strong obligation or necessity, **tener que** + an infinitive is used. The impersonal form is **hay (había, habrá**, etc.) **que** + an infinitive:

Ellos tienen que esperar.   They must (have to) wait.
Hay que hacer eso.   One must (It is necessary to) do that.

When *must* = *is (was) to, is (was) supposed to*, expressing a mild obligation or commitment, **haber de** + an infinitive is used:

Hemos de reunirnos esta noche.   We must (are to) meet tonight.
Habían de salir a las dos.   They were (supposed) to leave at two.

For a moral obligation, duty, customary action, etc., **deber** is used:

Ella debe llamar a su mamá.   She must (ought to) call her mother.

When *must* expresses probability in the present (or present perfect), it is indicated by the future (or future perfect) of the verb (see Lección seis, page 132), or by **deber (de)** + an infinitive:

Estarán en el salón.   They must be (probably are) in the lounge.
¿Qué les habrá pasado?   What can have happened to them?
Deben de ser las siete y media.   It must be (probably is) half past seven.
Carlos debe de habérselo llevado.   Charles must have taken it with him.

EJERCICIO

Después de oír una pregunta, oirán un verbo o una frase; contesten afirmativamente, usando la forma correcta del verbo correspondiente.

MODELOS: ¿*Son* las dos? (*deber de*)   Sí, deben de ser las dos.

¿*Has de* ir tú ahora? (*tener que*)   Sí, tengo que ir ahora.

1. ¿*Están* ellos en la biblioteca? (*deber de*)
2. ¿*Va* Juan *a* tocar la guitarra? (*haber de*)
3. ¿*Iban a* reunirse temprano? (*haber de*)
4. ¿*Es necesario* llegar a tiempo? (*haber que*)
5. ¿*Será preciso* colgar los cuadros en la pared? (*haber que*)
6. ¿*Debemos* ir al concierto esta noche? (*tener que*)
7. ¿Creían que *podían* esperar un rato? (*deber*)
8. ¿*Han de* pagar la cuenta ahora? (*tener que*)

5 Formas de mandato correspondientes a «vosotros, -as»

Recall that in this text we have followed the practice, which is common in Spanish America, of using the formal **ustedes** with the third person plural present subjunctive in familiar plural commands. Since the familiar plural forms are used in much of Spain, they are needed for recognition in reading. (For commands used with **usted, ustedes,** and **tú,** see Repaso tres, page 29.)

To form the affirmative familiar plural command (the plural imperative) of all verbs, drop **-r** of the infinitive and add **-d.** For the negative familiar plural command, use the second person plural of the present subjunctive. The subject **vosotros, -as,** is usually omitted. (See Appendix D, pages 288–303, for forms of all types of verbs.)

Infinitive	Affirmative	Negative
tomar:	tomad	no toméis
comer:	comed	no comáis
abrir:	abrid	no abráis
hacer:	haced	no **hagáis**
salir:	salid	no **salgáis**
tener:	tened	no **tengáis**
buscar:	buscad	no **busquéis**
cerrar:	cerrad	no cerréis
contar:	contad	no contéis
volver:	volved	no volváis
colgar:	colgad	no **colguéis**
sentir:	sentid	no **sintáis**
dormir:	dormid	no **durmáis**
pedir:	pedid	no **pidáis**

In forming the familiar plural commands of reflexive verbs, final **-d** is dropped before the reflexive pronoun **os,** except for **idos (irse).** All **-ir** reflexive verbs except **irse** require an accent on the **i** of the stem of the verb: **vestíos.**

Infinitive	Affirmative	Negative
levantarse:	levantaos	no os levantéis
sentarse:	sentaos	no os sentéis
ponerse:	poneos	no os **pongáis**
vestirse:	vestíos	no os **vistáis**
irse:	**id**os	no os **vayáis**

EJERCICIO

Cambien el infinitivo a la forma de mandato correspondiente a **vosotros, -as;** luego, expresen el mandato negativamente:

1. Hablar en inglés. 2. Comer antes de las seis. 3. Escribir las cartas hoy. 4. Venir a verme mañana. 5. Fijarse en la hora. 6. Ponerse los guantes. 7. Vestirse pronto. 8. Acercarse al coche.

RESUMEN

A. Repitan cada oración; luego, formen otra oración, empleando **no . . . tan . . . como,** siguiendo el modelo.

·MODELO: Elena es más alta que Ana.   Elena es más alta que Ana.
Ana no es tan alta como Ele.

1. Margarita lee más despacio que yo.
2. Yo me levanté más tarde que mis padres.
3. Esta música es más clásica que ésa.
4. Él pronuncia más correctamente que Ud.

Usen **no . . . tanto, -a (-os, -as) . . . como,** siguiendo el modelo.

MODELO: Yo tengo más flores que ella.   Yo tengo más flores que ella.
Ella no tiene tantas flores como yo.

5. Ramón cuelga más pinturas que su hermana.
6. Ana recibe más premios que Carmen.
7. Hay más fuentes allí que aquí.
8. Luis lleva más cuadros que Elena.

B. Usos de las formas comparativas de los adjetivos y de los adverbios. Para expresar en español:

1. This building is large; it is larger than that one (*distant*); it is the largest one in the state.
2. This painting is small; it is smaller than the one which is in the corner; it is the smallest one in the lounge.
3. We saw John's older brother and Mary's younger sister at the exhibition yesterday afternoon.
4. There are more than one hundred foreign students here; there are more than I imagined.
5. John says that he has already written more compositions this semester than he wrote last year.
6. Most of the students in (of) our class speak Spanish better than you (*pl.*) believe.

C. Comparaciones de igualdad. Para expresar en español:

1. This small painting is as beautiful as the larger one.
2. I have never seen so many excellent works in an exhibition.
3. There aren't so many students here as the last time.
4. Most students do not have so much interest in pictures as I.
5. I also like music very much. Robert plays the guitar better than I, but I do not practice so much.
6. Let's see if the second part of the concert is as interesting as the first.

D. Para traducir *must, to have to, to be to*, etc. Para expresar en español:

1. They must be (*two ways*) at the exhibition. 2. Jane and Paul must have arrived (*two ways*) late. 3. The students are (supposed) to deliver the works to the lounge before half past seven. 4. The jury is to announce the winners tomorrow. 5. We must always leave everything in order. 6. My roommate had to write a long composition last night. 7. One must remember that Chávez is a great composer and the most famous representative of Mexican music of our time. 8. Don't forget that the concert is to begin at eight o'clock.

E. Para expresar en español, empleando la forma de mandato correspondiente a **vosotros, -as:**

1. Hang the pictures. 2. Grant the prizes. 3. Say that in Spanish. 4. Sit down in the corner. 5. Don't get up yet. 6. Don't leave the room. 7. Pay attention to the time (hour). 8. Do that tomorrow morning.

Resumen de palabras y expresiones

¡adelante!   go on (ahead)! let's go!
al fondo   in the background
la **base**   rule (*of contest*)
el **brazo**   arm
el **Centro de Estudiantes**   Student Center
¡claro que no!   of course not!
clausurar   to close (*as an exhibition*)
colocar   to place, put
el **compositor**   composer
concurso de pintura   painting contest
   (competition)
de nuestros días   of today, in (of) our
   time
debajo de *prep.*   under, below
deber de + *inf.*   must, probably + *verb*
distinguido, -a   distinguished, famous
faltar   to be left
fijarse en   to notice, pay attention to
la **forma**   form
la **fuente**   fountain
el **ganador**   winner
iluminado, -a   illuminated, lighted
ilustre   illustrious, famous
impaciente   impatient(ly)

inaugurar   to inaugurate, open
el **jurado**   jury, judges (*of contest*)
lindo, -a   pretty; fine, perfect
olvidarse de que   to forget that
el **orden** (*pl.* **órdenes**)   order, arrangement
otorgar   to grant, award, confer
peninsular   peninsular (*of Spain*)
el **pintor**   painter
la **pintura**   painting
poner (el radio)   to turn on (the radio)
el **premio**   prize, award
presentar   to show, display, offer, enter
¿qué tal?   how are you? how goes it?
quitar (el radio)   to turn off (the radio)
el **representante**   representative
representar   to represent
el **rincón** (*pl.* **rincones**)   corner (*of a room*)
el **salón** (*pl.* **salones**)   salon, lounge, large
   hall, meeting room
sinfónico, -a   symphonic, symphony
   (*adj.*)
superior   superior, greater
tardar menos   to take less time
la **tarea**   task, job, work

Admirando un cuadro en el museo de la Fundación Miró,
Barcelona, España.

LA PINTURA
EN LA AMÉRICA ESPAÑOLA

Diego Rivera

•••

REVOLUCIÓN, GERMINACIÓN (mural), 1926–27
Cortesía, Escuela Nacional de Agricultura, Chapingo, México.
Fotografía de Bradley Smith, New York

Joaquín Torres García

•••

CONSTRUCTIVISMO, 1943
*Cortesía, Museum of Modern Art
of Latin America, Washington, D.C.
Gift of the Hon. Nelson Rockefeller*

1943 AMÉRICA 1943
*Cortesía, Museum of Art,
Rhode Island School of Design,
Providence, R.I.*

José Clemente Orozco

• • •

LAS SOLDADERAS, CA. **1930**
Cortesía, Museo Nacional de Arte Moderno, Chapultepec, I.N.B.A., México, D.F.
Fotografía de Bradley Smith, New York

José Sabogal
...

AGUADORAS, 1951
Cortesía, San Francisco Museum of Art. Gift of Mr. and Mrs. Garfield Warner

Carlos Mérida

• • •

BAJO EL CIELO DE TEXAS, 1943
Cortesía, Museum of Modern Art of Latin America,
Washington, D.C.

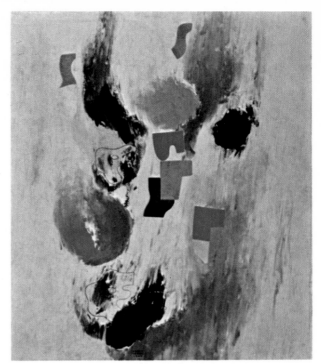

EL JOVEN REY, 1936
Cortesía, Carlos Mérida
From the collection of Mr. and Mrs. Stanley Marcus

Rufino Tamayo
• • •

MUJER CON PIÑA, 1941
*Extended loan from the Museum of Modern Art, New York
to the Museum of Modern Art of Latin America,
Washington, D.C.*

Amelia Peláez
• • •

MAR PACÍFICO, 1943
*Cortesía, Museum of Modern Art of Latin America,
Washington, D.C.*

Raquel Forner

. . .

ASTROSERES NEGROS, 1961
Cortesía, Museum of Modern Art of Latin America, Washington, D.C.

Roberto Matta

•••

HERMALA NÚMERO II, 1948
Cortesía, Museum of Modern Art of Latin America, Washington, D.C.

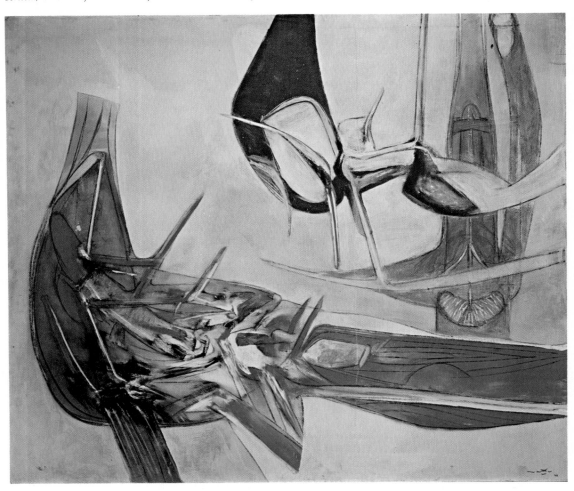

Vergara Grez
• • •

EL SOL EN LA LUNA, 1964
Cortesía, R. Vergara Grez y Antonio R.
Romera, Santiago, Chile

SIMETRÍA DINÁMICA
Cortesía, R. Vergara Grez
y Antonio R. Romera
Santiago, Chile

Héctor Poleo

• • •

FAMILIA ANDINA, 1943
*Cortesía, Museum of Modern Art
of Latin America, Washington, D.C.*

Alejandro Otero

• • •

COLORRITMO 34, 1957 (duco sobre tabla)
*Cortesía, Museum of Modern Art of Latin America,
Washington, D.C.*

CAMINANDO CON UN PARAGUAS AZUL, **1976**
Cortesía, Museum of Modern Art of Latin America, Washington, D.C.

Alejandro Obregón

• • •

COLUMBIA
Cortesía, Museum of Modern Art of Latin America, Washington, D.C.

Rafael Coronel

• • •

TODOS JUNTOS, 1965
Cortesía, Museum of Modern Art
of Latin America, Washington, D.C.

Angel Hurtado

• • •

SIGNO EN EL ESPACIO, 1962
Cortesía, Museum of Modern Art
of Latin America, Washington, D.C.

José Luis Cuevas
• • •

AUTORRETRATO
Cortesía, José Luis Cuevas y Galería de Arte Mexicano

Pedro Friedeberg
• • •

CONFESIONES DE UN ERIZO ICONOCLASTA
*Cortesía, Instituto Nacional de Turismo
de México y Galería Antonio Souza, México, D.F.*

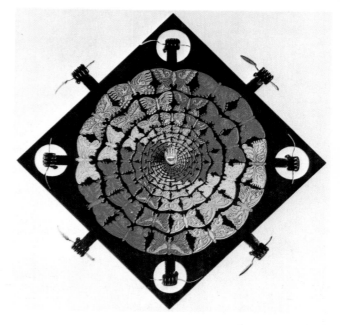

Mac Entyre
• • •

Untitled
Cortesía, Mac Entyre

Darío Suro

• • •

HOMENAJE A VELÁZQUEZ, 1959 (al temple)
Cortesía, Museum of Modern Art of Latin America, Washington, D.C.

Lectura 11

La pintura en la América española

Desde los primeros años del período colonial, se cultivó la pintura tan intensamente en la América española como en Europa. Los focos más importantes de actividad artística fueron la región ecuatoriana y los virreinatos de la Nueva España (México) y del Perú.

Durante la primera mitad del siglo actual surgió la gran escuela muralista de México, con Diego Rivera, José Clemente Orozco y David Alfaro Siqueiros. La Revolución de 1910 sirvió de base para la obra artística de estos pintores, que produjeron una larga serie de pinturas murales que decoran las paredes de muchos edificios públicos. Las artes, las fiestas populares, la vida de los indios y las nuevas ideas sociales les proporcionaron una gran variedad de temas.

Las ideas sociales y políticas de Rivera (1886–1957) lo llevaron a hacer de la pintura un medio de propaganda para educar al pueblo. El hombre y el mundo contemporáneo son también el tema general de Orozco (1883–1949). Se ha dicho que ningún otro pintor lo ha superado[1] en la expresión del aspecto eterno, humano y trágico de las luchas civiles de su país. Los temas revolucionarios adquirieron un vigor extraordinario en las obras de Siqueiros (1898–1974), quien se esforzó también por abrir nuevos caminos al muralismo. Experimentó con el uso de materiales nuevos, así como con la fusión de la pintura y la escultura.

---

[1] **ha superado**, has surpassed. On page 228, line 35, the verb form means *has gone beyond.*

Hacia 1920 empezó también en el Perú un movimiento indígena en el arte. Aunque se desarrolló bajo la influencia del muralismo mexicano, difiere de éste por su tono más moderado. José Sabogal (1888–1956), jefe de la nueva expresión artística de su país, ha buscado su inspiración en el paisaje, en los tipos indígenas y en las costumbres rurales del Perú, empleando como fondo los majestuosos Andes. Aunque ha interpretado la vida por los ojos del indio, no se observa en sus obras la nota de propaganda, como en los artistas mexicanos.

Durante la década siguiente empezaron a imponerse[2] en Hispanoamérica las corrientes artísticas de influencia europea. En la aceptación de las tendencias nuevas, el papel del pintor uruguayo Joaquín Torres García (1874–1948) fue de la mayor importancia. En 1928 creó un estilo nuevo, de formas rectangulares, por medio de las cuales aspiraba a expresar un simbolismo místico, de valor universal. Llegó a ser el exponente más notable del movimiento constructivista en Hispanoamérica. Su obra *Constructivismo* (1943)[3] es un ejemplo típico de las creaciones geométricas de este pintor.

Notables representantes de la pintura abstracta en Hispanoamérica son el pintor guatemalteco Carlos Mérida (1893–   ) y el mexicano Rufino Tamayo (1899–   ). Aunque ha desarrollado su carrera en México, Mérida ha buscado inspiración en la cultura indígena de su país de origen. En *Bajo el cielo de Texas* (1943), por ejemplo, se observan claras reminiscencias del arte maya.

Tamayo es, sin duda, el artista mexicano que ha ejercido mayor influencia sobre la pintura moderna en Hispanoamérica. Sin renunciar a la gran tradición muralista de su país—es un gran muralista también—, no ha dejado de participar en las tendencias principales del arte contemporáneo. Su óleo *Mujer con piña* (1941) muestra su predilección por el arte abstracto y su amor por los colores sonoros.[4]

Los pintores cubanos Amelia Peláez (1897–1968) y Wilfredo Lam (1902–   ) y la pintora argentina Raquel Forner (1902–   ) han desarrollado su obra artística en relación con los principios del surrealismo. Con Amelia Peláez la pintura cubana se incorporó a las corrientes principales del arte contemporáneo. La complejidad casi barroca del diseño y la exuberancia tropical del colorido caracterizan su pintura *Mar Pacífico* (1943). Las notas trágicas de la guerra y de la violencia se repiten en muchas de las obras de Raquel Forner, densas de materia. En *Astroseres[5] negros* (1961) se inventan personajes misteriosos, sin peso,[6] símbolos de su expresión figurada.

Hoy día se ensayan todas las corrientes de vanguardia en Hispanoamérica. El chileno Sebastián Roberto Matta (1912–   ), reconocido como uno de los primeros pintores surrealistas del mundo, ha superado su fase surrealista y cultiva una nueva figuración con infiltraciones relacionables con[7] la abstracción informal. Su óleo *Hermala Número 2* (1948) revela un conflicto entre lo orgánico y lo mecanístico, transmitido al lienzo[8] con gran libertad de pincel.[9] En otras obras sus formas dinámicas dan la impresión de volar más allá de los bordes del cuadro.

---

[2] **imponerse,** *take hold (dominate).* [3] For this painting and others mentioned in this Lectura, see art section between pages 226–227. [4] **sonoros,** *vibrant.* [5] **Astroseres,** *Astrobeings.* [6] **sin peso,** *weightless.* [7] **relacionables con,** *which can be related to.* [8] **lienzo,** *canvas.* [9] **libertad de pincel,** *freedom of brush work.*

En 1954 Ramón Vergara Grez (1923–   ) introdujo en Chile el movimiento constructivista, fundando el grupo *Rectángulo*. Ha rechazado[10] el informalismo y las demás derivaciones de la pintura surrealista (las cuales aspiraban a acabar con todas las normas en el arte) y se esfuerza por dar un enfoque[11] racionalista y un valor ético al arte. Desde 1963 el grupo se llama *Forma y espacio* y hace concesiones al arte cinético.[12]

Tendencias semejantes se encuentran en las producciones de un notable grupo de pintores venezolanos. Héctor Poleo (1918–   ) se ha destacado entre los vanguardistas neofigurativos abstractos. La obra *Familia andina* (1943) refleja una de las primeras fases de la actividad artística de este pintor. Aunque algo estilizada, la pintura es esencialmente de tipo naturalista.

Los pintores venezolanos Carlos Cruz Díez y Jesús Rafael Soto (1923–   ) figuran entre los artistas constructivistas y cinéticos más importantes que existen hoy en el mundo. Una creación interesante de Soto es *Escritura Hurtado* (1975), que pertenece a la serie *Firmas*. Delante de un fondo negro cruzado verticalmente de finas listas blancas,[13] se hallan suspendidos varios alambres[14] negros que forman curvas caprichosas; al moverse los alambres, se crean diseños moaré[15] que producen visiones deslumbrantes.[16]

Alejandro Otero (1921–   ) y Ángel Hurtado (1927–   ) también son exponentes del arte vanguardista en Venezuela. *Colorritmo*[17] 34 (duco sobre tabla, 1957), de Otero, es uno de los primeros ejemplos del arte geométrico-cinético. Consta de listas de colores dispuestas rítmicamente en líneas paralelas. Hurtado combina pinceladas[18] audaces en una variedad de estilos para crear su cuadro introspectivo *Señal en el espacio* (1962).

Alejandro Obregón (1920–   ), que nació en Barcelona, es uno de los representantes más notables de la pintura colombiana de hoy. *El velorio*[19] (1956) muestra su interés por los principios del expresionismo. Para representar el cuerpo del difunto,[20] Obregón emplea una gran variedad de colores brillantes; un gallo de alas verdes es el único acompañante.

Tres notables pintores mexicanos pueden representar las tendencias vanguardistas en su país: Rafael Coronel (1932–   ), José Luis Cuevas (1933–   ) y Pedro Friedeberg (1937–   ). Las obras sombrías y quiméricas[21] de Coronel tienen una calidad macabra que recuerda los lienzos de la última época de Goya. En *Todos juntos* (1965), sólo el color rosado de los rostros de los cuatro viejos rompe la triste uniformidad de los apagados[22] colores oscuros.

Entre los cultivadores del arte primitivo en Hispanoamérica, se destaca el pintor hondureño José Antonio Velázquez (1906–   ). En *San Antonio de Oriente* (1972) presenta una vista de su pueblo natal. Como en otras obras suyas, no faltan el sacerdote, un perro, un burro, algunas gallinas, gentes del pueblo y los tejados típicos.

---

[10] **Ha rechazado,** *He has rejected.*   [11] **enfoque,** *focus.*   [12] **cinético,** *kinetic (consisting in or depending upon motion).*   [13] **finas listas blancas,** *thin white stripes.*   [14] **alambres,** *wires.*   [15] **diseños moaré,** *moiré patterns (having a watered or clouded appearance, as silk, paper, etc.).*   [16] **deslumbrantes,** *dazzling.*   [17] **Colorritmo,** *Color-rhythm.*   [18] **pinceladas,** *brush strokes.*   [19] **El velorio,** *The Wake.*   [20] **del difunto,** *of the deceased.*   [21] **quiméricas,** *chimerical, fanciful.*   [22] **apagados,** *subdued.*

Otros importantes artistas del mundo hispánico son el pintor dominicano Darío Suro (1917–   ) y el puertorriqueño Julio Rosado del Valle. Suro es considerado como el más delicado intérprete del paisaje dominicano. En su pintura al temple,[23] *Homenaje a Velázquez* (1959), logra, con toques en espiral de color rosado, azul y negro, una armonía cromática que recuerda el efecto delicado característico del gran maestro español.

En nuestros días la vitalidad de las artes visuales en Hispanoamérica es extraordinaria. El hecho más importante es que el arte hispanoamericano ha dejado de ser nacional y se ha incorporado a la escena internacional.

EJERCICIO

Escriban un breve diálogo, de unas dieciséis líneas, sobre la pintura en la América española, empleando como elemento inicial las oraciones y preguntas siguientes:

María. ¡Hola, Carlos! ¿Has visto la exposición de cuadros de pintores hispanoamericanos que ha organizado el Departamento de Arte?

Carlos. ¡Ya lo creo! Me parece magnífica. ¿Qué obras te han interesado más, María?

En la página opuesta, arriba "Muchacho con paraguas," Enrique Grau, Colombia. Debajo "Entierro de un hombre ilustre," óleo de Mario Urteaga, 1936.

En esta página, "Guerreros Aztecas," José Clemente Orozco (en la Baker Library, Dartmouth College).

---

[23] **al temple,** *in distemper (tempera).*

Resumen de los usos de «para» y «por» ▪ Usos del participio pasado ▪ El pretérerito anterior de indicativo ▪ Usos del participio presente ▪ Las conjunciones «e» y «u» ▪ Usos de «pero, sino» y «sino que» ▪ El artículo neutro «lo» ▪ El pronombre neutro «lo» ▪ La formación de los adverbios ▪ Verbos auxiliares para expresar el modo

LECCIÓN DOCE

Los planes de Felipe

Va terminando el segundo semestre. Felipe, que estudia economía, va a graduarse en mayo, y hace varios meses que considera con seriedad sus planes para el futuro. Ha solicitado ingreso en varias Escuelas Graduadas y hoy tiene una cita con el jefe de su departamento, el profesor Gil, para consultarlo sobre sus planes.

Sr. Gil. Pase, Felipe, y siéntese. Hace tiempo que no me habla de sus planes.

Felipe. Pues, se alegrará de saber que dos universidades han respondido a mi solicitud de ingreso. No sólo me admitirán, sino que me informan que tienen algunas becas disponibles.

Sr. Gil. Pues no constituye ninguna sorpresa para mí. Lo único que me sorprende es que hayan tardado tanto en responder.

Felipe. Además, acabo de recibir una llamada telefónica del profesor Sáez, de la Universidad de . . .

Sr. Gil. Pero, ¿ha vuelto ya de la Argentina?

Felipe. Terminó su trabajo allí a fines de abril y apenas hubo regresado, me llamó. Pasará unas horas en San Francisco el lunes que viene y quiere que me encuentre con él en el aeropuerto.

Sr. Gil. No le debe sorprender lo cuidadosas que tienen que ser las universidades hoy día. Por desgracia, no hay becas para todos los que las merecen.

Felipe. Como usted sabe, primero quiero obtener el grado de Maestro en Artes[1] en economía y luego trabajar durante un par de años en alguna agencia del gobierno que tenga algo que ver con Hispanoamérica.

Sr. Gil. Y después es posible que usted piense en continuar sus estudios para el doctorado, ¿verdad?

Felipe. Exactamente.

Sr. Gil. Me parece un plan excelente. Sin experiencia práctica, es difícil darse a conocer en el campo de la economía. Dos o tres años de experiencia en una organización como el Banco Interamericano de Desarrollo, por ejemplo, serían de gran utilidad.

Felipe. Me interesaría muchísimo poder trabajar en una organización de ese tipo.

Sr. Gil. El Banco Interamericano de Desarrollo es una de las más activas en la tarea de renovar a[2] Hispanoamérica. Como usted sabe, ha concedido créditos no sólo para financiar proyectos agrícolas e industriales, sino para crear cooperativas campesinas y fincas experimentales.

Felipe. Es lástima que el público en general no esté enterado de todo lo que[3] se va haciendo día a día por transformar la estructura económica y social de Hispanoamérica.

Sr. Gil. Estoy seguro de que un joven con la preparación de usted podrá contribuir mucho a la labor de promover el desarrollo de los países del sur.

Felipe. Le estoy muy agradecido por todo lo que usted ha hecho por mí. Concluida la entrevista[4] con el profesor Sáez, volveré a consultarlo.

Sr. Gil. Le deseo mucho éxito, Felipe. No deje de llamarme si necesita ayuda.

Preparen un diálogo original, de unas quince líneas, para recitar en clase, empleando las frases y preguntas siguientes como elemento inicial:

1. *Jaime.* ¿Qué parte del concierto te ha gustado más, María?

   María. La composición de Chávez me ha parecido muy impresionante. Es la primera vez que oigo[5] una obra suya.

2. *Luisa.* Como Ud. sabe, me gustaría conseguir un puesto en algún país de la América española.

   Sr. Gil. No me parece difícil. Pero primero quiero que me dé Ud. algunos informes sobre sus estudios universitarios.

---

[1] **Maestro en Artes:** a literal translation of the degree offered by North American (and Canadian and British) universities, but which does not exist in Spanish America, where the only degree granted after the **licentiatura,** *licentiate,* is the **doctorado.** (The **doctorado** usually requires one additional year of advanced study and a doctoral dissertation.) The Spanish American degree called the **maestría** corresponds to our Teacher's Certificate.   [2] The personal **a** is often used before unmodified place names.   [3] The relative pronoun **cuanto** is encountered in literary usage for **todo lo que** but seldom in conversation.   [4] **Concluida la entrevista,** *After the interview [with Professor Sáez] is over* (lit., *the interview ended*). This absolute construction is rare in conversation, but it will be encountered in literary usage; see bottom, page 237.   [5] With expressions of time, such as **Es la primera vez que,** the present tense may be used in Spanish for the present perfect tense when present time is implied.

NOTAS GRAMATICALES

1 Resumen de los usos de «para» y «por»

A. **Para** is used:

1. To express the purpose, use, person, or place for which persons or things are intended or destined:

   Felipe considera sus planes para el futuro.   Philip considers his plans for the future.
   No hay becas para todos los que las merecen.   There aren't scholarships for all who deserve them.
   Ya han partido para México.   They have already left for Mexico.

2. To express a point or farthest limit of time in the future, often meaning *by*:

   Este diálogo es para mañana.   This dialogue is for tomorrow.
   Que estés aquí para las cinco.   May you be here by five o'clock.

3. With an infinitive to express purpose, meaning *to, in order to*:

   Tiene una cita con el jefe para consultarlo sobre sus planes. He has an appointment with the head to consult with him about his plans.
   Estamos para terminar el semestre. We are about to finish (on the point of finishing) the semester.

4. To express *for* in a comparison that may be understood or stated:

   Juanito habla bien para un niño.   Johnny talks well for a child.
   Para Uds., esto será fácil.   For you, this will be easy.

B. **Por** is used:

1. To express *for* in the sense of *because of, on account of, for the sake of, on behalf of, in exchange for, about, as*:

   Por falta de dinero él no pudo ir.   For lack of money he couldn't go.
   Quedo muy agradecido por todo lo que Ud. ha hecho por mí.   I am very grateful for all you have done for me.
   Pagué diez dólares por la camisa.   I paid ten dollars for the shirt.
   Lo tomaron por español.   They took him for (as) a Spaniard.

2. To express the space of time during which an action continues (*for, during*):

   Estaré en España por un mes.   I'll be in Spain for a month.
   Margarita saldrá mañana por la tarde.   Margaret will leave tomorrow afternoon.

3. To show *by what* or *by whom* something is done; also *through, along*:

Juan habló con Ana por teléfono.   John talked with Ann by telephone.
Pepe fue castigado por sus padres.   Joe was punished by his parents.

4. To indicate the object of an errand or search, *for*, after verbs such as **ir, enviar, mandar, preguntar, venir:**

Han enviado (venido, ido) por Marta.   They have sent (come, gone) for Martha.
Preguntaron por ella.   They asked for (about) her.

5. With an infinitive to express uncertain outcome (often to denote striving for something), or something yet to be done:

Carlos trabajaba por ganar una beca.   Charles was working to earn a scholarship.
La carta todavía está por escribir.   The letter is still to be written.

6. To form certain idiomatic expressions (some of which could be placed under the above headings):

por allí (around, along) there	**por falta de** for lack of
por aquí (around, by) here	**por favor** please
por ciento percent	**por fin** finally, at last
por cierto certainly, for sure	**por lo general** in general, generally
por completo completely	**por lo menos** at least
por consiguiente consequently	**por lo tanto** therefore
por desgracia unfortunately	**por medio de** by means of
¡por Dios! for heaven's sake!	**por primera vez** for the first time
por ejemplo for example	**por separado** separately
por encima de over, above	**por supuesto** of course, certainly
por eso because of that, therefore, that's why	**por último** finally, ultimately

¿Por qué? means *Why? For what reason?*, while **¿para qué?** means *why? for what purpose?*

EJERCICIO

Para leer en español, supliendo la preposición **para** o **por**:

1. ¿Cuándo partirán _____ la Argentina? 2. ¿Tiene Ud. muchos planes _____ las vacaciones? 3. Estamos muy agradecidos _____ todo. 4. Arturo me dijo que vendría _____ mí a las ocho. 5. ¿Por qué preguntaste _____ Ricardo? 6. La mamá de Isabel hizo el vestido _____ ella (*i.e., for her use*). 7. —¿ _____ quién es este

boleto? —Es _____ mí.   8. Es _____ el concierto que van a presentar el sábado _____ la noche.   9. Estoy seguro de que está _____ llover.   10. Tráeme tú una taza _____ té, _____ favor.   11. Los muchachos jugaron _____ dos horas? 12. Anduvieron despacio _____ la calle.   13. Escoja Ud. una tarjeta _____ Diana. 14. ¿Cuánto pagaste _____ ese reloj?   15. Parece que todo el mundo trabaja _____ ganar más dinero.   16. ¿Es verdad que comemos _____ vivir? 17. ¿Crees que lo tomaron _____ argentino?   18. _____ fin podemos hacer planes _____ la reunión.   19. Tendremos que darnos prisa _____ llegar a tiempo. 20. No constituye ninguna sorpresa _____ mí.   21. Voy a enviar _____ Antonio _____ entregarle estas cartas.   22. Que vuelvan Uds. _____ el almuerzo. 23. Este artículo, que fue escrito _____ Ana, es _____ el periódico de hoy. 24. _____ una persona que se siente muy bien, Carlota se queja mucho. 25. _____ desgracia, no hay beca disponible _____ Roberto.   26. Piense Ud. en continuar sus estudios _____ el doctorado.   27. El banco ha concedido créditos _____ financiar muchos proyectos.   28. Nuestra responsabilidad no puede olvidarse _____ completo.

2   Usos del participio pasado

A. The past participle is most commonly used with the appropriate tense of **haber** to form the perfect tenses, in which case the participle always ends in **-o.** It is also frequently used as an adjective, including its use with **estar** and similar verbs to express a state or condition which results from a previous action, and with **ser** to form the passive voice. In the latter two constructions, the past participle agrees in gender and number with the noun or pronoun it modifies:

> **Me ha parecido muy impresionante.**   It has seemed very impressive to me.
> **La puerta estaba (se encontraba) abierta.**   The door was open.
> **Los vasos fueron rotos por Juanito.**   The glasses were broken by Johnny.

B. The past participle also may be used independently with a noun or pronoun to express *time, manner, means,* and the like. (This is sometimes called the absolute use of the past participle.) Used thus, the participle precedes the noun or pronoun it modifies, and agrees with it in gender and number. The translation depends on the context:

> **Concluida la entrevista, volveré a consultarlo.**   Once (After) the interview is ended, I shall consult with you again.
> **Salido el avión, cenamos en el aeropuerto.**   After the plane had left (The plane having left), we ate supper at the airport.

NOTE: **De** often replaces **por** with verbs other than **estar** or **ser** to introduce an agent dependent upon a past participle: **Parto para Buenos Aires, acompañado de mi**

hermano Juan, *I am leaving (I'll leave) for Buenos Aires, accompanied by my brother John.*
Compare the normal use of **por** in the passive voice (see Lección primera, page 39).

EJERCICIO

Escuchen la oración; luego, cámbienla, usando el participio pasado, según el modelo.

MODELO: *Al escribir la carta,* Ana se la enseñó   Escrita la carta, Ana se la enseñó
                     a Marta   a Marta

1. *Al cerrar la puerta,* la profesora empezó a leer los exámenes.
2. *Al concluir sus estudios,* Felipe buscará un puesto.
3. *Después de envolver el regalo,* Luisa se lo envió a María.
4. *Después de hacer los planes,* los estudiantes los anunciaron.
5. *Al comprar los boletos,* Roberto se olvidó de su cita con el dentista.
6. *Después de entregar el informe,* Carolina fue a la biblioteca.

3   El pretérito anterior (*preterit perfect*) de indicativo

The preterit perfect tense is formed with the preterit of **haber** and the past participle. It is
translated like the English past perfect tense, but is used only after conjunctions such as
cuando, en cuanto, después que, apenas (*scarcely, hardly*). In the case of **apenas,** the word
when is carried over to the following clause in English; it is not expressed in Spanish:

Singular		*Plural*	
hube		**hubimos**	
hubiste	hablado, comido, vivido	**hubisteis**	hablado, comido, vivido
hubo		**hubieron**	

En cuanto (Cuando) ellos hubieron terminado, salieron de la casa.   As soon as
(When) they had finished, they left the house.
Apenas él hubo regresado, me llamó.   Scarcely had he returned, when he called
me.

In spoken Spanish, the simple preterit often replaces the preterit perfect. The Spanish
pluperfect is the equivalent of the English past perfect in other cases: **Habían vuelto,**
They had returned.

4   Usos del participio presente

The present participle, also called the gerund, has a number of important functions.

1. **Estar** is used with the present participle to express the progressive forms of the tenses, that is, to express the action of the verb as continuing at a given moment (see Lección primera, page 38):

   Los niños están (estaban) gritando.   The children are (were) shouting.
   ¿Qué estás leyendo ahora?   What are you reading now?

2. Verbs of motion, particularly **ir, andar, venir,** are used with the present participle to give a more graphic representation of an action in progress. These verbs normally retain something of their literal meaning. **Seguir** and **continuar,** *to continue, keep on,* are followed by the present participle. (The progressive forms of **ir, salir, venir** are seldom used.)

   Él iba (venía) cantando.   He was (went along, came) singing.
   Sigan (Continúen) Uds. charlando.   Continue *or* Keep on chatting.

   Ir + a present participle is also equivalent to the English *to go on* or *keep on* + present participle, *do something gradually (slowly, more and more):*

   Va terminando el segundo semestre.   The second semester is gradually ending.
   El público no está enterado de cuanto se va haciendo por transformar . . .   The public isn't informed of all that is slowly (gradually) being done to transform . . .

3. Referring to the subject, expressed or understood, the present participle may be used to convey a variety of adverbial relationships:

   Pasan mucho tiempo jugando en el parque.   They spend much time playing in the park.
   Andando rápidamente, llegué a tiempo.   By walking rapidly, I arrived on time.

EJERCICIO

Repitan cada oración; luego, al oír un verbo, substituyan la forma correcta del verbo seguida del participio presente, según los modelos.

MODELOS: Luis mira un mapa. (estar)   Luis mira un mapa. Luis está mirando un mapa.
           Andaban despacio. (ir)   Andaban despacio. Iban andando despacio.

1. Roberto visita a sus primos. (estar)
2. Luis hacía un viaje por Hispanoamérica. (estar)

3. Los jóvenes corren hacia nosotros. (venir)
4. Ellos se acercaban al patio. (ir)
5. Nosotros aprendemos la lengua poco a poco. (ir)
6. Ella anda rápidamente por la calle. (venir)
7. Juan solicita una beca para el año que viene. (estar)
8. Lea Ud. hasta las cuatro de la tarde. (seguir)

5 Las conjunciones «e» y «u»

Before words beginning with **i-, hi-** (but not **hie-**), Spanish uses **e**, *and*, for **y**. Before words beginning with **o-** or **ho-**, Spanish uses **u**, *or*, for **o**:

> **proyectos agrícolas e industriales** agricultural and industrial projects
> **Luis habla español e inglés.** Louis speaks Spanish and English.
> **Juanita hizo eso siete u ocho veces.** Jane did that seven or eight times.
>
> BUT: **nieve y hielo** snow and ice

6 Usos de «pero», «sino» y «sino que»

The English conjunction *but* is usually expressed by **pero** in Spanish. When *but* means *on the contrary, but instead*, **sino** is used in place of **pero** in an affirmative statement which contradicts a preceding negative statement. Usually no verb form—other than an infinitive—may be used after **sino**:

> **Me puse el traje, pero no lo compré.** I put on the suit, but I did not buy it.
> **No fueron en autobús, sino en avión.** They didn't go by bus, but by plane.
> **. . . no sólo para financiar proyectos, sino para crear cooperativas campesinas . . .** . . . not only to finance projects, but to create rural cooperatives . . .
> **Yo no quiero jugar, sino descansar.** I don't want to play, but to rest.

If the sentence contains different clauses, **sino que** is used:

> **No sólo me admitirán, sino que me informan que tienen algunas becas disponibles.** They will not only admit me, but they inform me that they have some scholarships available.

EJERCICIO

Para leer en español, supliendo la conjunción **pero, sino** o **sino que**:

1. Traté de llamar a Felipe, _____ nadie contestó. 2. A Carlos le gusta la música

clásica, _____ a mí no. 3. No vamos al banco, _____ a la biblioteca. 4. Ellos no fueron en autobús, _____ en taxi.   5. Los niños no andaban despacio, _____ corrían rápidamente. 6. Mis amigos van a México, _____ no pueden visitar a Monterrey. 7. Inés dice que no quiere estudiar, _____ dormir la siesta. 8. Carlos solicitó una beca, _____ no se la concedieron.

7   El artículo neutro «lo»

1. The neuter article **lo** is used with masculine singular adjectives, with adverbs, and with past participles used as adjectives, to form an expression almost equivalent to an abstract noun. The translation of this abstract idea or concept varies according to context:

   Lo malo es que no están aquí.   What is bad (The bad thing *or* part) is that they aren't here.
   Lea Ud. lo escrito.   Read what is (has been) written.
   Lo único que me sorprende es que hayan tardado tanto.   The only thing that surprises me is that it has taken them so long.

2. The neuter **lo** used with an adjective or adverb followed by **que** translates *how*:

   No le debe sorprender lo cuidadosas que tienen que ser las universidades.   It shouldn't surprise you how careful universities must be.

3. Remember the uses of the neuter article **lo** explained earlier: **lo que** meaning *what, that which*; **lo de** meaning *that (matter, affair) of* (see Lección diez, page 196); **de lo que,** *than,* in certain comparisons; and **lo más pronto posible,** *the soonest possible (as soon as possible)* (see Lección once, page 214).

EJERCICIO

Después de oír una oración, oirán una frase; substituyan la frase en la oración, según el modelo.

   MODELO: *Lo malo* es que ya han salido. (*Lo peor*)   Lo peor es que ya han salido.

   1. *Lo bueno* es que Luis ganó la beca. (*Lo mejor*)
   2. *Lo importante* es hablar correctamente. (*Lo necesario*)
   3. Hay que recordar *lo dicho*. (*lo hecho*)
   4. No traten Uds. de hacer *lo difícil*. (*lo imposible*)
   5. Repitan Uds. *lo escrito*. (*lo leído*)
   6. No se olvide Ud. de *lo nuestro*. (*lo suyo*)
   7. Siempre andan *lo más despacio* posible. (*lo más rápidamente*)

8. Parece que volverán *lo más tarde* posible. (*lo más pronto*)
9. Sabemos *lo contentos que* están ellos. (*lo tristes que*)
10. No puedes imaginarte *lo largas que* son las lecciones. (*lo difíciles que*)

8   El pronombre neutro «lo»

In addition to its use as a pronoun object meaning *it* (**No lo creo,** *I don't believe it*), the neuter pronoun **lo** is used:

1. To complete the sentence when no direct object is expressed, with verbs such as **advertir, decir, pedir, preguntar, saber,** and the like (see Lección tres, page 75):

   Como ellos no lo saben, yo se lo diré.   Since they don't know it, I'll tell them.
   —¿Podrías ir? —No lo sé. Pregúntaselo a ella.   "Could you go?" "I don't know.
   Ask her."

2. With certain verbs such as **ser** and **parecer,** in answer to a question or to refer back to a noun, adjective, or whole idea, sometimes with the meaning of *so:*

   —¿Es Ud. estudiante? —Sí, lo soy.   "Are you a student?" "Yes, I am."
   Él estará cansado, pero no lo parece.   He must be tired, but he doesn't seem so.

EJERCICIO

Para contestar afirmativamente, usando el pronombre neutro **lo.**

MODELO: ¿Es profesora la señorita Gómez?   Sí, lo es.

1. ¿Es ingeniero el señor Díaz?
2. ¿Son norteamericanos sus padres?
3. ¿Son Uds. estudiantes?
4. ¿Soy yo profesor (profesora)?
5. ¿Parecen ellos estar contentos?
6. ¿Parece ser práctico el plan?

9   La formación de los adverbios

In Spanish, adverbs of manner are formed by adding **-mente** (compare the English suffix *-ly*) to the feminine singular of adjectives. Adverbs may also be formed by using **con** plus a noun:

claro	clear	**claramente**	clearly	**con cuidado**	carefully
fácil	easy	**fácilmente**	easily	**con seriedad**	seriously

When two or more adverbs are used in a series, **-mente** is added only to the last one:

Ella habla rápida y correctamente.   She speaks rapidly and correctly.

Occasionally, adjectives are used in Spanish as adverbs, particularly in the spoken language and regularly in poetry, with no change in form other than the usual agreement:

Ellos vivían felices.   They were living happily.
Todas iban muy contentas.   All (*f.*) were going very contentedly.

EJERCICIO

Den los adverbios que correspondan a los adjetivos:

1. fuerte. 2. activo. 3. general. 4. preferible. 5. triste. 6. típico. 7. cortés. 8. exacto.
9. social y económico. 10. correcto y rápido.

10 Verbos auxiliares para expresar el modo (*modal auxiliaries*)

A. Translation of *can* and *may*

If *can* expresses physical ability, the present tense of **poder** is used; **saber** indicates mental ability:

Yo dudo que él pueda dirigir el concurso.   I doubt that he can direct the contest.
¿Sabe Ud. jugar al golf?   Can you (Do you know how to) play golf?

Some of the ways in which *may* is expressed are:

Puedes salir ahora si quieres.   You may go out now if you wish.
Es posible que no respondan a su solicitud.   They may (It is possible that they may) not reply to his application.
Puede (ser) que se vayan hoy.   They may (It may be that they will) leave today.
Aunque lo vea yo, no se lo diré.   Even though I may see him, I'll not tell him.
Que sean Uds. felices.   May you be happy.
¿Se puede entrar?   May I (we, one) come in?

B. Translation of *could* and *might*

Could, meaning *would be able to, might,* is translated by the imperfect, preterit, or conditional indicative, or by the imperfect subjunctive of **poder:**

Diana podía cantar bien.   Diane could (was able to) sing well.
Pablo no pudo terminar el trabajo.   Paul couldn't finish the work.

¿Podrías ayudarnos?   Could you (Would you be able to) help us?

Dijeron que podrían considerar el plan.   They said they could (might be able to) consider the plan.

Era posible que vinieran (pudiesen venir).   It was possible that they might come.

C. Translation of *should* (*ought to*), *should like*

Deber may be used in all tenses to express various degrees of obligation. When *should* indicates a mild obligation (not so strong as that expressed by the present tense of **deber**), the **-ra** imperfect subjunctive, the imperfect, or the conditional indicative tense of **deber** is used:

Ud. debiera ir a verlos.   You should (ought to) go (to) see them.

Yo sabía que debía buscarlo.   I knew that I should look for him.

Creíamos que Ana debía (debiera, debería) venir.   We thought (that) Ann should come.

The preterit of **deber** expresses an obligation at a time previous to another past action:

Ud. debió responder inmediatamente.   You should (ought to) have responded immediately.

In a sentence that expresses a contrary-to-fact condition or an improbable condition in the future (see Lección nueve, pages 183–184), *should* is translated by the conditional indicative tense in the main clause, and by the imperfect subjunctive tense in the **si**-clause:

Si yo tuviera tiempo, iría allá.   If I had (should have) time, I should (would) go there.

Should like may be translated by the **-ra** imperfect subjunctive forms of **querer,** or by the conditional indicative of **gustar:**

Yo quisiera (Me gustaría) ir con él.   I should like to go with him.

EJERCICIO

Para expresar en español:

1. Can you (*fam. sing.*) go to the office with me? 2. Jane can play the guitar well, but she cannot play it today because she is ill. 3. What can I do for you (*pl.*)? 4. You (*pl.*) may sit down if you wish. 5. May they have a good time tonight. 6. You (*fam. sing.*) should look at several brands of stereo sets if you should go to that store. 7. The clerk said last week that he could show you (*fam. sing.*) some new models. 8. Betty knows that she must call us today. 9. I should like (*two ways*) to drive your (*fam. sing.*) new car. 10. If I were John, I would apply for a scholarship in several universities.

RESUMEN

A. Escuchen el modelo; luego, formen dos frases nuevas, una empleando la voz pasiva, y la otra empleando **estar** con el participio pasado, según el modelo.

MODELO: Juan escribió la carta.   La carta fue escrita por Juan.
                                              La carta está escrita.

1. Un amigo mío hizo el estudio.
2. Ana vendió la bicicleta.
3. El banco concedió los créditos necesarios.
4. El público aceptó el plan.
5. Carlos abrió las ventanas.
6. La universidad los admitió en la Escuela Graduada.

B. Usos del participio pasado, del participio presente y del pretérito anterior de indicativo. Para expresar en español:

1. Continue (*pl.*) playing in the patio until I call you. 2. The students are (gradually) learning some Spanish songs. 3. Robert was walking (*progressive*) rapidly towards Jane's house. 4. As soon as they had returned home, they sent for us. 5. By working six or eight hours, I can finish this composition. 6. The composition written, I shall hand it to the teacher. 7. The exercises finished, I listened to some Mexican records. 8. The trip of Louise and Inez was suggested by their uncle. 9. Someone forgot to open the door; therefore, it was still closed. 10. Richard, accompanied by some friends of his, was making (*progressive*) plans for (the) vacation (*pl.*) in South America.

C. Usos del artículo y del pronombre neutro **lo.** Para expresar en español:

1. The best thing is to apply for entrance.
2. That matter of Robert seems very strange to me.
3. Come (*formal pl.*) to see us the soonest possible.
4. That is what Thomas and I intend to do.
5. "Is Mr. López the head of the department?" "Yes, he is."
6. "Is Mary's sister a teacher?" "No, she isn't."
7. "Can you (*fam. sing.*) tell Barbara that?" "Yes, I shall tell her (it)."
8. "Did he read the report?" "I did not ask him (it)."

D. Para contestar afirmativamente en español:

1. ¿Sabes jugar al golf? 2. ¿Puedes jugar conmigo hoy? 3. ¿Podrías llevarle a Ana el paquete? 4. ¿Deben Uds. escribirles a sus padres? 5. ¿Debieran Uds. visitar a sus tíos? 6. ¿Quisieran Uds. ir a México este verano? 7. ¿Es posible que tu padre te ofrezca el dinero para ir allá? 8. ¿Sería posible que él te lo ofreciera? 9. ¿Puede ser que tú consigas el puesto que deseas? 10. ¿Podría ser que tú lo consiguieras? 11. ¿Irá Ud. a la sierra si alguien lo (la) invita? 12. ¿Iría Ud. a México si alguien lo (la) invitara?

E. Repaso de algunas expresiones empleadas en el diálogo de esta lección. Para expresar en español:

1. Do you (*fam. sing.*) have anything to do now? 2. It is difficult to make oneself known nowadays. 3. For some time he hasn't talked to me about his plans. 4. I have just received a telephone call. 5. My friend finished his work at the end of April. 6. He wants me to meet him at the airport. 7. I shall consult with you (*formal*) after the interview with Mr. Gil. 8. You (*formal*) should think about continuing your studies for the doctorate. 9. Don't fail (*formal*) to call me. 10. The university didn't reply to his entrance application. 11. The public isn't informed of what is being done (*progressive*) day by day. 12. They are very grateful for all that you (*formal*) have done for them.

Resumen de palabras y expresiones

a fines de *prep.* at (toward) the end of
la **actividad** activity
activo, -a active
admitir to admit
agradecido, -a grateful
agrícola (*m. and f.*) agricultural, farm (*adj.*)
allá there (*often after verbs of motion*)
la **América española** Spanish America
el **banco** bank
campesino, -a peasant (*adj.*), rural
colaborar to collaborate
considerar to consider
constituir to constitute
la **cooperativa** cooperative (*society*)
crear to create
el **crédito** credit
cuanto *relative pron.* all that
cuidadoso, -a careful
darse a conocer to make oneself known, make a name for oneself
el **desarrollo** development
día a día day by day
discutir to discuss
disponible available
el **doctorado** doctorate
la **economía** economics
económico, -a economic
en general in general, generally

encontrarse (ue) con to meet, run across (into)
enterado, -a informed
la **entrevista** interview
la **estructura** structure
exactamente exactly
experimental experimental
financiar to finance
la **finca** farm, ranch
el **futuro** future
el **gobierno** government
graduado, -a graduate (*adj.*)
hace tiempo it is a long (some) time, for a long (some) time
hoy día nowadays, today
impresionante impressive
industrial industrial
el **ingreso** entrance, admission
interamericano, -a inter-American
el **jefe** head, chief
la **labor** labor, work
Maestro en Artes Master in (of) Arts
no sólo . . . sino que not only . . . but
la **oganización** (*pl.* **organizaciones**) organization
poco a poco little by little
práctico, -a practical
promover (ue) to promote, advance

el **proyecto** project
el **público** public
renovar (ue) to renew, rebuild, transform
responder (a) to answer, reply, respond (to)
la **responsabilidad** responsibility
la **solicitud** application, request

la **solicitud de ingreso** application for admission (entrance)
tardar tanto to delay (take) so long
tener algo que ver con to have anything (something) to do with
transformar to transform, change
único, -a only, sole
la **utilidad** utility, usefulness

Lectura 12

Hispanoamérica en el último tercio del siglo XX

Los problemas económicos y sociales que los países hispanoamericanos tendrán que resolver durante las próximas décadas son sumamente graves. A pesar de los esfuerzos de los últimos años, la América latina no ha logrado progresar con la rapidez deseada.

El problema más evidente es el de la debilidad económica y política de los países hispanoamericanos frente a la gran república norteamericana. En parte se debe al fraccionamiento geográfico[1] del territorio; pero también se debe a fuertes sentimientos nacionalistas que se han opuesto a[2] los intentos de unificación propuestos desde la época de Simón Bolívar, el libertador del norte de la América del Sur. Como veremos más adelante, alguna forma de integración económica será necesaria para garantizar un futuro de paz y de bienestar para nuestros vecinos al sur del Río Grande.

Otro problema urgente es el de la injusta distribución de la riqueza y del poder.[3] La mayoría de los hispanoamericanos todavía viven bajo regímenes en que el poder y la riqueza se encuentran concentrados en pocas manos. Para asegurar el bienestar de los países hispanoamericanos y fortalecer el desarrollo de los sistemas democráticos, habrá que emprender una serie de reformas económicas y sociales que eliminen los privilegios y la discriminación, den énfasis a la movilidad social y proporcionen a las generaciones

---

[1]**se debe . . . geográfico,** *it is due to the geographic fragmentation (division).*   [2]**que se han opuesto a,** *which have opposed.*   [3] **poder,** *power.*

jóvenes la motivación suficiente para adquirir la preparación científica y técnica necesaria para competir en la sociedad moderna.

Para que puedan desarrollarse en Hispanoamérica las ideas democráticas habrá que dedicar atención especial a la educación de las masas. En los últimos años se han construido miles de escuelas; pero es penoso[4] observar que el índice del analfabetismo[5] todavía excede el 50 por 100 en muchos países, sobre todo en aquellos en que la población indígena es numerosa.

Otro problema gravísimo es el del rápido aumento de la población, el cual, entre otras dificultades, ha creado la necesidad de aumentar proporcionalmente la producción alimenticia.[6] Si la población continúa creciendo al ritmo actual[7] (aproximadamente el 3 por 100 al año), llegará a los seiscientos millones de habitantes en el siglo entrante. Hispanoamérica no tiene hoy día los recursos económicos para construir las viviendas y las escuelas que se necesitan. ¿Qué medios podrán encontrarse para elevar el nivel de vida en el siglo XXI?

En general, se ha considerado la industrialización como el medio más eficaz para elevar el nivel de vida en las regiones subdesarrolladas. En la América hispana, sin embargo,[8] los obstáculos que encuentra la industrialización son muy graves. Uno de los más importantes es la falta de recursos económicos. En la economía de los países hispanoamericanos el comercio exterior[9] ha sido una de las principales fuentes de ingresos,[10] por el estímulo que constituye para las actividades industriales y comerciales. Pues, a pesar de los esfuerzos de los últimos años, el comercio exterior no sigue aumentando con suficiente rapidez. Desgraciadamente, la exportación de productos básicos—como el café o los minerales—no varía mucho de un año a otro. Además, en la nueva edad industrial y tecnológica en que vivimos, la exportación de productos básicos no tiene la importancia que tiene la de artículos manufacturados.

Para contrarrestar la disminución de las exportaciones ha habido un esfuerzo por aumentar la demanda interior,[11] por la creación de mercados nuevos. Es claro que para efectuar una intensa activación del comercio interior habrá que comenzar con una honda transformación de la sociedad, para hacer posible una distribución más equitativa de la riqueza. Las reformas sociales son urgentes no sólo por razones políticas y humanitarias, sino también por razones económicas.

Como ya hemos indicado, será difícil que los países hispanoamericanos puedan llevar a cabo las reformas y programas necesarios para satisfacer las aspiraciones del pueblo si continúan dentro de sus estrechas fronteras actuales. La integración económica de Hispanoamérica es necesaria no sólo para estimular las relaciones comerciales, sino también para hacer posibles las vastas operaciones científicas y técnicas que habrá que emprender en el futuro—operaciones que sólo pueden ser realizadas por naciones de grandes recursos económicos. Sin la integración indicada, los países hispanoamericanos no podrán asumir el puesto que les corresponde en la comunidad de naciones.

Entre las entidades internacionales que han contribuido a elevar el nivel de vida de Hispanoamérica y a fomentar el desarrollo económico general, la más importante es la Organización de los Estados Americanos (OEA). El resultado de un proceso evolutivo

---

[4]**penoso,** *distressing.*   [5]**analfabetismo,** *illiteracy.*   [6]**alimenticia,** *(of) food.*   [7]**al ritmo actual,** *at the present rate.*   [8]**sin embargo,** *however.*   [9]**comercio exterior,** *foreign trade.*   [10]**ingresos,** *income.*   [11]**demanda interior,** *domestic demand.*

que se inició hace más de un siglo, la OEA fue creada en su forma actual en 1948, como un organismo regional dentro de las Naciones Unidas. Desde entonces la OEA ha cumplido sus objetivos de manera ejemplar, [12] manteniendo la paz entre sus miembros, esforzándose por resolver los problemas políticos, jurídicos, sociales y económicos de los respectivos países e impulsando su desarrollo económico, social y cultural.

Al concluir esta larga, pero incompleta, discusión, hay que insistir en el hecho de que los problemas que hemos descrito son nuestros también; las soluciones y remedios que encuentren los países hispanoamericanos afectarán sus relaciones con todas las naciones del mundo libre. Los Estados Unidos ha demostrado que quiere cooperar en la busca de dichas soluciones—pero sin imponer condiciones y sin el papel dominante que ha dañado nuestras relaciones en el pasado. Es preciso que las dos Américas alcancen el máximo grado posible de cooperación y ayuda mutua.

EJERCICIO

Traduzcan al español las frases siguientes, tratando de imitar las construcciones y fraseología del texto:

1. Despite the efforts of the last few years, the Spanish-American countries have not been able to solve many of their social and economic problems.
2. The economic and political weakness of most of those countries is due in part to the geographic fragmentation of the territory.
3. It can also be explained by the strong nationalistic feelings which have opposed all plans of unification.
4. To strengthen the development of democratic systems, it will be necessary to eliminate privileges and discrimination and provide more opportunities for the younger generations.
5. The rapid increase of the population has created the need of increasing proportionately the production of food.
6. Although special attention has been given to the education of the masses, unfortunately the rate of illiteracy still exceeds fifty per cent in many Spanish-American countries.
7. In general, industrialization has been considered as the most effective means of raising the standard of living in underdeveloped regions.
8. In the economy of Spanish America, foreign trade has been one of the principal sources of income.
9. Unfortunately, however, the exportation of basic products has not varied a great deal from one year to another.
10. Since 1948 the OEA has made an effort to solve the various problems of the respective countries, and to promote their economic and cultural development.

---

[12]**de manera ejemplar,** *in an exemplary way.*

CORREOS Y TELEGRAFOS

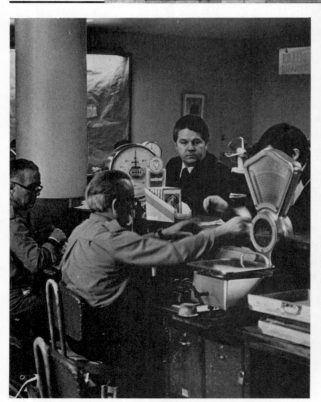

CARTAS ESPAÑOLAS

In the following pages some of the essential principles for business and personal letters in Spanish will be given. Even though many formulas used in Spanish letters are less formal and flowery than formerly, in general they are still less brief and direct than in English letters, and at times they may seem rather stilted. No attempt is made to give a complete treatment of Spanish correspondence, but study of the material included should suffice for ordinary purposes.

The new words and expressions whose English equivalents are given in this section (including the **Vocabulario útil**, page 265) are not listed in the Spanish-English vocabulary unless used elsewhere in the text. However, meanings are listed in the English-Spanish vocabulary for words used in Exercises A, B, and C (page 266).

A. Professional titles

Professional titles are more widely used in the Spanish-speaking countries than in the United States. Some titles are:

Arquitecto (Arq.) Architect
Doctor (Dr.) Doctor (*m.*)
Doctora (Dra.) Doctor (*f.*)
Ingeniero (Ing.) Engineer
Licenciado (Lic.) Licentiate (lawyer, or person who has a permit to practice a profession)

Profesor (Prof.)   Professor (*m.*)
Profesora (Profa.)   Professor (*f.*)

Normally these professional titles are accompanied by **señor (Sr.)**, **señora (Sra.)**, or **señorita (Srta.)**, and followed by **don** or **Don (D.)**, **doña** or **Doña (D^{a.})**:

Dr. D. Felipe Solís   **Lic. D. Ramón Estrada**
Ing. Don Luis Molina   **Profesora doña (D^{a.}) Carmen Valdés**

B. Address on the envelope

The title of the addressee begins with **Señor (Sr.,)**, **Señora (Sra.)**, or **Señorita (Srta.)**. **Sr. don (Sr. D.)** may be used for a man, **Sra. doña (Sra. D^{a.})** for a married woman, and **Srta.** for an unmarried woman:

Señor don Carlos Morelos   **Sr. D. Pedro Ortega y Moreno**[1]
Srta. Isabel Alcalá   **Sra. Dª. María López de Martín**

In the third example note that Spanish surnames often include the name of the father (**Ortega**), followed by that of the mother (**Moreno**). Often the mother's name is dropped (first two examples). A woman's married name is her maiden name followed by **de** and the surname of her husband (fourth example).

The definite article is not used with the titles **don** and **doña**, which have no English equivalents.

Two complete addresses follow:

Sr. D. Luis Montoya   **Srta. Elena Pérez**
Calle de San Martín, 25   **Avenida Bolívar, 245**
Santiago, Chile   **Caracas, Venezuela**

Business letters are addressed to a firm:

Suárez Hermanos (Hnos.)   **Señores (Sres.) López Díaz y Cía., S.A.**
Apartado (Postal) 867   **Paseo de la Reforma, 12**
Buenos Aires, Argentina   **México, D.F., México**

In an address in Spanish, one writes first **Calle** (**Avenida**, *Avenue*; **Paseo**, *Boulevard*; **Camino**, *Road*; **Plaza**, *Square*) **(de)**, then the house number. **Apartado (Postal)**, *Post Office Box*, may be abbreviated to **Apdo. (Postal)**; in Spanish America **Casilla postal** is commonly used for *Post Office Box*. The abbreviation **Cía.** = **Compañía**; **S.A.** = **Sociedad Anónima**, equivalent to English *Inc.* (*Incorporated*); and **D.F.** = **Distrito Federal**, *Federal District*.

---

[1]The conjunction **y** is often not used between the surnames: the person might prefer to be known as **D. Pedro Ortega Moreno.**

Airmail letters are marked **Vía aérea, Correo aéreo,** or **Por avión.** Special delivery letters are marked **Urgente** or **Entrega inmediata,** and registered letters, **Certificada.** Other directions on the envelope may be: **Particular,** *Private, Personal;* **Lista de correos,** *General Delivery;* **Para reexpedir,** *(Please) Forward;* **Impresos,** *Printed Matter;* **No doblar,** *Don't Fold.*

C. Heading of the letter

The usual form of the date line is:

México, D.F., 27 de enero de 1980

The month is usually not capitalized unless it is given first in the date. For the first day of the month, 1° **(primero)** is commonly used; the other days are written 2, 3, 4, etc. Other less common forms for the date line are:

Lima, a 15 de junio de 1979
Bogotá, 1° agosto 1978

The address which precedes the salutation of the business and formal social letter is the same as that on the envelope. In familiar letters only the salutation need be used.

D. Salutations

Appropriate salutations for business letters or those addressed to strangers, equivalent to *My dear Sir, Dear Sir, Dear Madam, Gentlemen, etc.,* are:

Muy señor (Sr.) mío: *(from one person to one gentleman)*
Muy señores (Sres.) míos: *(from one person to a firm)*
Muy señor nuestro: *(from a firm to one gentleman)*
Muy señores nuestros: *(from one firm to another firm)*
Muy señora (Sra.) mía: *(from one person to a woman)*
Muy señorita (Srta.) nuestra: *(from a firm to a young woman)*

Formulas which may be used in less formal letters are:

Estimado(s) señor(es):   Dear Sir (Gentlemen):
Distinguido(s) señor(es):   Dear Sir (Gentlemen):
Estimado profesor: Dear Professor:
Muy estimado Sr. Salas: Dear Mr. Salas:
Mi (Muy) distinguido amigo (colega):   Dear Friend (Colleague):
(Muy) apreciado señor (amigo):   Dear Sir (Friend):

Forms used in addressing relatives or close friends, equivalent to *(My) dear brother, friend, etc.,* are:

Querido hermano (Luis):   **(Mi) querida hija:**
Querida amiga mía: **Queridísima[1] mamá:**
Apreciado amigo: **Estimada amiga (Diana):**

---

[1]**Queridísima,** *Dearest.*

Great care must be taken to be consistent in the agreement of salutations and conclusions in Spanish letters, keeping in mind whether the letter is addressed to a man, woman, or firm, and whether it is signed by one person or by an individual for a firm.

E. The body of business letters

The Spanish business letter usually begins with a brief sentence which indicates the purpose of the letter. Some examples, with English translations, follow. Note that the sentences cannot always be translated word for word:

Acabo (Acabamos) de recibir su carta del 10 de septiembre.
I (We) have just received your letter of September 10.
Le acusamos recibo de su atenta[1] del 2 del corriente . . .
We acknowledge receipt of your letter of the 2nd (of this month) . . .
He (Hemos) recibido con mucho agrado su amable carta . . .
I was (We were) very glad to receive your (good) letter . . .
Nos referimos a su favor de . . .
We are referring to your letter of . . .
Tenemos a la vista su carta de fecha 8 del actual . . .
We have (at hand) your letter of the 8th (of this month) . . .
Tengo (Tenemos) el honor de acusar recibo de la mercancía . . .
I am (We are) happy to acknowledge receipt of the merchandise . . .
Tenemos el placer de informar a usted[2] que . . .
We are pleased to inform you that . . .
Me (Nos) es grato comunicarle(s) que . . .
I am (We are) pleased to inform you that . . .
Rogamos a Uds. se sirvan[3] enviarnos a vuelta de correo . . .
We ask that you kindly send us by return mail . . .
Les agradeceremos se sirvan comunicarnos . . .
We shall be grateful if you will please let us know . . .
Mucho agradeceré a Ud. el mandarme . . .
I shall be very glad if you will send me . . .
Obra en mi (nuestro) poder su grata de 30 de marzo p. pdo.[4] . . .
I (We) have at hand your letter of March 30 . . .
Le doy a Ud. las gracias por el pedido que se sirvió hacerme . . .
Thank you for the order which you kindly placed with me . . .
Le envío giro postal por $30.00 . . .
I am sending you a postal money order for $30.00 . . .

---

[1]**Carta** is often replaced with **favor, grata, atenta.**   [2]Since **usted** is technically a noun (coming from **vuestra merced,** *your grace*), the object pronoun **le** may be omitted. This practice is noted particularly in letter writing.   [3]After such verbs as **rogar, pedir, suplicar, esperar, agradecer** the conjunction **que** is often omitted.   [4]**p. pdo.** *or* **ppdo.** = **próximo pasado,** *last, past.*

Con fecha 8 del actual me permití escribir a usted, informándole . . .

On the 8th of this month I took the liberty of writing to you, informing you . . .

Tengo el agrado de dirigirme a usted para agradecerle el envío de . . .

I have the pleasure of writing to thank you for sending me . . .

En respuesta a su atenta carta del 15 del corriente, nos es grato remitirles adjunto lista de precios y condiciones de venta.

In reply to your letter of the 15th, we are pleased to send you (enclosed) our price list and conditions of sale.

Sírva(n)se reservarme para el 10 del corriente (del próximo) una habitación con dos camas y con baño. La estancia será de ocho días.

Please reserve for me for the 10th of this month (of next month) a room with two beds and with bath. The length of stay will be for one week.

F. Conclusions

The Spanish conclusion usually requires more than a mere *Very truly yours*, or *Sincerely yours*. However, there is a tendency nowadays to shorten conclusions of business letters, particularly as correspondence continues with an individual or firm. Appropriate conclusions for business letters or those addressed to strangers are:

Queda[1] (Quedo) de Ud(s). atento y seguro servidor,

I remain,

      Sincerely (Respectfully) yours,

Aprovecho esta oportunidad para saludarle(s)[2] atentamente,

I am taking advantage of this opportunity to remain,

                Sincerely yours,

Aprovechamos esta ocasión para ofrecernos sus attos.[3] y ss. ss.,

We take advantage of this occasion to remain,

                Sincerely yours,

Me repito[4] su afmo. s. s. *or* Nos repetimos sus afmos. ss. ss.,

I (We) remain,

      Sincerely,

---

[1]**Queda** is in the third person if the signee is the subject of the verb. Note similar use of other verbs in other examples.   [2]Several formulas used in the **Cartas españolas** section come from letters written in Spain. See page 55, including footnotes 1 and 2, for forms of third person direct object pronouns.   [3]Abbreviations used in the conclusions given are: **atto.** = **atento; attos.** = **atentos; s. s.** or **S. S.** = **seguro servidor** (*sing.*), lit., *your servant;* **ss. ss.** or **SS. SS.** = **seguros servidores** (*pl.*); **afmo. (afma.)** = **afectísimo (afectísima),** *sincere(ly), affectionate(ly);* **afmos. (afmas.)** = **afectísimos (afectísimas); atte.** = **atentamente.**   [4]After the first letter (in which the verb **approvechar** may have been used), **Me repito** is a good expression.

Quedamos de ustedes attos. y SS. SS.,
We remain,

      Very truly yours,

En espera de sus gratas noticias, les saluda atentamente,
Awaiting the expected good news from you, I remain,

      Sincerely,

Anticipándoles las gracias, nos reiteramos de Ud(s). atte.,
Thanking you in advance, we remain,

      Sincerely yours,

Les agradecemos su atención, y nos repetimos de Uds. attos. ss. ss.,
We thank you for your attention (to the matter), and we remain,

      Sincerely yours,

Lo saludan (muy) atentamente,
We are (remain),

      Sincerely yours,

Cartero repartiendo las cartas, Salamanca, España.

Some conclusions, with many possible variations, for informal social letters equivalent to *Cordially yours, Affectionately yours*, etc., are:

> Suyo (Tuyo) afectísimo (afmo.) *or* Suya (Tuya) afectísima (afma.),
> Suyos afectísimos (afmos.) *or* Suyas afectísimas (afmas.),
> Queda (Quedo) suyo afmo. (suya afma.),
> Le saluda cariñosamente[1] (muy atentamente),
> Le saluda muy cordialmente (su servidor y amigo),
> Se despide afectuosamente[2] (cordialmente),
> (Con el cariño[3] de) tu buen amigo (buena amiga),
> Cariñosos saludos[4] de tu amigo (amiga),
> Sinceramente, Cariñosamente, Afectuosamente,
> (Un abrazo[5] de) tu hijo, (*one boy signs*)
> Tu hijo (hija), que te quiere, (*one boy or girl signs*)
> Con todo el cariño (amor)[6] de tu hermano (hermana),
> Recibe todo mi cariño (amor), (*a young(er) person signs*)

Other phrases which may accompany these formulas are:

> Dé (Da) mis mejores recuerdos a toda su (tu) familia,
> Give my best regards to all your family,

> Salude afectuosamente de mi parte a sus padres,
> Give my affectionate (cordial) greetings to your parents,

> Con mis mejores deseos para Ud. y los suyos, me despido,
> With my best wishes for you and your family, I am (remain),

G. Sample letters

The following letters translated freely from Spanish to English will show how natural, idiomatic phrases in one language convey the same idea in another. Read the following letters aloud for practice, and be able to write any of them from dictation. The teacher may want to test comprehension by asking questions in Spanish on the content of the letters. At the end of this section are listed some words and phrases, not all of which are used in the sample letters, which should be useful in composing original letters.

---

[1]**cariñosamente,** *affectionately.*   [2]**afectuosamente,** *affectionately.*   [3]**cariño,** *affection.*   [4]**saludos,** *greetings.*   [5]**abrazo,** *embrace.*   [6]**amor,** *love.*

1

BIBLOGRAF, S.A.   DEPARTAMENTO EDITORIAL

Calle del Bruch, 151   -   Teléfonos   257 31 58/257 18 01   Telegramas: BIBLOGRAF

Barcelona, 3 de enero de 1979
Vía aérea

_____

_____

_____

Muy señores nuestros:

    Nos complacemos en acusar recibo de su atenta carta del día 18 de diciembre próximo pasado y de acuerdo con sus deseos les remitimos por correo aéreo aparte un catálogo, folletos y lista de precios de nuestras ediciones.

    Sobre los precios de esta lista les ofrecemos el 40% de descuento, con cargo de los gastos de embalaje, envío y seguro y pago por cheque a la recepción de la mercancía.

    Les rogamos se sirvan tomar nota de que nuestras obras son de libre adquisición en los Estados Unidos y que no tenemos concedida (ni por el momento entra en nuestros propósitos concederla) la exclusiva de su distribución en ese país.

    En espera de sus gratas órdenes, les saludamos muy atentamente,

BIBLOGRAF, S.A.

BIBLOGRAF, S.A.   PUBLISHING (EDITORIAL) DEPARTMENT

151 Bruch Street   Telephones   257 31 58/257 18 01   Telegrams: BIBLOGRAF

Barcelona, January 3, 1979
Air mail

_____

_____

_____

Gentlemen:

    We are pleased to acknowledge receipt of your (good) letter of (this past) December 18, and in accordance with your wishes we are sending you separately by air mail a catalogue, pamphlets, and a price list of our editions.

    We can offer 40 percent discount on prices of this list, less charge for packing, shipment, and insurance. Payment by check (is due) upon receipt of the merchandise.

    Please note that our works (publications) can be acquired freely in the United States and that we do not grant (nor for the moment are we thinking of granting) exclusive rights for their distribution in your country.

    Awaiting your kind orders, we remain,

Sincerely yours,

BIBLOGRAF, S.A.

2

Madrid, 8 de enero de 1977

_____

_____

_____

Muy Sres. nuestros:

Acusamos recibo de su atenta de fecha 26 de diciembre ppdo., y les notificamos que el precio bruto por un año de suscripción a nuestro diario ABC con destino a Estados Unidos, envío marítimo, es de 23,20$.[1]

La comisión máxima que se les puede abonar es del 10% de la cantidad ya citada.

Las órdenes de suscripción deberán venir acompañadas de su importe líquido, significándoles que el comienzo del servicio ha de ser siempre con el día primero de cada mes.

La remisión de los importes mencionados deberán hacerse por medio de cheque bancario a nombre de Prensa Española, S.A., Serrano, 61, Madrid.

Con este motivo, nos reiteramos suyos affmos. ss. ss.,

POR "PRENSA ESPAÑOLA" S.A.

Madrid, January 8, 1977

Gentlemen:

We acknowledge receipt of your letter of (this past) December 26, and we are notifying you that the gross price for a year's subscription to our newspaper ABC going to the United States by sea, is $23.20.

The maximum commission which can be granted is 10% of the amount mentioned above.

Subscription orders should be accompanied by the net amount, and we point out to you that the beginning of service (the subscription) must always be as of the first day of each month.

Remittance of the amounts mentioned must be made by (means of) bank check in the name of Spanish Press, S.A., 61 Serrano, Madrid.

(For this purpose), we remain,

Sincerely yours,

For "Spanish Press" S.A.

---

[1]Read **veintitrés dólares, veinte centavos.** While the comma between the **dólares** and **centavos** has largely been replaced in Spanish by a period, it is still used. (Also, the English comma is often written as a period in Spanish: 1.023,20.) The dollar sign is sometimes placed after the amount in Spanish.

3

AFRODISIO AGUADO, S.A.

Editores — Libreros

LIBRERÍA GENERAL   OFICINAS Y ALMACENES
Marqués de Cubas, 5   Bordadores, 5
Teléfonos   31 88 29 y 21 26 21   Teléfonos   48 63 19 y 48 59 29

MADRID

20 de junio de 1979

_____
_____
_____

Muy Sres. nuestros:

Nos referimos a su atenta del 12 del corriente que agradecemos.

Con esta fecha por correo aéreo, como impresos, les remitimos nuestro catálogo general y folletos de novedades para que se informen de nuestra producción editorial.

Rogamos presten atención a nuestras series "CLÁSICOS Y MAESTROS," donde recientemente hemos incorporado "AL MARGEN DE ESTOS CLÁSICOS," por Julián Marías, en una edición especial dedicada al universitario norteamericano, y "ASPECTOS DEL MUNDO ACTUAL," con tomos de gran interés.

La escala de descuentos que podemos aplicarles para sus encargos es la siguiente:

Pedidos hasta 10.000 Ptas. . . .   35% de descuento
Pedidos hasta 50.000 Ptas. . . .   40% de descuento
Pedidos superiores . . . . . .   45% de descuento

Nuestros envíos son efectuados por vía marítima en paquetes certificados y asegurados. Les cargamos únicamente los gastos de envío.

Quedamos, pues, en espera de sus noticias y tengan la seguridad de que atenderemos cualquier sugerencia que nos puedan hacer sobre el particular. Atentamente les saludamos,

AFRODISIO AGUADO, S.A.

Publishers—Book Dealers

GENERAL BOOKSTORE
5 Marqués de Cubas
Telephones   31 88 29 and 21 26 21

OFFICES AND WAREHOUSES
5 Bordadores
Telephones   48 63 19 and 48 59 29

MADRID

June 20, 1979

_____
_____
_____

Gentlemen:

Reference is to your letter of June 12 for which we thank you.

By air mail we are sending you today, as printed matter, our general catalogue and pamphlets on recent items in order that you may be informed of our publishing production.

We urge that you note (*lit.*, pay attention to) our series "CLASSICS AND (GREAT) TEACHERS," in which we have recently included "AL MARGEN DE ESTOS CLÁSICOS" (*Marginal Notes on these Classics*), by Julián Marías, in a special edition intended for the American university student, and "ASPECTOS DEL MUNDO ACTUAL" (*Aspects of Today's World*), with volumes of great interest.

The scale of discounts which we can apply for your orders is the following:

Orders up to 10,000 pesetas . . .   35% discount
Orders up to 50,000 pesetas . . .   40% discount
Larger orders . . . .   45% discount

Our shipments are made by sea in registered and insured packages. We charge you only for shipping expenses.

We await, then, word from you, and you may be sure that we shall take care of any suggestion you may wish to make to us concerning the matter.
We are (remain),

Sincerely yours,

4

Madrid, 26 de diciembre de 1978

_____
_____
_____

Muy señores nuestros:

Contestamos a su atenta carta de fecha 18 del corriente mes de diciembre.

Tomamos nota de la próxima visita del Sr. Hurtado de Mendoza, al cual tendremos mucho gusto en saludar personalmente.

Si ustedes desean que vayamos a buscarle al aeropuerto o cualquier otra gestión que podamos hacer desde aquí, saben estamos a su completa disposición.

Sin otro particular y en espera de sus siempre gratas noticias, aprovechamos la ocasión para saludarles muy atentamente y desearles unas Felices Navidades y un venturoso año 1979,

Madrid, December 26, 1978

_____
_____
_____

Gentlemen:

We are replying to your good letter of December 18.

We note the coming visit of Mr. Hurtado de Mendoza, whom we shall be very happy to greet personally.

If you want us to pick him up at the airport, or if there is anything else we can do here, we want you to know that we are completely at your service.

Without anything further and awaiting the good news we always have from you, we take advantage of this opportunity to remain sincerely yours, and to wish you a Merry Christmas and a happy 1979,

Vocabulario útil

abonar   to credit

adjunto, -a   enclosed, attached; *m. also adv.*

agradecer   to be grateful for, thank for

anexo, -a   enclosed, attached

aprovechar   to take advantage of

el **buzón**   mailbox

la **cantidad**   quantity, amount

cargar   to charge

la **casa de correos**   post office

el **catálogo**   catalogue

certificar   to register

comunicar   to inform, tell

dirigir   to address, direct

el **ejemplar**   copy

el **envío**   shipment, remittance

la **estampilla**   (postage) stamp (*Am.*)

la **factura**   bill, invoice

la **firma**   signature

el **franqueo**   postage

el **gerente**   manager

el **giro**   draft

grato, -a   kind, pleased

el **importe**   cost, amount

la **muestra**   sample

ofrecer(se)   to offer, be, offer one's services

el **pago**   payment

el **pasado**   last month

el **pedido**   order

permitirse   to take the liberty (to)

el **recibo**   receipt

referir (ie, i)   to refer

remitir   to remit, send

rogar (ue)   to ask, beg

el **saldo**   balance

el **sello**   (postage) stamp (*Spain*)

servirse (i,i)   to be so kind as to

el **sobre**   envelope

la **solicitud**   request

suplicar   to beg, ask

el **timbre**   (postage) stamp (*Am.*)

---

a la mayor brevedad posible   as soon as possible

a las órdenes de Ud(s).   at your service

a vuelta de correo   by return mail

acusar recibo de   to acknowledge receipt of

al cuidado de (a/c)   in care of (c/o)

anticipar las gracias   to thank in advance

dar(le) las gracias a (uno)   to thank (one)

de acuerdo con   in compliance with

del corriente (actual)   of the present month

echar al correo   to mail

en contestación a   in reply to

en espera de   awaiting

en pago de   in payment of

en su cuenta   to one's account

estar encargado, -a de   to be in charge of

giro postal   money order

hacer un pedido   to place (give) an order

haga(n) Ud(s). el favor de + *inf.*   please + *verb*

lista de precios   price list

me repito (nos repetimos)   I (we) remain

(nos) es grato   (we) are pleased

nos place   we are pleased

paquete postal   parcel post

por separado   under separate cover

sírva(n)se + *inf.*   please + *verb*, be pleased to + *inf.*

tener el agrado (gusto, placer) de + *inf.*   to be pleased (to) + *inf.*

tener la bondad de + *inf.*   to have the kindness to + *inf.*,   please + *verb*

EJERCICIOS

A. Address envelopes to the following:

1. Mr. Richard Castillo
   10 Santa Ana Square
   Madrid 10, Spain

3. Professor George Medina
   Box 546
   Buenos Aires, Argentina

2. Mrs. Louis Ortiz
   25 Bolívar Avenue
   Lima, Peru

4. López Brothers
   45 Madero Street
   Mexico City, Mexico

B. Give the following date lines and salutations:

1. Buenos Aires, December 10, 1979; Dear Mr. Aguilar: 2. Bogotá, January 1, 1977; Dear Mrs. Rivas: 3. La Paz, October 12, 1978; Dear Miss Ortega: 4. Mexico City, July 14, 1979; Dear Mother: 5. Sevilla, April 20, 1978; Dear Robert: 6. Barcelona, August 15, 1979; Dear daughter:

C. Give in Spanish:

1. Dear Sir: (*from one person*) 2. Dear Sir: (*from a firm*) 3. Dear Madam: (*from one person*) 4. Gentlemen: (*from one person*) 5. Gentlemen: (*from a firm*) 6. My dear Madam: (*to a young woman from one person*)

D. Read in Spanish, then give in correct business English:

1. He recibido su atenta carta del 9 de octubre.
2. Acabo de recibir el libro que se sirvió usted enviarme.
3. Le doy a Ud. las gracias por el pedido que se sirvió hacerme.
4. Tengo el gusto de comunicarle que me fue muy grato recibir su atenta del 16 del corriente.
5. De acuerdo con su solicitud, le remitimos hoy . . .
6. Adjunta le remitimos una muestra.
7. Ruego a ustedes tengan la bondad de darme informes . . .
8. Su carta del 11 del corriente fue referida a nuestro gerente.
9. Tengo el gusto de referirme a su atenta carta del 31 del pasado.
10. Acusamos a usted recibo de su giro postal por la cantidad de . . .

E. Give approximate translations for the following conclusions and indicate whether the signature would be that of an individual or a firm:

1. Aprovecho esta oportunidad para quedar de usted su afectísimo y s. s.,
2. Me pongo a las órdenes de ustedes para todo lo que pueda servirles,
3. En espera de sus noticias, quedo a sus órdenes y le saludo muy cordialmente,
4. Esperando poder servirles en otra ocasión, nos repetimos, atentamente,
5. Agradeciéndoles su atención, saluda a Uds. muy atentamente,

F. Suggestions for original letters in Spanish:

1. Write to a foreign student, describing some of your daily activities. Try to use words which you have had in this text or some previous text.
2. Write to a member of your family, describing some shopping you have done.
3. Assume that you are the Spanish secretary for an American exporting firm. Write a reply to a Spanish-American firm which has asked for a recent catalogue and prices.
4. Write to an individual, thanking him for his check, which has been received in payment of an invoice of a certain date. Give the balance which remains in his account.

APPENDICES

APPENDIX A

Pronunciation

The Spanish Alphabet

Letter	Name	Letter	Name	Letter	Name
a	a	j	jota	r	ere
b	be	k	ka	rr	erre
c	ce	l	ele	s	ese
ch	che	ll	elle	t	te
d	de	m	eme	u	u
e	e	n	ene	v	ve, uve
f	efe	ñ	eñe	w	doble ve
g	ge	o	o	x	equis
h	hache	p	pe	y	ye, i griega
i	i	q	cu	z	zeta

In addition to the letters used in the English alphabet, **ch, ll, ñ,** and **rr** represent single sounds in Spanish and are considered single letters. In dictionaries and vocabularies, words or syllables which begin with **ch, ll,** and **ñ** follow words or syllables that begin with **c, l,** and **n,** while **rr,** which never begins a word, is alphabetized as in English. **K** and **w** are used only in words of foreign origin. The names of the letters are feminine: **la be,** (*the*) *b*; **la jota,** (*the*) *j*.

The Spanish alphabet is divided into vowels **(a, e, i, o, u)** and consonants. The letter **y** represents the vowel sound **i** in the conjunction **y,** *and,* and when final in a word, as in **hay,** *there is, there are;* **ley,** *law;* **hoy,** *today;* **muy,** *very.*

The Spanish vowels are divided into two groups, strong vowels **(a, e, o)** and weak vowels **(i, u).**

General Remarks. Definition of Phonetic Terms

Even though Spanish uses practically the same alphabet as English, few sounds are identical in the two languages. In describing the Spanish sounds, it will sometimes be necessary to make comparisons between the familiar English sounds and the unfamiliar Spanish ones in order to show how Spanish is pronounced. The student should avoid, of course, the use of English sounds in Spanish words; he should strive to follow the explanations of the text and imitate the pronunciation of the teacher and of the tapes.

In general, Spanish pronunciation is much clearer and more uniform than the English. The vowel sounds are clipped short and are not followed by the diphthongal glide which is commonly heard in English, as in *no* (*no^u*), *came* (*ca^ime*), *why* (*why^e*). Even unstressed vowels are pronounced clearly and distinctly; the slurred sound of English *a* in *fireman*, for example, never occurs in Spanish.

Spanish consonants, likewise, are usually pronounced more precisely and distinctly than English consonants, although a few (especially **b, d,** and **g** between vowels) are pronounced very weakly. Several of them (**t, d, l,** and **n**) are pronounced farther forward in the mouth, with the tongue close to the upper teeth and gums. The consonants **p, t,** and **c** (before letters other than **e** and **i**) are never followed by the *h* sound that is often heard in English: *pen* (*p^hen*), *task* (*t^hask*), *can* (*c^han*).

To allow for greater accuracy in the description of Spanish speech sounds, it will be helpful to be familiar with the phonetic terms explained in the following paragraphs:

Voiced and voiceless sounds. A sound is said to be voiceless when, during its articulation, the breath passes through the larynx without the vibration of the vocal cords. When the sound is accompanied by the vibration of the vocal cords, it is called voiced. All vowels are normally voiced sounds; consonants, however, may be voiced or voiceless.[1]

Stop and continuant consonants. A stop consonant is one in the making of which the passage of the air through the mouth is for a brief moment entirely stopped, after which the stoppage is released and the air is allowed to pass; such are the consonants in English, *pat, cub, dog*. Continuants are consonants in the production of which there is a continuous passage of air and, consequently, a continuous sound, capable of being prolonged, such as the consonants in English *thief, save*.

Place of articulation. Sounds are also classified according to the position or place where the chief obstruction to the passage of the breath is made. If this obstruction is formed between the two lips, the sound is called bilabial: *p* in English *pen*. If the obstruction is made between the teeth, the sound is called interdental: English *th* in *thin*. If the tip of the tongue forms the obstruction back of the teeth, the sound is called dental: **t** in Spanish **tú**. If the obstruction is formed at the alveolar ridge (that is, the ridge that covers the base of the upper teeth), the sound is called alveolar: *t* in English *ten*. If the obstruction is between the tongue and the hard palate, the sound is called palatal: *ch* in English *church*. If it is between the tongue and the soft palate or velum, the sound is called velar: *c* in English *cut*.

Division of Words into Syllables

Spanish words are hyphenated at the end of a line and are divided into syllables according to the following principles:

a. A single consonant (including **ch, ll, rr**) is placed with the vowel which follows: **co-sa, mu-cha-cha, si-lla, co-rren.**

---

[1] The following Spanish consonants are normally voiced: **b, d, g, l, ll, m, n, ñ, r, rr, v, y.** One can easily learn to perceive the distinction between voiced and voiceless consonants by covering the ears with one's hands during the articulation of the sounds. After covering the ears, pronounce first, for example, the *z* of English *daze* and then the *ss* of English *hiss*; the distinction between voiced *z* and voiceless *ss* can be readily felt.

b. Two consonants are usually divided: **com-pa-ñe-ro, pre-sen-tan, gus-to, al-mor-zar.** Consonants followed by **l** or **r**, however, are generally pronounced together and go with the following vowel: **o-bra, pa-dre, a-pren-do.** The groups **nl, rl, sl, tl, nr,** and **sr,** however, are divided: **Car-los, En-ri-que.**

c. In combinations of three or more consonants, only the last consonant or the two consonants of the inseparable groups just mentioned (consonant plus **l** or **r,** with the exceptions listed) begin a syllable: **ins-pi-ra-ción, com-pran, in-glés, en-tra.**

d. Two adjacent strong vowels (**a, e, o**) are in separate syllables: **le-o, tra-en, cre-e.**

e. Combinations of a strong and weak vowel (**i,u**), or of two weak vowels, normally form single syllables: **Jai-me, gra-cias, vein-te, bien, sois, es-tu-dio, cau-sa, cuar-to, puer-ta, ciu-dad, Luis.** Such combinations of two vowels are called *diphthongs.* (See page 275 for further discussion of diphthongs.)

f. In combinations of a strong and weak vowel, a written accent mark on the weak vowel divides the two vowels into separate syllables: **dí-a, pa-ís, tí-o.** An accent on the strong vowel of such combinations does not result in two syllables: **lec-ción, tam-bién.**

Word Stress[1]

a. Most words which end in a vowel, or in **n** or **s** (plural endings of verbs and nouns, respectively), are stressed on the next to the last syllable: *di*-ce, ma-*le*-ta, *to*-mo, *en*-tran, *or*-den, *ca*-sas.

b. Most words which end in a consonant, except **n** or **s,** are stressed on the last syllable: **pro-fe-*sor*, ha-*blar*, ciu-*dad*, u-ni-ver-si-*dad*, ca-pi-*tal*, I-sa-*bel*, an-da-*luz*, e-fi-*caz*.**

c. Words not pronounced according to these two rules have a written accent on the stressed syllable: **ca-*fé*, in-*glés*, lec-*ción*, tam-*bién*, *lá*-piz, *mú*-si-ca.**

d. The written accent is also used to distinguish between two words spelled alike but different in meaning (**si,** *if,* **sí,** *yes;* **el,** *the,* **él,** *he,* etc.), and on the stressed syllable of all interrogative words (**¿*dón*-de?** *where?*), and a few exclamatory words (**¡*Qué* par-*ti*-do!** *What a game!*)

Vowels

a is pronounced between the *a* of English *ask* and the *a* of *father:* **al**-ta, *ca*-sa, *A*-na.
e is pronounced like *e* in *café,* but without the glide sound that follows the *e* in English: **a-pa-*re*-ce, *de*-be, us-*ted*.**
i (y) is pronounced like *i* in *machine:* **Fe-*li*-pe, *sí*, to-da-*ví*-a, y.**

---

[1] In this and the following four subsections, the stressed syllable of Spanish examples is italicized.

o is pronounced like *o* in *obey*, but without the glide sound that follows the *o* in English: *no, so-*lo, *to-*mo, co-*mi-*da.

u is pronounced like *oo* in *cool*: **us-***ted*, *u-***no**, *gus-*to.

The vowels **e** and **o** also have sounds like *e* in *let* and *o* in *for*. These sounds, as in English, generally occur when the **e** and **o** are followed by a consonant in the same syllable: *él*, *ser*, *son*, *es-pa-ñol*. In pronouncing the **e** in *él* and **ser** and the **o** in **son** and **español**, the mouth is opened wider and the distance between the tongue and the palate is greater than when pronouncing the **e** in **aparece** and **debe**, and the **o** in **no** and **solo**. These more open sounds of **e** and **o** occur also in contact with the strongly trilled **r (rr)**, before the **j** sound (written **g** before **e** or **i**, and **j**), and in the diphthongs **ei (ey)** and **oi (oy)**. Pay close attention to the teacher's pronunciation of these sounds.

Consonants

b and **v** are pronounced exactly alike. Each has two different sounds, a voiced stop sound and a voiced continuant sound. At the beginning of a breath-group (see pages 275–276), or after **m** or **n** (also pronounced **m** in this case), whether within a word or between words, Spanish **b** (or **v**) is a voiced bilabial stop, similar to English *b* in *boy*, but somewhat weaker: *bien*, *bue-***nas**, *va-***mos**, *un va-***so**. In all other positions, it is a voiced bilabial continuant; the lips do not close completely, as in stop **b**, but allow the breath to pass between them through a very narrow passage: *li-***bro**, *Cu-***ba**, *no va-***mos**. When between vowels, the articulation is especially weak. Avoid the English *v* sound.

c before **e** and **i**, and **z** in all positions, are pronounced like the English hissed *s* in *sent* in Spanish America and in southern Spain. In northern and central Spain, this sound is like *th* in *thin*. Examples: *cen-***tro**, *ci-***ne**, *gra-***cias**, *za-***pa**-to, ma-*íz*.

c before all other letters, **k**, and **qu** are like English *c* in *cat*, but without the *h* sound that often follows the *c* in English: *cam-***po**, *co-***sa**, *cla-***se**, ki-*ló-***me**-tro, *que-***dan**, *par-***que**. Note both sounds of **c** in *cin-***co**, *lec-***ción**.

ch is pronounced like English *ch* in *church*: *mu-***cho**, *co-***che**, *cho-co-la-***te**.

d has two sounds, a voiced stop sound and a voiced continuant sound. At the beginning of a breath-group, or when after **l** or **n**, Spanish **d** is a voiced dental stop, like a weak English *d*, but with the tip of the tongue touching the inner surface of the upper front teeth, rather than the ridge above the teeth, as in English: *dar*, *mun-***do**, *sal-***dré**. In all other cases the tongue drops even lower, and the **d** is pronounced as a voiced interdental continuant, like a weak English *th* in *this*: *ca-***da**, *ma-***dre**, *to-***do**. The sound is especially weak in the ending **-ado** and when final in a word before a pause: *es-***ta**-do, **us-***ted*, *Ma-***drid**.

f is pronounced like English *f*: *fá-***cil**, *Fe-li-***pe**.

g before **e** and **i**, and **j** in all positions, have no English equivalent. They are pronounced approximately like a strongly exaggerated *h* in *halt* (rather like the rasping German *ch* in *Buch*): *gen-***te**, *di-ri-***gir**, *hi-***jo**, *Jor-***ge**, *re-***gión**. (The letter **x** in the words **México** and **mexicano**, spelled **Méjico** and **mejicano** in Spain, is pronounced like Spanish **j**.)

g in other positions, and **gu** before **e** or **i**, are pronounced alike. Each has two sounds, a voiced stop sound and a voiced continuant sound. At the beginning of a breath- group, or when after **n**, Spanish **g** (written **gu** before **e** or **i**) is a voiced velar stop, like a weak English *g* in *go*: *gra*-**cias**, **gui**-*ta*-**rra**, **ten**-*go*. In all other cases, except before **e** or **i** in the groups **ge**, **gi**, Spanish **g** is a voiced velar continuant, that is, the sound is much weaker, and the breath continues to pass between the back of the tongue and the palate: **a**-*mi*-**ga**, *ha*-**go**, **la gui**-*ta*-**rra**. (In the combinations **gua** and **guo**, the **u** is pronounced like English **w** in *wet*: **a**-**gua**, *len*-**gua**, **an**-*ti*-**guo**; when the diaeresis is used over **u** in the combinations **güe**, **güi**, the **u** has the same sound: **ver**-*güen*-**za**, **ni**-**ca**-**ra**-*güen*-**se**.)

h is always silent: *ho*-**ra**, *ham*-**bre**, *hoy*.

l is pronounced like *l* in *leap,* with the tip and front part of the tongue well forward in the mouth: **lec**-*tu*-**ra**, **pa**-*pel*.

ll is pronounced like *y* in *yes* in most of Spanish America and in some sections of Spain; in other parts of Spain it is somewhat like *lli* in *million*: **e**-**lla**, **a**-**ma**-*ri*-**llo**, **lla**-*mar*.

m is pronounced like English *m*: **mi**-**ro**, **mo**-*men*-**to**.

n is pronounced like English *n*: **no**, **com**-*pren*-**den**. Before **b**, **v**, **m**, and **p**, however, it is pronounced like *m*: *un ban*-**co**, **in**-**vi**-*tar*. Before **c**, **qu**, **g**, and **j**, it is pronounced like English *n* in *sing*: *blan*-**co**, *ven*-**go**, **con**-**Jua**-*ni*-**ta**.

ñ is pronounced somewhat like the English *ny* in *canyon*: **se**-*ñor*, **ma**-*ña*-**na**, **a**-*ño*, **com**-**pa**-*ñe*-**ro**.

p is pronounced like English *p*, but without the *h* sound that often follows the *p* in English: *pa*-**so**, *pe*-**so**.

q (always written with **u**): see page 273, under **c**, **k**, and **qu**.

r and **rr** represent two different sounds. Single **r**, except when initial in a word and when after **l**, **n**, or **s**, is a voiced, alveolar, single trill, that is, it is pronounced with a single tap produced by the tip of the tongue against the gums of the upper teeth. The sound is much like *dd* in *eddy* pronounced rapidly: **ca**-**ra**, **o**-**ro**, **ha**-*blar*. When initial in a word, when after **l**, **n**, or **s**, and when doubled, the sound is a multiple trill, the tip of the tongue striking the gums in a series of very rapid vibrations: *ri*-**co**, *ro*-**jo**, **pi**-*za*-**rra**, **ca**-**rre**-*te*-**ra**, **En**-*ri*-**que**.

s is a voiceless, alveolar continuant, somewhat like the English hissed *s* in *sent*: **ca**-**si**, *es*-**tos**. Before the voiced **b**, **d**, **g**, **l**, **ll**, **m**, **n**, **ñ**, **r**, **v**, and **y**, however, Spanish **s** becomes voiced and is pronounced like English *s* in *rose*: **las** *blu*-**sas**, **des**-*gra*-**cia**, *mis*-**mo**, **los** **li**-**bros**, *es* **ver**-*dad*.

t is pronounced with the tip of the tongue touching the back of the upper front teeth (rather than the ridge above the teeth as in English); it is never followed by the *h* sound that is often heard in English: *to*-**ma**, *tar*-**des**, *tiem*-**po**, *tres*.

v: see page 273, under **b**.

x is pronounced as follows: (1) before a consonant it is pronounced like Spanish **s**, that is, it is a voiceless alveolar continuant sound, similar to English hissed *s* in *sent*: **ex**-**pli**-*car*, **ex**-**tran**-*je*-**ro**; (2) between vowels it is usually a double sound, consisting of a Spanish velar continuant **g** (as in *a*-**gua**) followed by a voiceless, hissed *s*: **e**-*xa*-**men** (eg-*sa*-**men**), *é*-**xi**-**to** (*ég*-**si**-**to**); (3) in a few words **x** may be pronounced *s* (a voiceless alveolar continuant sound) even between vowels, as in **e**-*xac*-**to**, **au**-**xi**-*liar* (and in words built on these words).

y is pronounced like a strong English *y* in *you*: *ya*, *yo*, **ma**-**yo**. The conjunction **y**, *and*, when combined with the initial vowel of a following word, is similarly pronounced: *Car*-**los**-*y* *A*-**na**.

Diphthongs

As stated on page 272, the weak vowels **i** (**y**) and **u** may combine with the strong vowels **a, e, o,** or with each other, to form single syllables. Such combinations of two vowels are called diphthongs. In diphthongs the strong vowels retain their full syllabic value, while the weak vowels, or the first vowel in the case of two weak vowels, lose part of their syllabic value.

As the first element of a diphthong, unstressed **i** is pronounced like a weak English *y* in *yes*, and unstressed **u** is pronounced like *w* in *wet*. The Spanish diphthongs which begin with unstressed **i** and **u** are: **ia, ie, io, iu; ua, ue, ui, uo,** as in *gra*-cias, *bien*, a-*diós*, ciu-*dad*; *cua*-tro, *bue*-no, *Luis*, an-*ti*-guo.

The diphthongs in which unstressed **i** and **u** occur as the second element of the diphthong are nine orthographically, but phonetically only six, since **i** and **y** have the same sound here. They are: **ai, ay; au; ei, ey; eu; oi, oy; ou.** They are pronounced as follows:

> **ai, ay** like a prolonged English *i* in *mine*: *bai*-le, *hay*
> **au** like a prolonged English *ou* in *out*: au-to-*bús*, *cau*-sa
> **ei, ey** like a prolonged English *a* in *fate*: *seis*, *ley*
> **eu** has no close equivalent in English. It consists of a clipped *e*, as in English *eh*, followed closely by a glide sound which ends in *oo*, to sound like *ehoo*: Eu-*ro*-pa
> **oi, oy** like a prolonged English *oy* in *boy*: *sois*, *soy*
> **ou** like a prolonged English *o* in *note*: lo u-*sa*-mos

Remember that two adjacent strong vowels within a word do not combine in a single syllable, but form two separate syllables: *cre*-o, te-*a*-tro. Likewise, when a weak vowel adjacent to a strong vowel has a written accent, it retains its syllabic value and forms a separate syllable: *dí*-a, pa-*ís*. An accent mark on a strong vowel merely indicates stress: *diá*-lo-go, tam-*bién*.

Triphthongs

A triphthong is a combination in a single syllable of a stressed strong vowel between two weak vowels. Four combinations are of frequent use: **iai, iei, uai (uay), uei (uey),** as in pro-nun-*ciáis*, es-tu-*diéis*, Pa-ra-*guay*, con-ti-*nuéis*. To indicate the mew of a cat and the bark of a dog the triphthongs **iau** and **uau** occur: *miau, guau*. In linking vowels between words, four and five vowels may be pronounced in one syllable.

Linking of Words

In reading or speaking Spanish, words are linked together, as in English, so that two or more may sound as one long word. These groups of words are called breath-groups. The pronunciation of certain Spanish consonants depends upon their position at the beginning of, or within, a breath-group. Similarly, the pronunciation of many individual sounds will be modified depending on the sounds with which they are linked within the breath-group. Since the words that make up the breath-group are pronounced as if they formed one long word, the principles which govern the structure of the syllable must be observed throughout the entire breath-group.

In speech, words normally are uttered in breath-groups. Thus it is necessary to practice pronouncing phrases and even entire sentences without a pause between words. Frequently a short sentence will be pronounced as one breath-group, while a longer one may be divided into two or more groups. The meaning of what is being pronounced will help you to determine where the pauses ending the breath-groups should be made.

The following examples illustrate some of the general principles of linking. The syllabic division in parentheses shows the correct linking; the syllable or syllables italicized bear the main stress.

a. Within a breath-group the final consonant of a word is joined with the initial vowel of the following word and forms a syllable with it: **el asiento (e-la-*sien*-to).**

b. Within a breath-group when two identical vowels of different words come together, they are pronounced as one: **el profesor de español (el pro-fe-*sor*-de es-pa-*ñol*).**

c. When unlike vowels between words come together within a breath-group, they are usually pronounced together in a single syllable. Two cases occur: (1) when a strong vowel is followed or preceded by a weak vowel, both are pronounced together in a single syllable and the result is phonetically a diphthong (see page 275): **su amigo (su a-*mi*-go), Juan y Elena (*Jua*-n y E-*le*-na), mi padre y mi madre (mi-*pa*-dre y-mi-*ma*-dre);** (2) if both vowels are strong, each loses a little of its syllabic value and both are pronounced together in one syllable: **vamos a la escuela (*va*-mo-sa-la es-*cue*-la); ¿Cómo está usted? (¿*Có*-mo es-*tá us*-ted?).**

Punctuation

Spanish punctuation is much the same as English. The most important differences are:

1. Inverted question marks and exclamation points precede questions and exclamations. They are placed at the actual beginning of the question or exclamation, not necessarily at the beginning of the sentence:

    ¿Hablan Carlos y Juan?   Are Charles and John talking?
    ¡Qué muchacha más bonita!   What a pretty girl!
    Usted es español, ¿verdad?   You are a Spaniard, aren't you?

2. In Spanish a comma is not used between the last two words of a series, while in English it usually is:

    Tenemos plumas, libros y lápices.   We have pens, books, and pencils.

3. A dash is generally used instead of the quotation marks of English. To denote a change of speaker in dialogue, it appears at the beginning of each speech, but is omitted at the end:

> —¿Es usted español? "Are you Spanish (a Spaniard)?"
> —Sí, señor. Soy de Toledo. "Yes, sir. I am from Toledo."

If a direct quotation is followed by its main clause, a second dash is used, to enclose the quotation and separate it from the main clause, just as quotation marks are used in English:

> —¿No viene usted con nosotros?— me preguntó Felipe. "Aren't you coming with us?" Philip asked me.

If Spanish quotation marks are used, they are placed on the line, as in the example which follows. In current practice English quotation marks are widely used in Spanish:

> Juan dijo: «Pasen ustedes». John said, "Come in."

Capitalization

Only proper names and the first word of a sentence begin with a capital letter in Spanish. The subject pronoun **yo** (*I* in English), names of months and days of the week, adjectives of nationality and nouns formed from them, and titles (unless abbreviated) are not capitalized. In titles of books or works of art, only the first word is ordinarily capitalized:

> Juan y yo hablamos. John and I are talking.
> Hoy es lunes. Today is Monday.
> Buenos días, señor (Sr.) Pidal. Good morning, Mr. Pidal.
> Son españoles. They are Spanish.
> El sol en la luna The Sun in the Moon

APPENDIX B

Frases para la clase (*Classroom Expressions*)

A number of expressions and grammatical terms which may be used in the classroom and laboratory are listed below. They are not included in the end vocabularies unless used in the preceding lessons. Other common expressions are used in the text.

Voy a pasar lista.	I am going to call the roll.
Presente.	Present.
¿Qué lección tenemos hoy?	What lesson do we have today?
Tenemos la Lección primera (dos).	We have Lesson One (Two).
¿En qué página empieza?	On what page does it begin?
¿Qué línea (renglón)?	What line?
(La lectura) empieza en la página . . .	(The reading) begins on page . . .
Al principio de la página . . .	At the beginning of (the) page . . .
En el medio (Al pie) de la página . . .	In the middle (At the bottom) of (the) page . . .
Abra(n) usted(es) el (los) libro(s).	Open your book(s).
Cierre(n) usted(es) el (los) libro(s).	Close your book(s).
Lea(n) usted(es) en español.	Read in Spanish.
Empiece(n) usted(es) a leer.	Begin to read.
Siga(n) usted(es) leyendo.	Continue (Go on) reading.
Traduzca(n) usted(es) al español (inglés) . . .	Translate into Spanish (English) . . .
Repita(n) usted(es) la frase modelo.	Repeat the model sentence.
Pronuncie(n) usted(es) . . .	Pronounce . . .
Basta.	That is enough, That will do.
Conteste(n) usted(es) (la pregunta) en español.	Answer (the question) in Spanish.
Vaya(n) usted(es) *or* **Pase(n) usted(es) a la pizarra.**	Go to the (black)board.
Escuche(n) usted(es) las instrucciones.	Listen to the directions.
Escriba(n) usted(es) (al dictado).	Write (at dictation).
Usted(es) ha(n) hecho una falta (un error).	You have made a mistake.
Corrija(n) usted(es) la falta.	Correct the mistake.
Borre(n) usted(es) la frase.	Erase the sentence.
Vuelva(n) usted(es) a su(s) asiento(s).	Return to your seat(s).
Siénte(n)se usted(es).	Sit down, Be seated.
Haga(n) usted(es) el favor de (+ inf.) . . .	Please (+ *verb*) . . .

Está bien.	All right, That's fine.
¿Qué significa (quiere decir) la palabra . . . ?	What does the word . . . mean?
¿Quién quiere hacer una pregunta?	Who wants to ask a question?
¿Cómo se dice . . . ?	How does one (do you) say . . . ?
Preste(n) usted(es) atención.	Pay attention.
Prepare(n) usted(es) para mañana . . .	Prepare for tomorrow . . .
Ha sonado el timbre.	The bell has rung.
La clase ha terminado.	The class has ended.
Ustedes pueden marcharse.	You may leave (You are excused).

Palabras y expresiones para el laboratorio (*Words and Expressions for the Laboratory*)

el	**alto parlante**	loudspeaker
la	**audición**	playback
los	**auriculares (audífonos)**	ear(head)phones
la	**cabina**	booth
el	**carrete**	reel
el	**cassette**	cassette
la	**cinta maestra (matriz)**	master tape
la	**cinta (magnetofónica)**	(magnetic) tape
la	**corriente (eléctrica)**	power; (electric) current
el	**disco (fonográfico)**	disc, (phonograph) record
	empalmar	to splice
el	**enchufe**	plug
la	**entrada**	input
	externo, -a	external
la	**grabadora (de cinta)**	(tape) recorder
	grabar	to record
el	**interruptor**	switch
el	**micrófono**	microphone
la	**perilla**	knob
	reparar	to repair
la	**salida**	output
el	**sonido**	sound
el	**volumen**	volume

Acérque(n)se usted(es) más al micrófono.	Get closer to the microphone.
Aleje(n) usted(es) más el micrófono.	Move the microphone away from you.
Apriete(n) usted(es) el botón.	Push the button.

Aumente(n) usted(es) el volumen.	Turn it louder (Increase the volume).
Cuelgue(n) usted(es) los auriculares.	Hang up the headphones.
Empuje(n) usted(es) el interruptor hacia la derecha (la izquierda).	Push the switch to the right (left).
Escuche(n) usted(es) la grabación.	Listen to the recording.
Hable(n) usted(es) en voz más alta (más baja, natural).	Speak in a louder (lower, natural) voice.
Hable(n) usted(es) más rápido (despacio).	Speak faster (slower).
Imite(n) usted(es) lo que oiga(n).	Imitate what you hear.
Mi máquina no funciona.	My machine doesn't work.
Pare(n) or Apague(n) usted(es) su máquina.	Stop or Turn off your machine.
Ponga(n) usted(es) en marcha or Encienda(n) usted(es) . . .	Start or Turn on . . .
Pónga(n)se or Quíte(n)se usted(es) los audífonos.	Put on or Take off your headphones.
Repita(n) usted(es) la respuesta.	Repeat the answer.
Se oirá or Usted(es) oirá(n) cada frase una vez (dos veces), seguida de una pausa.	You will hear each sentence once (twice), followed by a pause.
Se oirá or Usted(es) oirá(n) luego la respuesta (correcta).	Then you will hear the (correct) answer.
¿Se oye la señal claramente?	Is the signal clear?
Vuelva(n) usted(es) a enrollar la cinta.	Rewind the tape.

Términos gramaticales (*Grammatical Terms*)

el **adjectivo**	adjective
demostrativo	demonstrative
posesivo	possessive
el **adverbio**	adverb
el **artículo**	article
definido	definite
indefinido	indefinite
el **cambio ortográfico**	change in spelling
la **capitalización**	capitalization
la **cláusula**	clause
la **comparación**	comparison
el **comparativo**	comparative
el **complemento**	complement
directo	direct
indirecto	indirect

la	**composición**	composition
la	**concordancia**	agreement
la	**conjugación**	conjugation
la	**conjunción**	conjunction
la	**consonante**	consonant
el	**diptongo**	diphthong
el	**género**	gender
	femenino	feminine
	masculino	masculine
el	**gerundio**	gerund, present participle
el	**infinitivo**	infinitive
la	**interjección**	interjection
la	**interrogación**	interrogation, question
la	**letra**	letter (*of the alphabet*)
	mayúscula	capital
	minúscula	small
el	**modo indicativo (subjuntivo)**	indicative (subjunctive) mood
el	**nombre propio**	proper noun
el	**nombre (substantivo)**	noun (substantive)
el	**número**	numeral, number
	cardinal (ordinal)	cardinal (ordinal)
el	**objeto**	object
	directo	direct
	indirecto	indirect
la	**palabra (negativa)**	(negative) word
las	**partes de la oración**	parts of speech
el	**participio pasado (presente)**	past (present) participle
la	**persona**	person
	primera	first
	segunda	second
	tercera	third
el	**plural**	plural
la	**posición**	position
el	**predicado**	predicate
la	**preposición**	preposition
el	**pronombre**	pronoun
	interrogativo	interrogative
	personal	personal
	relativo	relative
la	**puntuación**	punctuation
el	**radical (la raíz)**	stem
el	**significado**	meaning
la	**sílaba**	syllable
	penúltima	next to last
	última	last
el	**singular**	singular

el **subjuntivo**	subjunctive (mood)
el **sujeto**	subject
el **superlativo (absoluto)**	(absolute) superlative
la **terminación**	ending
el **tiempo**	tense
el **tiempo simple (compuesto)**	simple (compound) tense
presente	present
imperfecto	imperfect
pretérito	preterit
futuro	future
condicional	conditional
pluscuamperfecto	pluperfect, past perfect
pretérito anterior	preterit perfect
pretérito perfecto	present perfect
futuro perfecto	future perfect
condicional perfecto	conditional perfect
el **triptongo**	triphthong
el **verbo**	verb
auxiliar	auxiliary
impersonal	impersonal
(in)transitivo	(in)transitive
irregular	irregular
reflexivo	reflexive
regular	regular
la **vocal**	vowel
la **voz**	voice
activa	active
pasiva	passive

Signos de puntuación (*Punctuation Marks*)

,	coma	( )	(los) paréntesis
;	punto y coma	« »	comillas
:	dos puntos	´	acento escrito
.	punto final	¨	(la) diéresis
. . .	puntos suspensivos	˜	(la) tilde
¿ ?	signo(s) de interrogación	-	(el) guión
¡ !	signo(s) de admiración	—	raya

Abreviaturas y signos (*Abbreviations and Signs*)

adj.	adjective	*lit.*	literally
adv.	adverb	*m.*	masculine
Am.	America	*Mex.*	Mexico
aux.	auxiliary	*obj.*	object
cond.	conditional	*part.*	participle
conj.	conjunction	*perf.*	perfect
dir.	direct	*pl.*	plural
e.g.	for example	*p.p.*	past participle
etc.	and so forth	*prep.*	preposition
f.	feminine	*pres.*	present
fam.	familiar	*pret.*	preterit
i.e.	that is	*pron.*	pronoun
imp.	imperfect	*reflex.*	reflexive
ind.	indicative	*sing.*	singular
indef.	indefinite	*subj.*	subjunctive
indir.	indirect	*trans.*	transitive
inf.	infinitive	*U.S.*	United States

( ) Words in parentheses are explanatory, or they are to be translated in the exercises.

— In the general vocabularies a dash indicates a word repeated, while in the exercises it usually is to be supplied by some grammatical form.

+ = followed by.

APPENDIX C

Cardinal numerals

0	cero	29	veintinueve (veinte y nueve)
1	un(o), una	30	treinta
2	dos	31	treinta y un(o), -a
3	tres	32	treinta y dos
4	cuatro	40	cuarenta
5	cinco	50	cincuenta
6	seis	60	sesenta
7	siete	70	setenta
8	ocho	80	ochenta
9	nueve	90	noventa
10	diez	100	ciento (cien)
11	once	101	ciento un(o), ciento una
12	doce	110	ciento diez
13	trece	200	doscientos, -as
14	catorce	300	trescientos, -as
15	quince	400	cuatrocientos, -as
16	dieciséis (diez y seis)	500	quinientos, -as
17	diecisiete (diez y siete)	600	seiscientos, -as
18	dieciocho (diez y ocho)	700	setecientos, -as
19	diecinueve (diez y nueve)	800	ochocientos, -as
20	veinte	900	novecientos, -as
21	veintiún, veintiuno, veintiuna	1.000	mil
	[veinte y un(o), -a]	1.020	mil veinte
22	veintidós (veinte y dos)	1.500	mil quinientos, -as
23	veintitrés (veinte y tres)	2.000	dos mil
24	veinticuatro (veinte y cuatro)	100.000	cien mil
25	veinticinco (veinte y cinco)	200.000	doscientos, -as mil
26	veintiséis (veinte y seis)	1.000.000	un millón (de)
27	veintisiete (veinte y siete)	2.000.000	dos millones (de)
28	veintiocho (veinte y ocho)	2.500.000	dos millones quinientos, -as mil

Uno and numerals ending in uno drop -o before a masculine noun: un soldado, *one soldier*; veintiún coches, *twenty-one cars*; treinta y un estudiantes, *thirty-one students*. Una is used before a feminine noun: una ciudad, *one city*; veintiuna señoritas, *twenty-one young ladies*; treinta y una páginas, *thirty-one pages*.

When a numeral ending in *one* follows a noun or is used alone, the numeral in Spanish agrees in gender with the noun: —¿Cuántos cuadros hay? —Veintiuno (Treinta y uno). *"How many pictures are there?" "Twenty-one (Thirty-one)."* —¿Cuántas obras hay? —Veintiuna (Treinta y una). *"How many works are there?" "Twenty-one (Thirty-one)."*

The cardinal numerals precede the nouns they modify unless they are used in a descriptive sense: **diez lecciones,** *ten lessons,* but **Lección dos (veintidós),** *Lesson Two* (*Twenty-two*).

Be sure to note that an accent mark must be written on the forms **dieciséis, veintiún, veintidós, veintitrés, veintiséis.** Numerals 16 through 19 and 21 through 29 may be written as three words, but they are pronounced as one: **diez y seis, diez y siete, veinte y un(o), -a, veinte y dos,** etc. Beginning with 31, numerals are written as separate words: **treinta y dos.**

Ciento becomes **cien** before nouns and before **mil** and **millones: cien dólares,** *one hundred dollars;* **cien mil habitantes,** *one hundred thousand inhabitants.*

Un is regularly not used with **cien(to)** and **mil: mil estudiantes,** *1,000 students;* however, one must say **ciento un mil habitantes,** *101,000 inhabitants.* **Un** is used with the noun **millón,** which requires **de** when a noun follows: **un millón de dólares,** *$1,000,000.* For *$2,000,000* one says **dos millones de dólares.**

The hundreds agree with a feminine noun: **doscientas muchachas,** *200 girls;* **quinientas cincuenta palabras,** *550 words.* Beyond nine hundred, **mil** must be used in counting: **mil novecientos setenta,** *1970.*

Regardless of the English use of *and* in numbers, **y** is regularly used in Spanish only between multiples of ten and numbers less than ten: **diez y seis,** *16;* **noventa y nueve,** *99;* but **seiscientos seis,** *606.*

In writing numerals in Spanish, a period is often used where a comma is used in English, and a comma is used for the decimal point: *$1.500,75.* In current commercial practice, however, the English method is being used more and more.

Ordinal Numerals

1st	**primero (primer), -a**	4th	**cuarto, -a**	8th	**octavo, -a**
2nd	**segundo, -a**	5th	**quinto, -a**	9th	**noveno, -a**
3rd	**tercero (tercer), -a**	6th	**sexto, -a**	10th	**décimo, -a**
		7th	**séptimo, -a**		

Ordinal numerals agree in gender and number with the nouns they modify. **Primero** and **tercero** drop final **-o** before a masculine singular noun: **el primer (tercer) edificio,** *the first (third) building,* but **los primeros días,** *the first days,* **la tercera parte,** *the third part (one-third).*

The ordinal numerals may precede or follow the noun. Contrast the following:

Lección primera	Lesson One (I)
el capítulo tercero	Chapter Three
la Calle Cuarta	Fourth Street

But:	
la primera lección	the first lesson
el tercer capítulo	the third chapter
la cuarta calle	the fourth street

A cardinal number precedes an ordinal when both are used together: **las tres primeras páginas,** *the first three pages.* (Note that Spanish says *the three first,* not *the first three,* as in English.)

With titles, chapters of books, volumes, etc., ordinal numerals are normally used through *tenth.* For higher numerals, they are regularly replaced by the cardinal numerals; in these cases all numerals follow the noun. With names of rulers and popes the definite article is also omitted in Spanish:

Felipe Segundo	Philip II (the Second)
la página sesenta	page 60
el tomo segundo	Volume Two
el siglo veinte	the twentieth century

Days of the Week/Months/Seasons

domingo	Sunday	**jueves**	Thursday
lunes	Monday	**viernes**	Friday
martes	Tuesday	**sábado**	Saturday
miércoles	Wednesday		

enero	January	**julio**	July
febrero	February	**agosto**	August
marzo	March	**septiembre**	September
abril	April	**octubre**	October
mayo	May	**noviembre**	November
junio	June	**diciembre**	December

la primavera	spring	**el otoño**	fall, autumn
el verano	summer	**el invierno**	winter

Dates

In expressing dates the ordinal numeral **primero** is used for the *first* (day of the month), and the cardinals are used in all other cases. The definite article translates *the, on the,* with the day of the month. (Remember that the definite article also translates *on* with a day of the week: **Yo saldré el lunes,** *I shall leave [on] Monday.)*

> **Hoy es el primero de enero.**   Today is the first of January (January 1).
> **Nació el dos de mayo.**   He was born (on) the second of May (May 2).

A complete date is expressed:

> **el diez de abril de mil novecientos setenta y nueve**   April 10, 1979

Time of Day

¿Qué hora es (era)?   What time is (was) it?

Es (Era) la una.   It is (was) one o'clock.

Son (Eran) las dos.   It is (was) two o'clock.

Es la una y cuarto (media).   It is a quarter after one (half-past one).

Son las nueve menos diez de la mañana.   It is ten minutes before (to) nine A.M. (in the morning).

Son las tres de la tarde en punto.   It is three P.M. (in the afternoon) sharp.

Eran las ocho de la noche.   It was eight at night (in the evening).

Ella saldrá a la una (a las cuatro).   She will leave at one (at four) o'clock.

Acaba de dar la una.   It has just struck one.

Ya han dado las dos.   It has already struck two.

Faltan diez minutos para las once.   It is ten minutes to eleven.

Estarán aquí hasta las cinco.   They will be here until five.

Yo trabajo desde las ocho hasta las doce.   I work from eight until twelve.

APPENDIX D

Regular Verbs

INFINITIVE

tomar, *to take*   **comer,** *to eat*   **vivir,** *to live*

PRESENT PARTICIPLE

tomando, *taking*   **comiendo,** *eating*   **viviendo,** *living*

PAST PARTICIPLE

tomado, *taken*   **comido,** *eaten*   **vivido,** *lived*

The Simple Tenses

Indicative Mood

PRESENT

I take, do take, am taking, etc.	*I eat, do eat, am eating, etc.*	*I live, do live, am living, etc.*
tomo	como	vivo
tomas	comes	vives
toma	come	vive
tomamos	comemos	vivimos
tomáis	coméis	vivís
toman	comen	viven

IMPERFECT

I was taking, used to take, took, etc.	*I was eating, used to eat, ate, etc.*	*I was living, used to live, lived, etc.*
tomaba	comía	vivía
tomabas	comías	vivías
tomaba	comía	vivía
tomábamos	comíamos	vivíamos
tomabais	comíais	vivías
tomaban	comían	vivían

PRETERIT

I took, did take, etc.	*I ate, did eat, etc.*	*I lived, did live, etc.*
tomé	comí	viví
tomaste	comiste	viviste
tomó	comió	vivió
tomamos	comimos	vivimos
tomasteis	comisteis	vivisteis
tomaron	comieron	vivieron

FUTURE

I shall (will) take, etc.	*I shall (will) eat, etc.*	*I shall (will) live, etc.*
tomaré	comeré	viviré
tomarás	comerás	vivirás
tomará	comerá	vivirá
tomaremos	comeremos	viviremos
tomaréis	comeréis	viviréis
tomarán	comerán	vivirán

CONDITIONAL

I should (would) take, etc.	*I should (would) eat, etc.*	*I should (would) live, etc.*
tomaría	comería	viviría
tomarías	comerías	vivirías
tomaría	comería	viviría
tomaríamos	comeríamos	viviríamos
tomaríais	comeríais	viviríais
tomarían	comerían	vivirían

Subjunctive Mood

PRESENT

(that) I may take, etc.	*(that) I may eat, etc.*	*(that) I may live, etc.*
tome	coma	viva
tomes	comas	vivas
tome	coma	viva
tomemos	comamos	vivamos
toméis	comáis	viváis
tomen	coman	vivan

-ra IMPERFECT

(that) I might take, etc.	(that) I might eat, etc.	(that) I might live, etc.
tomara	comiera	viviera
tomaras	comieras	vivieras
tomara	comiera	viviera
tomáramos	comiéramos	viviéramos
tomarais	comierais	vivierais
tomaran	comieran	vivieran

-se IMPERFECT[1]

(that) I might take, etc.	(that) I might eat, etc.	(that) I might live, etc.
tomase	comiese	viviese
tomases	comieses	vivieses
tomase	comiese	viviese
tomásemos	comiésemos	viviésemos
tomaseis	comieseis	vivieseis
tomasen	comiesen	viviesen

Imperative

take	eat	live
toma (tú)	come (tú)	vive (tú)
tomad (vosotros)	comed (vosotros)	vivid (vosotros)

The Compound Tenses

PERFECT INFINITIVE

haber tomado (comido, vivido), *to have taken (eaten, lived)*

PERFECT PARTICIPLE

habiendo tomado (comido, vivido), *having taken (eaten, lived)*

---

[1] There is also a future subjunctive, used rarely today except in proverbs, legal documents, etc., but which was common in Old Spanish. Forms are:

tomar: tomare tomares tomare tomáremos tomareis tomaren
comer: comiere comieres comiere comiéremos comiereis comieren
vivir: viviere vivieres viviere viviéremos viviereis vivieren

The future perfect subjunctive is: hubiere tomado (comido, vivido), etc.

Indicative Mood

PRESENT PERFECT	PLUPERFECT	PRETERIT PERFECT
I have taken, eaten, lived, etc.	*I had taken, eaten, lived, etc.*	*I had taken, eaten, lived, etc.*

PRESENT PERFECT

he
has
ha
hemos
habéis
han
} tomado comido vivido

PLUPERFECT

había
habías
había
habíamos
habíais
habían
} tomado comido vivido

PRETERIT PERFECT

hube
hubiste
hubo
hubimos
hubisteis
hubieron
} tomado comido vivido

FUTURE PERFECT

I shall (will) have taken, etc.

habré
habrás
habrá
habremos
habréis
habrán
} tomado comido vivido

CONDITIONAL PERFECT

I should (would) have taken, etc.

habría
habrías
habría
habríamos
habríais
habrían
} tomado comido vivido

Subjunctive Mood

PRESENT PERFECT

(that) I may have taken, etc.

haya
hayas
haya
hayamos
hayáis
hayan
} tomado comido vivido

-ra and -se PLUPERFECT

(that) I might have taken, etc.

hubiera *or* hubiese
hubieras *or* hubieses
hubiera *or* hubiese
hubiéramos *or* hubiésemos
hubierais *or* hubieseis
hubieran *or* hubiesen
} tomado comido vivido

Irregular Past Participles of Regular Verbs

| abrir: | **abierto** | describir: | **descrito** | escribir: | **escrito** |
| cubrir: | **cubierto** | descubrir: | **descubierto** | romper: | **roto** |

Comments Concerning Forms of Verbs

INFINITIVE	PRES. PART.	PAST. PART.	PRES. IND.	PRETERIT
decir	**diciendo**	**dicho**	**digo**	**dijeron**

IMP. IND.	PROGRESSIVE TENSES	COMPOUND TENSES	PRES. SUBJ.	IMP. SUBJ.
decía	**estoy,** etc. **diciendo**	**he,** etc. **dicho**	**diga**	**dijera** **dijese**

FUTURE			IMPERATIVE	
diré			**di** decid	

CONDITIONAL				
diría				

a. From five forms (infinitive, present participle, past participle, first person singular present indicative, and third person plural preterit) all other forms may be derived.

b. The first and second persons plural of the present indicative of all verbs are regular, except in the cases of **haber, ir, ser.**

c. The third person plural is formed by adding **-n** to the third person singular in all tenses, except in the preterit and in the present indicative of **ser.**

d. All familiar forms (second person singular and plural) end in **-s,** except the second person singular preterit and the imperative.

e. The imperfect indicative is regular in all verbs, except **ir (iba), ser (era), ver (veía).**

f. If the first person singular preterit ends in unaccented **-e,** the third person singular ends in unaccented **-o;** the other endings are regular, except that after **j** the ending for the third person plural is **-eron.** Eight verbs of this group, in addition to those which end in **-ducir,** have a **u-**stem preterit **(andar, caber, estar, haber, poder, poner, saber, tener);** four have an **i-**stem **(decir, hacer, querer, venir); traer** retains the vowel **a** in the preterit. (The third person plural preterit forms of **decir** and **traer** are **dijeron** and **trajeron,** respectively. The third person singular preterit form of **hacer** is **hizo.) Ir** and **ser** have the same preterit forms, while **dar** has second-conjugation endings in this tense.

g. The conditional always has the same stem as the future. Only twelve verbs have irregular stems in these tenses. Five drop **e** of the infinitive ending **(caber, haber, poder, querer, saber),** five drop **e** or **i** and insert **d (poner, salir, tener, valer, venir),** and two **(decir, hacer)** retain the Old Spanish stems **dir-, har- (far-).**

h. The stem of the present subjunctive of all verbs is the same as that of the first person singular present indicative, except for **dar, estar, haber, ir, saber, ser.**

i. The imperfect subjunctive of all verbs is formed by dropping **-ron** of the third person plural preterit and adding the **-ra** or **-se** endings.

j. The singular imperative is the same in form as the third person singular present indicative, except in the case of ten verbs (**decir, di; haber, he; hacer, haz; ir, ve; poner, pon; salir, sal; ser, sé; tener, ten; valer, val** *or* **vale; venir, ven**). The plural imperative is always formed by dropping final **-r** of the infinitive and adding **-d**. (Remember that the imperative is used only for familiar affirmative commands.)

k. The compound tenses of all verbs are formed by using the various tenses of the auxiliary verb **haber** with the past participle.

Irregular Verbs[1]

1. andar, andando, andado, *to go, walk*

PRETERIT	anduve	anduviste	anduvo	anduvimos	anduvisteis	anduvieron
IMP. SUBJ.	anduviera, etc.		anduviese, etc.			

2. caber, cabiendo, cabido, *to fit, be contained in*

PRES. IND.	quepo	cabes	cabe	cabemos	cabéis	caben
PRES. SUBJ.	quepa	quepas	quepa	quepamos	quepáis	quepan
FUTURE	cabré	cabrás, etc.		COND.	cabría	cabrías, etc.
PRETERIT	cupe	cupiste	cupo	cupimos	cupisteis	cupieron
IMP. SUBJ.	cupiera, etc.		cupiese, etc.			

3. caer, cayendo, caído, *to fall*

PRES. IND.	caigo	caes	cae	caemos	caéis	caen
PRES. SUBJ.	caiga	caigas	caiga	caigamos	caigáis	caigan
PRETERIT	caí	caíste	cayó	caímos	caísteis	cayeron
IMP. SUBJ.	cayera, etc.		cayese, etc.			

4. dar, dando, dado, *to give*

PRES. IND.	doy	das	da	damos	dais	dan
PRES. SUBJ.	dé	des	dé	demos	deis	den
PRETERIT	di	diste	dio	dimos	disteis	dieron
IMP. SUBJ.	diera, etc.		diese, etc.			

5. decir, diciendo, dicho, *to say, tell*

PRES. IND.	digo	dices	dice	decimos	decís	dicen
PRES. SUBJ.	diga	digas	diga	digamos	digáis	digan
IMPERATIVE	di				decid	
FUTURE	diré	dirás, etc.		COND.	diría	dirías, etc.
PRETERIT	dije	dijiste	dijo	dijimos	dijisteis	dijeron
IMP. SUBJ.	dijera, etc.		dijese, etc.			

---

[1] Participles are given with the infinitive; tenses not listed are regular.

6. **estar,** estando, estado, *to be*

PRES. IND.	**estoy**	**estás**	**está**	estamos	estáis	**están**
PRES. SUBJ.	**esté**	**estés**	**esté**	estemos	estéis	**estén**
PRETERIT	**estuve**	**estuviste**	**estuvo**	**estuvimos**	**estuvisteis**	**estuvieron**
IMP. SUBJ.	**estuviera,** etc.		**estuviese,** etc.			

7. **haber,** habiendo, habido, *to have* (auxiliary)

PRES. IND.	**he**	**has**	**ha**	**hemos**	habéis	**han**
PRES. SUBJ.	**haya**	**hayas**	**haya**	**hayamos**	**hayáis**	**hayan**
IMPERATIVE	**he**				habed	
FUTURE	**habré**	**habrás,** etc.		COND.	**habría**	**habrías,** etc.
PRETERIT	**hube**	**hubiste**	**hubo**	**hubimos**	**hubisteis**	**hubieron**
IMP. SUBJ.	**hubiera,** etc.		**hubiese,** etc.			

8. **hacer,** haciendo, **hecho,** *to do, make*

PRES. IND.	**hago**	haces	hace	hacemos	hacéis	hacen
PRES. SUBJ.	**haga**	**hagas**	**haga**	**hagamos**	**hagáis**	**hagan**
IMPERATIVE	**haz**				haced	
FUTURE	**haré**	**harás,** etc.		COND.	**haría**	**harías,** etc.
PRETERIT	**hice**	**hiciste**	**hizo**	**hicimos**	**hicisteis**	**hicieron**
IMP. SUBJ.	**hiciera,** etc.		**hiciese,** etc.			

Like **hacer:** deshacerse de, *to get rid of*; satisfacer, *to satisfy.*

9. **ir, yendo, ido,** *to go*

PRES. IND.	**voy**	**vas**	**va**	**vamos**	**vais**	**van**
PRES. SUBJ.	**vaya**	**vayas**	**vaya**	**vayamos**	**vayáis**	**vayan**
IMPERATIVE	**ve**				id	
IMP. IND.	**iba**	**ibas**	**iba**	**íbamos**	**ibais**	**iban**
PRETERIT	**fui**	**fuiste**	**fue**	**fuimos**	**fuisteis**	**fueron**
IMP. SUBJ.	**fuera,** etc.		**fuese,** etc.			

10. **oír, oyendo,** oído, *to hear*

PRES. IND.	**oigo**	**oyes**	**oye**	oímos	oís	**oyen**
PRES. SUBJ.	**oiga**	**oigas**	**oiga**	**oigamos**	**oigáis**	**oigan**
IMPERATIVE	**oye**				oíd	
PRETERIT	oí	oíste	**oyó**	oímos	oísteis	**oyeron**
IMP. SUBJ.	**oyera,** etc.		**oyese,** etc.			

11. **poder, pudiendo,** podido, *to be able*

PRES. IND.	**puedo**	**puedes**	**puede**	podemos	podéis	**pueden**
PRES. SUBJ.	**pueda**	**puedas**	**pueda**	podamos	podáis	**puedan**
FUTURE	**podré**	**podrás,** etc.		COND.	**podría**	**podrías,** etc.

PRETERIT	pude	pudiste	pudo	pudimos	pudisteis	pudieron
IMP. SUBJ.	pudiera, etc.		pudiese, etc.			

12. poner, poniendo, puesto, *to put, place*

PRES. IND.	pongo	pones	pone	ponemos	ponéis	ponen
PRES. SUBJ.	ponga	pongas	ponga	pongamos	pongáis	pongan
IMPERATIVE	pon				poned	
FUTURE	pondré	pondrás, etc.		COND.	pondría	pondrías, etc.
PRETERIT	puse	pusiste	puso	pusimos	pusisteis	pusieron
IMP. SUBJ.	pusiera, etc.		pusiese, etc.			

Like **poner**: componer, *to compose*; disponer, *to arrange, set up*; exponer, *to set forth*; imponer, *to impose*; oponer, *to oppose*; proponer, *to propose*; suponer, *to suppose*.

13. querer, queriendo, querido, *to wish, want*

PRES. IND.	quiero	quieres	quiere	queremos	queréis	quieren
PRES. SUBJ.	quiera	quieras	quiera	queramos	queráis	quieran
FUTURE	querré	querrás, etc.		COND.	querría	querrías, etc.
PRETERIT	quise	quisiste	quiso	quisimos	quisisteis	quisieron
IMP. SUBJ.	quisiera, etc.		quisiese, etc.			

14. saber, sabiendo, sabido, *to know*

PRES. IND.	sé	sabes	sabe	sabemos	sabéis	saben
PRES. SUBJ.	sepa	sepas	sepa	sepamos	sepáis	sepan
FUTURE	sabré	sabrás, etc.		COND.	sabría	sabrías, etc.
PRETERIT	supe	supiste	supo	supimos	supisteis	supieron
IMP. SUBJ.	supiera, etc.		supiese, etc.			

15. salir, saliendo, salido, *to go out, leave*

PRES. IND.	salgo	sales	sale	salimos	salís	salen
PRES. SUBJ.	salga	salgas	salga	salgamos	salgáis	salgan
IMPERATIVE	sal				salid	
FUTURE	saldré	saldrás, etc.		COND.	saldría	saldrías, etc.

Like **salir**: sobresalir, *to excel.*

16. ser, siendo, sido, *to be*

PRES. IND.	soy	eres	es	somos	sois	son
PRES. SUBJ.	sea	seas	sea	seamos	seáis	sean
IMPERATIVE	sé				sed	
IMP. IND.	era	eras	era	éramos	erais	eran
PRETERIT	fui	fuiste	fue	fuimos	fuisteis	fueron
IMP. SUBJ.	fuera, etc.		fuese, etc.			

17. tener, teniendo, tenido, *to have*

PRES. IND.	tengo	tienes	tiene	tenemos	tenéis	tienen
PRES. SUBJ.	tenga	tengas	tenga	tengamos	tengáis	tengan
IMPERATIVE	ten				tened	
FUTURE	tendré	tendrás, etc.		COND.	tendría	tendrías, etc.
PRETERIT	tuve	tuviste	tuvo	tuvimos	tuvisteis	tuvieron
IMP. SUBJ.	tuviera, etc.		tuviese, etc.			

Like tener: abstener, *to abstain*; contener, *to contain*; mantener, *to maintain*; obtener, *to obtain*; detener, *to detain, stop*; sostener, *to sustain*.

18. traer, trayendo, traído, *to bring*

PRES. IND.	traigo	traes	trae	traemos	traéis	traen
PRES SUBJ.	traiga	traigas	traiga	traigamos	traigáis	traigan
PRETERIT	traje	trajiste	trajo	trajimos	trajisteis	trajeron
IMP. SUBJ.	trajera, etc.		trajese, etc.			

Like traer: atraer, *to attract*.

19. valer, valiendo, valido, *to be worth*

PRES. IND.	valgo	vales	vale	valemos	valéis	valen
PRES. SUBJ.	valga	valgas	valga	valgamos	valgáis	valgan
IMPERATIVE	val (vale)				valed	
FUTURE	valdré	valdrás, etc.		COND.	valdría	valdrías, etc.

Like valer: equivaler, *to be equivalent to*.

20. venir, viniendo, venido, *to come*

PRES. IND.	vengo	vienes	viene	venimos	venís	vienen
PRES. SUBJ.	venga	vengas	venga	vengamos	vengáis	vengan
IMPERATIVE	ven				venid	
FUTURE	vendré	vendrás, etc.		COND.	vendría	vendrías, etc.
PRETERIT	vine	viniste	vino	vinimos	vinisteis	vinieron
IMP. SUBJ.	viniera, etc.		viniese, etc.			

Like venir: convenir, *to be fitting*; intervenir, *to take part, intervene*.

21. ver, viendo, visto, *to see*

PRES. IND.	veo	ves	ve	vemos	veis	ven
PRES. SUBJ.	vea	veas	vea	veamos	veáis	vean
PRETERIT	vi	viste	vio	vimos	visteis	vieron
IMP. IND.	veía	veías	veía	veíamos	veíais	veían

Verbs with Changes in Spelling

	a	o	u	e	i
Sound of *k*	ca	co	cu	que	qui
Sound of *g*	ga	go	gu	gue	gui
Sound of *s* (*th*)	za	zo	zu	ce	ci
Sound of Spanish **j**	ja	jo	ju	ge, je	gi, ji
Sound of *gw*	gua	guo		güe	güi

Changes in spelling are required in certain verbs to preserve the sound of the final consonant of the stem. The changes occur in only seven forms of each verb: in the first four types which follow the change is in the first person singular preterit, and in the remaining types in the first person singular present indicative, while all types change throughout the present subjunctive.

1. Verbs ending in **-car** change **c** to **qu** before **e: buscar,** *to look for*

PRETERIT	**busqué**	buscaste	buscó, etc.			
PRES. SUBJ.	**busque**	**busques**	**busque**	**busquemos**	**busquéis**	**busquen**

Like **buscar:** acercarse, *to approach*; atacar, *to attack*; colocar, *to place*; dedicar, *to dedicate*; desembarcar, *to disembark*; desempacar, *to unpack*; destacarse, *to stand out*; educar, *to educate*; equivocarse, *to be mistaken*; explicar, *to explain*; indicar, *to indicate*; invocar, *to invoke*; justificar, *to justify*; marcar, *to dial* (telephone); modificar, *to modify*; practicar, *to practice*; publicar, *to publish*; sacar, *to take out*; tocar, *to play* (music).

2. Verbs ending in **-gar** change **g** to **gu** before **e: llegar,** *to arrive*

PRETERIT	**llegué**	llegaste	llegó, etc.			
PRES. SUBJ.	**llegue**	**llegues**	**llegue**	**lleguemos**	**lleguéis**	**lleguen**

Like **llegar:** agregar, *to add*; castigar, *to punish*; colgar (ue),[1] *to hang* (*up*); encargarse de, *to take charge of*; entregar, *to hand* (*over*); investigar, *to investigate*; jugar (ue), *to play* (a game); negar (ie), *to deny*; obligar, *to oblige, force*; otorgar, *to grant*; pagar, *to pay* (*for*).

3. Verbs ending in **-zar** change **z** to **c** before **e: cruzar,** *to cross*

PRETERIT	**crucé**	cruzaste	cruzó, etc.			
PRES. SUBJ.	**cruce**	**cruces**	**cruce**	**crucemos**	**crucéis**	**crucen**

Like **cruzar:** aderezar, *to garnish*; alcanzar, *to reach*; almorzar (ue), *to take* (*eat*) *lunch*; aplazar, *to postpone*; avanzar, *to advance*; cazar, *to hunt*; centralizar, *to centralize*; comenzar (ie), *to commence, begin*; economizar, *to economize*; empezar (ie), *to begin*; esforzarse (ue) por, *to strive to*; especializarse, *to specialize*; garantizar, *to guarantee*; industrializar, *to industrialize*; lanzar, *to launch*; liberalizar, *to liberalize*; organizar, *to organize*; realizar, *to realize, carry out*; tropezar (ie) con, *to strike against*; utilizar, *to utilize*.

---

[1] See pages 300–303 for verbs with stem changes.

4. Verbs ending in **-guar** change **gu** to **gü** before **e: averiguar,** *to find out*

PRETERIT	**averigüé**	averiguaste	averiguó, etc.		
PRES. SUBJ.	**averigüe**	**averigües**	**averigüe**	**averigüemos**	**averigüéis**	**averigüen**

5. Verbs ending in **-ger** or **-gir** change **g** to **j** before **a** and **o: coger,** *to pick (up)*

PRES. IND.	**cojo**	coges	coge, etc.		
PRES. SUBJ.	**coja**	**cojas**	**coja**	**cojamos**	**cojáis**	**cojan**

Like **coger:** dirigir, *to direct*; elegir (i, i), *to elect*; escoger, *to choose, select*; exigir, *to demand*; proteger, *to protect*; recoger, *to pick up*; surgir, *to surge, arise*.

6. Verbs ending in **-guir** change **gu** to **g** before **a** and **o: distinguir,** *to distinguish*

PRES. IND.	**distingo**	distingues	distingue, etc.		
PRES. SUBJ.	**distinga**	**distingas**	**distinga**	**distingamos**	**distingáis**	**distingan**

Like **distinguir:** conseguir (i, i), *to obtain, attain*; seguir (i,i), *to follow*.

7. Verbs ending in **-cer** or **cir** preceded by a consonant change **c** to **z** before **a** and **o:**
vencer, *to overcome, conquer*

PRES. IND.	**venzo**	vences	vence, etc.		
PRES. SUBJ.	**venza**	**venzas**	**venza**	**venzamos**	**venzáis**	**venzan**

Like **vencer:** convencer, *to convince*; ejercer, *to exert*; torcer (ue), *to twist*.

8. Verbs ending in **-quir** change **qu** to **c** before **a** and **o: delinquir,** *to be guilty*

PRES. IND.	**delinco**	delinques	delinque, etc.		
PRES. SUBJ.	**delinca**	**delincas**	**delinca**	**delincamos**	**delincáis**	**delincan**

Verbs with Special Endings

1. Verbs ending in **-cer** or **cir** following a vowel insert **z** before **c** in the first person singular present indicative and throughout the present subjunctive: **conocer,** *to know, be acquainted with*

PRES. IND.	**conozco**	conoces	conoce, etc.		
PRES. SUBJ.	**conozca**	**conozcas**	**conozca**	**conozcamos**	**conozcáis**	**conozcan**

Like **conocer:** aparecer, *to appear*; crecer, *to grow*; desaparecer, *to disappear*; establecer, *to establish*; favorecer, *to* *favor*; florecer, *to flourish*; fortalecer, *to strengthen*; merecer, *to merit*; ofrecer, *to offer*; parecer, *to seem*; pertenecer, *to belong to*; reconocer, *to recognize*.

2. Verbs ending in **-ducir** have the same changes as **conocer,** with additional changes in the preterit and imperfect subjunctive: **conducir,** *to conduct, drive*

PRES. IND.	**conduzco**	conduces	conduce, etc.		
PRES. SUBJ.	**conduzca**	**conduzcas**	**conduzca**	**conduzcamos**	**conduzcáis**	**conduzcan**
PRETERIT	**conduje**	**condujiste**	**condujo**	**condujimos**	**condujisteis**	**condujeron**
IMP. SUBJ.	**condujera,** etc.		**condujese,** etc.		

Like **conducir:** deducir, *to deduce*; introducir, *to introduce*; producir, *to produce*; reducir, *to reduce*; traducir, *to translate*.

3. Verbs ending in **-uir** (except **-guir** and **-quir**) insert **y** except before **i,** and change unaccented **i** between vowels to **y: huir,** *to flee*

PARTICIPLES	**huyendo**		huido		
PRES. IND.	**huyo**	**huyes**	**huye**	huimos	huís	**huyen**
PRES. SUBJ.	**huya**	**huyas**	**huya**	**huyamos**	**huyáis**	**huyan**
IMPERATIVE	**huye**				huid
PRETERIT	huí	huiste	**huyó**	huimos	huisteis	**huyeron**
IMP. SUBJ.	**huyera,** etc.		**huyese,** etc.		

Like **huir:** concluir, *to conclude, end*; constituir, *to constitute*; construir, *to construct*; contribuir, *to contribute*; destruir, *to destroy*; disminuir, *to diminish*; distribuir, *to distribute*; incluir, *to include*; instruir, *to instruct*; obstruir, *to obstruct*; substituir, *to substitute*.

4. Certain verbs ending in **-er** preceded by a vowel replace unaccented **i** of the ending by **y: creer,** *to believe*

PARTICIPLES	**creyendo**		creído		
PRETERIT	creí	**creíste**	**creyó**	**creímos**	**creísteis**	**creyeron**
IMP. SUBJ.	**creyera,** etc.		**creyese,** etc.		

Like **creer:** leer, *to read.*

5. Some verbs ending in **-iar** require a written accent on the **i** in the singular and third person plural in the present indicative and present subjunctive and in the singular imperative: **enviar,** *to send*

PRES. IND.	**envío**	**envías**	**envía**	enviamos	enviáis	**envían**
PRES. SUBJ.	**envíe**	**envíes**	**envíe**	enviemos	enviéis	**envíen**
IMPERATIVE	**envía**				enviad

Like **enviar:** ampliar, *to enlarge*; esquiar, *to ski*; variar, *to vary*. However, such common verbs as the following do not have the accented **i:** anunciar, *to announce*; cambiar, *to change*; estudiar, *to study*; iniciar, *to initiate*; limpiar, *to clean*; pronunciar, *to pronounce*.

6. Verbs ending in **-uar** have a written accent on the **u** in the same forms as verbs in section 5 above:[1] **continuar,** *to continue*

PRES. IND.	**continúo**	**continúas**	**continúa**	continuamos	continuáis	**continúan**
PRES. SUBJ.	**continúe**	**continúes**	**continúe**	continuemos	continuéis	**continúen**
IMPERATIVE	**continúa**				continuad	

Like **continuar:** efectuar, *to carry out;* evaluar, *to evaluate;* graduarse, *to graduate;* situar, *to put, place.*

7. Verbs whose stems end in **ll** or **ñ** drop the **i** of the diphthongs **ie (ié)** and **ió.** Examples are:

bullir, *to boil*

PRES. PART.	**bullendo**					
PRETERIT	bullí	bulliste	**bulló**	bullimos	bullisteis	**bulleron**
IMP. SUBJ.	**bullera,** etc.		**bullese,** etc.			

reñir (i, i), *to scold*

PRES. PART.	**riñendo**					
PRETERIT	reñí	reñiste	**riñó**	reñimos	reñisteis	**riñeron**
IMP. SUBJ.	**riñera,** etc.		**riñese,** etc.			

Stem-Changing Verbs

Class I (-ar, -er)

Many verbs of the first and second conjugations change the stem vowel **e** to **ie** and **o** to **ue** when the vowels **e** and **o** are stressed, *i.e.,* in the singular and third person plural of the present indicative and present subjunctive and in the singular imperative. Class I verbs are designated: **cerrar (ie),**[2] **volver (ue).**[3]

---

[1] **Reunir(se),** *to gather, meet,* has a written accent on the **u** in the same forms as **continuar:**

PRES. IND.	reúno reúnes reúne . . . reúnen	
PRES. SUBJ.	reúna reúnas reúna . . . reúnan	
IMPERATIVE	reúne	

[2] **Errar,** *to err, miss* (a shot), is designated: **errar (ye).** At the beginning of a verb the initial **i** of the diphthong **ie** is changed to **y,** since no Spanish word may begin with **ie:**

PRES. IND.	yerro	yerras	yerra	erramos	erráis	yerran
PRES. SUBJ.	yerre	yerres	yerre	erremos	erréis	yerren
IMPERATIVE	yerra					

[3] Forms of **oler (ue),** *to smell* (an odor) follow. Spanish words do not begin with **u** followed by **a, e,** or **o;** thus **h** is written before **ue:**

PRES. IND.	huelo	hueles	huele	olemos	oléis	huelen
PRES. SUBJ.	huela	huelas	huela	olamos	oláis	huelan
IMPERATIVE	huele					

cerrar, *to close*

PRES. IND.	**cierro**	**cierras**	**cierra**	cerramos	cerráis	**cierran**
PRES. SUBJ.	**cierre**	**cierres**	**cierre**	cerremos	cerréis	**cierren**
IMPERATIVE	**cierra**					

Like **cerrar:** comenzar, *to commence, begin;* despertar, *to awaken;* empezar, *to begin;* negar, *to deny;* pensar, *to think;* recomendar, *to recommend;* sentarse, *to sit down;* tropezar con, *to strike against.*

perder, *to lose, miss*

PRES. IND.	**pierdo**	**pierdes**	**pierde**	perdemos	perdéis	**pierden**
PRES. SUBJ.	**pierda**	**pierdas**	**pierda**	perdamos	perdáis	**pierdan**
IMPERATIVE	**pierde**					

Like **perder:** defender, *to defend;* desatender, *to disregard;* entender, *to understand;* extender, *to extend;* tender, *to tend.*

contar, *to count; to relate*

PRES. IND.	**cuento**	**cuentas**	**cuenta**	contamos	contáis	**cuentan**
PRES. SUBJ.	**cuente**	**cuentes**	**cuente**	contemos	contéis	**cuenten**
IMPERATIVE	**cuenta**					

Like **contar:** acordarse, *to remember;* acostarse, *to go to bed;* almorzar, *to take (eat) lunch;* aprobar, *to approve;* colgar, *to hang (up);* costar, *to cost;* demostrar, *to demonstrate;* encontrar, *to find;* esforzarse por, *to strive to;* mostrar, *to show;* probar, *to try out, test;* recordar, *to recall;* renovar, *to renew.*

volver,[1] *to return*

PRES. IND.	**vuelvo**	**vuelves**	**vuelve**	volvemos	volvéis	**vuelven**
PRES. SUBJ.	**vuelva**	**vuelvas**	**vuelva**	volvamos	volváis	**vuelvan**
IMPERATIVE	**vuelve**					

Like **volver:** devolver, *to return, give back;* doler, *to ache, pain;* envolver, *to wrap up;* llover, *to rain;* promover, *to promote;* resolver, *to resolve;* soler, *to be accustomed to;* torcer, *to twist.*

jugar, *to play* (a game)

PRES. IND.	**juego**	**juegas**	**juega**	jugamos	jugáis	**juegan**
PRES. SUBJ.	**juegue**	**juegues**	**juegue**	juguemos	juguéis	**jueguen**
IMPERATIVE	**juega**					

---

[1] The past participles of **volver, devolver, envolver, resolver** are: **vuelto, devuelto, envuelto, resuelto,** respectively.

Class II (-ir)

Certain verbs of the third conjugation have the changes in the stem indicated below.
Class II verbs are designated: **sentir (ie, e), dormir (ue,u).**

PRES. IND.	1, 2, 3, 6	} e > ie	PRES. PART.			} e > i
PRES. SUBJ.	1, 2, 3, 6	o > ue	PRETERIT	3, 6		o > u
IMPERATIVE	Sing.		PRES. SUBJ.	4, 5		
			IMP. SUBJ.	1, 2, 3, 4, 5, 6		

sentir, *to feel*

PRES. PART.	**sintiendo**					
PRES. IND.	**siento**	**sientes**	**siente**	sentimos	sentís	**sienten**
PRES. SUBJ.	**sienta**	**sientas**	**sienta**	**sintamos**	**sintáis**	**sientan**
IMPERATIVE	**siente**					
PRETERIT	sentí	sentiste	**sintió**	sentimos	sentisteis	**sintieron**
IMP. SUBJ.	**sintiera,** etc.		**sintiese,** etc.			

Like **sentir:** adquirir, [1] *to acquire;* advertir, *to notice;* consentir, *to consent;* convertir, *to convert;* diferir, *to differ;* divertirse, *to amuse oneself;* preferir, *to prefer;* referirse a, *to refer to;* sugerir, *to suggest.*

dormir, *to sleep*

PRES. PART.	**durmiendo**					
PRES. IND.	**duermo**	**duermes**	**duerme**	dormimos	dormís	**duermen**
PRES. SUBJ.	**duerma**	**duermas**	**duerma**	**durmamos**	**durmáis**	**duerman**
IMPERATIVE	**duerme**					
PRETERIT	dormí	dormiste	**durmió**	dormimos	dormisteis	**durmieron**
IMP. SUBJ.	**durmiera,** etc.		**durmiese,** etc.			

Like **dormir;** morir, [2] *to die.*

Class III (-ir)

Certain verbs in the third conjugation change **e** to **i** in all forms in which changes occur in Class II verbs. These verbs are designated: **pedir (i, i).**

pedir, *to ask*

PRES. PART.	**pidiendo**					
PRES. IND.	**pido**	**pides**	**pide**	pedimos	pedís	**piden**
PRES. SUBJ.	**pida**	**pidas**	**pida**	**pidamos**	**pidáis**	**pidan**

---

[1]Forms of **adquirir (ie)** are:

PRES. IND.	**adquiero**	**adquieres**	**adquiere**	adquirimos	adquirís	**adquieren**
PRES. SUBJ.	**adquiera**	**adquieras**	**adquiera**	adquiramos	adquiráis	**adquieran**
IMPERATIVE	**adquiere**					

[2]Past participle: **muerto.**

IMPERATIVE	**pide**					
PRETERIT	pedí	pediste	**pidió**	pedimos	pedisteis	**pidieron**
IMP. SUBJ.	**pidiera,** etc.		**pidiese,** etc.			

Like **pedir:** competir, *to compete*; conseguir, *to obtain, attain*; despedirse, *to take leave*; elegir, *to elect*; impedir, *to prevent*; repetir, *to repeat*; seguir, *to follow*; servir, *to serve*; vestir, *to dress*.

reír, *to laugh*

PARTICIPLES	**riendo**		reído			
PRES. IND.	**río**	**ríes**	**ríe**	reímos	reís	**ríen**
PRES. SUBJ.	**ría**	**rías**	**ría**	**riamos**	**riáis**	**rían**
IMPERATIVE	**ríe**				reíd	
PRETERIT	reí	reíste	**rió**	reímos	reísteis	**rieron**
IMP. SUBJ.	**riera,** etc.		**riese,** etc.			

APPENDIX E

1 Verbs Followed by an Infinitive and Those Whose Meanings Change When Used Reflexively

I. Verbs Followed by an Infinitive, with or without a Preposition

Many verbs in Spanish are followed directly by an infinitive, as in English. Also, many verbs, as well as certain adjectives and nouns, require a preposition, especially **a, con, de, en,** or **por,** before an infinitive. An occasional verb may be followed by more than one preposition. (Remember that an infinitive is used after many idiomatic expressions, for example, **hay [había] que,** *it is [was] necessary to;* **tener que,** *to have to, must.*) Since the list is long, only the verbs (including a few which appear in idiomatic expressions) used in this text are listed below.

A. Verbs which may be followed directly by an infinitive

aconsejar to advise	**merecer** to merit, deserve
acostumbrar to be accustomed to	**necesitar** to need
bastar to be enough, be sufficient	**oír** to hear
conseguir (i, i) to succeed in	**olvidar** to forget
convenir to be fitting, be advisable	**parecer** to appear, seem
deber should, ought to, must	**pensar (ie)** to intend, plan
decidir to decide	**permitir** to permit, allow to, let
dejar to let, allow, permit	**poder** to be able, can
desear to desire, wish, want	**preferir (ie, i)** to prefer
esperar to hope, expect	**prometer** to promise
faltar to be lacking	**querer** to wish, want
gustar to like, be pleasing to	**resolver (ue)** to resolve
hacer to make, have	**saber** to know how (to), can
impedir (i, i) to prevent	**sentir (ie,i)** to regret, be sorry
importar to matter, be important	**soler (ue)** to be accustomed to
interesar to interest	**temer** to fear
lograr to succeed in	**ver** to see
mandar to command, have, order	

B. Verbs followed by certain prepositions before an infinitive or other object

a. Verbs which require **a** before an infinitive are:

acudir a to resort (come) to	**ayudar a** to help (aid) to
aprender a to learn to	**bajar a** to come (go) down to
aspirar a to aspire to	**comenzar (ie) a** to commence to
atreverse a to dare to	**contribuir a** to contribute to

correr a   to run to
decidirse a   to make up one's mind to
dedicarse a   to dedicate (devote) oneself to
dirigirse a   to turn to, direct oneself to
empezar (ie)   to begin to
enseñar a   to teach (how) to, show to
enviar a   to send to
incorporarse a   to be incorporated into
invitar a   to invite to
ir a   to go to

llegar a   to come to, become
obligar a   to oblige (force) to
oponerse a   to oppose
pasar a   to go to
salir a   to go (come) out to
tender (ie) a   to tend to
venir a   to come to
volver (ue) a   to return to;
  to . . . again

Verbs which require **a** before an object are:

acercarse a   to approach
ajustarse a to adjust to
asistir a   to attend
corresponder a   to correspond to

jugar (ue) a   to play (*a game*)
llegar a   to reach, arrive (at)
referirse (ie) a   to refer to

b. Verbs which require **con** before an infinitive (but more commonly before an object) are:

amenazar con   to threaten to (with)
casarse con   to marry, get
  married to

preocuparse con   to be concerned
  with (about), be preoccupied with
relacionarse con   to be related to

In addition to the four verbs mentioned, other verbs which require **con** before an object are:

encontrarse (ue) con   to run
  across

enfrentarse con   to face
tropezar (ie) con   to strike against

c. Verbs which require **de** before an infinitive are:

abstenerse de   to refrain from
acabar de   to have just
acordarse (ue) de   to remember to
alegrarse de   to be glad to
cansarse de   to become tired of
deber de   must (*probability*)

dejar de   to stop (cease), fail to
encargarse de   to take charge of
haber de   to be (be supposed) to
olvidarse de   to forget to
tratar de   to try to
tratarse de   to be a question of

Verbs which require **de** before an object are:

apoderarse de   to take possession of
burlarse de   to make fun of
constar de   to consist of
deshacerse de   to get rid of
despedirse (i, i) de   to take leave of

gozar de   to enjoy
partir de   to leave
salir de   to leave
servir (i,i) de   to serve as (a)
tratar de   to treat of, deal with

d. Verbs which require **en** before an infinitive are:

consentir (ie, i) en   to consent to, agree to
insistir en   to insist on

pensar (ie) en   to think of (about)
tardar en   to delay in, take long to

Verbs which require **en** before an object are:

entrar en   to enter
fijarse en   to notice

reparar en   to pay attention to

e. Verbs followed by **por** before an infinitive are:

esforzarse (ue) por   to make an
   effort to, strive to
estar por   to be to

interesarse por   to become interested in

II. Verbs (Not Listed in Lección dos) Whose Meanings Change When Used Reflexively

acostumbrar   to accustom

acostumbrarse a   to be *or* become
   accustomed to

decidir   to decide
dedicar   to dedicate
desarrollar   to develop
destacar   to make stand out,
   emphasize
dirigir   to direct, address
distinguir   to distinguish
encontrar (ue)   to find
establecer   to establish
interesar   to interest

ir   to go
llevar   to take, carry

marchar   to march
ocupar   to occupy
preparar   to prepare

presentar   to present, introduce
quitar   to remove, take away
reunir   to collect
sentir (ie,i)   to feel, regret
tratar de   to try to (+ *inf.*); to
   treat of, deal with
ver   to see
volver (ue)   to return

decidirse a   to make up one's mind to
dedicarse a   to dedicate oneself to
desarrollarse   to be developed
destacarse   to stand out

dirigirse a   to direct oneself (turn) to
distinguirse   to become distinguished
encontrarse (ue)   to find oneself, be
establecerse   to establish oneself, settle
interesarse (por)   to become
   interested (in)
irse   to go away, leave
llevarse   to take away, take (with
   oneself)
marcharse   to leave, go away
ocuparse de   to take care of
prepararse   to be prepared, prepare
   oneself
presentarse   to present oneself, appear
quitarse   to take off (oneself)
reunirse   to meet, gather
sentirse (ie, i) (bien)   to feel (well)
tratarse de   to be a question of

verse   to be (seen)
volverse (ue)   to become

VOCABULARIES

Spanish-English

A

a to, at, in, into, on, from, by, after, *etc.; not translated when used before a personal dir. obj.*
  a clase to class
  a fin de que *conj.* in order that
  a finales de at the end of
  a la derecha (izquierda) to *or* on the right (left)
  a la iglesia to church
  a la orden yes, at your service
  a las once at eleven o'clock
  a lo lejos in the distance
  a menos que *conj.* unless
  a menudo often, frequently
  a mitad del camino halfway
  a partir de beginning with
  a pesar de in spite of, despite
  ¿a qué hora? at what time?
  a veces at times
abarcar to embrace, include
abierto, -a *p.p. of* **abrir** *and adj.* open, opened
la **abogacía** law, legal profession
el **abogado** lawyer, attorney
el **abrazo** embrace
el **abrigo** topcoat, overcoat
  abril April
  abrir to open, open up
  abrumado, -a overwhelmed
  absorber to absorb

la **abstención** abstention
  abstener to abstain
    abstenerse de to abstain (refrain) from
la **abstracción** abstraction
  abstracto, -a abstract
la **abundancia** abundance
  abundante abundant
  abundar to abound, be in abundance
el **abuso** abuse
  acabar to end, finish
    acabar con + *obj.* to put an end to, wipe out
    acabar de + *inf.* to have just + *p.p.*
la **academia** academy
  académico, -a academic
  acaso perhaps
  accesible accessible
el **accidente** accident
la **acción** (*pl.* **acciones**) action
el **aceite** olive oil
  acelerar to accelerate, speed up; *reflex.* to be accelerated, speeded up
la **aceptación** acceptance
  aceptar accept
la **acera** sidewalk
  acerca de *prep.* about, concerning
  acercar to bring (draw) near
    acercarse (a + *obj.*) to approach, draw near (to)
    acercarse más to draw nearer, approach, come closer

acompañado, -a (de)   accompanied (by)

el **acompañante**   companion, attendant

acompañar   to accompany, go with

acondicionado: el aire—,   air conditioning

aconsejar   to advise

el **acontecimiento**   event, happening

acordarse (ue) (de + *obj.*)   to remember, recall

  acordarse de + *inf.*   to remember to

acostar (ue)   to put to bed; *reflex.* to go to bed, lie down

acostumbrar   to be accustomed to, be in the habit of

  acostumbrarse a   to become accustomed to

la **actitud**   attitude

la **activación**   activation, promotion

activamente   actively

la **actividad**   activity

activo, -a   active

el **acto**   act

actual *adj.*   present, present-day

  el actual   the present one (*m.*)

el **acuerdo**   accord, agreement

  estar de acuerdo   to agree, be in agreement

acumular(se)   to accumulate, gather

adecuadamente   adequately

adelante   ahead

  ¡adelante!   go on (ahead)! let's go!

  más adelante   later (farther) on

el **adelanto**   advance(ment)

además *adv.*   besides, furthermore

  además de *prep.*   besides, in addition to

aderezar   to garnish

adicional   additional

adiós   goodbye

la **adivinanza**   riddle

adjetivo, -a   adjective, adjectival

el **adjetivo**   adjective

la **administración**   administration

  Administración de Negocios   Business Administration

administrativo, -a   administrative

el **admirador**   admirer

admirar   to admire

la **admisión (*pl.* admisiones)**   admission

admitir   to admit

adobar   to prepare; to pickle

¿adónde?   where? (*with verbs of motion*)

adoptar   to adopt

adornar   to adorn, decorate

adquirir (ie)   to acquire

el **adulto**   adult

adverbial *adj.*   adverbial

el **adverbio**   adverb

adverso, -a   adverse

advertir (ie, i)   to notice

aeroespacial   air-space *adj.*

el **aeropuerto**   airport

  en el aeropuerto   at (in) the airport

afectar   to affect

aficionado,-a a   fond of

el **aficionado**   fan; amateur

  aficionado a los deportes   sports fan

afirmar   to affirm

  puede afirmarse   it can be affirmed (stated)

afirmativamente   affirmatively

afirmativo, -a   affirmative(ly)

afortunadamente   fortunately

el **África**   Africa

la **agencia**   agency

agigantado, -a   gigantic, extraordinary

agotar   to exhaust, use; *reflex.* to become exhausted, be used up

  se van agotando   (they) are gradually being used up

agradable   agreeable, pleasant

  lo más agradable   the most pleasant thing

agradecido, -a   grateful, thankful

agregar   to add

agrícola (*m. and f.*)   agricultural, farm (*adj.*)

la **agricultura**   agriculture

el **agua (*f.*)**   water

  vaso para agua   water glass

el **aguacate**   avocado, alligator pear

agudo, -a   high(-pitched) (*tone*)

la **aguadora**   water bearer

ahora   now

  ahora mismo   right now, right away

ahorrar   to save

el **aire**   air

  al aire libre   in the open air, outdoors

  el aire acondicionado   air conditioning

aislado, -a   isolated

el **ají**   chili, pepper (*vegetable*)

ajustar   to adjust; *reflex.* to be adjusted

  ajustarse a   to adjust to

al = a + el   to the

  al + *inf.*   on, upon + *pres. part.*

  al aire libre   in the open air, outdoors

  al año siguiente   (in) the following year

  al día siguiente   (on) the following (next) day

  al fondo   in the background

al horno   in the oven
al lado de   beside, at the side of
al margen de   on the fringe of
al mismo tiempo   at the same time
al parecer   apparently
al poco rato   after a short time
al poco tiempo   after (in) a short time
al servicio de   in the service of
al vapor   steamed, in steam
el **ala** (*f.*)   wing
  de alas verdes   green-winged
el **alambre**   wire
el **alcantarillado**   sewerage, sewerage system
  alcanzar   to reach, attain
  alegrar   to make glad
    alegrarse (de + *obj.***)**   to be glad (of, to)
    ¡cuánto me alegro (de)!   how glad I am (to)!
    ¡cuánto me alegro de que . . . !   how glad I am that . . . !
  Alejandro   Alexander
  algo *pron.*   something, anything; *adv.* somewhat, rather
  alguien *pron.*   someone, somebody, anyone, anybody
  algún   *used for* **alguno** *before m. sing. nouns*
  alguno, -a *adj. and pron.*   some, any (one), someone; *pl.* some, several, a few
    alguna cosa   something, anything
  Alicia   Alice
la **alimentación**   nourishment, food, nutrition
  alimenticio, -a   (of) food
  almacenar   to store (up)
la **almeja**   clam
la **almendra**   almond
  almorzar (ue)   to take (eat) lunch
el **almuerzo**   lunch
    para el almuerzo   for lunch
  ¡aló!   hello! (*telephone*)
  alrededor *adv.*   around
los **alrededores**   environs, outskirts, vicinity
la **alteración** (*p.* **alteraciones**)   alteration, disturbance
  alterar   to disturb, upset
  alto, -a   high, tall
la **altura**   height, altitude
    salto de altura   high jump
el **alumno**   pupil, student
el **alza** (*f.*)   rise, advance (*in prices*)
  allá   there (*often after verbs of motion*)

  más allá de   beyond
  allí   there
    por allí   (around, along) there
    por allí vienen   there they come
  amarillo, -a   yellow
el **Amazonas**   Amazon (River)
el **ambiente**   environment, atmosphere
    el medio ambiente   environment
la **amenaza**   threat
  América   America
    la **América Central**   Central America
    la **América del Sur**   South America
    la **América española**   Spanish America
    la **América hispana**   Spanish (Hispanic) America
    la **América latina**   Latin America
  americano, -a   American
la **amiga**   friend (*f.*)
el **amigo**   friend
el **amor**   love, affection
  ampliar   to enlarge, extend, broaden
  amplio, -a   large, extensive, broad
  Ana   Ann, Anne, Anna
el **analfabetismo**   illiteracy
  andaluz, -uza   Andalusian (*of southern Spain*)
  andar   to go, walk
los **Andes**   Andes (*mountains in South America*)
  andino, -a   Andean
  angloamericano, -a (*also noun*)   Anglo-American
  anglosajón, -ona (*also noun*)   Anglo-Saxon
    la **anglosajona**   the Anglo-Saxon one (*f.*)
el **ángulo**   angle, corner
el **animal**   animal
  anoche   last night
el **Antártico**   Antarctic (Ocean)
  ante *prep.*   before (*position*), in the presence (face) of
  anterior *adj.*   earlier, previous
    el **pretérito anterior**   preterit perfect (*tense*)
  antes *adv.*   before, formerly
    antes de *prep.*   before
    antes (de) que *conj.*   before
  anticipación: con horas de—,   hours in advance (ahead of time)
  antiguo, -a   old, ancient
  Antonio   Anthony
  anual   annual
  anunciar   to announce, advertise
  añadir   to add
el **año**   year

al año yearly, each year
al año siguiente (in) the following year
¿cuántos años tienes (tiene Ud.)? how old
  are you?
de estos (los) últimos años of (in) recent
  years, of the last (past) few years
durante estos (los) últimos años during
  (in) the last few years, recently
en estos últimos años recently, (in) the
  last few years, in recent years
tener . . . años to be . . . years old
todo el año all year, the whole (entire)
  year
todos los años every year
apagado, -a subdued
el **aparato** (piece of) apparatus, device
aparecer to appear, show up
el **apartamento** apartment
el **apasionamiento** enthusiasm, intense
  emotion
el **apellido** surname, last name
apenas scarcely, hardly
aplazar to postpone
la **aplicación** application
apolítico, -a apolitical
Apolo 11 Apollo 11 (*a U.S. space mission in
  1969*)
apoyar to support, second, back
apreciablemente appreciably
aprender (a + inf.) to learn (to + *inf.*)
aprobar to approve, pass (*a course or
  examination*)
apropiado, -a appropriate, fitting
aproximadamente approximately
aproximado, -a approximate
apto, -a competent
apuntar to note, take note of
apurarse to hurry (up)
aquel, aquella (-os, -as) *adj.* that, those
  (*distant*)
aquél, aquélla (-os, -as) *pron.* that (one),
  those; the former
aquello *neuter pron.* that
aquí here
  por aquí here, around (by, along) here
árabe (*m. and f.*) Arabic
el **árbol** tree
la **Argentina** Argentina
argentino, -a Argentine
el **argumento** argument

la **armonía** harmony
el **arquitecto** architect
la **arquitectura** architecture
arriba above
el **arroz** rice
  arroz (con leche) rice (pudding)
el **arte** art; (*f. pl.*) arts, crafts
  artes y oficios arts and crafts
  Bellas Artes Fine Arts
  Maestro en Artes Master of Arts
el **Ártico** Arctic (Ocean)
el **artículo** article
artificial artificial
el (la) **artista** artist
artístico, -a artistic
Arturo Arthur
asado, -a roast(ed)
la **ascendencia** ancestry
asegurado, -a assured
asegurar to assure
asequible accessible, available
así so, thus
  así como just as, as well as
  así que *conj.* as soon as
el **asiento** seat
la **asignatura** subject (*of study*)
asistir a to attend, be present at, witness
la **asociación** (*pl.* **asociaciones**) association
  Asociado: Estado Libre—, Commonwealth
  (Associated Free State)
el **asopao de pollo** *dish of chicken, rice, vegetables,
  and herbs*
el **aspecto** aspect
la **aspiración** (*pl.* **aspiraciones**) aspiration
aspirar a to aspire to
el **astronauta** astronaut
la **astronave** space ship (vehicle)
el **Astroser** Astrobeing
asumir to assume, take on
el **asunto** matter, subject; affair
el **ate** preserve, sweetmeat
la **atención** attention
el **aterrizaje** landing
aterrizar to land
atlético, -a athletic
el **atletismo** athletics, track (and field sports)
la **atmósfera** atmosphere
la **atracción** (*pl.* **atracciones**) attraction
atraer to attract
atraído, -a *p.p. of* **atraer** *and adj.* attracted

atreverse (a)   to dare (to)
audaz (*pl.* **audaces**)   bold
aumentar   to increase, augment
  va aumentando   (it) is (gradually)
    increasing
el **aumento**   increase, growth
aun, aún   even, still
aunque   although, even though, even if
el **auricular**   receiver (*telephone*)
el **autobús** (*pl.* **autobuses**)   bus
  autobús de la universidad   university bus
  autobús de las dos   two-o'clock bus
  en autobús   by (in a) bus
automático, -a   automatic
el **automóvil**   automobile
la **autonomía**   autonomy
el **autor**   author
la **autoridad**   authority
el **autorretrato**   self-portrait
auxiliar *adj.*   auxiliary
el **auxilio**   aid, help
el **avance**   advance
avanzado, -a   advanced
avanzar   to advance
averiguar   to find out
el **avión** (*pl.* **aviones**)   (air)plane
  avión de las dos   two-o'clock plane
  en avión   by (in a) plane
ayer   yesterday
  ayer (por la tarde)   yesterday (afternoon)
la **ayuda**   aid, help
ayudar (**a** + *inf.*)   to help (to)
azteca (*m. and f.*)   Aztec
el (la) **azúcar**   sugar
azul   blue

B

el **bachiller**   bachelor (*holder of a degree*)
  título de bachiller   bachelor's degree
el **bachillerato**   baccalaureate, bachelor's degree
la **bahía**   bay
bailar   to dance
el **baile**   dance, dancing
bajar   to lower
bajo *prep.*   below, under
bajo, -a   low, lower
  piso bajo   lower (first) floor
el **balompedista**   football player (*soccer*)
el **balompié**   football, soccer

el **baloncesto**   basketball
el **banco**   bank
  banco de hielo   iceberg
el **banquero**   banker
el **banquete**   banquet
el **baño de sol**   sunbath
Bárbara   Barbara
el **barril**   barrel
barroco, -a   baroque
la **base**   base, basis (*pl.* bases); rule (*of contest*)
  a base de   on the basis of
básicamente   basically
básico, -a   basic
el **básquetbol**   basketball
la **basura**   garbage, trash, rubbish
bastante *adj. and adv.*   quite, rather, enough,
  sufficient
bastar   to be enough (sufficient)
la **beca**   scholarship
el **béisbol**   baseball
bello, -a   beautiful, pretty; fine
  Bellas Artes   Fine Arts
beneficio: en—de   for the benefit of
la **biblioteca**   library
la **bicicleta**   bicycle
bien *adv.*   well
  decir bien   to be right
  ¡qué bien!   how well!
el **bien**   good
el **bienestar**   well-being, welfare
el **biftec**   (beef)steak
el **billete**   ticket
la **biología**   biology
biológico, -a   biological
  las biológicas   the biological ones (*f.*)
blanco, -a   white
  las blancas   the white ones (*f.*)
la **blusa**   blouse
la **bocina**   speaker (*machine*)
el **boleto**   ticket (*Mex.*)
la **bombilla**   bulb (*light*)
bonito, -a   beautiful, pretty
el **borde**   edge, border
el **bosque**   forest, wood(s)
la **botánica**   botany
el **Brasil**   Brazil
el **brasileño**   Brazilian
el **brazo**   arm
breve   brief, short
brevemente   briefly
brillante   brilliant

brindar to offer

la **broma** joke

buen *used for* **bueno** *before m. sing. nouns*

bueno *adv.* well, well now (then), all right, fine, good

  ¡bueno! hello! *(telephone)*

bueno, -a good, well

  buenos días good morning (day)

  lo bueno what is good, the good thing (part)

bullir to boil

burlarse (de) to make fun (of)

el **burro** burro, donkey

la **busca** search

buscar to look (for), search (for), seek

C

Caballeros: San Juan de los—, *town north of Sante Fe, New Mexico*

caber to fit, be contained in

la **cabeza** head

  tener dolor de cabeza to have a headache

el **cabo** end

  llevar a cabo to accomplish, carry out; *reflex.* to be carried out

cada each

caer to fall

el **café** coffee; café

  taza para café coffee cup

la **cafetera** coffeepot

caído *p.p. of* **caer**

la **caja** box, case

la **cajeta** *a kind of jelly*

el **calamar** squid

calcular to calculate, estimate

el **cálculo** calculation

la **calefacción** heating

la **calidad** quality, grade

caliente warm, hot

el **calor** heat, warmth

  hacer más calor to be warmer (warmest) *(weather)*

  hacer (mucho) calor to be (very) warm *(weather)*

  tener (mucho) calor to be (very) warm *(living beings)*

el **Callao** Callao *(port near Lima, Peru)*

la **calle** street

la **cama** bed

la **cámara** camera

cambiar to change

  van cambiando (they) are changing

el **cambio** change

  en cambio on the other hand

caminar to walk

el **camino** road, way, path

  por el camino along the way

la **camisa** shirt

el **campamento** camp

  campamento de muchachos boys' camp

el **campeonato** championship

campesino, -a peasant *(adj.)*, rural

el **campo** country, field; area

  casa de campo country house (home)

  por el campo in (through) the country

el **Canadá** Canada

la **canción** *(pl.* **canciones)** song

el **candado** lock

la **canela** cinnamon

el **cangrejo** crab

cansado, -a tired

  estar cansado, -a (de + *inf.)* to be tired (of + *pres. part.*)

cansar to tire (someone); *reflex.* to become tired

cantar to sing

la **cantidad** quantity, amount

el **cañón** *(pl.* **cañones)** canyon

  Gran Cañón Grand Canyon

la **capacidad (de)** capacity (to)

capacitado, -a competent, qualified

capacitar to qualify, enable

capaz *(pl.* **capaces)** capable

la **capital** capital *(city)*

el **capitán** captain

caprichoso, -a changeable, whimsical

la **cápsula** capsule

la **cara** face

el **carácter** *(pl.* **caracteres)** character, nature

característico, -a characteristic

el **carbón** coal

cardinal cardinal

Carlos Charles

Carlota Charlotte

Carmen Carmen

la **carne** meat

  carne asada roast, roasted meat

carne de cerdo   pork
carne de vaca   beef
carne picada   ground meat
Carolina   Caroline
la carrera   career, profession; race
    carrera del espacio   space race
    carreras de vallas   hurdles
la carretera   highway, road
el carro   car (*railroad*)
la carta   letter
la cartera   purse
el cartero   postman
la casa   house, home
    a casa de (Ramón)   to (Raymond's) house
    en casa   at home
    fuera de casa   outside (of) the house
    (ir) a casa   (to go) home
    salir de casa   to leave home
casado, -a (con)   married (to)
el casado   married man
casarse (con + *obj.*)   to marry, get married
    (to)
casi   almost
el caso   case
    en todo caso   in any case
    hacer caso de   to take into account, pay
        attention to
castigar   to punish
la cátedra   professorship
    libertad de cátedra   academic freedom
la caza   hunting
cazar   to hunt
el cebiche   seviche (*pickled fish*)
la cebolla   onion
la ceguera   blindness
Celaya   *city northwest of Mexico City*
celebrar   to celebrate, hold
célebre   celebrated, famous
celeste   celestial
celestial   celestial, heavenly
cenar   to eat (take) supper
el centavo   cent (*U.S.*)
centenario, -a   centennial
centralizar   to centralize
el centro   center
    Centro de Estudiantes   Student Center
    (estar) en el centro   (to be) downtown
    (ir) al centro   (to go) downtown
cerca *adv.*   near, close
    cerca de *prep.*   near
    más de cerca   more (most) closely

cerdo: carne de—,   pork
cerrado, -a   closed
cerrar (ie)   to close
cesar   to cease, stop
el cielo   sky
la ciencia   science
    Ciencias Físico-Matemáticas   Physical-
        Mathematical Sciences
    ciencias físico-químicas   physical-
        chemical sciences
    ciencias políticas (sociales)   political
        (social) sciences
científico, -a   scientific
el científico   scientist
ciento (cien)   a (one) hundred
    (uno) por ciento   (one) percent
cierto, -a (a)   certain, true
    por cierto   certainly, for sure
la cifra   figure
el cigarro   cigar
cinco   five
cincuenta   fifty
el cine   movie(s)
cinético, -a   kinetic (*consisting in or depending
        on motion*)
la cinta   tape
circular   to circulate
la circunstancia   circumstance
la cita   date, appointment
citado, -a   cited, above-mentioned
    las citadas   the ones mentioned (listed) (*f.*)
citar   to cite, mention, give
la ciudad   city
    ciudad de México   Mexico City
el ciudadano   citizen
civil   civil
la civilización   civilization
Clara   Clara, Clare
claramente   clearly
claro, -a   clear
¡claro que no!   of course not!
la clase   class; kind
    a clase   to class
    clase de español   Spanish class
    de ninguna clase   not . . . of any kind
    en clase   in class
    ¿qué clase de . . . ?   what kind of . . . ?
    sala de clase   classroom
clásico, -a   classic
la clasificación   classification, rating
la cláusula   clause

clausurar   to close (*as an exhibition*)
al clausurarse   when (it) closes (is closed)
el **clérigo**   cleric, clergyman, priest
la **clínica**   clinic, hospital
clínica de la universidad   university clinic
el **club**   club
cocer (ue)   to cook
la **cocina**   kitchen
cocinar   to cook
la **cocinera**   cook (*f.*)
el **coche**   car
en coche   by (in a) car
la **coexistencia**   coexistence
coger   to pick (up)
la **colaboración**   collaboration
colaborar   to collaborate
el (la) **colega**   colleague
el **colegio**   school (*a secondary school which prepares for the university*)
colgar (ue)   to hang (up)
colmado, -a de   crowded (filled) with, full of
la **colocación**   position, place
colocar   to place, put
colombiano, -a (*also noun*)   Colombian
la **colonia**   colony
colonial   colonial
la **colonización**   colonization
el **color**   color
el **colorido**   coloring
Colorritmo   Colorhythm
la **columbia**   pigeon (archaic)
combatir   to combat, fight
combinado, -a   combined
combinar   to combine
el **combustible**   combustible, fuel
el **comedor**   dining room
el **comentario**   commentary, comment
comenzar (ie) (a + *inf.*)   to commence (to), begin (to), start (to)
comer   to eat
comercial   business, commercial
el **comerciante**   merchant, businessman
el **comercio**   commerce, trade, business
comercio exterior (interior)   foreign (domestic) trade
la **comida**   meal, food, dinner
el **comienzo**   beginning
la **comisión** (*pl.* **comisiones**)   committee, commission
como   as (a), like; since
así como   as well as, just as

como si   as if
como último recurso   as a last resort
tanto . . . como   as (so) well . . . as, both . . . and
¿cómo?   how? what? in what way?
¡cómo no!   of course! certainly!
cómodo, -a   comfortable
la **compañera**   companion (*f.*)
compañera de cuarto   roommate (*f.*)
el **compañero**   companion (*m.*)
compañero de cuarto   roommate (*m.*)
la **compañía**   company
la **comparación** (*pl.* **comparaciones**)   comparison
comparar   to compare
comparativo, -a   comparative
la **competencia**   competition
competir (i,i)   to compete
la **complejidad**   complexity
completar   to complete
completo, -a   complete
por completo   completely
complicado, -a   complicated
el **componente**   component
componer   to compose
la **composición** (*pl.* **composiciones**)   composition, makeup
el **compositor**   composer
la **compra**   purchase
ir de compras   to go shopping
comprar   to buy; *reflex.* to buy (for oneself)
comprender   to comprehend, understand
el **compromiso**   commitment, pledge
compuesto, -a   *p.p. of* **componer** *and adj.* composed
común (*pl.* **comunes**)   common
la **comunidad**   community
con   with
con éxito   successfully
con frecuencia   frequently
con horas de anticipación   hours in advance (ahead of time)
con seriedad   seriously
conceder   to grant, give
concentrar   to concentrate
se ha concentrado   (it) has been concentrated
la **concesión** (*pl.* **concesiones**)   concession
el **concierto**   concert
concluir   to conclude, end, finish
la **concordancia**   agreement
la **concurrencia**   crowd, competition

concurso de pintura   painting contest
(competition)

la **condición** (*pl.* **condiciones**)   condition
   en muy malas condiciones   in very bad
   condition
   condicional *adj.*   conditional
el **condicional**   conditional (*tense*)
el **condimento**   condiment, seasoning
   conducir   to conduct, drive, lead, guide
el **conejo**   rabbit
la **conferencia**   conference; lecture
   conferir (ie,i)   to confer
la **confesión** (*pl.* **confesiones**)   confession
   confirmar   to confirm
el **conflicto**   conflict
la **conjunción** (*pl.* **conjunciones**)   conjunction
el **conjunto**   group; team
   conmigo   with me
   conocer   to know, be acquainted with, meet;
      to recognize
      dar a conocer   to make known
      darse a conocer   to make oneself known,
      make a name for oneself
      mucho gusto (en conocerlo *or* **-la)**   (I'm
      very) pleased to know (meet) you
   conocido, -a   known, well-known,
      recognized, familiar
      más conocido, -a   best known
el **conocimiento**   knowledge
la **conquista**   conquest, winning
   consciente   conscious
la **consecuencia**   consequence
   conseguir (i,i)   to get, obtain, attain, bring
      about
el **consejero**   counsellor, adviser
el **consejo**   advice
el **consentimiento**   consent
   consentir (ie, i) en   to consent to, agree to
la **conservación**   conservation, preservation
   conservador, -ora   conservative
   conservar   to conserve, preserve; *reflex.* to be
      preserved
las **conservas**   preserves
   considerable   considerable
   considerablemente   considerably
la **consideración**   consideration, regard, respect,
      significance
   considerar   to consider, assume
   consigo   with himself, herself, itself, *etc.*
   consiguiente: por—,   consequently, therefore
   consistir en   to consist of

   constante   constant
   constar de   to consist of, be composed of
   constituir   to constitute, make up, include,
      set up
la **construcción** (*pl.* **construcciones**)
      construction
el **constructivismo**   constructivism
   constructivista (*m. and f.*)   constructivist
   constructivo, -a   constructive
   construido, -a   constructed, built
   construir   to construct, build
   consultar   to consult; to discuss, take up
      (with)
el **consumidor**   consumer
   consumir   to consume, use
el **consumo**   consumption, use
el **contacto**   contact
      en contacto con   in contact (touch) with
la **contaminación**   contamination, pollution
   contaminar   to contaminate
   contar (ue)   to count; to tell, relate
      contar con   to count on
   contemporáneo, -a   contemporary
   contener   to contain
   contento, -a   contented, happy, pleased; *adv.*
      contentedly
      estar contento, -a (de que)   to be happy
      (that)
      lo contentos que están   how happy they
      are
la **contestación** (*pl.* **contestaciones**)   answer,
      reply
   contestar   to answer, reply
   contigo   with you (*fam. sing.*)
la **continuación**   continuation
   continuar   to continue, go (keep) on
   contra   against, at (*the opponent's goal in soccer*)
   contraído, -a   made, entered into
   contrario, -a   opposite, enemy, of one's
      opponent
      al contrario   on the contrary
   contrarrestar   to counteract, offset
el **contraste**   contrast
   contribuir   to contribute
   convencer (de que)   to convince (that)
   convencido, -a de que   convinced that
   conveniente   useful, desirable
   convenir   to be fitting (advisable)
la **conversación** (*pl.* **conversaciones**)
      conversation
   conversar   to converse, talk

para conversar for conversation
convincente convincing
la **cooperación** cooperation
cooperar to cooperate, take part
la **cooperativa** cooperative (*society*)
la **copla** popular song
la **corbata** necktie
Coronado, Francisco Vázquez de (1510–1549)
    Spanish explorer of the southwestern U.S.
correctamente correctly
correcto, -a correct
correr to run
la **correspondencia** correspondence
corresponder a to belong to, correspond to
correspondiente (a) corresponding (to)
corriente *adj.* current, common, popular,
    well-known
    los más corrientes the most common ones
    (*m.*)
la **corriente** current
cortar to cut (off)
cortés (*pl.* **corteses**) courteous
la **cortesía** courtesy
corto, -a short
la **cosa** thing
    alguna cosa something, anything
    algunas cosas más a few more things
    cualquier cosa anything (*at all*)
la **cosecha** harvest, crop
Cosmos *name of a soccer team in New York City*
la **costa** coast
    Costa del Sol Southern Coast (*Spain*)
costar (ue) to cost
el **coste** cost
costoso, -a costly, expensive
la **costumbre** custom
la **creación** (*pl.* **creaciones**) creation,
    construction
crear to create
la **creatividad** creativity
crecer to grow, increase
    irá creciendo (it) will continue to increase
    va creciendo (it) continues to increase, is
    gradually increasing
el **crecimiento** growth
el **crédito** credit
creer to believe, think
    creer que sí (no) to believe so (not)
    ¡ya lo creo! of course! certainly!
creído *p.p. of* **creer**
la **crisis** crisis

la **crítica** criticism
crítico, -a critical
el **crítico** critic
cromático, -a chromatic
la **cruz** (*pl.* **cruces**) cross
cruzar to cross
el **cuaderno** notebook
la **cuadra** block (*city*)
el **cuadro** picture painting
cual: el—, la—, (los, las cuales) that, which,
    who, whom
    lo cual which (fact)
¿cuál(es)? which one (ones)? what?
cualquier(a) (*pl.* **cualesquier[a]**) any *or*
    anyone (at all), just anyone
    cualquier cosa anything (at all)
cuando when
¿cuándo? when?
cuanto *neuter pron.* all that
    en cuanto *conj.* as soon as
    en cuanto a *prep.* as for, concerning
cuanto, -a all that (who)
    unos(-as) cuantos(-as) some, a few
¿cuánto, -a (-os, -as)? how much (many)?
    ¿cuánto tiempo? how long (much time)?
    ¿cuántos años tienes (tiene Ud.)? how old
    are you?
¡cuánto + *verb!* how . . . !
¡cuánto, -a (-os, -as)! how much (many)!
cuarenta forty
cuarto, -a fourth
    tres cuartas partes three fourths
    una cuarta parte one fourth
el **cuarto** room; quarter
    compañero (compañera) de cuarto
    roommate
    (son las nueve) y cuarto (it is) a quarter
    after (nine)
cuatro four
cubano, -a (*also noun*) Cuban
cubierto, -a (de) *p.p. of* **cubrir** *and*
    adj. covered (with)
cubrir to cover, include
    cubrirse de to be covered with
la **cuenta** account, bill
    darle cuenta a uno to give one an account of
    darse cuenta de to realize
    tener en cuenta to bear in mind, take into
    account
el **cuento** (short) story, tale
el **cuerpo** body

mente sana en cuerpo sano   a healthy (sound) mind in a healthy (sound) body

la **cuestión** (*pl.* **cuestiones**)   question

el **cuidado**   care

con cuidado   carefully

tener (mucho) cuidado   to be (very) careful

cuidadoso, -a   careful

lo cuidadosas que tienen que ser   how careful (they) must be

la **culpa**   fault, blame

tener la culpa   to be at fault, be to blame

el **cultivador**   cultivator

cultivar   to cultivate

el **cultivo**   crop

la **cultura**   culture; education

cultural   cultural

el **cumpleaños**   birthday

regalo de cumpleaños   birthday gift

cumplir   to fulfill, perform, carry out, discharge

cursiva: en—,   in italics

el **curso**   course

la **curva**   curve

cuyo, -a   whose, of whom, of which

el **Cuzco**   Cuzco (*Andean city in Peru, former capital of the Inca empire*)

Ch

charlar   to chat

Chávez, Carlos (1899–1978)   *Mexican composer and conductor*

el **cheque**   check

el **chile**   chili, pepper

salsa de chile   chili sauce

chileno, -a (*also noun*)   Chilean, of Chile

la **chimenea**   chimney, smokestack, hearth

el **chocolate**   chocolate

chutar   to kick (*soccer*)

D

dale = da (tú) + le   give him (her)

dañar   to harm, hurt

dar   to give; *reflex.* to give oneself

dale recuerdos míos   give him (her) my regards (best wishes)

dar a conocer   to make known

dar la mano (a)   to shake hands (with)

dar mucho gusto a   to please a lot, give much pleasure to

dar un paseo   to take a walk (stroll)

dar paseos   to take walks

darle cuenta a uno   to give one an account of

darse a conocer   to make oneself known, make a name for oneself

darse cuenta de   to realize

darse prisa   to hurry (up)

lo damos a   we are selling (offering) it for (at)

los **datos**   data, facts

de   of, from, by, about, to, concerning, with, as; in (*after a superlative*); than (*before numerals*)

de manera ejemplar   in an exemplary way

de manera (modo) que   so that

de parte de   on the part of

de todos modos   at any rate, by all means

de veras   really, truly

no . . . más de   not . . . more than (*before a numeral*)

debajo *adv.*   below

debajo de *prep.*   under, below

debatido, -a   debated, discussed

deber   to owe; must, ought to, should

deber de + *inf.*   must, probably + *verb*

debería   I (he, she, you *formal*) should

debiera   I (he, she, you) should, ought to

debiéramos   we should, ought to

se debe a   it is due to

el **deber**   duty, debt, obligation

debido, -a   just, proper, due

como es debido   as is proper, as is only right

debiera   I (he, she, you) should, ought to

la **debilidad**   weakness

la **década**   decade

el **decano**   dean

decidir   to decide; *reflex.* to decide, make a decision

decidirse a   to make up one's mind to

decir   to say, tell

decir bien   to be right

decir que sí (no)   to say yes (no)

diga, dígame   hello (*telephone*)
es decir   that is (to say)
querer decir   to mean
se lo dije   I told him (her, you *formal,* them)
se lo diré (a ellos)   I'll tell them
la **decisión**   decision
tomar una decisión   to make a decision
declarar   to declare; *reflex.* to declare oneself (itself)
decorar   to decorate
dedicar   to dedicate, devote; to give
deducir   to deduce, infer
defectuoso, -a   defective
defender (ie)   to defend
la **defensa**   defense
definido, -a   definite
definitivo, -a   definitive
degenerar   to degenerate
dejar   to leave (*behind*); to let, allow, permit
deja mucho que desear   (it) leaves much to be desired
dejar de + *inf.*   to stop (cease) + *pres. part.,* fail *or* cease to + *inf.*
no dejar de + *inf.*   not to stop + *pres. part.,* not to fail to + *inf.*
del = de + el   of (from) the
delicado, -a   delicate, scrupulous
delicioso, -a   delicious
delinquir   to be guilty
la **demanda**   demand
demanda interior   domestic demand
demás: los (las) —,   the other, the rest (of the)
demasiado *adv.*   too, too much
la **democracia**   democracy
democrático, -a   democratic
la **democratización**   democratization
demostrar (ue)   to demonstrate, show
demostrativo, -a   demonstrative
denso, -a   dense, crowded
el **dentista**   dentist
dentro de *prep.*   within, in, inside
el **departamento**   department
Departamento de Español   Spanish Department
depender (de)   to depend (on)
el (la) **dependiente**   clerk
el **deporte**   sport
aficionado, -a a los deportes   sports fan
sección de deportes   sports section

el **deportista**   sportsman
derecho, -a   right (*direction*)
a la derecha   to (on) the right
el **derecho**   right; law
Escuela (Facultad) de Derecho   Law School
el **Derecho**   Law
la **derivación** (*pl.* **derivaciones**)   derivation
el **desafío**   challenge
desaparecer   to disappear
desarrollar(se)   to develop, be developed
el **desarrollo**   development
la **desatención**   lack of attention
desatender (ie)   to disregard, pay no attention to
desatendido, -a   disregarded
desayunarse   to eat (take) breakfast
descansar   to rest
el **descenso**   decline
describir   to describe; *reflex.* to be described
descrito, -a *p.p. of* **describir** *and adj.* described
descubierto, -a *p.p. of* **descubrir** *and adj.* discovered
descubrir   to discover
vamos descubriendo   we are (gradually) discovering
desde *prep.*   from, since; for (*time*)
desde hace varios años   for several years
desde . . . hasta   from . . . (up) to
desde que *conj.*   since
deseado, -a   desired
desear   to desire, wish, want
deja mucho que desear   (it) leaves much to be desired
desembarcar   to disembark, land
el **desembarco**   landing
desempacar   to unpack
el **deseo**   desire
tener muchos deseos de   to be very eager (wish very much) to
desfavorable   unfavorable
la **desgracia**   misfortune
por desgracia   unfortunately
desgraciadamente   unfortunately
deshabitado, -a   uninhabited
deshacerse de   to get rid of
designar   to designate, denote
deslumbrante   dazzling
despacio   slowly

lo más despacio posible   the slowest possible

despedirse (i,i) (de)   to take leave (of), say goodbye (to)

despejado, -a   clear (*weather*)

los **desperdicios**   waste products

despertar (ie)   to awaken, wake up, arouse; *reflex.* to wake up (oneself)

la **despreocupación**   lack of concern

después *adv.*   afterward(s), then, later

   después de *prep.*   after

   después (de) que *conj.*   after

destacar   to make stand out, emphasize; *reflex.* to stand out

el **destino**   destiny, fate, future

la **destrucción**   destruction

destruido, -a   destroyed

destruir   to destroy; *reflex.* to be destroyed, destroy oneself (itself)

detener   to detain, stop

el **deterioro**   deterioration

detrás de *prep.*   behind

devolver (ue)   to return, give back

devuelto *p.p. of* **devolver**

el **día**   day

   al día siguiente   (on) the following (next) day

   buenos días   good morning (day)

   de nuestros días   of today, in (of) our time

   día a día   day by day

   hoy día   nowadays, today

   todo el día   all day, the whole (entire) day

   todos los días   every day

el **diálogo**   dialogue

diario, -a   daily

el **diccionario**   dictionary

el **dictado**   dictation

dicho, -a *p.p. of* **decir** *and adj.*   (the) said, (the) aforementioned

   lo dicho   what is (was) said

dieciocho   eighteen

dieciséis   sixteen

Diego   James

diez   ten

la **diferencia**   difference

   a diferencia de   unlike

diferente   different

diferir (ie,i)   to differ

difícil   difficult, hard

   lo difícil   what is difficult, the difficult thing (part)

lo difíciles que (son)   how difficult (they are)

la **dificultad**   difficulty

el **difunto**   deceased

la **difusión**   diffusion

dile = di (tú) + le   tell him (her)

la **dimensión** (*pl.* **dimensiones**)   dimension

el **diminutivo**   diminutive

dinámico, -a   dynamic

el **dinero**   money

Dios   God

   ¡Dios mío!   heavens! for heaven's sake!

   ¡por Dios!   for heaven's sake!

directamente   directly

Directiva: Junta—,   governing board (committee), officers

directo, -a   direct

el **director**   director, manager; editor (*of a newspaper*)

dirigir   to direct, manage

   dirigirse (a + obj.)   to go *or* turn (to), direct oneself (to), address (*a person*)

la **disciplina**   discipline

disciplinado, -a   disciplined

el **disco**   record (*phonograph*)

la **discriminación**   discrimination

la **discusión**   discussion

discutir   to discuss, argue about

el **diseño**   design, pattern

la **disminución**   diminution, decrease

disminuir   to diminish, decrease

disponer   to arrange, set up

disponible   available

dispuesto, -a *p.p. of* **disponer** *and adj.*   arranged, set up

distinguido, -a   distinguished, famous

distinguir   to distinguish; *reflex.* to distinguish oneself, be distinguished; to shine

distinto, -a   different

la **distribución**   distribution

distribuir   to distribute

la **diversidad**   diversity

diverso, -a   diverse, different, varied

divertir (ie,i)   to amuse; *reflex.* to have a good time, amuse oneself

   divertirse mucho   to have a very good time

   ¡diviértete mucho!   have a very good (fine) time!

doblar   to fold

doce   twelve

a las doce   at twelve o'clock
son las doce (menos cuarto)   it is (a quarter to) twelve
la **docena (de)**   dozen (of)
docente   educational
el **doctorado**   doctorate, doctor's degree
doctoral   doctoral
la **documentación**   documentation, papers
el **documento**   document, paper
el **dólar**   dollar (*U.S.*)
doler (ue)   to ache, pain, hurt
me (le) duele la cabeza   my (his) head aches
el **dolor**   ache, pain
tener dolor de cabeza   to have a headache
doméstico, -a   domestic
dominante   dominant, dominating, prevailing
Domingo   Dominic
Santo Domingo   St. Dominic
el **domingo**   (on) Sunday
dominicano, -a   Dominican, of the Dominican Republic
don   Don (*title used before first names of men*)
donde   where, in which
¿dónde?   where?
¿por dónde se va . . . ?   how does one go . . . ? (*by what route?*)
doña   Doña (*title used before first names of women*)
dormir (ue,u)   to sleep; *reflex.* to fall asleep, go to sleep
dormir la siesta   to take a nap
Dorotea   Dorothy
dos   two
(avión) de las dos   two-o'clock (plane)
los (las) dos   the two, both
doscientos, -as   two hundred
el **duco**   duco
la **ducha**   shower (*bath*)
la **duda**   doubt
sin duda   doubtless, without a doubt
sin duda alguna   without any doubt (whatever)
dudar   to doubt
dudoso, -a   doubtful
el **dulce**   sweet(meat); candy
dulce en pasta   fruit paste
la **duración**   duration; life
durante   during, in, for
durar   to last

E

e   and (*used for* y *before* i-, hi-, *but not* hie-)
la **ecología**   ecology
ecológico, -a   ecological
la **economía**   economics, economy
económico,-a   economic
economizar   to economize, save
el **Ecuador**   Ecuador
ecuatoriano, -a   Ecuadorian, of Ecuador
la **edad**   age
el **edificio**   building
la **educación**   education
la Educación Física   Physical Education
el **educador**   educator
educar   to educate
educativo, -a   educational
efectivo, -a   effective
el **efecto**   effect
efectuar   to effect, carry out (on), bring about
eficaz   effective
ejemplar   exemplary
el **ejemplo**   example
por ejemplo   for example
ejercer   to exercise, exert
el **ejercicio**   exercise, practice
el (*pl.* **los**)   the (*m.*)
del (de los) que   than
el (los) de   that (those) of, the one(s) of (with, in)
el (los) que   that, who, which, he (those) who (whom), the one(s) who (that, which)
él   he; him, it (*m.*) (*after prep.*)
electivo, -a   elective
la **electricidad**   electricity
eléctrico, -a   electric
elegante   elegant
elegido, -a   selected, chosen
elegir (i,i)   to elect, choose, select
el **elemento**   element
Elena   Ellen, Helen
elevado, -a   high, lofty, elevated
elevar   to elevate, raise, lift
la **eliminación**   elimination
eliminar   to eliminate
ella   she; her, it (*f.*) (*after prep.*)
ellos, -as   they; them (*after prep.*)
embargo: sin—,   nevertheless, however
emocionante   thrilling, exciting
la **empanada**   *small meat* (or *fish*) *pie*

la **empanadita**   small turnover
empatado, -a   tied
el **empate**   tie (*in game*)
empezar (ie) (a + *inf.*)   to begin (to), start (to)
el **empleado**   employee
emplear   to employ, use
  ha obligado a emplear   (he) has forced
    into use
el **empleo**   use, employment
emprender   to undertake
en   in, on
  en autobús (avión, coche, taxi)   in a *or* by
    bus (plane, car, taxi)
  en cuanto   as soon as
  en (el aeropuerto)   at *or* in (the airport)
  en favor de   in favor of, for
  en fin   in short
  en lugar de   instead of, in place of
  en seguida   at once, immediately
  en suma   in short, in a word
  en otras partes   elsewhere
  en todas partes   everywhere
  en todo caso   in any case
  en voz alta   aloud
encantado, -a   delighted
encargarse de   to take charge of, undertake
encima: por—de *prep.*   over, above
encontrar (ue)   to encounter, find, meet;
  reflex. to be, be found, find oneself
  encontrarse con   to meet, run across (into)
la **encuesta**   poll, inquiry
la **enchilada**   corn cake with chili
el **enemigo**   enemy
la **energía**   energy
  la crisis de la energía   energy crisis
enero   January
el **énfasis**   emphasis
enfermo, -a   ill, sick; sickly (*with* **ser**)
el **enfermo**   patient, sick person
el **enfoque**   focus
enfrentarse con   to face, cope with
enfrente de *prep.*   in front of
enorme   enormous, large
Enrique   Henry
enrollado, -a   rolled
la **ensalada**   salad
ensayar   to try to, attempt
el **ensayo**   essay
la **enseñanza**   education, instruction, teaching
enseñar   to show, point out

enseñar a + *inf.*   to show (teach) how to
entender (ie)   to understand
enterado, -a   informed
entero, -a   entire, whole
la **entidad**   entity, body, organization
el **entierro**   burial
entonces   then, at that time
la **entrada**   entrance, admission
entrante   coming, next
entrar (en + *obj.*)   to enter, come (go) in
  ¿se puede entrar?   may I (we, one) come in?
entre *prep.*   between, among, in
entregar   to hand (over), deliver
el **entremés** (*pl.* **entremeses**)   appetizer
la **entrevista**   interview
entusiasta (*m. and f.*)   enthusiastic
enviar   to send
la **envoltura**   wrapping
  sin envoltura   unwrapped
envolver (ue)   to wrap up
envuelto *p.p. of* **envolver**   wrapped (up)
la **época**   epoch, period, time
equipados: van—,   (they) are equipped
el **equipaje**   baggage, luggage
el **equipo**   team; set, system; equipment
  equipos (de muchachos)   (boys') teams
  equipos de sonido   sound equipment
equitativo, -a   equitable
equivalente *adj. and m. noun*   equivalent
equivaler a   to be equivalent to
equivocarse   to be mistaken
el **erizo**   hedgehog
errar (ye)   to err, miss (*a shot*)
la **erre**   *the letter* "rr"
el **escabeche**   pickled fish
escalonar   to stagger
el **escaparate**   show window
la **escena**   scene
escoger   to choose, select
escolar   school (*adj.*)
escribir   to write
  escribir a máquina   to type(write), write on
    a (the) typewriter
  está por escribir   (it) is to be written
escrito, -a *p.p. of* **escribir** *and adj.*   written
  lo escrito   what is (has been) written
la **escritora**   writer (*f.*)
la **escritura**   script, (hand) writing
escuchar   to listen (to)
la **escuela**   school

a (en) la escuela to (at, in) school
Escuela de Derecho Law School
Escuela Graduada Graduate School
escuela superior high school
la **escultura** sculpture
ese, esa (-os, -as) *adj.* that, those (*nearby*)
ése, ésa, (-os, -as) *pron.* that (one), those
  (*nearby*)
esencial essential
esencialmente essentially
la **esfera** sphere
esforzarse (ue) por to strive to, make an
  effort to
el **esfuerzo (por)** effort (to)
eso *neuter pron.* that
  a eso de at about (*time*)
  por eso therefore, because of that, for that
    reason, that's why
espacial spatial, (pertaining to) space
el **espacio** space, room
  carrera del espacio space race
España Spain
español, -ola (*also noun*) Spanish; Spaniard
  de habla española Spanish-speaking
el **español** Spanish (*language*)
  (clase) de español Spanish (class)
  Departamento de Español Spanish
    Department
especial special
el **especialista** specialist
especializarse to specialize
especialmente especially
la **especie** kind, species
específico, -a specific
el **espectador** spectator
la **esperanza** (*also pl.*) hope
esperar to wait (for), await; to hope, expect
  esperar mucho to wait long
  espero tu llamada I'll expect your call
  (no) esperar más (not) to wait (any) longer
espiral: toques en—, swirls
espléndido, -a splendid
el **esposo** husband, spouse; *pl.* husband and
  wife, spouses
la **esquina** corner (*street*)
el **establecimiento** establishment, place of
  business, institution
  establecer to establish, set up, settle; *reflex.*
    to establish oneself, settle
la **estación** (*pl.* **estaciones**) station; season

el **estadio** stadium
el **estado** state, condition
  Estado Libre Asociado Commonwealth
    (Associated Free State)
  los Estados Unidos United States
estar to be; to look, taste, feel
  está bien all right, that's fine
  está por escribir (it) is to be written
  estar al tanto de to be aware of
  estar de acuerdo to agree, be in agreement
  estar en favor to be in favor
  estar para to be about to, be on the point of
este, esta (-os, -as) *adj.* this, these
éste, ésta (-os, -as) *pron.* this (one), these; the
  latter
estereofónico, -a stereophonic
estilizado, -a stylized
el **estilo** style
estimar to esteem
estimular to stimulate
el **estímulo** stimulus
esto *neuter pron.* this
  esto es this (that) is
estratégico, -a strategic
estrecho, -a narrow, close, rigid
la **estructura** structure
el **(la) estudiante** student
  Centro de Estudiantes Student Center
  residencia de estudiantes student
    residence hall (dormitory)
estudiantil student (*adj.*)
estudiar to study
el **estudio** study
  comisión de estudio study committee
  plan de estudios curriculum
  programa de estudio program of study,
    curriculum (*pl.* curricula)
etcétera et cetera, etc., and so forth
eterno, -a eternal
ético, -a ethical
Europa Europe
europeo, -a European
la **evaluación** (*pl.* **evaluaciones**) evaluation
evaluar to evaluate
evidente evident, obvious
la **evolución** evolution, change
evolutivo, -a evolutionary
exactamente exactly
exacto, -a exact
exagerar to exaggerate

el **examen** (*pl.* **exámenes**) exam(ination), test
examinar to examine
exceder to exceed
excedido, -a exceeded
la **excelencia** excellence
excelente excellent, fine
excepcional exceptional
excesivo, -a excessive, great
la **exclamación** (*pl.* **exclamaciones**) exclamation
la **excursión** (*pl.* **excursiones**) excursion, trip
hacer una excursión to make (take) an excursion
exigir to require, demand
el **exiliado** exile
la **existencia** existence
existir to exist, be, be in existence
el **éxito** success
con éxito successfully
tener (mucho) éxito to be (very) successful
la **expansión** expansion, spread
la **expedición** (*pl.* **expediciones**) expedition
la **experiencia** experience
experimental experimental
experimentar to experiment
el **experimento** experiment
la **explicación** explanation
explicar to explain
la **exploración** (*pl.* **exploraciones**) exploration
explorar to explore
la **explotación** exploitation
el **exponente** exponent
la **exportación** (*pl.* **exportaciones**) export, exportation
la **exposición** (*pl.* **exposiciones**) exposition, exhibition
expresar to express
la **expresión** (*pl.* **expresiones**) expression
el **expresionismo** expressionism
extender (ie) to extend, expand
extenso, -a extensive, vast
exterior *adj.* exterior, outer; foreign
comercio exterior foreign trade
extranjero, -a strange, foreign
dos jóvenes extranjeros two foreign young men
en el extranjero abroad
el **extranjero** foreigner
extraño, -a strange, unusual
extraordinario, -a extraordinary
la **exuberancia** exuberance

F

la **fábrica** factory
la **fabricación** manufacture
la **faceta** facet, face, aspect
fácil easy
fácilmente easily
el **factor** factor
la **facultad** school (*in a university*)
Facultad de Derecho Law School
la **fachada** façade, front
la **falta** fault, mistake; lack
incurrir en falta to draw (incur) a penalty
por falta de *prep.* for lack of
faltar to be lacking (missing), need; to be left
no puede faltar it must appear, it cannot be missing
la **fama** fame, reputation
la **familia** family
famoso, -a famous
fantástico, -a fantastic
la **farmacia** pharmacy, drugstore
la **fase** phase
la **fauna** fauna (*animals of a region*)
el **favor** favor
en favor de in favor of, for
estar en favor to be in favor
por favor please (*at end of request*)
favorable favorable
favorecer to favor, help
favorito, -a favorite
febrero February
fecundo, -a fruitful
la **fecha** date
federal federal
la **felicidad** happiness
felicitar to congratulate; *reflex.* to congratulate oneself; *reciprocal* to congratulate each other (one another)
Felipe Philip
feliz (*pl.* **felices**) happy; *adv.* happily
femenino, -a feminine, women's
feminista (*m. and f.; also f. noun*) feminist
fenomenal phenomenal
el **ferrocarril** railroad
fértil fertile
el **fichero** file, filing case
la **fiebre** fever
la **fiesta** fiesta, festival, party, holiday

la **figura** figure, person
la **figuración** figuration
figurado, -a figurative, imaginary
figurar to figure, appear
fijado, -a fixed, determined, established
fijar to fix, establish, determine
  fijarse en to notice, pay attention to
la **filosofía** philosophy
el **fin** end, purpose
  a fin de que *conj.* in order that
  a fines de *prep.* at (toward) the end of
  en fin in short
  fin de semana weekend
  por fin finally, at last
  finales: a—de at the end of
la **finalidad** end, purpose
financiar to finance
financiero, -a financial
la **finca** farm, ranch
fino, -a fine, thin
la **Física** Physics
físico, -a physical
  la Educación Física Physical Education
  las físicas the physical ones (*f.*)
físico-químico, -a physical-chemical
el **flan** custard
flexible flexible
la **flor** flower
la **flora** flora (*plants of a region*)
la **Florida** Florida
el **foco** focus, center
folklórico, -a folklore (*adj.*)
el **folleto** pamphlet, folder
fomentar to foment, encourage, promote, foster
el **fondo** background
  al fondo in the background
la **forma** form, way
  forma de vida way of living
la **formación** formation
formar to form, make (up); to educate, train
  formar parte de to form (make up) a part of
la **fórmula** formula
fortalecer to strengthen, support
la **foto** photo
  sacar fotos to take photos
el **fraccionamiento** fragmentation, division
la **fractura** fracture
francés, esa French
el **francés** French (*language*)

  profesora de francés French teacher (*f.*)
Francia France
Francisco Francis
la **frase** phrase, sentence
la **fraseología** phraseology
Fray Friar (*title*), Father
la **frecuencia** frequency
  con frecuencia frequently
frente a *prep.* in the face (presence) of
la **fresa** strawberry
el **fresco** coolness
  hacer (mucho) fresco to be (very) cool (*weather*)
los **frijoles (refritos)** (refried) kidney beans
frío, -a cold
el **frío** cold
  hacer más frío to be colder (*weather*)
  hacer (mucho) frío to be (very) cold (*weather*)
  tener (mucho) frío to be (very) cold (*living beings*)
frito, -a fried
la **frontera** frontier, border, boundary
las **frutas** fruit(s)
  conservas de frutas fruit preserves
el **fruto** fruit, benefit, product
la **fuente** fountain; source
fuera de *prep.* outside of
fuerte strong
la **función** (*pl.* **funciones**) function
el **funcionario** official, public official
la **fundación** foundation
fundar to found, establish
la **fusión** fusion
el **fútbol** football
  (partido) de fútbol football (game)
el **futbolista** football player
futuro, -a future
el **futuro** future; future tense

G

la **gallina** hen
el **gallo** cock, rooster
la **gana** desire
  tener (muchas) ganas de to desire *or* wish (very much) *or* to be (very) eager to
la **ganadería** livestock raising
el **ganado vacuno** cattle

el **ganador**   winner
ganar   to gain, earn, win
  va ganando   (it) is gradually winning
    (gaining)
la **ganga**   bargain
garantizar   to guarantee
la **garganta**   throat
el **gas**   gas
la **gasolina**   gas(oline)
  estación de gasolina   gas (service) station
gastar   to spend (*money*), waste, use (up)
el **gasto**   cost, expense
el **gato**   cat
el **gazpacho**   *cold vegetable soup*
la **generación** (*pl.* **generaciones**)   generation
general   general (*adj.*)
  en general   in general, generally
  por lo general   in general, generally
la **generalización**   generalization
generalmente   generally
el **género**   gender
la **gente**   people
  gentes del pueblo   townspeople
  mucha gente   many people
geográfico, -a   geographic
la **geología**   geology
geométrico, -a   geometrical
la **germinación**   germination
el **gimnasio**   gym(nasium)
Ginastera, Alberto (1916–   )   *Argentine composer*
el **glaciar**   glacier
global   global
glorioso, -a   glorious
el **glosario**   glossary
glotón, -ona   gluttonous
el **gobierno**   government
  funcionario del gobierno   government official
el **gol**   goal (*soccer*)
el **golf**   golf
el **golpe**   blow
Goya: (Francisco de) (1746–1828)   *Spanish painter*
gozar (**de** + *obj.*)   to enjoy
la **gracia**   grace
  gracias (a)   thanks (to)
  gracias por   thanks *or* thank you for
  mil gracias   many (a thousand) thanks

  muchas gracias   many thanks, thank you very much, thanks a lot
el **grado**   degree
graduado, -a   graduate
  Escuela Graduada   Graduate School
graduarse   to graduate
la **gramática**   grammar
  curso de gramática   grammar course
gramatical   grammatical
gran *used for* **grande** *before sing. nouns*   great, grand
  Gran Cañón   Grand Canyon
grande   large, big, great
la **granja**   farm
grave   grave, serious; deep, low (*tone*)
gravísimo, -a   very grave (serious)
gritar   to shout, cry out
  se gritaron el uno al otro   they shouted to each other (one another)
el **grupo**   group, class
Guadalupe Hidalgo   *town near Mexico city where the treaty of February 2, 1848, ceding California, Arizona, and New Mexico to the U.S., was signed*
el **guajolote**   turkey (*Mex.*)
Guanajuato   *a state of Mexico*
el **guante**   glove
guapo, -a   handsome, good-looking, pretty
la **guardería infantil**   day nursery
guatemalteco, -a   Guatemalan
gubernamental   governmental
la **guerra**   war
el **guerrero**   warrior
la **guía**   guide, guidance
el **guisado**   stew
la **guitarra**   guitar
gustar   to be pleasing (to), like
  ¿cómo (te) gusta?   how do (you) like?
  gustar más   to like better (best), prefer
  me gustaría   I should like
el **gusto**   pleasure
  con mucho gusto   gladly, with great (much) pleasure
  dar mucho gusto a   to please a lot, give much pleasure to
  mucho gusto (en conocerlo *or* **-la)**   (I'm) very glad *or* pleased to meet (know) you
  tener mucho gusto en + *inf.*   to be very glad to + *inf.*, have much pleasure in + *pres. part.*

H

la **Habana**   Havana
haber   to have (*auxiliary*); to be (*impersonal*)
   ha habido   there has (have) been
   haber de + *inf.*   to be (be supposed) to
   había   there was (were)
   habrá   there will be
   habrá que + *inf.*   it will be necessary to
   habría   there would be
   hay   there is (are)
   hay (mucho) sol   it is (very) sunny, the sun is shining (brightly)
   hay que + *inf.*   it is necessary to, one must
   hubo   there was (were)
   ¿qué hay de nuevo?   what's new?
habitable   (in)habitable
el **habitante**   inhabitant
el **hábito**   habit
habla: de—española (hispana)   Spanish-speaking
hablador, -ora   talkative
hablar   to speak, talk
   habla (Elena)   this is (Helen), (Helen) is speaking
   hablar por teléfono   to talk by (on the) telephone
habrá   *future of* **haber**
habría   *conditional of* **haber**
hacer   to do, make
   ¿cuánto tiempo hace?   how long (much time) has it been?
   desde hace varios años   for several years
   hace (media hora)   (a half hour) ago
   hace media hora que llegamos   it is a half hour since we arrived (we arrived a half hour ago)
   hace (mucho) sol   it is (very) sunny, the sun is shining (brightly)
   hace mucho tiempo   it is a long time, for a long time
   hacer buen (mal) tiempo   to be good (bad) weather
   hacer (mucho) calor (fresco, frío, viento)   to be (very) warm (cool, cold, windy)
   hacer un viaje (una excursión)   to make (take) a trip (an excursion)
   hacerse + *noun*   to become

   ¿qué tiempo hace?   what kind of weather is it?
   se están haciendo   (they) are being made
   se va haciendo   (it) is slowly (gradually) being done
   todo lo que se va haciendo   all that is being done
hacia *prep.*   toward, to
hallar   to find; *reflex.* to be, be found, find oneself
el **hambre** (*f.*)   hunger
   tener (mucha) hambre   to be (very) hungry
la **harina**   flour
   harina de maíz   corn meal
hasta *prep.*   until, to, up to, as far as; *adv.* even
   desde . . . hasta   from . . . (up) to
   hasta la vista   until (I'll see you) later, so long
   hasta luego   see you later, until (I'll see you) later
   hasta mañana   until (I'll see you) tomorrow
   hasta que *conj.*   until
hay   there is (are)
   hay que + *inf.*   it is necessary to, one must
   ¿qué hay de nuevo?   what's new?
la **hayaca**   tamale (*Venezuela*)
la **hazaña**   deed; feat
hecho, -a *p.p. of* **hacer** *and adj.*   made, done
   hecho, -a de   made with
   lo hecho   what is (was) done
el **hecho**   fact; deed, event
el **hemisferio**   hemisphere
la **hermana**   sister
la **hermanita**   little sister
el **hermanito**   little brother
el **hermano**   brother; *pl.* brothers, brother(s) and sister(s)
hermosísimo, -a   very pretty (beautiful)
hermoso, -a   pretty, beautiful
hidráulico, -a   hydraulic
   la hidráulica   the hydraulic (one) (*f.*)
el **hielo** (*also pl.*)   ice
   banco de hielo   iceberg
la **hija**   daughter
el **hijo**   son; *pl.* children
hinchado, -a   swollen
hispánico, -a (*also noun*)   Hispanic

la **hispánica** the Hispanic (one) (*f.*)
hispano, -a Hispanic, Spanish
de habla hispana Spanish-speaking
el **hispano** Spaniard, person of Hispanic origin
Hispanoamérica Spanish America
hispanoamericano, -a (*also noun*) Spanish (Hispanic) American
la **hispanoamericana** the Spanish American (one) (*f.*)
hispanoparlante *adj.* Spanish-speaking
el (la) **hispanoparlante** speaker of Spanish
la **historia** history
el **historiador** historian
histórico, -a historical
el **hogar** home
la **hoja** leaf
¡hola! hello! hi!
el **hombre** man
¡hombre! man (alive)! upon my word!
el **homenaje** homage
hondo, -a deep, profound, far-reaching
hondureño, -a Honduran
el **honor** honor
la **hora** hour, time (*of day*)
¿a qué hora? at what time (hour)? when?
con horas de anticipación hours in advance (ahead of time)
¡ya era hora! it was about time!
el **horno** oven
al horno in the oven
hoy today
hoy día nowadays, today
hubo *pret. of* **haber** there was (were)
el **hueso** bone
el **huésped de honor** guest of honor
huir to flee
la **humanidad** humanity; *pl.* Humanities
humanitario, -a humanitarian
humano, -a human
la **humita** tamale (*South America*)
el **humo** smoke

I

iconoclasta (*m. and f.*) iconoclastic
la **idea** idea

ideal *adj.* ideal
el **idealismo** idealism
la **identificación** identification
ido *p.p. of* **ir** gone
la **iglesia** church
a la iglesia to church
igual equal, uniform, the same
la **igualdad** equality
igualitario, -a equalitarian, egalitarian
igualmente equally
ilimitado, -a unlimited
iluminado, -a illuminated, lighted
ilusorio, -a illusory
ilustrar to illustrate
ilustre illustrious, famous
la **imagen** (*pl.* **imágenes**) image, picture
la **imaginación** imagination
imaginarse to imagine
imitar to imitate
impaciente impatient(ly)
el **impedimento** impediment
impedir (i,i) to prevent
el **imperfecto** imperfect (*tense*)
el **imperio** empire
impersonal impersonal
imponer to impose; *reflex.* to take hold, dominate
la **importancia** importance
importante important
lo importante what is important, the important thing (part)
importar to import; to be important, matter
imposible impossible
lo imposible what is impossible, the impossible thing (part)
la **impresión** (*pl.* **impresiones**) (**de que**) impression (that)
impresionante impressive, moving
impresionar to impress
imprudente imprudent, unwise
impulsar to impel, promote
inagotable inexhaustible
inaugurar to inaugurate, open
al inaugurarse . . . when (it) opens (is opened) . . .
incluir to include
incompleto, -a incomplete
incorporarse a to be incorporated in
incurrir to incur
incurrir en falta to draw a penalty

indefinido, -a indefinite
la independencia independence
indicar to indicate, show
el indicativo indicative (mood)
  (presente) de indicativo (present)
    indicative (tense)
el índice index, rate
indígena (m. and f.) native, Indian,
    indigenous
indio, -a (also noun) Indian
indirecto, -a indirect
individual individual
el individuo individual
indudable certain, doubtless
la industria industry
industrial industrial
el industrial industrialist
la industrialización industrialization
industrializar to industrialize
Inés Inez, Agnes
la infancia infancy
infantil: guardería—, day nursery
la infiltración (pl. infiltraciones) infiltration
el infinitivo infinitive
la influencia influence
informal informal
el informalismo informalism (art movement)
informar to inform, tell
el informe report; pl. information
la ingeniería engineering
el ingeniero engineer
inglés, -esa English
el inglés English (language)
el ingrediente ingredient
ingresar (en + obj.) to enter (a university)
el ingreso entrance, admission; pl. income,
    revenue
  solicitud de ingreso application for
    admission (entrance)
inicial initial
iniciar to initiate, start, begin
la injusticia injustice
injusto, -a unjust
inmediatamente immediately
inmediato, -a immediate
la inmigración immigration
el inmigrante immigrant
la innovación (pl. innovaciones) innovation
inscribirse (en) to enroll, register (in)
inseparable inseparable

insistir (en + obj.) to insist (on)
  insistir en que to insist that
la inspiración (pl. inspiraciones) inspiration
la instalación (pl. instalaciones) installation,
    facility, plant
instalar to install, set up
la institución (pl. instituciones) institution
el instituto institute
instruido, -a well-educated, informed,
    trained
instruir to instruct, inform, advise
el instrumento instrument, tool
el insulto insult
la integración integration
inteligente intelligent
intensamente intensely
intenso, -a intense, intensive, active
el intento intent, design, plan
interamericano, -a inter-American
el interés (por) interest (in)
interesado, -a interested
interesante interesting
  la más interesante the most interesting
    one (f.)
interesar to interest
  interesarse por to be (become) interested
    in
  me interesan (los equipos) (the sets)
    interest me, I am interested in (the sets)
interino, -a interim, temporary
interior adj. interior, domestic
  la demanda (el comercio) interior
    domestic demand (trade)
el interior interior, inside
internacional international
interpretar to interpret
el intérprete interpreter
el interrogado person (party) questioned
interrogativo, -a interrogative
la intervención intervention
intervenir to intervene, participate, take part
íntimamente intimately
la introducción introduction
introducir to introduce
  introducido, -a por introduced by
introdujeron, introdujo pret. of introducir
introspectivo, -a introspective
la inundación (pl. inundaciones) flood
  aguas de las inundaciones flood waters
inventar to invent

la **investigación** (*pl.* **investigaciones**)
investigation
investigar   to investigate
la **invitación** (*pl.* **invitaciones**)   invitation
invitar (a + *inf.*)   to invite (to)
invocar   to invoke
ir (a + *inf.*)   to go (to); *reflex.* to go away,
leave
   ir + *pres. part.*   to be (*progressive form*), go
on, keep on, be gradually (+ *pres. part.*)
   ir a la iglesia   to go to church
   ir al centro   to go downtown
   ir de compras   to go shopping
   ir en autobús (avión, coche, taxi)   to go by
bus (plane, car, taxi)
   se va haciendo   (it) is slowly (gradually)
being done
   va creciendo   it is gradually increasing, it
continues to increase
   vámonos   let's go (be going)
   vamos a + *inf.*   we are going to *or* let's
(let's go to)
   vamos a ver   let's see
   van cambiando   (they) are changing
   van equipados   (they) are equipped
la **ironía**   irony
irregular   irregular
irremediablemente   irremediably
Isabel   Isabel, Betty, Elizabeth
Israel   Israel
el **istmo**   isthmus
Italia   Italy
el **italiano**   Italian (*language*)
izquierda: a la—,   to (on) the left

J

jactarse (de)   to boast (of)
Jaime   James, Jim
la **jalea**   jelly
jamás   ever, never, (not) . . . ever
el **jamón** (*pl.* **jamones**)   ham
el **jardín** (*pl.* **jardines**)   garden
el **jefe**   head, chief, leader
Jorge   George
joven (*pl.* **jóvenes**)   young, younger, youthful
   dos jóvenes extranjeros   two foreign
young men

el **(un) joven**   the (a) young man
la **(una) joven**   the (a) young lady (woman)
las **jóvenes**   young women (ladies)
los **jóvenes**   young people, young men
un joven   a young man (person)
Juan   John
Juanita   Juanita, Jane
Juanito   Johnny
el **juego**   game
el **jueves**   (on) Thursday
el **jugador**   player
jugar (ue) (a + *obj.*)   to play (*a game*)
   jugar al (tenis)   to play (tennis)
julio   July
Julio   Julius
junio   June
la **junta**   board
   Junta Directiva   governing board
(committee), officers
   Junta de Síndicos   Board of Trustees
juntos, -as   together
el **jurado**   jury, judges (*of contest*)
jurídico, -a   juridical, legal
justificar   to justify
la **juventud**   youth

K

el **kilogramo**   kilogram (2.2 *pounds*)
el **kilómetro**   kilometer (5/8 *mile*)
Kino: Eusebio Francisco   *Jesuit, explorer,
founder of missions and forts in Mexico and
southwestern U.S.*

L

la (*pl.* **las**)   the (*f.*)
   de la(s) que   than
   la(s) de   that (those) of, the one(s) of (with,
in)
   la(s) que   who, that, which, she who, the
one(s) *or* those who (that, whom, which)
la *obj. pron.*   her, it (*f.*), you (*formal f.*)
la **labor** (*also pl.*)   labor, work
el **lado**   side
   al lado de   beside, at the side of

por lado for each side
el **lago** lake
la **lámpara** lamp
la **langosta** lobster
el **langostino** prawn, crawfish
el **lanzamiento** launching
lanzar to launch, land
lograron lanzar (they) succeeded in
launching (landing)
el **lápiz** (*pl.* **lápices**) pencil
largo, -a long
lo largas que (son) how long (they are)
las *obj. pron.* them (*f.*), you (*formal f.*) (*also see*
la)
la **lástima** pity, shame
es lástima it's a pity (too bad)
¡qué lástima! what a pity (shame)!
latino, -a Latin
la América latina Latin America
el **lazo** tie, bond
lavar to wash; *reflex.* to wash (oneself)
le *obj. pron.* him, you (*formal m.*); to him, her,
it, you
la **lección** (*pl.* **lecciones**) lesson
Lección primera Lesson One
toda la lección all the lesson, the whole
(entire) lesson
la **lectura** reading, reading selection
la **leche** milk
la **lechuga** lettuce
leer to read
leído *p.p. of* **leer** *and adj.* read
lo leído what is (was) read
lejos: a lo—, in the distance
la **lengua** tongue, language
lento, -a slow
les *obj. pron.* (to) them, you (*pl.*)
las **letras** letters (= literature)
levantar to raise, lift (up); *reflex.* to rise, get
up
la **ley** law
la **liberación** liberation, freedom
liberación de la mujer women's "lib"
liberal liberal
liberalizar to liberalize; *reflex.* to be
liberalized
la **libertad** liberty, freedom
el **libertador** liberator
libre free
al aire libre in the open air, outdoors

la **librería** bookstore
el **libro** book
libro de español Spanish book
la **licencia** license
sacar la licencia to get (obtain) the license
el **licenciado** licentiate (*holder of a licentiate or
master's degree*)
el **liceo** = French lycée, *a secondary school which
prepares for the university*
el **lienzo** canvas (*painting*)
la **liga** league
ligado, -a bound, tied
ligados entre sí bound (tied) together
limitado, -a limited
limitarse a to limit oneself to
el **límite** limit
la **limpieza** cleaning
lindísimo, -a very pretty
lindo, -a pretty; fine, perfect
la **línea** line
la **lista** list; stripe
listo, -a ready; clever (*with* **ser**)
literario, -a literary
la **literatura** literature
la **litografía** lithograph
lo *neuter article* the; what is (was), *etc.*
a lo lejos in the distance
de lo que than
lo + *adj. or adv.* + **que** how . . .
lo cuidadosas que tienen que ser how
careful they must be
lo de that (matter, affair) of
lo (malo) what is (bad) the (bad) thing *or*
part
lo más agradable the most pleasant thing
lo más pronto posible the soonest
possible, as soon as possible
lo (nuestro) what is (ours), (our) part
lo (órganico) the *or* what is (organic)
lo peor what is worse (worst), the worse
(worst) thing *or* part
lo que what, that which, whatever
lo único the only thing
por lo general in general, generally
por lo tanto therefore
lo *obj. pron.* him, it (*m. and neuter*), you (*formal m.*)
lo soy I am
no lo parece he doesn't seem so
la **localidad** locality, place
la **locura** madness

el **lodo**   mud
   había (mucho) lodo   it was (very) muddy
lograr   to attain, get, obtain, produce;
   + *inf.*   to succeed in + *pres. part.*
   lograron (establecerse)   (they) succeeded
     in (settling)
Londres   London
los   the (*m.*)
   de los que   than
   los de   those of, the ones of (with, in)
   los dos   the two, both
   los que   who, that, which, the ones *or*
     those who (that, whom, which)
los *obj. pron.*   them (*m.*), you (*m. pl.*)
Los Ángeles   Los Angeles
lucrativo, -a   lucrative, profitable
la **lucha**   struggle
luchar (por)   to struggle *or* strive (for)
luego   then, next, later
   hasta luego   (I'll) see you later, until later
   luego que *conj.*   as soon as
el **lugar**   place
   en lugar de   instead of, in place of
   en primer lugar   in the first place
   tener lugar   to take place, occur
   todo el lugar   the whole place
Luis   Louis
Luisa   Louise
la **luna**   moon
   hay luna   the moon is shining
lunar   lunar
el (los) **lunes**   (on) Monday(s)
   el lunes que viene   next Monday

Ll

la **llamada**   call
llamado, -a   called
llamar   to call, knock; *reflex.* to call oneself,
   be named
   ¿cómo se llama . . . ?   what's the name
     of . . . ?
   ¿cómo se llama Ud. (él, ella)?   what is your
     (his, her) name?
   lo mandó llamar   (he) had him called, (he)
     sent for him
   me llamo   my name is
   te llamo   I'll call you

la **llegada**   arrival
llegar (a)   to arrive (at), reach, come *or* go (to)
   llegar a   to come to (go so far as to) + *inf.*,
     succeed in + *pres. part.*
   llegar a ser   to become, come to be
   llegar tarde   to arrive (be) late
lleno, -a   full
llevadero, -a   bearable, tolerable
llevar   to take, carry, lead; to wear; *reflex.* to
   take (with oneself), take away
   llevar a cabo   to carry out, accomplish
   llevarse a cabo   to be carried out
llover (ue)   to rain
la **lluvia**   rain
   agua de las lluvias   rain water

M

macabro, -a   macabre, hideous
macerar   to steep, soak
la **maestría**   mastery, skill
el **maestro**   master, teacher
   Maestro en Artes   Master of Arts
   profesión de maestro   teaching profession
magnífico, -a   magnificent, fine, wonderful,
   great
el **maíz**   maize, corn
   harina de maíz   corn meal
majestuoso, -a   majestic
mal   *used for* **malo** *before m. sing. nouns*
mal *adv.*   bad, badly
la **maleta**   suitcase, bag
malgastar   to waste, squander
malo, -a   bad; ill (*with* **estar**)
   lo malo   what is bad, the bad thing (part)
la **mamá**   mama, mother
mandar   to send, order, command, have
   lo mandó llamar   (he) had him called, (he)
     sent for him
   mandar llamar   to send for, have (one)
     called
el **mandato**   command
la **manera**   manner, way
   de dos maneras   in two ways
   de manera ejemplar   in an exemplary way
   de manera que *conj.*   so that
   de una manera más eficaz   in a more
     effective way

la **manifestación** (*pl.* **manifestaciones**)
  manifestation
maniobrar to maneuver, work
la **mano** hand
  dar la mano (a) to shake hands (with)
  ¡manos a la obra! (let's get) to work!
mantener to maintain, keep; *reflex.* to keep
  (oneself), stay
manufacturar to manufacture
mañana *adv.* tomorrow
  hasta mañana until (I'll see you)
    tomorrow
  mañana (por la noche) tomorrow (night *or*
    evening)
la **mañana** morning
  de la mañana in the morning, a.m.
  por la mañana in the morning
el **mapa** map
  máquina: escribir a—, to type(write), write
    on a (the) typewriter
el **mar** sea
maravilloso, -a marvelous, wonderful
la **marca** brand, make, kind
marcado, -a made, scored
marcar to dial (*telephone*); to make (*a score*)
marciano, -a of Mars
la **marcha** march
marchar to go, proceed, come along; *reflex.*
  to leave, go away
Margarita Margaret, Marguerite
margen: al—de on the fringe of
María Mary
el **mariachi** *member of Mexican popular orchestra*
el **marido** husband
el **marisco** shellfish; *pl.* seafood, shellfish
marítimo, -a maritime
Marta Martha
Marte Mars (*a planet*)
el (los) **martes** (on) Tuesday(s)
más more, most; other
  alguna orquesta más another (an
    additional) orchestra
  algunas cosas más a few more things
  lo más (agradable) the most (pleasant)
    thing
  lo más (pronto) posible the (soonest)
    possible, as (soon) as possible
  más conocido, -a best-known
  más o menos more or less, approximately
  (no) esperar más (not) to wait (any) longer

no más . . . de not . . . more than
  (*before a numeral*)
no . . . más que only
¡qué muchacha más bonita! what a pretty
  girl!
valer más to be better
la **masa** mass, crowd; *pl.* masses (*people*)
matemático, -a mathematical
la **materia** matter, material, subject
el **material** material
materno, -a maternal, mother (*tongue*)
matricularse to matriculate, register, enroll
el **matrimonio** marriage
máximo, -a maximum, greatest
maya (*m. and f.*) Maya, Mayan
mayo May
mayor greater, greatest; older, oldest
  la mayor parte de most (of), the greater
    part of
la **mayoría** majority
  en su mayoría in its majority, for the
    most part
la **mazorca** ear (*of corn*)
  hojas de mazorca del maíz corn husks
me *obj. pron.* me, to (from) me, (to) myself
el **mecanismo** mechanism, (piece of)
  machinery
mecanístico, -a mechanistic
  lo mecanístico the (what is) mechanistic
la **medicina** medicine (*remedy*)
la **Medicina** Medicine (*science*)
el **médico** doctor, physician
la **medida** measure, step, means
medio, -a half, a half; average, middle
  a (las siete) y media at half past (seven), at
    (7):30
  hace media hora a half hour ago
el **medio** means, medium; environment
  el medio ambiente environment
  por medio de *prep.* by means of
mejor better, best
la **mejora** betterment, improvement
mejorar to better, improve
mencionado, -a mentioned,
  above-mentioned
menor smaller, smallest; younger, youngest;
  lesser, least
menos less, least, fewer; except
  a menos que *conj.* unless
  más o menos more or less, approximately

por lo menos   at least
son las doce menos cuarto   it is a quarter
  to twelve
la **mente**   mind
  mente sana en cuerpo sano   a healthy
    (sound) mind in a healthy (sound) body
el **menú**   menu
  menudo: a—,   often, frequently
el **mercado**   market
  merecer   to merit, deserve
el **mes**   month
la **mesa**   table, desk
  meteorológico, -a   meteorological
    los meteorológicos   the meteorological
      (ones) (*m.*)
el **método**   method
la **metrópoli**   metropolis
  mexicano, -a   Mexican
  México   Mexico
    ciudad de México   Mexico City
  mi   my
  mí *pron.*   me, myself (*after prep.*)
el **miedo**   fear
    tener miedo (de que)   to be afraid (that)
    tener (mucho) miedo (de)   to be (very)
      afraid *or* frightened (of, to)
el **miembro**   member
  mientras (que) *conj.*   while, as long as
el (los) **miércoles**   (on) Wednesday(s)
  Miguel   Michael, Mike
  mil   a (one) thousand; *pl.* thousands
    mil gracias   many (a thousand) thanks
el **millón** (*pl.* **millones**)   million
    (dos) millones de (personas)   (two) million
      (persons)
el **millonario**   millionaire
el **mineral**   mineral
  minero, -a   mining
  ministerial   ministerial, in the ministry
    (government)
el **ministerio**   ministry
la **minoría**   minority
el **minuto**   minute
  mío, -a *adj.*   my, (of) mine
    ¡Dios mío!   heavens! for heaven's sake!
    (el) mío, (la) mía, (los) míos, (las) mías
      pron.   mine
  mirar   to look (at)
la **misión** (*pl.* **misiones**)   mission
  misionero, -a   missionary

mismo, -a   same; -self
  ahora mismo   right now, right away
  él mismo   he himself
  las mismas   the same ones (*f.*)
  las mismas (oportunidades) que   the same
    (opportunities) as
  los estudiantes mismos   the students
    themselves
  misterioso, -a   mysterious
  místico, -a   mystical
la **mitad**   half
  a mitad del camino   halfway
  moaré (*m. and f.*)   moiré
la **moción** (*pl.* **mociones**)   motion
el **modelo**   model
  moderado, -a   moderate
  moderar   to moderate
  modernamente   recently, lately
  modernizar   to modernize
  moderno, -a   modern
la **modificación** (*pl.* **modificaciones**)
    modification, change
  modificar   to modify, change
el **modo**   mode, manner, way; mood (*grammar*)
    de modo que *conj.*   so that
    de todos modos   at any rate, by all means
el **módulo**   module
el **mole**   *a sauce*
    mole poblano   *a sauce in the style of Puebla*
      (*Mexico*)
  molestar   to bother, molest, trouble
    no te molestes   don't bother, never mind
el **momento**   moment
    en este (ese) momento   at this (that) moment
la **montaña**   mountain
  mordaz   biting
  morir (ue,u)   to die
el **moro**   Moor
el **mosaico**   mosaic
  mostrar (ue)   to show
la **motivación**   motivation
el **motivo**   motive, reason
  mover(se) (ue)   to move
la **movilidad**   mobility
el **movimiento**   movement
la **muchacha**   girl
    equipos de muchachas   girls' teams
el **muchacho**   boy; *pl.* boys, boy(s) and girl(s)
    (campamento) de muchachos   boys'
      (camp)

muchísimo *adv.*   very much

muchísimo, -a (-os, -as)   very much (many)

mucho *adv.*   much, very much, a great deal, a lot of

  esperar mucho   to wait long

  (trabajar) mucho   (to work) hard

mucho, -a (-os, -as)   much, many; very

  mucho gusto   (I'm) very glad *or* pleased to meet you

mudar   to change

  mudarse (de)   to change (*one's clothing, etc.*)

la muerte   death

muerto, -a *p.p. of* morir *and adj.*   died, dead

la muestra   sample

la mujer   woman

  liberación de la mujer   women's "lib"

la multiplicación   multiplication, large increase

mundial *adj.*   world(-wide), universal

el mundo   world

  todo el mundo   everybody, the whole (entire) world

el municipio   municipality, city

mural *adj. and m. noun*   mural

el muralismo   muralism (*painting of murals*)

muralista (*m. and f.*)   muralist, of murals

el muralista   muralist, painter of murals

el museo   museum

la música   music

mutuo, -a   mutual

muy   very

N

nacer   to be born

la nación (*pl.* naciones)   nation

  las Naciones Unidas   United Nations

nacional   national

nacionalista (*m. and f.*)   nationalist(ic)

nada *pron.*   nothing, (not) . . . anything; *adv.* (not) at all

  nada de particular   nothing special

  (no) . . . nada más   anything more

nadie   no one, nobody, (not) . . . anybody (anyone)

NASL = Asociación Nacional de Ligas de Soccer   National Association of Soccer Leagues

natal   native

natural   natural

la naturaleza   nature

naturalista (*m. and f.*)   naturalistic

la navegación   navigation

el navío   ship

la neblina   mist

  había neblina   it was misty

necesario, -a   necessary

la necesidad   necessity, need

  la necesidad de que   the necessity that

necesitar   to need

negar (ie)   to deny, refuse

negativamente   negatively

negativo, -a   negative

la negligencia   negligence

los negocios   business

  Administración de Negocios   Business Administration

negro, -a   black, Negro

neofigurativo, -a   Neo-Figurative

nervioso, -a   nervous

neutro, -a   neuter

ni *conj.*   neither, nor

  ni . . . ni   neither . . . nor, (not) . . . either . . . or

la niebla   fog

  había niebla   it was foggy

la nieve   snow

ningún   *used for* ninguno *before m. sing. nouns*

ninguno, -a *adj. and pron.*   no, no one, none, (not) . . . any (anybody, anyone)

la niña   little girl

el niño   little boy, child; *pl.* children

el nivel   level

  en todos los niveles   at all levels

  nivel de vida   standard of living

no *adv.*   no, not

  todavía no   not yet

  yo no   not I

nocivo, -a   harmful

la noche   night

  de la noche   in the evening, p.m.

  de noche   at night

  (el sábado) por la noche   (Saturday) night

  esta noche   tonight

  mañana por la noche   tomorrow night (evening)

  todas las noches   every night

el nombre   name

la norma   norm

normalmente

nombrado, -a named

el **norte** north

norteamericano, -a (*also noun*) (North) American

nos *obj. pron.* us, (to) us, (to) ourselves, *reciprocal pron.* (to) each other, one another

no-servibles non-useful, non-usable

nosotros, -as we, us (*after prep.*); ourselves

la **nota** note

notable notable, noteworthy

　lo más notable the most notable thing

notablemente notably

la **noticia** news (item), information, notice; *pl.* news, information

la **novela** novel

el **novelista** novelist

noventa ninety

la **novia** sweetheart, fiancée, girlfriend

el **novio** sweetheart, boyfriend, fiancé

la **nube** cloud

nublado, -a cloudy

nuclear nuclear

　la nuclear nuclear (one) (*f.*)

nuestro, -a *adj.* our, (of) ours

　(el) nuestro, (la) nuestra, (los) nuestros, (las) nuestras *pron.* ours

　lo nuestro what is ours, our part

nueve nine

nuevo, -a new, brand-new

　Nueva España New Spain (= Mexico)

　Nueva York New York

　Nuevo México New Mexico

　¿qué hay de nuevo? what's new?

el **número** number, numeral

numeroso, -a numerous, many, large

nunca never, (not) . . . ever

O

o or

　o . . . o either . . . or

Oaxaca *city southeast of Mexico City*

objetivamente objectively

el **objetivo** objective

el **objeto** object

la **obligación** (*pl.* **obligaciones**) obligation

obligado, -a obligated, obliged

obligar (a + *inf.*) to oblige *or* force (to)

obligatorio, -a obligatory, required

la **obra** work (*art, literature, etc.*)

　¡manos a la obra! (let's get) to work!

　¡qué obra más (tan) interesante! what an interesting work!

obscuro, -a dark

la **observación** (*pl.* **observaciones**) observation

observar to observe, note, see

el **observatorio** observatory

el **obstáculo** obstacle

obstruir to obstruct

obstruyan *pres. subj. of* **obstruir**

obtener to obtain, get

la **ocasión** (*pl.* **ocasiones**) occasion, opportunity

occidental west, western

el **océano** ocean, sea

　Océano Pacífico Pacific Ocean

ocupado, -a occupied, busy

ocupar to occupy

ocurrir to occur, happen, take place

ochenta eighty

ocho eight

ochocientos, -as eight hundred

OEA = Organización de los Estados Americanos Organization of the American States

la **ofensiva** offensive

oficial *adj.* official

la **oficina** office

　oficina de policía police department (station)

el **oficio** craft, trade; office, occupation

　artes y oficios arts and crafts

ofrecer to offer

　ofrecerse a + *inf.* to offer to

oído *p.p. of* **oír**

oír to hear

　oye (tú) (*fam. command*) listen, hey, say

el **ojo** eye

el **óleo** oil, oil painting

oler (hue) to smell (*an odor*)

olvidar to forget

　no debe olvidarse one shouldn't forget

　olvidarse (de + *obj.*) to forget (to)

　olvidarse de que to forget that

once eleven

　a las once at eleven o'clock

Oñate: Juan de *Spanish explorer and founder of present New Mexico*

la **opción** option

la **operación** (*pl.* **operaciones**) operation

opinar to be of the opinion, think
la **opinión** (*pl.* **opiniones**) opinion
oponer to oppose, face
  oponerse a to oppose
la **oportunidad** opportunity, chance
opuesto *p.p. of* **oponer** opposed
la **oración** (*pl.* **oraciones**) sentence
la **órbita** orbit
el **orden** (*pl.* **órdenes**) order, arrangement
la **orden** (*pl.* **órdenes**) order, command
  a la orden yes, here, present, at your service
  por orden de at the order of
el **ordenador** computer
orgánico, -a organic
  lo orgánico the (what is) organic
el **organismo** organism; agency, organization
la **organización** (*pl.* **organizaciones**) organization
Organización de los Estados Americanos Organization of American States
organizar to organize
la **orientación** orientation
  curso de orientación orientation course
orientado, -a orientated
Oriente: San Antonio de—, *town in Cuba*
el **origen** (*pl.* **orígenes**) origin
original original
  la original the original (one) (*f.*)
el **oro** gold
  de oro (of) gold
la **orquesta** orchestra
os *obj. pron.* you (*fam. pl.*), to you, (to) yourselves, (*reciprocal pron.*) (to) one another, each other
oscuro, -a dark, shadowy
el **oso** bear
el **ostión** (*pl.* **ostiones**) oyster
la **ostra** oyster
el **otoño** fall, autumn
otorgar to grant, award, confer
otro, -a other, another
  el otro the other one (*m.*)
¡oye! *fam. command of* **oír** listen! hey! say!

P

Pablo Paul
pacífico, -a pacific

Océano Pacífico Pacific Ocean
el **padre** father; *pl.* fathers, parents, father and mother
la **paella** *a rice dish containing meat, vegetables, and shellfish*
pagar to pay (for)
  pagar (tres dólares) por to pay (three dollars) for
la **página** page
el **pago** pay(ment)
el **país** country, nation
el **paisaje** landscape, countryside
el **pájaro** bird
la **palabra** word
pálido, -a pale
el **papá** papa, father, dad
el **papel** paper; role
el **paquete** package
el **par** pair
  un par de a couple (pair) of
para *prep.* for, to, in order to, by (*time*)
  estar para to be about to, be on the point of
  para que *conj.* in order that
  ¿para qué? why? for what purpose?
  taza para café coffee cup
  taza para té teacup
  vaso para agua water glass
el (los) **parabrisas** windshield(s)
el (los) **paraguas** umbrellas
el **Paraguay** Paraguay
paralelo, -a parallel
parecer to appear, seem, appear *or* seem to be
  al parecer apparently
  (me) parece que (I) think or believe that, it seems to (me) that
  me parece que no I think (believe) not
  ¿qué (te, os) parece . . . ? what do (you) think of . . . ? how do (you) like . . . ?
la **pared** wall
el (los) **paréntesis** parenthesis (*pl.* parentheses)
el **parque** park
el **párrafo** paragraph
la **parrilla** grill
la **parrillada** barbecued beef
la **parte** part, place
  de parte de on the part of
  en otras partes elsewhere, in other places
  en (por) todas partes everywhere
  formar parte de to form (make up) a part of

la mayor parte de   most (of), the greater part of
por su parte   on his (its) part
tres cuartas partes   three fourths
una cuarta (tercera) parte   one fourth (third)
la **participación**   participation
participar en   to participate in, take part in
el **participio**   participle
particular   particular; private
nada de particular   nothing special
el **partidario**   partisan, supporter
el **partidarismo**   partisanship
el **partido**   party; game, match
partido (de fútbol)   (football) game
treinta puntos el partido   thirty points a (per) game
partir (de + obj.)   to leave, depart
a partir de   beginning with
partiendo de allí   beginning (leaving) there
la **pasa**   raisin
pasado, -a   past, last
el **pasado**   past
pasar   to pass, pass on; to spend (*time*); to happen, go on
pasa (tú), pase(n) Ud(s).   come in
pasar a   to pass into (on), go on to
pasar por   to pass (go, come) by *or* along, drop by (in), stop by
¿qué pasó?   what happened?
¿qué tal lo pasó?   how did he fare (do)?
¿qué (te) pasa?   what's the matter with (you)?
el **paseo**   walk, stroll, ride, drive
dar un paseo   to take a walk (stroll)
dar paseos   to take walks
pasivo, -a   passive
el **paso**   stop, pace
a pasos agigantados   at a gigantic (an extraordinary) pace
la **pasta**   paste (*confection*), dough
dulce en pasta   a fruit paste
el **patio**   patio, courtyard
la **pausa**   pause
el **pavo**   turkey (*Spain*)
la **paz**   peace
la **pedagogía**   pedagogy, teaching
pedir (i,i)   to ask, ask for, request
Pedro   Peter
Pelé   *famous Brazilian soccer player who, after*

retiring in Brazil, played on the Cosmos team in New York City
la **película**   film
el **peligro**   danger
hay el peligro (de que)   there is the danger (that)
el **pelo**   hair
peninsular   peninsular (*of Spain*)
penoso, -a   distressing
pensar (ie)   to think; + *inf.* to intend, plan
manera de pensar   way of thinking
pensar en + *obj. or inf.*   to think of (about)
peor   worse, worst
lo peor   what is worse (worst), the worse (worst) thing *or* part
Pepe   Joe
pequeño, -a   small, little (*size*)
perder (ie)   to lose, miss
perdido, -a   lost
perdonar   to pardon
perfecto, -a (*also m. noun*)   perfect
pretérito perfecto   present perfect
el **periódico**   newspaper
el **período**   period
permitir   to permit, allow, let
pero   but
el **perro**   dog
la **persona**   person; *pl.* persons, people
el **personaje**   person (*of importance*), personage
personal *adj.*   personal
el **personal**   personnel
pertenecer   to belong
el **Perú**   Peru
pesar: a — de *prep.*   in spite of, despite
el **pescado**   fish (*prepared*)
el **peso**   peso (*monetary unit of several countries*); weight
sin peso   weightless
el **petróleo**   petroleum, oil
picado, -a   minced, chopped, ground
picante   hot, highly seasoned
el **pie**   foot
poner el pie   to set foot
la **piedra**   stone
de piedra   (of) stone
la **piel**   skin, hide
la **pierna**   leg
la **pimienta**   black pepper
el **pimiento**   pepper (*vegetable*)
el **pincel**   brush, brush work

la **pincelada**   brush stroke
el **pintor**   painter (*m.*)
la **pintora**   painter (*f.*)
la **pintura**   painting
   concurso de pintura   painting contest (competition)
la **piña**   pineapple
el **piso**   floor, story
   piso bajo   lower (first) floor
la **pista**   court (*tennis*)
la **pizarra**   chalkboard
el **plan**   plan
   plan de estudios   curriculum
la **plana**   page (*printing*)
el **planeta**   planet
   planetario, -a   planetary
la **planta**   plant
el **plátano**   plantain, banana
   hojas de plátano   banana leaves
el **plato**   plate, dish, course (*at meals*); turntable
la **playa**   beach
la **plenitud**   fullness, abundance
la **pluma**   pen
el **plural**   plural
el **pluscuamperfecto**   pluperfect, past perfect
la **población**   population
   poblano: mole—,   *a sauce in the style of Puebla (Mexico)*
pobre   poor
poco, -a   *adj., pron., and adv.*   little (*quantity*); *pl.* (a) few
   al poco rato   after a short while
   al poco tiempo   after (in) a short time
   poco a poco   little by little
   un poco   a little, a little while
   un poco de   a little (of)
poder   to be able, can
   ¿pudieras esperar?   could you wait?
   puede ser (que)   it may be (that)
   ¿se puede (entrar)?   may I (we, one) come in?
el **poder**   power
el **poeta**   poet
la **policía**   police
   oficina de policía   police department (station)
   político, -a   political
   ciencias políticas   political science(s)
el **polvo**   dust
   había (mucho) polvo   it was (very) dusty

el **pollo**   chicken
   poner   to put, place, put on (*record*); *reflex.* to put on (oneself); + *adj.* to become
   poner el pie   to set foot
   poner (el radio)   to turn on (the radio)
   poner en práctica   to put into practice
popular   popular
la **popularidad**   popularity
   concurso de popularidad   popularity contest
populoso, -a   populous
poquito: un—,   a little (tiny) bit
por *prep.*   for, during, in, through, along, by, for the sake of, on behalf of, about, around, over, per, in exchange for, as (a), (+ *inf.*) to be + *p.p.*
   por allí   around (along) there
   por allí vienen   there they come
   por aquí   here, around (by, along) here
   por ciento   percent
   por ejemplo   for example
   por el camino   along the way
   por encima de   *prep.* over, above
   por eso   therefore, because of that, for that reason, that's why
   por falta de   *prep.* for lack of
   por favor   please (*at end of request*)
   por fin   finally, at last
   por la tarde   in the afternoon
   por lado   for each side
   por lo general   in general, generally
   por lo menos   at least
   por lo tanto   therefore
   por medio de   *prep.* by means of
   por orden de   at the order of
   ¿por qué?   why? for what reason?
   por semana   per (each) week
   por separado   separately
   por su parte   on his (its) part
   por supuesto   of course, certainly
   por todas partes   everywhere
   por teléfono   by (on the) telephone
   por último   finally, ultimately
el **porcentaje**   percentage
porque   because, for
la **portería**   goal (*soccer*)
portugués, -esa   Portuguese
el **portugués**   Portuguese (*language*)
poseer   to possess, have
posesivo, -a   possessive
la **posibilidad**   possibility

posible possible
  lo más (pronto) posible the (soonest) possible, as (soon) as possible
la **posición** position
el **postre** dessert
  postrer(o), -a last
el **postulado** postulate, assumption
  potable drinkable, potable
la **potencia** power
la **práctica** practice, skill
  poner en práctica to put into practice
  practicar to practice, go in for, carry on
  práctico, -a practical
el **precio** price
  preciso, -a necessary
la **predilección** predilection, preference
  predominantemente predominantly
la **preferencia** preference
  preferible preferable
  preferiblemente preferably
  preferido, -a preferred
    la preferida the preferred one (f.)
  preferir (ie,i) to prefer
la **pregunta** question
  preguntar to ask (a question)
    preguntar por to ask for (about), inquire (about)
    pregúntaselo a ella ask her (fam. command)
    se lo preguntaré I shall ask them (him, her, you formal)
el **premio** prize, award
la **preocupación** (pl. **preocupaciones**) (**por**) preoccupation, worry, concern (with, about)
  preocupar to preoccupy, worry
    ¿qué le preocupa a Ud.? what are you worried (concerned) about?
la **preparación** (pl. **preparaciones**) preparation
  preparado, -a prepared, ready
  preparar to prepare, fix
    preparar el terreno to pave the way
    prepararse para to prepare oneself for, be prepared for
  preparatorio, -a preparatory
la **preposición** (pl. **preposiciones**) preposition
  preposicional prepositional
la **presencia** presence
  presentar to present, introduce; to show, display, offer, enter; reflex. to present oneself, appear

  las obras presentadas the works that have been entered (presented)
  presente adj. present
el **presente** present, present tense
la **presidenta** president (f.)
el **presidente** president (m.)
el **presidio** garrison of soldiers; fort
  presidir to preside over, dominate
la **presión** pressure
  prestar to lend
el **prestigio** prestige
  los mejores prestigios the highest prestige
  prestigioso, -a prestigious
el **pretérito** preterit (tense)
    pretérito anterior preterit perfect
    pretérito perfecto present perfect
  primario, -a primary
    la primaria the primary (one) (f.)
  primer used for **primero** before m. sing. nouns first
  primero adv. first
  primero, -a first
    Lección primera Lesson One
    los primeros the first ones (m.)
    Repaso primero Review One
  primitivo, -a primitive
el **primo** cousin
  principal principal, main
    las principales the principal ones (f.)
  principalmente principally
el **principio** principle
la **prisa** haste
    darse prisa to hurry (up)
    tener (mucha) prisa to be in a (big) hurry
  privilegiado, -a privileged
el **privilegio** privilege
la **probabilidad** probability
  probable probable
el **problema** problem
el **proceso** process, progressive movement
la **producción** (pl. **producciones**) production
  producir to produce, turn out
el **producto** product
la **profesión** (pl. **profesiones**) profession
  profesional professional
el **profesional** professional, professional person (man)
el **profesor** professor, teacher, instructor
    profesor de español Spanish teacher
la **profesora** professor, teacher, instructor (f.)

profesora de francés   French teacher (f.)
el **profesorado**   faculty, teaching staff
el **programa**   program, schedule
    programa de estudio   program of study,
        curriculum (pl. curricula)
progresar   to progress
el **progreso**   progress
prohibido, -a   prohibited, forbidden
prohibir   to prohibit, forbid
el **promedio**   average
prometer   to promise
promover (ue)   to promote, advance
promulgar   to promulgate, proclaim
el **pronombre**   pronoun
pronto   soon, quickly
    lo más pronto posible   the soonest
        possible, as soon as possible
la **pronunciación**   pronunciation
pronunciar   to pronounce
la **propaganda**   propaganda
propenso, -a   prone, disposed
propio, -a   (one's) own
proponer   to propose
proporcionalmente   proportionately
proporcionar   to furnish, provide
la **propuesta**   proposal, proposition
propuesto, -a p.p. of **proponer** and
    adj.   proposed
propulsado, -a   propelled
el **proselitismo**   proselytism
próspero, -a   prosperous
la **protección**   protection
proteger   to protect
la **protesta**   protest
provechoso, -a   advantageous, beneficial
la **provincia**   province
la **provocación**   provocation
próximo, -a   next, coming
el **proyecto**   project, plan
prudente   prudent, wise
la **psicología**   psychology
publicar   to publish
público, -a   public
el **público**   public
    los intereses del público   public interests
pudieras   you could
el **pueblecito**   small town, village
el **pueblo**   town, village; people, nation
    gentes del pueblo   townspeople
la **puerta**   door

puertorriqueño, -a (also noun)   Puerto Rican
pues adv.   well, well then (now); why; conj.
    since, for, because
puesto p.p. of **poner**   placed, put
el **puesto**   place, position, post, job
la **pulsera**   bracelet
    reloj de pulsera   wristwatch
el **puma**   puma, cougar
el **punto**   point
    en punto   sharp (time)
    puntos adicionales   bonus points
puro, -a   pure

que   that, which, who, whom; as; than; since;
    indir. command have, let, may, etc.
    antes (de) que conj.   before
    de lo que   than (what)
    del (de la, de los, de las) que   than
    el (la, los, las) que   that, which, who,
        whom, he (she, those) who (etc.), the
        one(s) who (etc.)
    las mismas (oportunidades) que   the same
        (opportunities) as
    lo + adj. or adv. + **que**   how . . .
    lo largas que (son)   how long (they are)
    lo que   what, that which, whatever
    no . . . más que   only
    tener que + inf.   to have to, must
¿qué?   what? which?
    ¿para qué?   why? for what purpose?
    ¿por qué?   why? for what reason?
    ¿qué hay de nuevo?   what's new?
    ¿qué tal?   how . . . ? how are you? how
        goes it?
¡qué + adj. or adv.!   how . . . ! what . . . !;
    + noun what (a, an) . . . !
    ¡qué bien!   how well!
    ¡qué obra más (tan) interesante!   what an
        interesting work!
quebrado, -a   broken
quedar(se)   to remain, stay; to be, be left
    quedan algunas cosas más   some more
        (other) things remain (are left)
quejarse (de)   to complain (of)
    ¿se quejaban uno de otro?   were they
        complaining of each other?
querer   to wish, want; to be willing

no quieren (quedarse) (they) won't *or* are unwilling (to stay)
no quisieron esperar (they) refused to (would not) wait
querer (a) to love, like
querer decir to mean
¿quieres (quiere Ud.) + *inf.*? will you + *verb*?
quisiera (I) should *or* would like
quiso hacer eso (he) tried to do that
querido, -a dear
querida mía my dear
el **queso** cheese
quien (*pl.* **quienes**) who, whom, he (those) who, the one(s) who
¿quién(es)? who? whom?
¿de quién(es) es (esta cinta)? whose (tape) is this?
¡quién! who!
quimérico, -a chimerical, fanciful
la **química** chemistry
químico, -a chemical
quince fifteen
quisiera (I) should *or* would like
quitar to take away (off), remove; *reflex.* to take off (oneself)
quitar (el radio) to turn off (the radio)
quizá(s) perhaps

R

el **rabo** tail
racionalista (*m. and f.*) rationalistic
racionar to ration
radical stem *adj.*
el **radio** radio, radio set
la **radio** radio (*as a means of communication*)
Rafael Raphael
rallado, -a grated
la **rama** branch
Ramón Raymond
rápidamente rapidly, fast
lo más rápidamente posible the fastest possible, as fast (rapidly) as possible
la **rapidez** rapidity, speed
rápido, -a rapid(ly), fast
Raquel Rachel
raro, -a rare, unusual

el **rato** while, short time (while)
al poco rato after a short while
la **razón** (*pl.* **razones**) reason
no tener razón to be wrong
tener razón to be right
la **realidad** reality
en realidad in reality, in fact
la **realización** achievement, accomplishment
realizar to realize, carry out, accomplish; *reflex.* to be carried out (made, taken), become fulfilled
el **receptor** receiver
la **receta** recipe
recibir to receive
reciente recent
recientemente recently
recitar to recite, give
la **reclamación** reclamation, demand, claim
recoger to pick (up), gather, collect
la **recomendación** (*pl.* **recomendaciones**) recommendation
recomendado, -a recommended
recomendar (ie) to recommend
la **recompensa** recompense, reward
reconocer to recognize
reconocido, -a recognized, known
recordar (ue) to recall, remember
recordar (a uno) to remind (one) of
recorrer to go (travel) over
recreo: de—, recreational
rectangular rectangular
rectángulo, -a rectangular
el **rector** rector, president
el **recuerdo** remembrance
dale recuerdos míos give him (her) my regards (best wishes)
el **recurso** resource, recourse, resort; *pl.* resources
rechazar to reject
la **reducción** reduction
reducir to reduce
redundante redundant
referirse (ie,i) a to refer to
reflejar to reflect
reflexivo, -a reflexive
la **reforma** reform
el **refrán** (*pl.* **refranes**) proverb
el **refresco** refreshment, cold (soft) drink
refrito, -a refried
regalar to give (*as a gift*)

el **regalo** gift
el **régimen** (*pl.* **regímenes**) regime, rule
la **región** (*pl.* **regiones**) region
regional regional
la **regla** rule
el **reglamento** regulation(s)
regresar to return, come back
regular regular
reído *p.p. of* **reír** laughed
el **Reino Unido** United Kingdom
reír (i,i) to laugh
la **relación** (*pl.* **relaciones**) relation
  en relación con in relation to
relacionables con which can be related to
relacionado, -a (con) related (to)
  relacionados unos con otros related to
    one another
relativo, -a relative
religioso, -a religious
el **reloj** watch, clock
  reloj de pulsera wristwatch
rellenar to fill, stuff
  rellenarse de to be filled (stuffed) with
relleno, -a stuffed, filled
el **remedio** remedy
la **reminiscencia** reminiscence
remoto, -a remote
remunerativo, -a remunerative
renovar (ue) to renew, rebuild, remodel
renunciar to renounce
reñir (i,i) to scold
reparar en to notice, pay attention to
repartir deliver, distribute
repasar to review
  para repasar for review
el **repaso** review
  Repaso primero Review One
repetir (i,i) to repeat
la **represa** dam
la **representación** representation
el **representante** representative
representar to represent
la **república** republic
reservar to reserve
el **resfriado** cold (*disease*)
la **residencia** residence, residence hall
  residencia de estudiantes student
    residence hall (dormitory)
residir to reside, live
la **resolución** solution (*of a problem*)

resolver (ue) to resolve; to solve, settle,
  decide; *reflex.* to be solved (resolved)
respectivo, -a respective
respecto de with respect to, concerning
respirar to breathe
responder (a) to answer, reply, respond (to)
la **responsabilidad** responsibility
la **respuesta** reply, answer
el **restaurante** restaurant
el **resto** rest
la **restricción** (*pl.* **restricciones**) restriction
resuelto, -a *p.p. of* **resolver** *and adj.* resolved,
  settled
el **resultado** result
el **resumen** (*pl.* **resúmenes**) summary
retirar to retire, withdraw
la **reunión** (*pl.* **reuniones**) meeting
reunir to collect; *reflex.* to meet, gather
revelar to reveal
revisar to revise, check
la **revista** magazine, journal
la **revolución** (*pl.* **revoluciones**) revolution
revolucionario, -a revolutionary
el **rey** king; *pl.* kings, king(s) and queen(s)
Ricardo Richard
rico, -a rich, wealthy; tasty (*food*)
el **riesgo** risk
el **rincón** (*pl.* **rincones**) corner (*of room*)
el **río** river
  el Río Grande *river between the U.S. and
    Mexico*
la **riqueza** wealth, riches
rítmicamente rhythmically
el **ritmo** rhythm; rate
  al ritmo (actual) at the (present) rate
la **rivalidad** rivalry
robar to rob, steal
  robármela to steal it (*f.*) from me
Roberto Robert
rodeado, -a de surrounded by
rojo, -a red
el **romance** ballad
romper to break
la **ropa** clothing, clothes
  mudarse de ropa to change clothes
la **rosa** rose
rosado, -a rose, rose-colored
el **rostro** face
  roto *p.p. of* **romper** broken
rubio, -a blond(e)

rural   rural
Rusia   Russia

S

el **sábado por la noche**   Saturday night (evening)
saber   to know (*facts*), know how, can (*mental ability*); *in pret.* to learn, find out
sabido, -a   known
Sabogal, José (1888–1956)   *Peruvian painter*
sacar   to take, take out
  sacar (fotos)   to take (photos)
  sacar (la licencia)   to get *or* obtain (the license)
el **sacerdote**   priest
la **sala**   living room, classroom
  sala (de clase)   classroom
  salir (de + *obj.*)   to leave, go out (of)
  salir de casa   to leave home
el **salón** (*pl.* **salones**)   salon, lounge, (large) hall, meeting room
la **salsa**   sauce
el **salto de altura**   high jump
saludar   to greet, speak to, say hello to
El Salvador   El Salvador, The Savior
salvaje   wild
salvo, -a   safe
  sano y salvo   safe and sound
san   *used for* **santo** *before m. saint's name not beginning with* Do- *or* To-
  San Antonio de Oriente   *town in Cuba*
  San Juan (de los Caballeros)   *town north of Santa Fe, New Mexico*
  San Roque (1295?–1327)   *a French saint venerated for his work in a plague in Italy*
sano, -a   sane; healthy, sound
  sano y salvo   safe and sound
santo, -a   saint, holy, St(e).
el **satélite**   satellite
la **sátira**   satire
satisfacer   to satisfy
se *pron. used for* **le** *or* **les**   (to) him, her, it, them , you (*formal*); *reflex. pron.* (to) himself, herself, *etc.*; *reciprocal pron.* (to) each other, one another; *indef. subject* one, people, *etc.*
Sebastián   Sebastian
la **sección** (*pl.* **secciones**)   section, part

la **secretaria**   secretary (*f.*)
el **secretario**   secretary (*m.*)
el **sector**   sector
  secundario, -a   secondary
    la secundaria   the secondary (one) (*f.*)
la **sed**   thirst
  tener (mucha) sed   to be (very) thirsty
el **sedimento**   sediment
  seguida: en—,   at once, immediately
    vuelvo en seguida   I'll return at once (be right back)
  seguido, -a de   followed by
  seguir (i,i)   to follow, continue, go (keep) on
    se sigue estudiando   people (they) are continuing to study
    seguir + *pres. part.*   to continue (go on) + *pres. part.*
  según   according to
  segundo, -a   second
    por segunda vez   for the second time
  seguro, -a   sure, certain
    estar seguro, -a de que   to be sure that
seis   six
  a las seis   at six o'clock
  son las seis   it is six o'clock
  seiscientos, -as   six hundred
  seleccionar   to select
  selecto, -a   select
la **semana**   week
  fin de semana   weekend
  por semana   per (each) week
  semejante   similar
el **semestre**   semester
  sencillamente   simply
  sentado, -a   seated
  sensacional   sensational
el **sensor**   sensor
  sentar (ie)   to seat; to set, establish; *reflex.* to sit down
el **sentimiento**   sentiment, feeling
  sentir (ie,i)   to feel, regret, be sorry
    ¡cuánto lo sentimos!   how we regret it (sorry we are)!
    sentirse bien   to feel well
la **señal**   sign, signal
  señalar   to point out (at), indicate
  señor   Mr., sir
    los señores (Gómez)   Mr. and Mrs. (Gómez)
el **señor**   gentleman
la **señora**   lady, woman
la **señorita**   Miss, young lady (woman)

separado, -a separated
  por separado separately
separar to separate
septentrional northern
septiembre September
ser to be
  es ella it is she
  es que the fact is that
  llegar a ser to become, come to be
  podría ser que it could be that
  puede (ser) que it may be that
  sea . . . o whether it be . . . or
  sigue siendo (it) continues to be
  soy yo it is I
la **serie** series
seriedad: con—, seriously
serio, -a serious
Serra: Fray Junípero *founder of California missions*
la **Serranía** sierra, mountainous country
servible useful, usable, serviceable
el **servicio** service
  al servicio de in the service of
servir (i,i) to serve
  al servirse upon being served
  ¿en qué puedo servirle(s)? what can I do for you?
sesenta sixty
setenta seventy
el **sexo** sex
si if, whether
sí yes
sí *reflex. pron.* himself, herself, *etc. (after prep.)*
siempre always
  siempre que *conj.* provided that
la **sierra** mountain range, mountains
la **siesta** nap, siesta
  dormir (ue,u) la siesta to take a nap
siete seven
  a las siete y media at 7:30, at half past seven
el **siglo** century
el **significado** meaning
significativo, -a significant, meaningful
el **signo** sign
siguiente following, next
  al año siguiente (in) the following year
  al día siguiente (on) the next (following) day
silencioso, -a silent
silvestre wild
la **silla** chair

el **simbolismo** symbolism
el **símbolo** symbol
la **simetría** symmetry
simpático, -a likeable, charming, nice
simple simple
sin *prep.* without
  sin peso weightless
  sin que *conj.* without
el **síndico** trustee
  Junta de Síndicos Board of Trustees
sinfónico, -a symphonic, symphony (*adj.*)
el **singular** singular
sino but
  no sólo . . . sino *or* **sino que (también)** not only . . . but (also)
  que no es otro, -a que which is none other than
  sino que *conj.* but
el **sistema** system
el **sitio** site, place
la **situación** (*pl.* **situaciones**) situation
situar to put, place
sobre on, upon, on top of, over, about
  sobre todo above all, especially
sobresalir to excel
social social
  ciencias sociales social sciences
la **sociedad** society
el **sofá** sofa
el **sol** sun
  hace *or* **hay (mucho) sol** it is (very) sunny, the sun is shining (brightly)
solar solar
la **soldadera** wife of a soldier, camp follower (*f.*)
el **soldado** soldier
soler (ue) + *inf.* to be accustomed to
solicitar to solicit, apply for
la **solicitud** petition, request, application
  solicitud de ingreso application for admission (entrance)
solo, -a sole, single, lone, alone
sólo *adv.* only
  no sólo . . . sino *or* **sino que (también)** not only . . . but (also)
el **soltero** bachelor
la **solución** (*pl.* **soluciones**) solution
el **sombrero** hat
sombrío, -a somber, gloomy
someter to submit
el **sonido** sound
  equipo de sonido sound equipment
sonoro, -a vibrant

sorprender to surprise
  me sorprende (it) surprises me, I'm
    surprised
sorprendido, -a surprised
la **sorpresa** surprise
  ¡qué sorpresa! what a surprise!
sostener to sustain, maintain
soviético, -a Soviet
Sr. = **señor**
Sra. = **señora**
Srta. = **señorita**
su his, her, your (formal), its, their
suave soft
subdesarrollado, -a underdeveloped
subjuntivo, -a subjunctive
el **subjuntivo** subjunctive (mood)
  el (presente) de subjuntivo (present)
    subjunctive
subordinado, -a subordinate
subrayado, -a underlined
subsistir to subsist, last, exist
substantivo, -a (also m. noun) substantive,
    noun
substituir to substitute
  substitúyan (lo) substitute (it)
  substituyendo substituting
el **suceso** happening, event
el **suelo** ground, soil
el **sueño** sleep
  tener (mucho) sueño to be (very) sleepy
la **suerte** luck
  ¡qué suerte has tenido! how lucky
    (fortunate) you have been!
  tener (mucha) suerte to be (very) lucky or
    fortunate
suficiente sufficient, enough
sufrido, -a suffered, undergone
la **sugerencia** suggestion
sugerido, -a suggested
sugerir (ie,i) to suggest
sujeto, -a subject, liable
el **sujeto** subject
  suma: en—, in short, in a word
sumamente extremely, exceedingly
suministrar to provide, supply
superar to surpass, exceed
la **superficie** surface
superior superior, greater, upper
  escuela superior high (secondary) school
la **supervivencia** survival

suplir to supply
suponer to suppose
supuesto: por—, of course, certainly
el **sur** south
  la América del Sur South America
  Suramérica South America
surgir to surge, arise, appear
el **suroeste** southwest
el **surrealismo** surrealism (literary and artistic
    type of the 20th century)
surrealista (m. and f.) surrealist
suscitar to raise, stir up, arouse
suspendido, -a suspended
suyo, -a adj. his, her, its, your (formal), their
    of his (hers, its, yours, theirs)
  (el) suyo, (la) suya, (los) suyos, (las) suyas
    pron. his, hers, its, yours (formal), theirs
  lo suyo what is his (hers, etc.), his (her,
    etc.) part

T

la **tabla** board
el **taco** a rolled corn cake
  tal such (a)
  con tal (de) que conj. provided that
  ¿qué tal? how are you? how goes it?
  ¿qué tal . . . ? how . . . ?
  tal vez perhaps
el **tamal** tamale
también also, too
tampoco neither, (not or nor) . . . either
  ni (a mí) tampoco neither do (I), nor (I)
    either
  tan as, so
  ¡qué día tan (más) hermoso! what a
    beautiful day!
  tan + adj. or adv. + **como** as (so) . . . as
  una exposición tan excelente such an
    excellent exhibition
  tanto, -a (-os, -as) adj. and pron. as (so) much
    (many); adv. as (so) much
  estar al tanto de to be aware of (informed
    of)
  por lo tanto therefore
  tanto . . . como as (so) much . . . as, as
    (so) well as, both . . . and
  tanto como as (so) much as

tanto, -a (-os, -as) + *noun* + **como**   as (so)
much (many) . . . as
tapatío, -a   *associated with Guadalajara, Mexico*
tardar   to delay
   tardar menos   to take less time
   tardar (mucho) en   to take (very) long to,
   be (very) long in, delay (long) in
   tardar tanto   to delay (take) so long
tarde   late
   lo más tarde posible   the latest possible, as
   late as possible
la **tarde**   afternoon
   (ayer) por la tarde   (yesterday) afternoon
   de la tarde   in the afternoon, p.m.
   por la tarde   in the afternoon
la **tarea**   task, job, work
la **tarjeta**   card (*postal*)
el **taxi**   taxi
   en taxi   by (in a) taxi
la **taza**   cup
   taza para café   coffee cup
   taza para té   teacup
te *obj. pron.*   you (*fam.*), to you, (to) yourself
el **té**   tea
   taza para té   teacup
el **teatro**   theater
la **técnica**   technique
técnico, -a   technical
el **técnico**   technician
la **tecnología**   technology
tecnológico, -a   technological
el **tejado**   tile roof
   Tejas   Texas
la **telecomunicación**   telecommunication
   servicios de telecomunicación
      telecommunication services
   telefónico, -a   telephone (*adj.*)
el **teléfono**   telephone
   por teléfono   by (on the) telephone
el **telespectador**   television viewer (spectator)
   televisado, -a   televised
la **televisión**   television
   programa de televisión   TV program
el **televisor**   television set
el **tema**   theme, subject, topic
   temer   to fear
la **temperatura**   temperature
   temple: al —,   in distemper (tempera)
la **temporada**   season
   temprano   early

la **tendencia**   tendency
tender (ie) a   to tend to
tener   to have (*possess*), hold; *in pret.* to get,
   receive; to consider
   aquí la tienes (tiene Ud.)   here it is
   ¿cuántos años tienes (tiene Ud.)?   how old
   are you?
   no tener razón   to be wrong
   ¿qué tiene (Carlos)?   what's the matter
   with (Charles)?
   tener . . . años   to be . . . years old
   tener algo que ver con   to have something
   to do with
   tener cuidado   to be careful
   tener dolor de cabeza   to have a headache
   tener en cuenta   to bear in mind, take into
   account
   tener éxito   to be successful
   tener hambre (sed)   to be hungry (thirsty)
   tener la culpa   to be at fault, be to blame
   tener lugar   to take place
   tener miedo de que   to be afraid that
   tener (mucha) suerte   to be (very) lucky *or*
   fortunate
   tener (muchas) ganas de   to desire or wish
   (very much) to, be (very) eager to
   tener (mucho) calor   to be (very) warm
   (*living beings*)
   tener mucho gusto en   to be very glad
   (pleased) to + *inf.*, have much pleasure
   in + *pres. part.*
   tener (mucho) miedo (de)   to be (very)
   frightened *or* afraid (of, to)
   tener (muchos) deseos de   to wish (very
   much) *or* be (very) eager to
   tener prisa   to be in a hurry
   tener que + *inf.*   to have to, must + *inf.*
   tener razón   to be right
   tener sueño   to be sleepy
   tener tiempo para   to have time to
   tener vergüenza   to be ashamed
el **tenis**   tennis
   jugar (ue) al tenis   to play tennis
   pista de tenis   tennis court
la **teoría**   theory
   tercer *used for* **tercero** *before m. sing. nouns*
   tercero, -a   third
   una tercera parte   one (a) third
el **tercio**   third
   Teresa   Teresa, Theresa

Santa Teresa de Ávila   St. Theresa (1515–1582) *Spanish mystic writer*

terminar   to end, finish

  antes de terminar la década   before the end of the decade

  va terminando   (it) is slowly (gradually) ending

término: en primer   in the foreground

el **termóstato**   thermostat

el **terreno**   terrain, area; field (*sports*)

  preparar el terreno   to pave the way

terrestre   terrestrial, land

el **territorio**   territory

la **tesis**   thesis

el **texto**   text, textbook

ti *pron.*   you (*fam. sing.*), yourself (*after prep.*)

la **tía**   aunt

el **tiempo**   time (*in general sense*); tense; weather

  al mismo tiempo   at the same time

  al poco tiempo   after (in) a short time

  ¿cuánto tiempo?   how long (much time)?

  ¿cuánto tiempo hace?   how long (much time) has it been?

  hace buen (mal) tiempo   it is good (bad) weather

  hace (mucho) tiempo   it is a long (some) time, for a long (some) time

  mucho tiempo   much (a long) time

  ¿qué tiempo (hace)?   what kind of weather (is it)?

  tener tiempo para   to have time to

la **tienda**   store, shop

la **tierra**   land, earth

el **tío**   uncle; *pl.* uncle(s) and aunt(s)

típico, -a   typical

el **tipo**   type

el **título**   title, degree

  título de bachiller   bachelor's degree

el **tobillo**   ankle

el (los) **tocadiscos**   record player(s)

tocar   to touch, play (*music*)

todavía   still, yet

  todavía no   not yet

todo, -a   all, every; *pl.* all, all of them, everybody, everyone; *pron.* all, everything

  en todo caso   in any case

  sobre todo   above all, especially

  toda la (lección)   all the *or* the whole (lesson)

  todas las noches (tardes)   every night *or* evening (afternoon)

  todos los días   every day

  todos los que   all those who

tomar   to take, drink, eat

  tomar una decisión   to make a decision

  tomar por   to take for *or* take as (a)

Tomás   Thomas

el **tomate**   tomato

el **tono**   tone

el **toque en espiral**   swirl

la **torcedura**   sprain

torcer (ue)   to twist, turn, sprain

el **torneo**   tourney, tournament, match, contest

la **tortilla**   omelet (*Spain*); corn pancake (*Mexico*)

la **tostada**   toasted corn cake

tostado, -a   toasted

totalmente   totally, entirely

el **trabajador**   worker

trabajar   to work

  trabajar mucho   to work hard

el **trabajo**   work

  horas de trabajo   working hours

la **tradición** (*pl.* **tradiciones**)   tradition

tradicionalmente   traditionally

la **traducción**   translation

traducir   to translate

  (para) traducir al español   (to) translate into Spanish

traduzcan *pres. subj. of* **traducir**

traer   to bring

trágico, -a   tragic

traído *p.p. of* **traer**   brought

el **traje**   suit

la **transformación**   transformation, change

transformar   to transform, change

la **transmisión**   transmission

transmitir   to transmit

la **transparencia**   transparency, slide

transportar   to transport

el **transporte**   transportation

trasladar   to move

  trasladarse a   to move (take oneself) to

el **tratado**   treaty

tratar   to treat

  tratar de + *inf.*   to try to; + *obj.* to deal with, treat of

  tratarse de   to be a question of

el **trecho**   stretch

treinta   thirty

  treinta (y seis)   thirty(-six)

tremendo, -a   tremendous, heavy

tres   three

a las tres   at three o'clock
trescientos, -as   three hundred
tripulado, -a   manned
triste   sad
  lo tristes que están   how sad they are
tristemente   sadly
el **triunfo**   triumph; success
tropezar (ie) con   to stumble (strike) against
tropical   tropical
tu   your (*fam.*)
tú   you (*fam.*)
el **turno**   turn
tuyo, -a *adj.*   your (*fam.*), of yours
  (el) tuyo, (la) tuya, (los) tuyos, (las) tuyas
    pron. yours

U

u   or (*used for* **o** *before* **o-, ho-**)
Ud(s). = **usted(es)**   you (*formal*)
último, -a   last (*in a series*), final
  de estos últimos años   of (in) recent years,
    of the last (past) few years
  durante estos (los) últimos años   during
    (in) the last few years, recently
  en estos últimos años   recently, (in) the
    last few years, in recent years
  este (el) último   this (the) last one (*m.*)
  por último   finally, ultimately
un, uno, -a,   a, an, one
  es la una   it is one o'clock
  hasta la una   until one o'clock
  se gritaron el uno al otro   they shouted to
    each other (one another)
unánime   unanimous
únicamente   only
único, -a   only, sole
  lo único   the only thing
unido, -a   united, joined
  el Reino Unido   the United Kingdom
  los Estados Unidos   United States
  las Naciones Unidas   United Nations
  unido, -a con   joined to, united with
la **unificación**   unification
la **uniformidad**   uniformity
la **unión** (*pl.* **uniones**)   union
  Unión Soviética   Soviet Union
unir(se)   to unite, join

universal   universal
la **universidad**   university
  (autobús) de la universidad   university
    (bus)
  universitario, -a   university (*adj.*)
    la universitaria   the university (one) (*f.*)
  unos, -as   some, a few, any, several; about
    (*quantity*)
    unos con otros   with (to) one another
    unos (-as) cuantos (-as)   some, a few
urbano, -a   urban, city (*adj.*)
urgente   urgent
el **Uruguay**   Uruguay
uruguayo, -a (*also noun*)   Uruguayan
usado, -a   used
usar   to use
el **uso**   use
usted   you (*formal*)
útil   useful
la **utilidad**   use, usefulness, utility
la **utilización**   utilization, use
utilizado, -a   utilized, used
utilizar   to use, utilize

V

vaca: carne de—,   beef
las **vacaciones**   vacation
vacilar en + *inf.*   to hesitate to + *inf.*
vacuno: ganado—,   cattle
valenciano, -a   Valencian, of Valencia (*Spain*)
valer   to be worth
  más vale (vale más)   it is better
  ¿qué valdría más?   what would be better?
  valer más   to be better
válido, -a   valid
valioso, -a   valuable
el **valor**   value
vallas: carrera de—,   hurdles
vámonos *see* **irse**
vamos   we are going, let's go
  vamos a + *inf.*   we are going to *or* let's
    (let's go) to
  (vamos) a ver   let's see
vanguardia: de—,   vanguardist,
    avant-guardist (*term applied to many "new"
    movements in the 20th century*)

vanguardista (*m. and f.*) (*also noun*) vanguardist
el **vapor**   steam
  al vapor   steamed, in steam
varía *pres. ind. of* **variar**
variar   to vary
la **variedad**   variety
varios, -as   various, several
el **vaso**   glass
  vaso para agua   water glass
vasto, -a   vast, huge, very large
Vd(s). = **usted(es)**   you (*formal*)
el **vatiaje**   wattage
el **vecino**   neighbor
veinte   twenty
veinticinco   twenty-five
veintidós   twenty-two
velar por   to watch over
Velázquez: (Diego) (1599–1660)   *Spanish painter*
el **velorio**   wake
el **venado**   deer
vencer   to overcome, conquer, win out
vender   to sell
venezolano, -a   Venezuelan, of Venezuela
venir (a + *inf.*)   to come (to)
  (el semestre) que viene   next (semester)
  por allí vienen   there they come
la **ventana**   window
la **ventanilla**   ticket window
Venus   Venus (*a planet*)
ver   to see; *reflex.* to be (seen)
  nos vemos   we'll see (be seeing) each other
  se ve que   it is evident (apparent) that
  se ven (obligados)   (they) are (obliged)
  tener algo que ver con   to have anything (something) to do with
  (vamos) a ver   let's see
el **verano**   summer
veras: de —,   really, truly
el **verbo**   verb
la **verdad**   truth
  es verdad   it is true, that's right
  ¿no es verdad? *or* **¿verdad?**   isn't it true? aren't you? etc., (*after negative*) isn't that so?
verdadero, -a   true, real
verde   green
la **vergüenza**   shame

tener vergüenza   to be ashamed
verticalmente   vertically
el **vestíbulo**   vestibule, lobby, hall
el **vestido**   dress
vestir (i,i)   to dress (*someone*); *reflex.* to dress (oneself), get dressed
la **vez** (*pl.* **veces**)   time (*in a series*)
  a veces   at times
  alguna vez   some time, ever, (at) any time
  cada vez más   more and more
  dos veces   twice, two times
  muchas veces   many times, often
  otra vez   again, another time
  por primera vez   for the first time
  tal vez   perhaps
viajar   to travel
el **viaje**   trip
  hacer un viaje   to make (take) a trip
Vicente   Vincent
la **vida**   life
  el nivel de vida   standard of living
  forma de vida   way of living
viejo, -a   old
  el viejo   the old man
el **viento**   wind
  hacer (mucho) viento   to be (very) windy
el (los) **viernes**   (on) Friday(s)
el **vigor**   strength
el **vinagre**   vinegar
la **violencia**   violence
el **virreinato**   viceroyalty
la **visión** (*pl.* **visiones**)   vision, fantasy, sight
la **visita**   visit
visitar   to visit, call on
la **vista**   sight, view
  en vista de   in view of
  hasta la vista   so long, until (I'll see you) later
visto *p.p. of* **ver**   seen
visual   visual
la **vitalidad**   vitality
la **vivienda**   dwelling, house
vivir   to live
la **vocal**   vowel
volar (ue)   to fly; to project
el **volumen**   volume
volver (ue)   to return, come back; *reflex.* to become
  volver a (levantar)   (to lift) again

vuelvo en seguida   I'll return at once (be right back)

vosotros, -as *pron.*   you (*fam. pl.*), yourselves

la **votación**   vote, voting

votar (por)   to vote (for)

el **voto**   vote

la **voz** (*pl.* **voces**)   voice

en voz alta   aloud

el **vuelo**   flight

la **vuelta**   return

dar una vuelta   to take a walk (stroll)

vuelto *p.p. of* **volver**   returned

vuestro, -a *adj.*   your (*fam. pl.*), of yours

(el) vuestro, (la) vuestra, (los) vuestros, (las) vuestras *pron.*   yours

Y

y   and

ya   already, now, soon, later, in due time, then; *sometimes used for emphasis and not translated*

¡ya era hora!   it was about time!

¡ya lo creo!   of course! certainly!

ya no   no longer

Z

la **zapatería**   shoe store

el **zapato**   shoe

la **zona**   zone

la **zoología**   zoology

English-Spanish

A

a, an   un, una; *often not translated*
able: be—,   poder
abound   abundar
about *prep.*   ˜de, acerca de, sobre; *for probability use future or cond. tense*
abuse   el abuso
academic   académico, -a
accept   aceptar
accident   el accidente
accompanied by   acompañado, -a de
accompany   acompañar
according to *prep.*   según
accustomed: be—to   acostumbrar
ache   doler (ue)
  (my) head aches   (me) duele la cabeza, (tengo) dolor de cabeza
acquainted: be well—with   conocer bien
actively   activamente
admission   el ingreso
  application for admission   solicitud de ingreso
admit   admitir
advanced   avanzado, -a
advertise   anunciar
adviser   el consejero
afraid: be—,   tener miedo
after *prep.*   después de

after a short time   al poco tiempo (rato)
  at a quarter after (eight)   a las (ocho) y cuarto
afternoon   la tarde
  yesterday afternoon   ayer por la tarde
afterwards   después, más tarde
again   otra vez, volver (ue) a (+ *inf.*)
agency   la agencia
ago: (six months)—,   hace (seis meses)
agree   estar de acuerdo
agreement: be in—,   estar de acuerdo
agriculture   la agricultura
airport   el aeropuerto
  at the airport   en el aeropuerto
all   todo, -a; *pl.* todos, -as
  all (day)   todo (el día)
  all that   todo lo que, cuanto
almond   la almendra
almost   casi
alone   solo, -a
already   ya
also   también
  not only . . . but also   no sólo . . . sino también
although   aunque
always   siempre
America   América
  South America   la América del Sur
  Spanish America   la América española (hispana), Hispanoamérica

American: North—, norteamericano, -a
among entre
amuse divertir (ie, i)
and y, (*before* i-, hi-, *but not* hie-) e
animal el animal
ankle el tobillo
Ann Ana
announce anunciar
annual anual
another otro, -a
answer contestar
any *adj. and pron.* alguno, -a, (*before m. sing. nouns*) algún, (*after negative or comparative*) ninguno, -a (ningún); *often not translated*
  any boy (at all) cualquier muchacho
  anyone of us cualquiera de nosotros
  in any case en todo caso
  without any doubt (whatever) sin duda alguna
  anyone alguien, (*after negative or comparative*) nadie
anything algo, alguna cosa, (*after negative*) nada, ninguna cosa
  anything (at all) cualquier cosa
apartment el apartamento
apparatus el aparato
apparently al parecer
appear aparecer
appetizer el entremés
application la solicitud
  application for admission, entrance application solicitud de ingreso
apply for solicitar
approach acercarse (a)
appropriate apropiado, -a
approximately más o menos
April abril
Argentina la Argentina
Argentine *adj.* argentino, -a
arouse despertar (ie)
arrive llegar
  (they) must have arrived habrán (deben de haber) llegado
Arthur Arturo
article el artículo
as tan, como
  as . . . as tan . . . como
  as if como si
  as soon as tan pronto como, en cuanto, así

que, luego que
  the same (opportunities) as las mismas (oportunidades) que
ask (*question*) preguntar; (*request*) pedir (i,i)
  ask for (*request*) pedir (i,i); (*inquire about*) preguntar por
  I did not ask him (it) no se lo pregunté
asopao el asopao
association la asociación (*pl.* asociaciones)
at a, en
  at (eight) o'clock a las (ocho)
  at once en seguida
  at the end of a fines de
  at (the exhibition) en (la exposición)
athletic atlético, -a
attend asistir a
attention la atención
  give special attention to dedicar atención especial a
  pay attention to fijarse en
August agosto
available disponible
average medio, -a
avocado el aguacate
  avocado salad ensalada de aguacate
awaken (*someone*) despertar (ie)
award otorgar
away: right—, ahora mismo

B

bad malo, -a, (*before m. sing. nouns*) mal
  not at all bad (no) . . . nada malo, -a
bank el banco
Barbara Bárbara
bargain la ganga
basic básico, -a
basketball el baloncesto, el básquetbol
  basketball team equipo de baloncesto (básquetbol)
  play basketball jugar (ue) al baloncesto (básquetbol)
be estar, ser; encontrarse (ue), hallarse; (*visible phenomena*) haber; (*weather*) hacer
  be able poder
  be afraid tener miedo
  be at fault tener la culpa

be hungry (thirsty)   tener hambre (sed)
be in agreement   estar de acuerdo
be in a hurry   tener prisa
be mistaken   equivocarse
be necessary to   haber que (ser necesario *or* preciso) + *inf.*
be right   tener razón, decir bien
be to, be necessary to   haber de + *inf.*
be (very) careful   tener (mucho) cuidado
be (very) cool (*weather*)   hacer (mucho) fresco
be very eager to   tener muchas ganas (muchos deseos) de + *inf.*
be (very) fortunate *or* **lucky**   tener (mucha) suerte
be very glad (to)   alegrarse (de)
be (very) sleepy   tener (mucho) sueño
be (very) successful   tener (mucho) éxito
be wrong   no tener razón
here (it) is   aquí (lo) tienes (tiene Ud.)
how old is (he)?   ¿cuántos años tiene (él)?
isn't it?   ¿(no es) verdad?
it is sunny, the sun is shining   hace (hay) sol
there is (are)   hay
there was (were)   había, hubo
there will not be time to   no habrá tiempo para
what is being done   lo que se va haciendo
what's the matter with (Paul)?   ¿qué tiene (Pablo)?
bear   el oso
beautiful   bonito, -a, hermoso, -a
because   porque
become + *noun*   hacerse
  become a member of   formar parte de
  become interested in   interesarse por
bed   la cama
beef   la carne de vaca
  ground beef   carne picada de vaca
before *adv.*   antes; *conj.* antes (de) que; *prep.* antes de
  before eight o'clock   antes de las ocho
begin (to)   comenzar (ie) (a + *inf.*), empezar (ie) (a + *inf.*)
believe   creer
  I believe that   creo que, me parece que
besides *prep.*   además de
best   mejor
  the best (*f. pl.*)   las mejores
  the best thing   lo mejor
better   mejor

Betty   Isabel
between   entre
bicycle   la bicicleta
bill   la cuenta
bird   el pájaro
birthday   el cumpleaños
  birthday gift   regalo de cumpleaños
bit: quite a—,   bastante
black   negro, -a
  black pepper   la pimienta
blond(e)   rubio, -a
blouse   la blusa
blow   el golpe
  give oneself a blow   darse un golpe
bone   el hueso
book   el libro
bookstore   la librería
  at (in) the bookstore   en la librería
botany   la botánica
box   la caja
boy   el muchacho
  any boy (at all)   cualquier muchacho
  boys' camp   campamento de muchachos
bracelet   la pulsera
brand   la marca
break   romper
breakfast   el desayuno
  eat breakfast   tomar el desayuno, desayunarse
bring   traer
broaden   ampliar
broken   roto, -a
brother   el hermano
building   el edificio
bulb   la bombilla
bus   el autobús (*pl.* autobuses)
  by bus   en autobús
  the (ten o'clock) bus   el autobús (de las diez)
  the university bus   el autobús de la universidad
business   los negocios
busy   ocupado, -a
but   pero, sino, sino que
  not only . . . but (+ *verb*)   no sólo . . . sino que
  not only . . . but also   no sólo . . . sino también
buy   comprar
  buy herself   comprarse
by   por, de, para, en
  by all means   de todos modos
  by car   en coche

by working trabajando
day by day día a día

C

çake: corn—, la tortilla
call la llamada; llamar
  call again llamar otra vez, volver (ue) a llamar
camera cámara
camp el campamento
can poder (*mental ability*) saber; *for conjecture use future tense*
capital (*city*) la capital
captain el capitán
car el coche
  by car en coche
card (*postal*) la tarjeta
career la carrera
careful: be (very)—, tener (mucho) cuidado
Carmen Carmen
case el caso
cattle el ganado vacuno
celebrate celebrar
center el centro
  Student Center Centro de Estudiantes
chair la silla
change el cambio; cambiar
charge: take—of encargarse de
Charles Carlos
Charlotte Carlota
cheese el queso
  cheese turnover empanadita de queso
chicken el pollo
  chicken asopao asopao de pollo
children los niños
chili el chile, el ají
  chili sauce salsa de chile
chocolate el chocolate
choose escoger
church la iglesia
  go to church ir a la iglesia
city la ciudad
class la clase
  to class a clase
  who doesn't have a class que no tiene clase
classroom la sala de clase
clerk el dependiente
clinic la clínica
close cerrar (ie)

closed cerrado, -a
closer más cerca
  come closer acercarse más
cloud la nube
cloudy nublado, -a
club el club
coffee el café
cold *adj.* frío, -a; (*disease*) el resfriado
collaboration la colaboración
colleague el (la) colega
combat combatir
come venir
  come closer acercarse más
  come in (*fam. sing.*) pasa (tú); *pl.* pasen Uds.
  may I come in? ¿se puede?
comfortable cómodo, -a
comment el comentario
committee la comisión (*pl.* comisiones)
common corriente, común (*pl.* comunes)
compare comparar
competition el concurso
complain quejarse
composed: be—of constar de
composer el compositor
composition la composición (*pl.* composiciones)
concerning respecto de, acerca de, sobre
concert el concierto
condition la condición (*pl.* condiciones)
  in (very) bad condition en (muy) malas condiciones
congratulate felicitar
consider considerar
consist of constar de
consult (with) consultar (a)
consumption el consumo
contact el contacto
  in contact with en contacto con
contain contener
contest el concurso
continue continuar, seguir (i, i)
contribute contribuir
cook la cocinera; cocinar
cool fresco, -a; *noun* el fresco
  be (very) cool (*weather*) hacer (mucho) fresco
corn el maíz
  corn cake la tortilla
  corn husks hojas de la mazorca del maíz
corner (*of room*) el rincón (*pl.* rincones)
cost costar (ue)
cougar el puma

could   *imp., pret., or cond. of* poder
counsellor   el consejero
count   contar (ue)
  count on   contar con
country (*nation*)   el país
course   el curso
course: of—!   ¡cómo no! ¡por supuesto!
cousin   el primo, la prima
crab   el cangrejo
create   crear
critic   el crítico
cultural   cultural
custard   el flan

D

dance   el baile
  for dancing   para el baile
danger   el peligro
  in danger of   en peligro de
  there is danger that   hay el peligro de que
date (*appointment*)   la cita
day   el día
  all day   todo el día
  day by day   día a día
  every day   todos los días
  on the following day   al día siguiente
  what a beautiful day!   ¡qué día más (tan)
    hermoso *or* bonito!
deal: a great—of   mucho, -a
  deal with   tratar de
December   diciembre
decide   decidir
decision   la decisión (*pl.* decisiones)
  make a decision   tomar una decisión
decorate   decorar
deer   el venado
degenerate   degenerar
degree   el grado; el título
delay so long   tardar tanto
delighted   encantado, -a
deliver   entregar
democratic   democrático, -a
department   el departamento
  police department   oficina de policía
  Spanish Department   Departamento de
    Español

describe   describir
despite *prep.*   a pesar de
dessert   el postre
development   el desarrollo
  International Development Bank   Banco
    Internacional de Desarrollo
dial (*telephone*)   marcar
dialogue   el diálogo
Diane   Diana
different   diferente, distinto, -a, diverso, -a
difficult   difícil
difficulty   la dificultad
diminish   disminuir
dining room   el comedor
direct   dirigir
director   el director
disappear   desaparecer
discover   descubrir
discrimination   la discriminación
discuss   discutir
dish   el plato
distinguish oneself   distinguirse
distinguished   distinguido, -a
distribute   distribuir
do   hacer; *not translated as auxiliary*
  didn't they? don't they (you)?   ¿(no es) verdad?
  have (something) to do with   tener (algo) que
    ver con
  what can I do for you?   ¿en qué puedo
    servirle(s)?
  what is being done   lo que se va haciendo
doctor   el médico
doctorate   el doctorado
dollar   el dólar
door   la puerta
doubt   la duda; dudar
  without any doubt (whatever)   sin duda
    alguna
down: sit—,   sentarse (ie)
downtown   el centro
  (be) downtown   (estar) en el centro
  (go) downtown   (ir) al centro
drastic   radical
dress   el vestido
dressed: get—,   vestirse (i, i)
drive   conducir
drop by   pasar por
drugstore   la farmacia
due: be—to   deberse a
during   durante

E

each   cada
  (see) each other   (ver) se
eager: be (very)—to   tener (muchas) ganas *or*
    (muchos) deseos de
early   temprano
earn   ganar
easily   fácilmente
easy   fácil
eat   tomar, comer
  eat breakfast   tomar el desayuno, desayunarse
  eat supper   cenar
  eat (take) lunch   almorzar (ue), tomar el
    almuerzo
ecology   la ecología
  ecology (class)   (clase) de ecología
economic   económico, -a
economics   la economía
economize   economizar
economy   la economía
edge   el borde
editor (*of a newspaper*)   el editor
education   la educación
  Physical Education   la Educación Física
effective   eficaz
effort   el esfuerzo
eight   ocho
  at a quarter after eight   a las ocho y cuarto
  at eight o'clock   a las ocho
  (before) eight o'clock   (antes de) las ocho
  it must be eight o'clock   serán (deben de ser)
    las ocho
eighteen   diez y ocho
eighty   ochenta
  eighty (-nine)   ochenta (y nueve)
electricity   la electricidad
eleven   once
eliminate   eliminar
elimination   la eliminación
emphasis   el énfasis
enchilada   la enchilada
encounter   encontrar (ue)
end   el fin; terminar, concluir
  at the end of   a fines de
energy   la energía
engineer   el ingeniero
engineering   la ingeniería
enough   bastante

enter   entrar (en + *obj.*)
entire: the—place   todo el lugar
entrance   el ingreso
  entrance application   la solicitud de ingreso
environment   el ambiente, el medio ambiente
especially   especialmente, sobre todo
evaluate   evaluar
evaluation   la evaluación (*pl.* evaluaciones)
even   aún
even though   aunque
ever   jamás, alguna vez, (*after negative*) nunca,
    jamás, (*at any time*) alguna vez
every   todo, -a
every day   todos los días
every night   todas las noches
everybody   todo el mundo, todos
everything *pron.*   todo
  leave everything   dejarlo todo
exam   el examen (*pl.* exámenes)
example   el ejemplo
  for example   por ejemplo
exceed   exceder
excel   sobresalir
excellent   excelente
excessive   excesivo, -a
excursion   la excursión (*pl.* excursiones)
  make (take) an excursion   hacer una excursión
exercise   el ejercicio
exert   ejercer
exhibition   la exposición (*pl.* exposiciones)
expect   esperar
expense   el gasto
expensive   caro, -a
experience   la experiencia
explain   explicar
exportation   la exportación
exposition   la exposición

F

face   la cara
faculty   el profesorado
fail: (not) to—to   (no) dejar de + *inf.*
fall (*season*)   el otoño; caer
family   la familia
famous   famoso, -a, distinguido, -a
fantastic   fantástico, -a
father   el padre, el papá

fault   la culpa
  be at fault   tener la culpa
favor   el favor
  be in favor   estar en favor
favorable   favorable
favorite   favorito, -a
February   febrero
feel well   sentirse (ie, i) bien
feeling   el sentimiento
fever   la fiebre
few: (a)—,   unos, -as
  of the last few years   de los últimos años
field   el campo
fiesta   la fiesta
fifteen   quince
fifty   cincuenta
  fifty-one   cincuenta y un(o), -a
  fifty percent   el cincuenta por ciento
file   el fichero
fill   rellenar
  be filled with   rellenarse de
film   la película
finally   por fin
find   encontrar (ue), hallar
  find out (*in pret.*)   saber
finish   terminar, concluir, acabar
first   primero, -a (*before m. sing. nouns*) primer
  first floor   piso bajo
  the first one (*m.*)   el primero
  the first page (*printing*)   la primera plana
fish   el pescado
  pickled fish   el escabeche
five   cinco
  at five   a las cinco
  five hundred   quinientos, -as
flan   el flan
floor   el piso
  first floor   piso bajo
flower   la flor
folder   el folleto
following   siguiente
  on the following day   al día siguiente
fond: be (very)—of   ser (muy) aficionado, -a a
food   la comida
  of food *adj.*   alimenticio, -a
foot   el pie
football   el fútbol
  football game   partido de fútbol
for   para, por
  for (an hour)   desde hace (una hora) *or* hace

(una hora) que + *verb*
  for some time he hasn't talked to me   hace
    tiempo que él no me habla (ha hablado)
forbidden   prohibido, -a
foreign   extranjero, -a
  foreign trade   el comercio exterior
forget   olvidar, olvidarse de (+ *obj.*)
  forget that   olvidarse de que
form   formar
fortunate: be (very)—,   tener (mucha) suerte
  how fortunate (our team) is!   ¡qué suerte tiene
    (nuestro equipo)!
forty   cuarenta
  forty-seven   cuarenta y siete
four   cuatro
fourteen   catorce
fragmentation   el fraccionamiento
French (*language*)   el francés
fried   frito, -a
friend   el amigo, la amiga
  girl friend   la novia
from   de, desde
front: in—of *prep.*   enfrente de
fruit   las frutas
  fruit preserves   conservas de frutas
full   lleno, -a
fun: make—of   burlarse de
  they were making fun of each other   se
    burlaban uno de otro
furthermore   además
future   el futuro

G

game (*match*)   el partido
garnished (with)   aderezado, -a (con)
gas   el gas
general: in—,   en general
generation   la generación (*pl.* generaciones)
gentleman   el señor
geographic   geográfico, -a
geology   la geología
George   Jorge
get   conseguir (i,i), obtener
  get dressed   vestirse (i,i)
  get the license   sacar la licencia
  get up   levantarse
  let's get to work!   ¡manos a la obra!

gift   el regalo
girl   la muchacha
  girl friend   la novia
  girls' teams   equipos de muchachas
give   dar, (*as a gift*) regalar
  give oneself a blow   darse un golpe
  give special attention to   dedicar atención
  especial a
glad: be (very)—to   alegrarse (mucho) de + *inf.*
  glad to meet you   mucho gusto (en conocerlo,
  -la)
  how glad I am (to) . . . !   ¡cuánto me alegro
  (de) . . . !
gladly   con mucho gusto
glove   el guante
go   ir (a + *inf.*)
  don't (*fam. sing.*) go to so much trouble   no te
  molestes tanto
  go out to   salir a
  go over   recorrer
  go shopping   ir de compras
  let's go to class   vamos a clase
gold   el oro
  gold (watch)   (reloj) de oro
good   bueno, -a, (*before m. sing. nouns*) buen
  have a (very) good time   divertirse (ie, i)
  (mucho)
government   el gobierno
  government agency   agencia del gobierno
gradually   *use* ir + *pres. part.*
  (they) are gradually learning   van aprendiendo
graduate *adj.*   graduado, -a; graduarse
  Graduate School   Escuela Graduada
grammar   la gramática
  grammar course   curso de gramática
grant   conceder, otorgar
great   gran (*before sing. nouns*); *pl.* grandes
  a great deal   mucho
green   verde
ground   picado, -a; el suelo
guest of honor   el huésped de honor
guitar   la guitarra

H

hair   el pelo
  the one (*m.*) with red hair   el del pelo rojo
  what beautiful hair she has!   ¡qué pelo tan

(más) hermoso *or* bonito tiene (ella)!
half   medio, -a
  a half degree   medio grado
  a half hour   media hora
  half past (seven)   (las siete) y media
half   la mitad
hall   el salón
  residence hall   la residencia
hand   la mano
  my hand is swollen   tengo la mano hinchada
  shake hands (with)   dar la mano (a)
hand (over)   entregar
handsome   guapo, -a
hang (up)   colgar (ue)
happen   pasar
happy   feliz (*pl.* felices), contento, -a
hat   el sombrero
have   tener; (*auxiliary*) haber
  have (*causative*)   hacer *or* mandar + *inf.*
  have *indir. command*   que + *pres. subj.*
  have a headache   tener dolor de cabeza
  have a (very) good time   divertirse (ie, i)
  (mucho)
  have (*something, anything*) to do with   tener
  (algo) que ver
  have just   acabar de + *inf.*
  have to   tener que + *inf.*
he   él
head   la cabeza, (*of department*) el jefe
  (my) head aches   (me) duele la cabeza, (tengo)
  dolor de cabeza
headache: have a—,   tener dolor de cabeza
hear   oír
heavens!   ¡Dios mío!
Helen   Elena
help   la ayuda
  help (to)   ayudar (a + *inf.*)
  help each other   ayudarse
Henry   Enrique
her *adj.*   su(s); su(s) *or* el (la, los, las) . . . de ella
her *dir. obj.*   la; *indir. obj.* le, se; *after prep.* ella
here   aquí
  here (it) is   aquí (lo) tienes (tiene Ud.)
hers *pron.*   (el) suyo, (la) suya, (los) suyos, (las)
  suyas *or* (el, la, los, las) de ella
  of hers   suyo(s), -a(s), de ella
herself: buy—,   comprarse
high   alto, -a, elevado, -a
him   *dir. obj.* le, lo; *indir. obj.* le, se; *after prep.* él
his   *adj.* su(s); su(s) *or* el (la, los, las) . . . de él;
  pron. (el) suyo, (la) suya, (los) suyos, (las)
  suyas *or* (el, la, los, las) de él

of his   suyo(s), -a(s), de él
hold (*meeting*)   celebrar
home   la casa
  at home   en casa
  (go) home   (ir) a casa
honor   el honor
  guest of honor   el huésped de honor
hope   esperar
hot   caliente
hour   la hora
house   la casa
how + *adj. or adv.*!   ¡qué . . . !
  how + *verb*!   ¡cuánto . . . !
  how glad I am (to)!   ¡cuánto me alegro (de)!
  how pretty Betty is!   ¡qué bonita (hermosa) es Isabel!
how?   ¿cómo?
  how do you (*fam. sing.*) **like the game?**   ¿qué tal te parece el partido?
  how long?   ¿cuánto tiempo?
  how much (many)?   ¿cuánto, -a (-os, -as)?
  how old is (he)?   ¿cuántos años tiene (él)?
however   sin embargo
Humanities   las humanidades
hundred: a (one)—,   cien(to)
  five hundred   quinientos, -as
  four (nine, six, seven, three, two) hundred   cuatro- (nove-, seis-, sete-, tres-, dos-) cientos, -as
  one hundred (sixteen)   ciento (diez y seis)
hungry: be—,   tener hambre
hunt   cazar
hurry: be in a—,   tener prisa
hurry (up)   apurarse, darse prisa
hurt   doler (ue)
  does your (*fam. sing.*) *or* **his (throat) hurt?**   ¿te *or* le duele (la garganta)?
husks: corn—,   hojas de la mazorca del maíz

in   en, de, a, por; (*after a superlative*) de
  in order to   *prep.* para
include   incluir
income   los ingresos
increase   el aumento; aumentar
industrialization   la industrialización
Inez   Inés
influence   la influencia
inform   informar
information   los informes, las noticias
informed of   enterado, -a de
  be informed of   enterarse de
ingredient   el ingrediente
injustice   la injusticia
insist on   insistir en
instrument   el instrumento
intend   pensar (ie) + *inf.*
Inter-American   Interamericano, -a
interest   el interés; interesar
  interest in   interés por
interested: become—in   interesarse por
  we shall be interested in (the birds)   nos interesarán (los pájaros)
interesting   interesante
international   internacional
  International Day   Día Internacional
interview   la entrevista
into   en
introduce   presentar
invitation   la invitación (*pl.* invitaciones)
invite   invitar (a + *inf.*)
isolated   aislado, -a
it *dir. obj.*   lo (*m. and neuter*), la (*f.*); *indir. obj.* le; (*usually omitted as subject*) él (*m.*), ella (*f.*); *after prep.* él (*m.*), ella (*f.*)
item: news—,   la noticia

I

I   yo
ice   el hielo
idea   la idea
ideal   ideal
if   si
ill   enfermo, -a
illiteracy   el analfabetismo
imagine   imaginarse

J

James   Jaime
Jane   Juanita
January   enero
job   el puesto
Joe   Pepe
John   Juan
Johnny   Juanito
Joseph   José
July   julio

June junio
jury el jurado
just: have—, acabar de + *inf.*

K

kind la clase
  what kind of? ¿qué clase de?
kitchen la cocina
knock at llamar a
know (*facts*) saber, (*be acquainted with*) conocer
known: make oneself—, darse a conocer

L

lack faltar
  be lacking faltar
  is there anything lacking? ¿falta algo?
lady: young—, la joven, la señorita
lamp la lámpara
large gran(de), numeroso, -a
  a larger one (*m.*) uno más grande
  the larger ones (*m.*) los más grandes
last pasado, -a (*in a series*) último, -a
  of the last few years de los últimos años
  last night anoche
  last page la última página
  last (year) el (año) pasado
  the last time la última vez
  this last one (*m.*) este último; (*f.*) esta última
late tarde
later más tarde
latter: the—, éste, ésta (-os, -as)
law el derecho
  Law School Facultad de Derecho
lawyer el abogado
learn aprender (a + *inf.*)
  (they) are gradually learning van aprendiendo
least menos
leave salir (de + *obj.*), partir (de + *obj.*), irse, marcharse (de + *obj.*); *trans.* dejar
  leave everything dejarlo todo
  leave for salir (partir) para
lecture la conferencia
left: be—, quedar

to (on) the left a la izquierda
less menor, menos
let dejar, permitir
  let (*formal sing.*) **me** + *verb.* déjeme Ud. *or* permítame Ud. + *inf.*
  let's (let us) + *verb* vamos a + *inf.*, or first pl. *pres. subj.*
  let's get to work! ¡manos a la obra!
  let's go to class vamos a clase
  let us (let's) see (vamos) a ver
letter la carta
library la biblioteca
license la licencia
lift levantar
like como; gustar, (*person*) querer (a)
  he would like le gustaría (a él)
  how do you (*fam. sing.*) **like (the game)?** ¿qué tal te parece (el partido)?
  I should like yo quisiera, me gustaría
  would you (*fam. sing.*) **like . . . ?** ¿quisieras (tú) . . . ? ¿te gustaría . . . ?
line la línea
list la lista
listen (to) escuchar
little (*quantity*) poco, -a
  little by little poco a poco
live vivir
living: standard of—, el nivel de vida
lobby el vestíbulo
lock el candado
long largo, -a
  delay so long tardar tanto
  have you (*fam. pl.*) **been waiting for us (for) a long time?** ¿hace mucho tiempo que nos esperáis?
  how long? ¿cuánto tiempo?
  wait long esperar mucho
longer: stay—, quedarse más
look at mirar
look for buscar
lose perder (ie)
Louis Luis
Louise Luisa
lounge el salón (*pl.* salones)
love querer (a)
  love each other quererse
lower bajar
lucky: be (very)—, tener (mucha) suerte
lucrative lucrativo, -a
lunch el almuerzo

eat (take) lunch   almorzar (ue), tomar el almuerzo
  for lunch   para el almuerzo

M

made   hecho, -a
magazine   la revista
main   principal
majority   la mayoría
make   la marca; hacer
  (he) was making (*progressive*)   (él) estaba haciendo
  make fun of   burlarse de
  make oneself known   darse a conocer
  make the trip   hacer el viaje (la excursión)
  they were making fun of each other   se burlaban uno de otro
man   el hombre
  young man   el joven
  young men   los jóvenes
many   muchos, -as
  how many?   ¿cuántos, -as?
  so (as) many   tantos, -as
map   el mapa
March   marzo
Margaret   Margarita
maritime   marítimo, -a
Martha   Marta
marvelous   maravilloso, -a
Mary   María
masses (*people*)   las masas
matter   el asunto
  that matter (of Robert)   lo (de Roberto)
  what's the matter with (Paul)?   ¿qué tiene (Pablo)?
may *indir. command* (*wish*)   que + *pres. subj.; sign of pres. subj.;* poder
  may I come in?   ¿se puede?
  may they have a good time   que se diviertan
  you (*formal*) **may sit down**   Ud(s). puede(n) sentarse
May   mayo
me *dir. and indir. obj.*   me; *after prep.* mí
  with me   conmigo
meal   la comida
means   el medio
meat   la carne
  meat pie   la empanada

medicine   la medicina
meet   encontrar (ue), encontrarse (ue) (con); (*gather*) reunirse, (*be introduced to*) conocer
  glad (pleased) to meet you   mucho gusto (en conocerlo, -la)
meeting   la reunión (*pl.* reuniones)
member   el miembro
  become a member of   formar parte de
menu   el menú
Mexican   mexicano, -a
Mexico   México
Michael   Miguel
midnight   la medianoche
might   *sign of the imp. subj.*
million   el millón (*pl.* millones)
  five million(s)   cinco millones de
mind: never—(*fam. sing.*)   no te molestes
mine *pron.*   (el) mío, (la) mía, (los) míos, (las) mías
  of mine *adj.*   mío(s), mía(s)
minute   el minuto
mistaken: be—,   equivocarse
model   el modelo
moment   el momento
  at this (that) moment   en este (ese) momento
money   el dinero
month   el mes
  next month   el mes que viene, el próximo mes
more   más
morning   la mañana
  good morning   buenos días
  tomorrow (yesterday) morning   mañana (ayer) por la mañana
most   más
  for the most part   en su mayoría
  most of   la mayor parte de, la mayoría de
mother   la madre, la mamá
motion   la moción
mountains   las montañas, la sierra
movie(s)   el cine
Mr.   (el) señor, Sr.
much *adj.*   mucho, -a; *adv.* mucho
  how much?   ¿cuánto, -a?
  so (as) much *adv.*   tanto
  so (as) much + *noun*   tanto, -a
  so much as   tanto como
  so (as) much + *noun* + **as**   tanto, -a . . . como
  very much *adv.*   mucho, muchísimo
music   la música

must   deber, haber de + *inf.*, tener que + *inf.*; *(for probability use future cond., future perf.) or* deber de + *inf.*

    it must be eight o'clock   serán (deben de ser) las ocho

    one must remember   hay que recordar

my   mi(s)

N

name   el nombre

nap   la siesta

    take a nap   dormir (ue, u) la siesta

nationalistic   nacionalista (*m. and f.*)

near *prep.*   cerca de

necessary   necesario, -a, preciso, -a

    be necessary to   haber que (ser necesario *or* preciso) + *inf.*

need   la necesidad; necesitar

never   nunca

    never mind *(fam. sing.)*   no te molestes

new   nuevo, -a

    New York   Nueva York

news   las noticias

    news item   la noticia

newspaper   el periódico

next   próximo, -a, siguiente

    next (semester)   el (semestre) que viene

    next year   el próximo año, el año que viene

night   la noche

    every night   todas las noches

    last night   anoche

    tomorrow night   mañana por la noche

nine   nueve

    before nine o'clock   antes de las nueve

    it was nine o'clock   eran las nueve

    nine hundred   novecientos, -as

ninety   noventa

    ninety-two   noventa y dos

no, not *adv.*   no; *adj.* ninguno, -a, *(before m. sing. nouns)* ningún; *often not translated*

    no one   nadie

noon   el mediodía

    at noon   al mediodía

    before noon   antes del mediodía

North American   norteamericano, -a

not   no

not only . . . but (+ *verb*)   no sólo . . . sino que

not only . . . but also   no sólo . . . sino también

note   observar

noteworthy   notable

notice   fijarse en

novel   la novela

November   noviembre

now   ahora

nowadays   hoy día

number   el número

numerous   numeroso, -a

O

observation   la observación (*pl.* observaciones)

observe   observar

obtain   conseguir (i,i), obtener

occur   ocurrir

o'clock: at (ten)—,   a las (diez)

    before (eight) o'clock   antes de las (ocho)

    the (ten) o'clock (bus)   el (autobús) de las (diez)

October   octubre

OEA =   la Organización de los Estados Americanos

off: take—(*oneself*)   quitarse

offer   ofrecer, (*oneself*) ofrecerse (a + *inf.*)

office   la oficina

often   a menudo

oil: olive—,   el aceite

old   viejo, -a

    how old is (he)?   ¿cuántos años tiene (él)?

older   mayor

olive oil   el aceite

on   en, sobre

    on (Sundays)   los (domingos)

    put on (*oneself*)   ponerse

once: at—,   en seguida

one   un, uno, una; *indef. subject* se, uno

    one must remember   hay que recordar

    the one in (of, with)   el (la) de

    the one(s) who (which, that)   el (la) que; *pl.* los (las) que, quien(es) (*persons only*)

    the other one (*f.*)   la otra

    visit one another   visitarse

onion   la cebolla

only *adj.*   único, -a
  the only thing   lo único
only *adv.*   solamente, sólo, no . . . más que
  not only . . . but (+ *verb*)   no sólo . . . sino
  que
  not only . . . but also   no sólo . . . sino
  también
open *adj.*   abierto, -a; abrir
opportunity   la oportunidad
oppose   oponerse a
or   o, (*before* o-, ho-) u
orchestra   la orquesta
order (*arrangement*)   el orden (*pl.* órdenes)
  in order   en orden
  in order that *conj.*   para que
  in order to *prep.*   para
organization   la organización
organize   organizar
origin   el origen (*pl.* orígenes)
other   otro, -a
  (see) each other   (ver)se
  the other one (*m.*)   el otro; (*f.*) la otra
  the others   los otros
ought: you (*formal sing.*)**—to**   Ud. debiera + *inf.*
our   nuestro, -a
ours *pron.*   (el) nuestro, (la) nuestra, (los)
  nuestros, (las) nuestras
  of ours *adj.*   nuestro(s), nuestra(s)
out: find—, (*in pret.*)   saber
  go out to   salir a
outdoors   al aire libre
over: go—,   recorrer
own   propio, -a

P

package   el paquete
paella   la paella
painter   el pintor
painting   la pintura, el cuadro
  painting competition   concurso de pintura
pale   pálido, -a
pamphlet   el folleto
paragraph   el párrafo
parents   los padres, los papás
park   el parque
part   la parte
  for the most part   en su mayoría

participate in   participar en
participation   la participación
pass   pasar
  pass by   pasar por
past: half—(seven)   (las siete) y media
patio   el patio
Paul   Pablo
pay (for)   pagar
  pay attention to   fijarse en
people *indef. subject*   se, uno
  young people   los jóvenes
pepper   el chile, la pimienta
  black pepper   la pimienta
  stuffed pepper   el chile relleno
percent   por ciento
percentage   el porcentaje
perhaps   tal vez, quizá(s), acaso
person   la persona
  a young person   un (una) joven
Philip   Felipe
photo   la foto
  take photos   sacar fotos
photograph   la fotografía
  take photographs   sacar fotografías
physical   físico, -a
  Physical Education   la Educación Física
pickled fish   el escabeche
picture   el cuadro
picturesque   pintoresco, -a
pie: meat—,   la empanada
place   el lugar, el sitio; colocar
plan   el plan, el intento; pensar (ie) + *inf.*
plane   el avión (*pl.* aviones)
plant   la planta
play (*music*)   tocar, (*game*) jugar(ue) (a + *obj.*)
  play (tennis)   jugar al tenis
player   el jugador
pleasant   agradable
  the most pleasant thing   lo más agradable
please   por favor (*at end of request*)
pleased to meet you   mucho gusto (en conocerlo,
  -la)
pleasure   el gusto
  what a pleasure it gives me!   ¡qué gusto
  me da!
p.m.   de la noche (tarde)
point   el punto
police department   la oficina de policía
political   político, -a
poll   la encuesta

poor   pobre
popular   popular
popularity   la popularidad
  popularity contest   concurso de popularidad
population   la población
pork   la carne de cerdo
  ground pork   carne picada de cerdo
Portuguese (*language*)   el portugués
possible   posible
  the soonest possible   lo más pronto posible
postpone   aplazar
practical   práctico, -a
practice   practicar
prefer   preferir (ie,i), gustar más
preferred: those (*f.*)—by   las preferidas por
prepare   preparar
  prepare oneself   prepararse
prepared   preparado, -a
preserves   las conservas
  fruit preserves   conservas de frutas
president (*woman*)   la presidenta
pretty   bonito, -a, hermoso, -a
price   el precio
principal   principal
privilege   el privilegio
prize   el premio
probably   probablemente; *use future, cond., or future perfect tense*
problem   el problema
product   el producto
production   la producción
profession   la carrera, la profesión (*pl.* profesiones)
  teaching profession   profesión de maestro
professional   profesional
professor   el profesor, la profesora
progress   el progreso
project   el proyecto
promote   fomentar, impulsar
prone   propenso, -a
proportionately   proporcionalmente
proposal   la propuesta
propose   proponer
protection   la protección
provide   proveer
public   el público
pudding: rice—,   el arroz con leche
Puerto Rican (*also noun*)   puertorriqueño, -a
puma   el puma
purpose   el fin

purse   la pulsera
put   poner
  put on (*oneself*)   ponerse
  put on (*record*)   poner

Q

quarter   el cuarto
  at a quarter after (eight)   a las (ocho) y cuarto
  it is a quarter to twelve   son las doce menos cuarto
question   la pregunta
quite a bit   bastante

R

rabbit   el conejo
radical   radical
radio (*set*)   el radio; (*communication*) la radio
rain   llover (ue)
raise   elevar
raisin   la pasa
rapid   rápido, -a
rapidly   rápidamente
rate   el índice, el ritmo
  at any rate   de todos modos
Raymond   Ramón
read   leer
receive   recibir
receiver   el auricular
recent   reciente
  in recent years   durante (en) los *or* estos últimos años
recipe   la receta
recommend   recomendar (ie)
recommendation   la recomendación (*pl.* recomendaciones)
record (*phonograph*)   el disco
rector   el rector
red   rojo, -a
  the red ones (*f.*)   las rojas
reduce   reducir
reduction   la reducción
reflected: be—,   reflejarse
refreshment   el refresco
regards   los recuerdos

region   la región (*pl.* regiones)
register   matricularse
regret   sentir (ie,i)
remember   recordar (ue)
remind (one of)   recordar (ue) (a uno)
remote   remoto, -a
repeat   repetir (i,i)
reply   contestar, responder
report   el informe
representation   la representación
representative   el representante
required   obligatorio, -a
reserve   reservar
residence hall   la residencia
respective   respectivo, -a
rest   el resto, descansar
restaurant   el restaurante
result   el resultado
return (*come back*)   volver (ue), regresar; (*give back*)
   devolver (ue)
   return home   volver *or* regresar a casa
rice   el arroz
   rice pudding   el arroz con leche
Richard   Ricardo
right   derecho, -a
   be right   tener razón, decir bien
   right away   ahora mismo
river   el río
road   el camino, la carretera
roast(ed)   asado, -a
Robert   Roberto
rolled   enrollado, -a
room   el cuarto
   dining room   el comedor
roommate   el compañero (la compañera) de
   cuarto
rose   la rosa

S

salad   la ensalada
same   mismo, -a
   the same (opportunities) as   las mismas
      (oportunidades) que
Saturday   el sábado
   on Saturday   el sábado
sauce   la salsa

say   decir
   say yes   decir que sí
scholarship   la beca
school   la escuela, (*of a university*) la facultad
   go to school   ir a la escuela
   Graduate School   Escuela Graduada
   Law School   Facultad de Derecho
season (*period of time*)   la temporada
seasoning   el condimento
seated   sentado, -a
second   segundo, -a
secretary   la secretaria
see   ver
   let's (let us) see   (vamos) a ver
seem (to be)   parecer
select   escoger
sell   vender
semester   el semestre
   next semester   el semestre que viene
send   mandar, enviar
   send for   enviar (mandar) por
sentence   la frase, la oración, (*pl.* oraciones)
   the following sentences and questions   las
      frases y preguntas siguientes
September   septiembre
serve   servir (i,i)
   serve as   servir de
service: at your—,   a la orden
set (*stereo*)   el equipo
   stereo set   el equipo estereofónico
   television set   el televisor
seven   siete
   half past seven   las siete y media
   seven hundred   setecientos, -as
seventeen   diez y siete, diecisiete
seventy   setenta
   seventy(-nine)   setenta (y nueve)
several   varios, -as
shake hands (with)   dar la mano (a)
sharp   en punto
she   ella
shellfish   los mariscos
shining: the sun is—,   hace (hay) sol
shoe   el zapato
shopping: go—,   ir de compras
short: after a—time   al poco tiempo (rato)
should   *sign of cond. ind. and imp. subj.;* deber
   I should like   (yo) quisiera, me gustaría
   they should form   deberían formar
   you should   Ud. debiera, (tú) debieras

show enseñar (a + *inf.*), mostrar (ue), indicar
shower la ducha
sidewalk la acera
sierra la sierra
since como, pues; (*time*) desde
sing cantar
sister la hermana
sit down sentarse (ie)
   let's sit down vamos a sentarnos, sentémonos
six seis
   before six o'clock antes de las seis
   six hundred seiscientos, -as
sixteen diez y seis, dieciséis
sixty sesenta
   sixty(-five) sesenta (y cinco)
sky el cielo
sleep dormir (ue,u)
sleepy: be (very)—, tener (mucho) sueño
slide la transparencia
slowly despacio
small pequeño, -a
   the (this) small one (*m.*) el (este) pequeño
snow la nieve
so tan
   delay so long tardar tanto
   so (as) many tantos, -as
   so (as) much *adv.* tanto
   so (as) much + *noun* + **as** tanto, -a
social social
society la sociedad
solve resolver (ue)
some *adj. and pron.* alguno, -a (*before m. sing.*
   nouns) algún; *pl.* algunos, -as, unos, -as; *often*
   not translated
   for some time he hasn't talked to me hace
   tiempo que él no me habla (ha hablado)
someone alguien
   someone (of them) alguno, -a (de ellos, -as)
son el hijo
song la canción (*pl.* canciones)
source la fuente
south el sur
   South America la América del Sur
southwest el suroeste
Spain España
Spanish *adj.* español,-ola, hispano,-a; (*language*)
   el español
   Spanish America la América española
   (hispana), Hispanoamérica
   Spanish Club Club Hispano (Español)

(Spanish) Department Departamento (de
   Español)
Spanish-American hispanoamericano, -a
Spanish-speaking hispanoparlante, de habla
   española (hispana)
speak hablar
speaker (*stereo*) la bocina
special especial
spend (*time*) pasar
splendid espléndido, -a
sport el deporte
   sports section la sección de deportes
sprain torcer (ue)
   I sprained my ankle me torcí el tobillo
staff: teaching—, el profesorado
standard el nivel
start (to) empezar (ie) (a + *inf.*), comenzar (ie) (a
   + *inf.*)
state el estado
   United States los Estados Unidos
stay quedarse
   stay longer quedarse más
steep macerar
stereo *adj.* estereofónico, -a
   stereo set equipo estereofónico
still todavía
store la tienda
strange extraño, -a
street la calle
strengthen fortalecer
stretch el trecho
strong fuerte
structure la estructura
student el (la) estudiante, el alumno, la alumna;
   adj. estudiantil
   Student Center Centro de Estudiantes
study el estudio; estudiar
stuffed relleno, -a
stumble against tropezar(ie) con
style el estilo
   soccer style de estilo *soccer*
successful: be (very)—, tener (mucho) éxito
such (a) tal
   such as tal(es) como
suggest sugerir (ie,i)
suggestion la sugerencia
suitcase la maleta
summer el verano
   summer vacation vacaciones de verano
sun el sol

the sun is shining   hace (hay) sol
Sunday(s): on—,   el (los) domingo(s)
sunny: it is—,   hace (hay) sol
supper: eat—,   cenar
support   apoyar
suppose   *for conjecture use future or cond. tense*
supposed: be—to   haber de + *inf.*
sure   seguro, -a
  be sure (that)   estar seguro, -a (de que)
surname   el apellido
surprise   la sorpresa; sorprender
  what a surprise!   ¡qué sorpresa!
surrounded by   rodeado, -a de
swollen   hinchado, -a
  his (ankle) is swollen   él tiene (el tobillo) hinchado
  my hand is swollen   tengo la mano hinchada
system   el sistema

T

table   la mesa
taco   el taco
take   tomar, (*carry*) llevar, (*photos*) sacar, (*poll*) realizarse
  take a nap   dormir (ue,u) la siesta
  take a trip   hacer un viaje (una excursión)
  take a walk   dar un paseo (una vuelta)
  take a while to   tardar un rato en
  take charge of   encargarse de
  take lunch   almorzar (ue), tomar el almuerzo
  take off (*from someone*)   quitar
  take off (*from oneself*)   quitarse
talk   hablar
  for some time he hasn't talked to me   hace tiempo que él no me habla (ha hablado)
  talk on the telephone   hablar por teléfono
tall   alto, -a
tamale   el tamal
task   la tarea
teacher   el profesor, la profesora
teaching profession   la profesión de maestro
teaching staff   el profesorado
team   el equipo
technique   la técnica
telephone   el teléfono; *adj.* telefónico, -a
  on the telephone   en el teléfono

talk on the telephone   hablar por teléfono
television   la televisión
  television program   el programa de televisión
  television set   el televisor
tell   decir, contar (ue)
  I shall tell her (it)   se lo diré a ella
temperature   la temperatura
  take one's temperature   tomar la temperatura a uno
ten   diez
  at ten o'clock   a las diez
  the ten-o'clock bus   el autobús de las diez
tennis   el tenis
  play tennis   jugar (ue) al tenis
terrible   terrible
territory   el territorio
text   el texto
than   que, (*before a numeral*) de, (*before a clause*) del (de la, de los, de las) que, de lo que
thanks for   gracias por
that *adj.* (*near person addressed*) ese, esa (-os, -as); (*distant*) aquel, aquella (-os, -as); *pron.* ése, ésa (-os, -as), aquél, aquélla (-os, -as); (*neuter*) eso, aquello; *relative pron.* que
  that of   el (la) de
  that which   lo que
the   el, la, los, las; (*neuter article*) lo
  the (best thing)   lo (mejor)
their *adj.*   su(s), de ellos, -as
theirs *pron.*   (el) suyo, (la) suya, (los) suyos, (las) suyas *or* (el, la, los, las) de ellos, -as
  of theirs *adj.*   suyo(s), -a(s), de ellos, -as
them *dir. obj.*   los, las; *indir. obj.* les, se; *after prep.* ellos, -as
themselves: the students—,   los estudiantes mismos
there   allí
  there is (are)   hay
  there was (were)   hubo, había
therefore   por eso, por lo tanto
thermostat   el termóstato
these *adj.*   estos, estas; *pron.* éstos, éstas
they   ellos, -as
thing   la cosa
  the best thing   lo mejor
  the most pleasant thing   lo más agradable
  the only thing   lo único
think about   pensar (ie) en + *obj. or inf.*
thirsty: be—,   tener sed

thirty treinta
    thirty-one treinta y un(o), -a
this *adj.* este, esta; *pron.* this (one) éste, ésta,
    (*neuter*) esto
Thomas Tomás
those *adj.* (*near person addressed*) esos (-as),
    (*distant*) aquellos (-as); *pron.* ésos, (-as),
    aquéllos (-as)
    those which los (las) que
thousand: a (one)—, mil
three tres
    three hundred trescientos, -as
throat la garganta
    does your (*fam. sing.*) *or* **his throat hurt?** ¿te
    (le) duele la garganta?
through por
ticket el billete, el boleto (*Mex.*)
time (*in a general sense*) el tiempo; (*of day*) la hora;
    (*series*) la vez (*pl.* veces)
    after a short time al poco tiempo (rato)
    at times a veces
    at what time? ¿a qué hora?
    have a (very) good time divertirse (ie,i)
    (mucho)
    have time to tener tiempo para + *inf.*
    have you (*fam. pl.*) **been waiting for us (for) a
    long time?** ¿hace mucho tiempo que nos
    esperáis?
    of our time de nuestros días
    for some time he hasn't talked to me hace
    tiempo que él no me habla (ha hablado)
    may they have a good time que se diviertan
    the last time la última vez
    there will not be time to no habrá tiempo
    para
    what time can it be? ¿qué hora será?
to a, de, con, para, que
    have to tener que + *inf.*
    it is a quarter to twelve son las doce menos
    cuarto
today hoy, hoy día
    today's game el partido de hoy
together juntos, -as
tomorrow mañana
    tomorrow morning (night) mañana por la
    mañana (noche)
tone el tono
tonight esta noche
tostada la tostada

toward(s) *prep.* hacia
trade el comercio
    foreign trade el comercio exterior
trip el viaje, la excursión (*pl.* excursiones)
    make *or* **take the (a) trip** hacer el (un) viaje (la
    and una excursión)
try to tratar de + *inf.*
turn el turno
turn on (*radio, stereo*) poner
    turn to dirigirse a
turnover la empanadita
twelve doce
    it is a quarter to twelve son las doce menos
    cuarto
twenty veinte
    twenty-nine veinte y nueve, veintinueve
    twenty-one veinte y un(o), -a (veintiún,
    veintiuno, veintiuna)
two dos
    at two o'clock a las dos
    the two los (las) dos
    two hundred doscientos, -as
type el tipo
typewriter: write on the—, escribir a máquina
typical típico, -a

U

uncle el tío
underdeveloped subdesarrollado, -a
understand entender (ie)
unfortunately desgraciadamente, por desgracia
unification la unificación
United States los Estados Unidos
university la universidad; *adj.* universitario, -a
    the university (bus) (el autobús) de la
    universidad
unpack desempacar
until *prep.* hasta; *conj.* hasta que
up: get—, levantarse
    hurry (up) apurarse, darse prisa
    wake up (*oneself*) despertarse (ie)
upon + *pres. part.* al + *inf.*
us *dir. and indir. obj.* nos; *after prep.* nosotros, -as
use el uso; emplear, usar
useful útil

V

Valencian   valenciano, -a
valuable   valioso, -a
various   varios, -as
vary   variar
very   *adv.* muy, mucho; *adj.* mucho, -a
   very much   *adv.* mucho, muchísimo
vinegar   el vinagre
visit   visitar
   visit one another   visitarse
vote   el voto
   vote (for)   votar (por)

W

wait (for)   esperar
   wait long   esperar mucho
   wait longer (for)   esperar más
wake up (*oneself*)   despertarse (ie)
walk   el paseo, la vuelta; andar, caminar
   take a walk   dar un paseo (una vuelta)
   (he) was walking (*progressive*)   (él) iba
      andando (caminando)
wall   la pared
want   querer, desear
wash   lavar, (*oneself*) lavarse
watch   el reloj; mirar
   gold watch   reloj de oro
water   el agua (*f.*)
wattage   el vatiaje
we   nosotros, -as
weakness   la debilidad
Wednesday   el miércoles
week   la semana
weekend   el fin de semana
well   bien, pues
what   lo que
what?   ¿qué?
what + *noun*!   ¡qué . . . !
   what a surprise!   ¡qué sorpresa!
   what pleasure it gives me!   ¡qué gusto me da!
whatever   lo que
when   cuando
when?   ¿cuándo?

where?   ¿dónde?   (*with verbs of motion*) ¿adónde?
whether   si
which *relative pron.*   que, el (la) cual, los (las)
      cuales, el (la, los, las) que
   that which   lo que
   the one(s) which   el (la) cual, los (las) cuales,
      el (la, los, las) que
   those which   los (las) que
   which (fact)   lo cual, lo que
which?   ¿qué? ¿cuál?
   which one(s)?   ¿cuál(es)?
while   el rato
   take a while to   tardar un rato en
white   blanco, -a
   the white ones (*f.*)   las blancas
who *relative pron.*   que, quien(es), el (la) cual, los
      (las) cuales, el (la, los, las) que
   he (the one) who   quien, el (la) que
   those (the ones) who   quienes, los (las) que
who?   ¿quién(es)?
whom   que, a quien(es)
whom?   ¿quién(es)? ¿a quién(es)?
whose *relative adj.*   cuyo, -a (-os, -as)
whose?   ¿de quién(es)?
   whose (records) are these?   ¿de quién(es) son
      estos (discos)?
why?   ¿por qué?
wild   salvaje
will   querer; *sign of future tense*
   will you bring . . . ?   ¿quieres (quiere Ud.)
      traer . . . ?
win   ganar
winner   el ganador
wish   querer, desear
   I wish that (would that) . . . !   ¡ojalá (que) +
      subj.!
with   con, de, en
withdraw   retirar
woman   la mujer
wonder   *for conjecture use future or cond. tense*
word   la palabra
work (*of art*)   la obra; (*labor*) el trabajo, la labor;
      trabajar
   by working   trabajando
   let's get to work!   ¡manos a la obra!
worth: be—,   valer
   be worth more   valer más
would   *sign of imp. ind. or cond. tense*
   would that . . . !   ¡ojalá (que) + *subj.*!

wrap   envolver (ue)

write   escribir

write on the typewriter   escribir a máquina

written   escrito, -a

the composition written   escrita la composición

wrong: be—,   no tener razón

Y

year   el año

for many years   desde hace muchos años *or* hace muchos años que + *verb*

from one year to another   de un año a otro

in recent years   durante (en) los *or* estos últimos años

of the last few years   de los últimos años

next year   el próximo año

yellow   amarillo, -a

yes   sí

say yes   decir que sí

yesterday   ayer

yesterday morning (afternoon)   ayer por la mañana (tarde)

yet   todavía

not yet   todavía no

you   (*fam. sing.*) tú, (*pl.*) vosotros, -as; *dir. and indir. obj.* te, os; *after prep.* ti, vosotros, -as

with you   contigo

you   (*formal*) *subject pron. and after prep.* usted (Ud.), ustedes (Uds.); *dir. obj.* lo (le), la, los, las; *indir. obj.* le, les, se

young   joven (*pl.* jóvenes)

young lady   la joven, la señorita

young man   el joven

young men (people)   los jóvenes

younger   menor, más joven

younger generations   generaciones jóvenes

your *adj.*   (*fam.*) tu(s), vuestros(s), -a(s); (*formal*) su(s), de Ud. (Uds.)

yours *pron.*   (*fam.*) (el) tuyo, (la) tuya, (los) tuyos, (las) tuyas, (el) vuestro, (la) vuestra, (los) vuestros, (las) vuestras; (*formal*) (el) suyo, (la) suya, (los) suyos, (las) suyas *or* (el, la, los, las) de Ud. (Uds.)

of yours *adj.*   (*fam.*) tuyo(s), -a(s), vuestro(s), -a(s); (*formal*) suyo(s), suya(s), de Ud. (Uds.)

MAPS

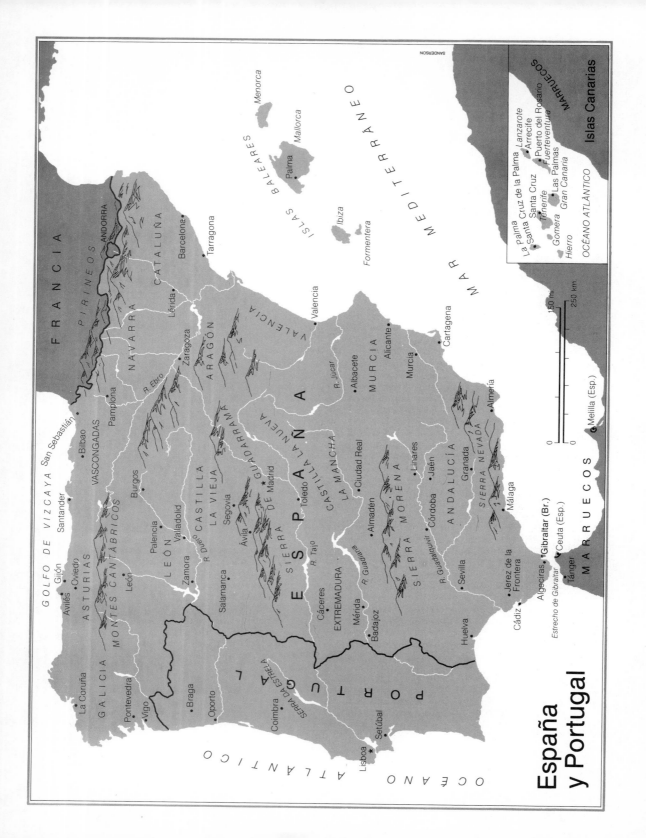

España y Portugal

FRANCIA

PIRINEOS

ANDORRA

GOLFO DE VIZCAYA

San Sebastián

Bilbao

VASCONGADAS

Santander

Gijón

Oviedo

Avilés

ASTURIAS

MONTES CANTÁBRICOS

GALICIA

La Coruña

Pontevedra

Vigo

Braga

Oporto

PORTUGAL

Coimbra

SERRA DA ESTRELA

Lisboa

Setúbal

OCÉANO ATLÁNTICO

Pamplona

NAVARRA

Zaragoza

ARAGÓN

R. Ebro

Lérida

Barcelona

Tarragona

CATALUÑA

VALENCIA

Valencia

Burgos

Palencia

Valladolid

León

LEÓN

Zamora

CASTILLA LA VIEJA

R. Duero

Salamanca

Segovia

Ávila

SIERRA DE GUADARRAMA

Madrid

E S P A Ñ A

CASTILLA LA NUEVA

Toledo

R. Tajo

Cáceres

EXTREMADURA

Mérida

Badajoz

R. Guadiana

R. Júcar

Albacete

LA MANCHA

Ciudad Real

MURCIA

Murcia

Alicante

Cartagena

Almería

SIERRA NEVADA

Almadén

SIERRA MORENA

Linares

Jaén

Córdoba

R. Guadalquivir

ANDALUCÍA

Granada

Málaga

Sevilla

Huelva

Jerez de la Frontera

Cádiz

Algeciras

Gibraltar (Br.)

Ceuta (Esp.)

Tánger

Estrecho de Gibraltar

MARRUECOS

MAR MEDITERRÁNEO

ISLAS BALEARES

Menorca

Mallorca

Palma

Ibiza

Formentera

SANDERSON

0   150 mi
0   250 km.

Melilla (Esp.)

Islas Canarias

MARRUECOS

La Palma

Santa Cruz de la Palma

Lanzarote

Arrecife

Puerto del Rosario

Fuerteventura

Santa Cruz

Tenerife

Gomera

Las Palmas

Gran Canaria

Hierro

OCÉANO ATLÁNTICO

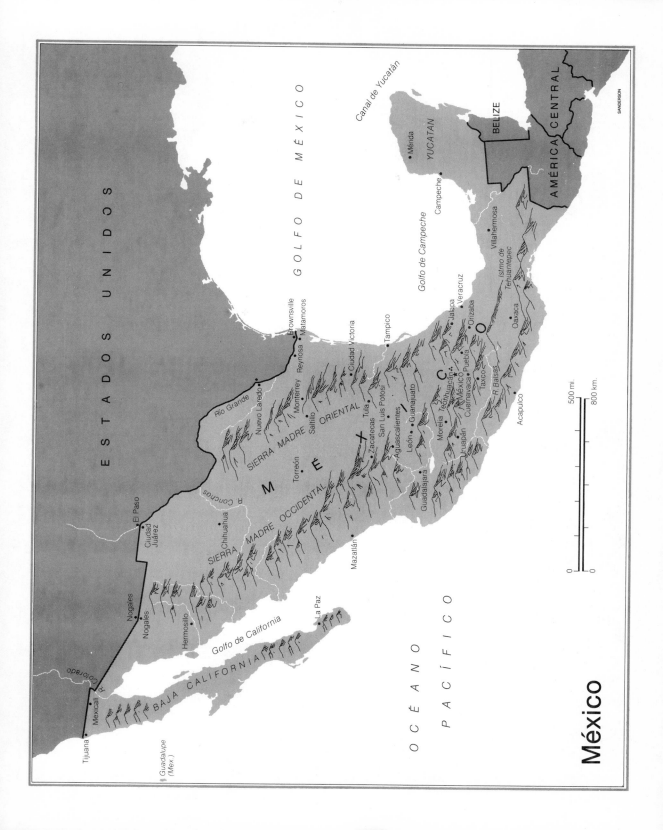

México

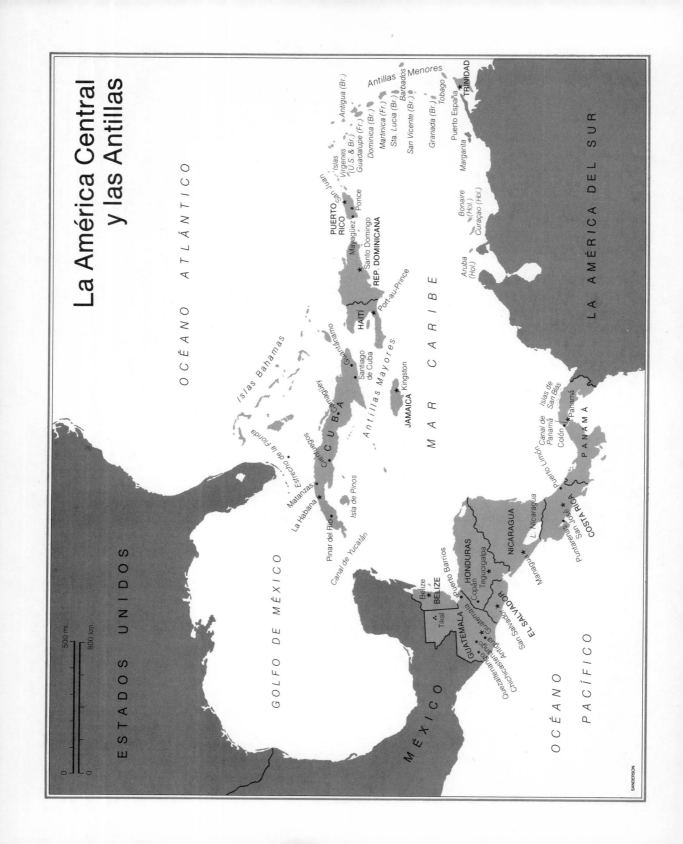

La América Central y las Antillas

ESTADOS UNIDOS

OCÉANO ATLÁNTICO

GOLFO DE MÉXICO

MÉXICO

Estrecho de la Florida

Islas Bahamas

Pinar del Río
La Habana
Matanzas
Cienfuegos
CUBA
Isla de Pinos
Canal de Yucatán

Camagüey
Guantánamo
Santiago de Cuba

Antillas Mayores

JAMAICA
Kingston

HAITÍ
Port-au-Prince

REP. DOMINICANA
Santo Domingo
Mayagüez
Ponce
PUERTO RICO
San Juan

Islas Vírgenes (U.S. & Br.)
Guadalupe (Fr.)
Dominica (Br.)
Martinica (Fr.)
Sta. Lucia (Br.)
San Vicente (Br.)
Barbados (Br.)
Granada (Br.)
Tobago

Antillas Menores

Antigua (Br.)

TRINIDAD
Puerto España
Margarita

MAR CARIBE

Bonaire (Hol.)
Curaçao (Hol.)
Aruba (Hol.)

LA AMÉRICA DEL SUR

Belize
BELIZE
Tikal
Puerto Barrios
GUATEMALA
Guatemala
Antigua
Chichicastenango
Quetzaltenango
San Salvador
EL SALVADOR
Copán
Tegucigalpa
HONDURAS
Managua
NICARAGUA
L. Nicaragua
Puerto Limón
San José
Puntarenas
COSTA RICA
Canal de Panamá
Colón
Islas de San Blas
PANAMÁ
Panamá

OCÉANO PACÍFICO

500 mi
800 km

SANDERSON

MAR CARIBE

OCÉANO ATLÁNTICO

Barranquilla
Cartagena
Caracas
TRINIDAD
Puerto España
Maracaibo
VENEZUELA
GUAYANA
Georgetown
SURINAM
Paramaribo
Medellín
R. Orinoco
GUAYANA FRAN.
Cayenne
COLOMBIA
Bogotá
Cali

Quito
Ecuador
ECUADOR
Guayaquil
Manaus
R. Amazonas
Belem

CORDILLERA DE LOS ANDES
Iquitos
R. Madeira
BRASIL
Recife

PERÚ
Lima
Machu Picchu
Cuzco
BOLIVIA
Salvador
L. Titicaca
La Paz
Brasilia
Arequipa
Belo Horizonte
Arica
Sucre
Iquique
PARAGUAY
Rio de Janeiro
Antofagasta
Asunción
São Paulo
Santos
Trópico de Capricornio
Tucumán
CHILE
ARGENTINA
R. Paraná
Córdoba
Pôrto Alegre
OCÉANO PACÍFICO
Rosario
URUGUAY
Valparaíso
Mendoza
Buenos
Santiago
CORDILLERA DE LOS ANDES
Aires
Montevideo
La Plata
Río de la Plata
Concepción
Bahía Blanca

Puerto Montt

0   1000 mi.
0   1600 km.

Islas
Malvinas

Punta Arenas
Estrecho de
Magallanes
Tierra del
Fuego
Cabo de
Hornos

La América del Sur

SANDERSON

INDEX

a: gender of nouns ending in, 91; omission of personal **a**, 43, 166; personal **a**, 43, 94, 163, 166, 234 note; plus **el**, 34 note, 89; preposition, 108–109; verbs which take **a** before an infinitive, 108–109, 304–305; verbs which take **a** before an object, 305

abbreviations and signs, 29 note, 54, 253–254, 256 note, 257 note, 283

absolute: superlative, 215–216; use of the past participle, 234 note, 237–238

address: forms of, 29, 31, 54, 221

adjective clauses, 162–164; subjunctive in, 138 note, 165–166

adjectives: agreement of, 38, 39, 40, 111, 122 note, 125–128, 164, 195, 197, 202, 213, 237, 243, 284–285; comparison of, 213–216; demonstrative, 195; feminine of, 125–126; forms of, 125–128; past participle used as, 38, 40, 237; plural of, 125–126; position of, 37 note, 126–128, 197–198, 215; possessive (short forms), 197–198, (long forms), 197–198; prepositional phrase used as, 39, 128; shortened forms of, 94, 127–128, 284–285; used as adverbs, 243; used as nouns, 202; with **estar**, 37, 39–40, 111, 237–238; with **ser**, 38, 39–40, 111, 237–238

adquirir: forms of, 302 note

adverbial clauses, subjunctive in, 180–182, 194 note

adverbs: adjectives used as, 243; **algo** and **nada** used as, 95; comparison of, 214–216; formation of, 6 note, 30 note, 242-243

agreement: of adjectives, 38, 39, 40, 111, 122 note, 125–128, 164, 195, 197, 202, 213, 237, 243, 284–285; of cardinal numerals, 284–285; of ordinal numerals, 285–286

al: + infinitive, 107

alphabet: Spanish, 270

andar: with present participle, 239

"any," 90, 94–95

aquél, "the former," 196

article, definite: contraction of **el** with **a, de**, 34 note, 89; **el** with feminine nouns, 89; for the possessive, 88, 167; forms, 87; in comparison of adjectives, 213–214; in dates, 88, 286; **lo,** see neuter **lo**; omission of, 88–89, 199; omission with names of rulers and popes, 286; omission with seasons, 88; summary of uses, 87–89; to form possessive pronouns, 199; used as a demonstrative, 163–164, 196; used to form compound relative pronouns, 163–164; used with adjectives to form nouns, 202; used with the name of a language, 88–89

article, indefinite: forms of, 89–90; omission of, 90, 285; summary of uses, 89–90

"become," 59

breath-group, 14, 24–25, 53, 160–161, 275–276

"by," translated by **para**, 235; translated by **por**, 236; with passive, 39, 236, 237; with present participle, 239

caer: forms of, 18, 28, 243

"can," 243

PHOTOGRAPH CREDITS

Title page: *Familia Andina* by Héctor Poleo (Venezuela), 1943 *Courtesy of the Permanent Collection of the Museum of Modern Art of Latin America, OAS, Washington, D.C.*

3 University of the Andes, Bogotá, Colombia *Photo by P. Menzel* University of Costa Rica, San José, Costa Rica *Photo by P. Menzel*

9 University of Sevilla, Spain *Photo by P. Menzel*

10 University student, Spain *Photo by P. Menzel*

13 Restaurant interior, Madrid, Spain *Photo by P. Menzel*

23 University of the Andes, Bogotá, Colombia *Photo by P. Menzel*

23 Secretary, Madrid, Spain *Photo by P. Menzel*

32 University of Mexico *Courtesy of American Airlines, photo by Bob Takis*

35 University of the Andes, Bogotá, Colombia *Photo by P. Menzel* University of Costa Rica, San Juan, Costa Rica *Photo by P. Menzel*

46 Boy reading, Asunción, Paraguay *Photo by P. Menzel* Girl at blackboard, Asunción, Paraguay *Photo by P. Menzel*

48 Classroom, San Juan, Puerto Rico *Photo by P. Menzel*

49 University classroom, Spain *Photo by P. Menzel*

51 Mission, Lompac, California *Photo by P. Menzel* Mission, New Mexico *Photo by P. Menzel*

52 Costa Brava, Spain *Photo by P. Menzel*

62 Lithograph of Caracas, Venezuela *Courtesy of Creole Petroleum Corporation*

64 Mission, California *Photo by P. Menzel* Farm worker, Lompac, California *Photo by P. Menzel*

67 Strawberry harvest, California *Photo by P. Menzel*

69 Physical education class, France *Photo by P. Menzel* Tennis player *Courtesy of Stock, Boston, Inc.*

80 Laboratory technician in wine distillery, Spain *Photo by P. Menzel* Computer center, University of Guadalajara, Mexico *Photo by P. Menzel*

83 Computer center, University of Guadalajara, Mexico *Photo by P. Menzel*

85 Paella, Valencia, Spain *Photo by P. Menzel* Eating paella, Spain *Photo by P. Menzel*

97 Folk dancers, Bogotá, Colombia *Photo by P. Menzel*

98 Outdoor café, Macuto, Venezuela *Photo by P. Menzel*

100 "Tasca," Spain *Photo by P. Menzel* Latin Quarter, Paris, France *Photo by P. Menzel*

105 Tennis player, Spain *Photo by P. Menzel* Soccer players, Spain *Photo by P. Menzel*

115 Boys playing basketball in León Park, Tegucigalpa, Honduras *Photo by P. Menzel*

116 Soccer players, Chapala, Mexico *Photo by P. Menzel*

118 Soccer stadium, Colombia *Courtesy of Colombia National Tourist Board* Soccer match, University of Mexico stadium *Courtesy of Fotografía Ferronales, Mexico*

123 Bariloche, Argentina *Courtesy of Pan American Photo Library* Tree with moss, San José, Costa Rica *Photo by P. Menzel*

124 View of San José, Costa Rica *Photo by P. Menzel*

136 Pollution sign, San Juan, Puerto Rico *Photo by P. Menzel* Billboard, Spain *Photo by P. Menzel*

141 University of Costa Rica, San Juan, Costa Rica *Photo by P. Menzel*

154 Student demonstration, Barcelona, Spain *Photo by P. Menzel*

159 Doctors' nameplates, Chile *Photo by P. Menzel* Hospital de San Juan de Dios, Bogotá, Colombia *Photo by P. Menzel*

170 Nameplates, Lima, Peru *Photo by P. Menzel*

175 Solar furnace, France *Photo by P. Menzel* University of Venezuela students, Caracas, Venezuela *Photo by P. Menzel*

188 Oil derricks, Maracaibo, Venezuela *Photo by P. Menzel*

193 Shops on Florida Street, Buenos Aires, Argentina *Photo by P. Menzel* Department store floor plan, Spain *Photo by P. Menzel*

194 Record store, Bogotá, Colombia *Photo by P. Menzel*

Color Section (Between pages 226 and 227)